Gender Lens

Gender Lens

Women's Issues and Perspectives

Edited by

Rekha Pande

RAWAT PUBLICATIONS

Jaipur • New Delhi • Bangalore • Hyderabad • Guwahati • Kolkata

ISBN 978-81-316-0628-5

Published by
Prem Rawat for **Rawat Publications**
Satyam Apartments, Sector 3, Jawahar Nagar, Jaipur 302 004 (India)
Phone: 0141 265 1748/7006; Fax: 0141 265 1748
E-mail: info@rawatbooks.com
Website: www.rawatbooks.com

New Delhi Office
4858/24, Ansari Road, Daryaganj, New Delhi 110 002
Phone: 011 2326 3290

Also at *Bangalore, Hyderabad, Guwahati* and *Kolkata*

Typeset by
Mukesh Technologies Pvt. Ltd., Puducherry

Printed at
Chaman Enterprises, New Delhi

Dedicated to all the women
who strive through action, research and advocacy for the creation of
an equitable society in which gender justice is realized.

Contents

Acknowledgements

During the slow and often interrupted evolution of this book, I have accumulated many debts, only a proportion of which I have space to acknowledge here. I have been extremely fortunate and acknowledge the assistance extended to me by many scholars involved in this project. Finalizing essays for a book of this genre can be a daunting task, a challenge, given the need to incorporate all the varieties that characterize the diverse issues related to women in today's world. This task becomes even more difficult in the third world and particularly in a country like India which is a byword for diversity. Thematically, the papers are organized into five headings, titled Women's Movements, Governance, Caste, Class and Race, Work and Labour, Violence and Sexual Harassment, Women in Margins and Health Issues and the response that I received was overwhelming, and it was difficult to select the papers. On this dissimilar template, the forces of modernity and, of late, the knowledge economy via the cyberspace as the most visible forms have generated new forms of patriarchy, and yet the traditional areas such as ideology, work and health can also be approached from a new angle in the light of the changes that are occurring in today's world. Therefore, we now have a rainbow of struggles to reclaim women's space in all these domains that make a colourful mosaic, which cannot be reduced to a melting pot like the American dream. The challenge here is to give voice to the narratives that use very different categories that cannot be understood without the context or also cannot be fully reduced to writing.

Many of my friends are responsible for making this book a reality. First and foremost, I acknowledge them for they have been involved with the women's movement in different parts of the world and helping to build the capacities of women, men and children towards achieving gender equality through teaching, research, publication, training and consultation. Their commitment and enthusiasm motivated me a lot to go ahead with this book. Without their support, this book would not have seen the light of the day. To all of you a big thanks. I also acknowledge the help received from Prasad in the Centre of Women's Studies who carried correspondence with the authors unceasingly. I thank Dr M.N. Rajesh for helping me with the proofreading and corrections in the manuscript. This book could not have been written without his encouragement. I thank Rawat Publications for helping in bringing out this volume at such a quick pace.

I acknowledge and extend my heartfelt gratitude to my husband Dr Suresh Pande, who has always been my anchor. He has provided me a quiet space to write, cooked meals as and when required while I was working, brought me tea when I needed a break and also read pages of the manuscript and made corrections and provided an insight. My elder son, Sankalp, and twins Tarun and Varun have always been my major pillars of support. I also want to add that the new addition to my new-found daughter-in-law Neha has brought me immense joy and happiness. Words alone cannot express what I owe them for their warmth and love and for providing all the technical support from long distance in the United States, China and Canada. Last but not least, my thanks to God, who made all things possible.

Rekha Pande

Introduction

The present book, *Gender Lens: Women's Issues and Perspectives,* explores the cultural meanings of gender and gender differences. It makes us think critically not only about gender but about other social divisions as well. It aims to expand our knowledge and understanding of women in our own society and also those living in societies very different from ours. This book is an interdisciplinary work that places gender at the intersection of society, caste, race, sexuality and work. These structural forces have shaped the individual and collective lives of women across diverse cultures and times, as well as provide analytical categories for critically examining the worlds in which we live.

There is a very close relationship between the contemporary feminist movement and the social, political and economic status of women. All over the world, the women's movement evolved out of social reform movements such as the abolition of slavery, the social purity and temperance movements, in the West. Women began to realize that in order to transform society, they would need their own organizations. They campaigned upon a whole range of issues; from guardianship of infants, property rights, divorce, access to higher education and the medical professions, to equal pay and protective legislation for women workers. Many of these issues continue to be relevant even today. The role of women, their position and status in society and their nature have been issues of debate and discussion informed by religion, tradition and culture, misogyny, feminism and many times, downright ignorance and bigotry.

In India, during the first few decades of post-Independence period, the major concern was for overall economic growth. This was immediately followed by another decade, which witnessed an increased concern for equity and poverty alleviation. Gender issues were subsumed under poverty-related concerns, and there were no programmes specifically aimed at women. Women during this period were involved in such movements as the anti-price, law and famine relief movement but did not start to pick up issues involving their oppression as women until the 1970s. The myth of equality for women was shattered by the path-breaking *Towards Equality Report* of 1975. It focused attention on the fact that despite many progressive social legislations and constitutional guarantees, women's status had indeed not improved much. Women continued to have an inferior status in many areas such as political, economic and social. The increasing incidence of practices such as dowry indicates a further lowering of the status of women. They also indicate a process of regression from some of the norms developed during the freedom movement. In the post-Independence era, there has not been any dearth of documents or policies relating to women. There has been a shift from welfare, to development, to integrating women in development, to empowerment, and yet there is a lot that has to be achieved in order to provide for the creation of an equitable society in which gender justice is realized. This book attempts to bring some such issues on a common platform. The introductory paper by Rekha Pande gives an overview of the scope and problems and prospects of the women's movement in India. Far from seeing it only from a conventional view where the focus is on victimhood, she has mapped the terrain of the diverse strands to reveal how the agents at different levels negotiate and articulate their agendas drawing from a cross-section of people to make the women's movement work. This book looks at the historical background of the rise of feminism and women's movement in India, how the concerns with gender were generally equated with poverty alleviation and the need to go beyond it.

We are living in a world of unprecedented change where the forces of a restructured global capitalism seek to establish their hegemony over all parts of the globe in the name of globalization. This is a period where the overarching power—the global hegemony—is being understood as the Empire that has acquired new meanings. However, the establishment of this capitalism and change in all societies and all regions is not uniform and in many places it is distorted, where the forms of women's oppression are starkly visible and naked. In some other places, the problem seems to be local like in the case of women trafficking in India and in Myanmar; but after going beyond a surface analysis, we see that it is tied to the larger forces of criminal networks which are as much part of the globalization trend as the legitimate business. This trend also shows the emergence of human trafficking as a transnational activity, reflecting the dark underside of globalization. While some papers such as Lipi Ghosh's paper and Ajailiu Niumai's piece touch on aspects regarding the distortions of these new developments in regions far removed from the happening places of the United States and Europe, we also have papers that try to understand women's problems in the heartland of globalization—Europe and Canada. Here, the authors trace the different fragments in the Western societies and also the role of immigrants and the new notions of work. These regimes have raised important questions that have been effectively grappled by women, yet a lot needs to be done particularly in terms of employment and equality in these countries and also the problem of difference, with a large number of non-whites immigrating there. Another paper extends this scope of enquiry to South Africa, which is again a transitional society where the burden of transition is accompanied by the deadweight of apartheid and racial divide. This paper focuses on the problems associated with a new regime against the background of unresolved problems, but with a historic beginning—the Truth and Reconciliation Committee.

In the context of South Africa, U. Joan Fairhurst shows how women's activism and an unconditional stance against discriminatory practice of all kinds have been rewarded. She provides evidence to show that women are taking their rightful place in society today, serving in all walks of life: not just the traditional sectors of care, health and education, but also as decision-makers in homes, communities and in a variety of social, political and economic spheres. Increasingly, women are being afforded opportunities and recognition for their integral role in a balanced and well-functioning society at local, national and international level. N.A. Flipsen and Th.P. van der Weide highlight the women's movement in the Netherlands in the period 1870–2009. They point out that these movements can only be fully appreciated when seen in the context of the overall women's movements in Western countries in the same period.

This paper looks at the development of the women's movement in three phases and concludes that progress has been made towards equality and equity of men and women. Up to now, this process has already taken a century and is still ongoing. Societal changes, human traditions and values seem to need a lot of time and need to be pushed from various angles. Role models are needed to break barriers and existing thinking patterns, and often, changes do not come easily, but come with power and force. For the Western societies, in particular, the Dutch society women have been able to place themselves in all layers and have taken important positions, similar to men. Shauna Wilton's chapter explores the English–Canadian women's movement from the beginning of the twentieth century until today, with a focus on women's legal and political issues and advances. At the beginning of the twenty-first century, advocates of gender equality are finding it increasingly difficult to mobilize women despite the rolling back of the Canadian welfare state and successive policies that undermine women's position in Canadian society. In fact, the situation of Canadian women—particularly Aboriginal women, minority women and single-parent women—is more vulnerable than it has been for many decades. This chapter reinforces the necessity and urgency of developing new frames and calls to action for women that meet the combined challenges of neo-liberalism, neo-conservatives and globalization. In conclusion, several alternatives for the future of the Canadian women's movement are proposed.

Besides South Africa, Canada, the Netherlands, other countries that are also analyzed here are Bangladesh, Nigeria, Philippines and Brazil. In Brazil, feminization of poverty is an area of enquiry. Thematically, the papers are organized into five parts, titled Women's Movement; Caste, Class and Governance; Work and Labour; Violence and Sexual Harassment; and Marginality and Health Issues. Some papers from the same region fall in different categories, and a typical example of this trend is a set of papers on the tribal regions of North-East India, where literacy has penetrated recently, but the residual customs of the Mizo and Naga tribes are fused into Christianity with a high literacy rate, and exhibit a considerable degree of tension that has not been problematized. The existence of scant records, fieldwork or recent data that have helped to usher in a new understanding of these concerns is the object of enquiry by Hminthanzuali in her paper. This region stands as a contrast to the image of India as a Hindu caste society, which is the focus of another set of papers that seek to problematize the notion of caste via a gender lens and see its operation in the present day.

An understanding of the present day is critical as the dynamics of caste have undergone a considerable change both at the ground level and also in terms of fresh academic understanding, where new ground has been broken. Of significant mention would be the disuse of outmoded categories such as *varna,* that have only theoretical significance, and the recognition of categories such as *dalit,* that has entered the parlance of discussion in the Indian civil society. A series of papers try to tackle these problems and demonstrate that while issues of caste are important, they are not of the same mould as the 1960s when the stereotype of caste in Hindu society was set in academia. The caste situation has morphed, and we also see its operation in urban India albeit in different forms. This shows that both rural and urban India have changed but still have to confront these primordial problems. It would be too unfair to typecast India in the same mould for we now have a strong and articulate middle class with a booming economy and an educated workforce. How this workforce is staffed by women managers who have to battle the glass ceiling is another area of enquiry. Such questions are also raised in a set of articles pertaining to entrepreneurship that seek to pin down the pitfalls staving off women entrepreneurs in an unequal marketplace. A fundamental conflict between different sets of data prepared by the governmental agencies and others, coupled with the diverse perceptions generated in part by the different expectations, shape the views of the actors, and this is neatly brought out in the form of strong arguments that seek to unravel the access of women to the marketplace and higher jobs and the patterns behind such structures. While the economy has expanded and the world of work has changed qualitatively, there is still a glass ceiling and there are also problems of credit and lending, etc., that stunt women's growth. Work and women managers are always addressed in terms of being an upper-class reality that is now shaken and there is a discussion on even women walking the ramp in Bollywood. A woman entrepreneur in a free market where everything is supposed to be equal in terms of market forces is an area of analysis concerning one paper. Sita Vanka's paper examines the problems, performance and perceptions of women in sustaining business in the Indian context. Education and recognition are the reasons which lend strength to women in business. Finance, competition, labour and HRM are the problems that women face in the process of managing business but women strongly believe that these are not real but perceptive in nature. Lalit Joshi's paper looks at the transformation of urban India into gargantuan manifestations of steel, brick and mortar in the seventies and the eighties, accompanied by the rise of a middle class which displayed an evergrowing appetite for consumer products, even though economic liberalization and globalization were a few years away. Taking an example of a film, he has argued that the filmic narrative is not only constructed along gendered lines and spectatorship designed to manipulate male gaze, but gay interludes are also thrown in to bring the narrative in sync with the contemporary discourse on sexuality.

A series of papers examine themes related to work and another series on gender inequality, health and poverty. Issues of access to food and nutrition and gender and poverty alleviation are also addressed here. Bangladesh is a theme that is investigated although it is seen as a part of South Asia; the framework obscures certain diversities and here an attempt is made to look at the specifics of Bangladeshi women who are divorced. The paper on divorce in Bangladesh finds place in the section on Violence and Sexual Harassment because the divorced women and their children are becoming vulnerable within the society and face a lot of problems due to their poor socio-economic conditions. Gender empowerment in administration is a reality that has entered the political rhetoric but how much of it is lip service is a topic investigated in detail with some suggestions. Faisal Ahmmed and Tofayel Ahmed's paper explores the health status of rural pregnant women and their medical support-seeking behaviour in general and looks at how the situation of pregnancy- and childbirth-related morbidity and mortality is worse in Bangladesh because of low utilization of maternal health services. No discourse on feminism in India would be complete without reference to Muslims, who make up one of India's largest minorities. The problems stemming from being Muslim women in a largely Hindu society and doubly burdened with personal laws is the focus of K.M. Ziyauddin's paper. This is particularly relevant since India has the second largest number of Muslims in the world, and the significant fact is that they have not been drawn to the larger politics of West Asia. In India, the Muslim situation is very peculiar since it is not part of the global Islamic agenda though the Muslims were one of the ruling classes for centuries in India; and also the fact that in terms of ethnicity, the second and the third largest groups of Muslims—the Bengalis and the Urdu-speaking Muslims—are found in the Indian subcontinent. As minorities, governed by their personal law boards, the Muslims as a minority are in a special situation. The vibrant debate on the minorities in the Indian social sphere and the academia has also thrown important observations since the past two decades, and the characterization of the Hindus as a majority is also being problematized with region playing an important role as a marker of identity. Further, with India being seen as a series of extended minorities rather than as a simple majority–minority dichotomy brings out certain realities. Indira Mahendravada looks at the role of caste and its association with governance as articulated through family and other structures. Swain's paper rounds off the discussion by looking at the dominant caste ideology as a form of dominance. Although some papers focused on the mainstream knowledge economy and others complemented it with the linkages between new forms of oppression and the global criminal economy, some grey areas were also left out. M.N. Rajesh's paper looks at the phenomena of the open moment. Beginning with an overview of the transitions, the article elaborates on the range of changes and how many regions and sectors have emerged, as well as the decline of other stable regions and industries. Having established that this is an open moment, the paper appeals for an urgency to seize the moment and gender the knowledge economy because in the open moment, the possibilities for many changes are open, but the fact that the future may soon be colonized and out of bounds is also a looming reality. It proceeds to argue based on examples that the newly-emerging economies have grasped the enormity of this opportunity to catch up with the West and have become a potent power in the making with special reference to the BRICS countries and the East Asian Tigers. However, the catch is that gender is not taken here as a category at all, thereby marginalizing a vast majority. Olugu Ukpai's paper shows how recent efforts at the official international level, particularly by the United Nations agencies, have successfully put Female Genital Cutting (FGC) on women's health and human rights agendas and labelled it as a form of violence against women, and while many governments and national leaders have publicly denounced the practice, only a few translated their oratory into effective and practical laws prohibiting violence, or into programmes to empower practitioners to abandon it. His article investigates why decades of legal efforts towards the abolition of violence practices such as FGC against the Nigerian women remain an illusion. Sexual harassment in Kerala is also investigated in detail and Rebecca John's paper problematizes what is popularly known as the 'Kerala Model of Development' in relation to gender equality by arguing that the statistical optimism about the status of women in Kerala belies the everyday experience of violence women face. Two similar papers on desertion in Andhra Pradesh by R. Jayasree and stalking by B. Ratna Kumari take up new forms of violence against women and give more support to the argument in the form of good documentation of phenomena that is widespread. Attitudinal changes are a clear indicator of the direction in which the society is moving, and this is best conceptualized in many articles taking into account a host of factors that condition us and which are also in a flux.

To sum up, gender is about relationships between men and women. Gender equality is about equal valuing of women and men—of their similarities and their differences. We need equal, respectful partnerships between men and women for the creation of an equitable society in which gender justice is realized. Gender lens then become the spectacles. Out of one lens of the spectacles, one can see the participation, needs and realities of women. Out of the other lens, one can see the participation, needs and realities of men. One's sight or vision is the combination of what each eye sees. We need both eyes to see best. This book is an interdisciplinary work that places gender at the intersection of society, caste, race, sexuality and work. It becomes an interesting exercise at looking at a variety of other socially constructed categories of difference and inequality such as ethnicity, culture, work, religion and sexuality shaping gender. As is the case with prisms in a kaleidoscope, the interaction of gender with other social prisms creates complex patterns of identity and relationships for people across groups and situations. Gender is a complex and multifaceted array of experiences and meanings that cannot be understood without considering the social context within which they are situated and wearing the gender lens.

Part I

Women's Movements

CHAPTER 1

Feminism and Women's Movement in India: Historical Context

Rekha Pande

The present chapter looks at the historical background of the rise of feminism and the women's movement in India. Not only in India, but all over the world, there has been a close link between the two, each inspiring and enriching the other. Any basic definition of feminism or feminisms can start with the assertion that at the centre of feminism are the concerns for women's subordinate status in society, and with the discrimination encountered by women because of their sex. Further, feminists call for changes in the social, economic, political or cultural order to reduce and eventually overcome this discrimination against women and create an equitable society in which gender justice is achieved.

FEMINISM AND WOMEN'S MOVEMENT

While the women's movement is a much earlier phenomenon, the term 'feminism' is a modern one. Yet, there is a very close connection between the two. Feminism is said to be the movement to end women's oppression (hooks, 2000: 26). The term 'feminism' seems to have been first used in 1871 in a French medical text to describe a cessation in development of the sexual organs and characteristics in male patients who were perceived as suffering from 'feminization' of their bodies (Fraisse, 1995). The term was then picked up by Alexander Dumas, a French writer, republican and anti-feminist, to describe women who behaved in a supposedly masculine way. The term became widely used in the mid-nineteenth century when the Women's Rights Movement emerged in the United States of America with the Seneca Falls Convention of 1848. This was followed by the writings of Elizabeth Candy Stanton and Mary Wollstonecraft, who questioned many injustices meted out to women. Hence, the term 'feminism' emerged long after women started questioning their inferior status and demanding an amelioration of their social position. In the Indian context, many groups were not comfortable with the use of the term 'feminists' and did not identify their struggle for women's rights with this term. But today, by and large, 'feminism' as a term is understood to denote the political stance of someone committed to changing the social position of women.

Feminism comprises a number of social, cultural and political movements, theories and moral philosophies concerned with gender inequalities and equal rights for women. One can clearly see the history of feminism as consisting of three waves. The apparent pattern of rise and fall of feminism over time has led to the wave analogy in which the peaks and troughs of the feminist movement are characterized as following the motion of tidal waters, with its ongoing cycle of gradual swelling, eventual cresting and final subsiding (Pilcher and Whelehan, 2004: 52). The first wave was in the mid-nineteenth and early twentieth century and was primarily concerned with gaining equal rights for women, particularly the rights to suffrage. In Britain, the Suffragettes campaigned for the women's vote. In 1918, the Representation of the People Act was passed granting the franchise to propertied women over the age of 30 years. In 1928, this was extended to all women over 18 years (Phillips, 2004). The second wave was in the 1960s and 1970s when protests were centred on women's inequality, not only in the context of women's political rights, but also in the areas of family, sexuality and work. Second-wave feminism has existed continuously since then and continues to coexist with what is termed 'third wave'.

The second-wave feminism saw cultural and political inequalities as inextricably linked. The movement encouraged women to understand aspects of their own personal lives as deeply politicized, and reflective of a sexist structure of power. If the first-wave feminism focused upon absolute rights such as suffrage, the second-wave feminism was largely concerned with other issues of equality, such as the end to discrimination (ibid.). Carol Hanisch, with her essay *The Personal is Political,* coined a slogan that became synonymous with the second wave and was related to the women's liberation movement (DuBois, 1997).

The third-wave feminism extends from the 1990s to the present. The movement arose in the early 1990s as a response to the perceived failures of second-wave feminism. The third wave was also a response to the backlash against initiatives and movements created by the second wave. Third-wave feminism seeks to challenge or avoid what it deems the second wave's 'essentialist' definitions of feminity, which (according to them) overemphasized the experiences of upper-middle-class white women. A post-structuralist interpretation of gender and sexuality is central to the third wave's ideology.

Third-wave feminists often focus on 'micro-politics' and challenged the second wave's paradigm as to what is, or is not, good for females. Post-feminism is a term that is used to describe a range of viewpoints reacting to feminism. The term was first used in the 1980s to signify a backlash against the second-wave feminism. It now denotes a wide range of theories, some of which argued that postmodernism has destabilized the notion of a universal feminity, and takes a critical approach to previous feminist discourses, including challenges to the second-wave ideas (Gillis et al., 2007). One of the earliest uses of the term was in Susan Bolotin's 1982 article 'Voices of the Post-Feminist Generation', published in *The New York Times Magazine*. This article was based on a number of interviews with women who largely agreed with the goals of feminism, but did not identify themselves as feminists (Rosen, 2000). Some contemporary feminists, like Pollitt Katha, consider feminism to hold simply that 'women are people'. Views that separate the sexes rather than uniting them are considered by these writers to be *sexist* rather than *feminist* (Pollitt, 1995).

Although one talks about the different phases of feminism, one cannot divide them into water-tight compartments. Rather, there has been a continuum of thought and activities across the three periods. Feminist theory developed from the feminist movement. It takes a number of forms in a variety of disciplines such as feminist geography, feminist history, feminist literary criticism and so on. The link between the rise of certain ideologies and social movements is clearly seen in the case of the shifts in the feminist movements the world over. Such currents have impacted India also to a large extent. In the Indian context, we can see the rise of feminism and the women's movement in two distinct phases: the pre-Independence era and the post-Independence era.

WOMEN'S MOVEMENT IN PRE-INDEPENDENCE INDIA

Pre-colonial social structures and women's role in them reveal that feminism was theorized differently in India than in the West. Colonial essentialization of 'Indian culture' and reconstruction of Indian womanhood as the epitome of that culture through social reform movements resulted in political theorization in the form of nationalism rather than as feminism alone (Chatterjee, 1989). In the pre-Independence era, the women's movement began as a social reform movement in the nineteenth century. At this time, the Western ideas of liberty, equality and fraternity were being imbibed by our educated elite through the study of English and the contact with the West. This Western liberalism was extended to the women's question and was translated into a social reform movement. The reform movements however were not homogeneous and varied a lot in terms of the ideas and changes that were to be fostered. They did, however, share a common concern for rooting out social evils, partly in response to charges of barbarity from the colonial rulers. This was a period of the hegemonic control and influence of colonial ideology. It was a time of transition; one of the emerging bourgeois society and values; and of new modes of thought.

The colonial intervention in the nineteenth century was no longer confined only to the market or polity, but it was intruding into the areas of culture and society, effecting transformation in the social fabric of Indian society. This potential threat was sensed by the Indian intellectual reformers, exposed to the Western ideas and values. Sensitive to the power of colonial domination and responding to the Western ideas of rationalism, liberalism and civilized society, they also sought ways and means of resisting this colonial hegemony by resorting to what K.N. Panikkar refers to as the cultural defence (Panikkar, 1975).

This cultural defence resulted in a paradoxical situation. Spurred by new European ideas of rationalism and progress, the reformers tried to create a new society, modern yet rooted in Indian tradition. They began a critical appraisal of Indian society in an attempt to create a new ethos devoid of all overt social aberrations such as polytheism, polygamy, casteism, *sati*, child marriage and illiteracy—all of which they believed were impediments to the progress of women. All the social reformers shared a belief common to many parts of the world in the nineteenth century that no society could progress if its women were backward. To the reformers, the position of Indian women, as it was in the nineteenth century, was abysmally low, and hence their efforts were directed at an overall improvement in the status of women through legislation, political action and propagation of education. This was mainly spurred by the first-wave feminism of the West and concentrated on achieving basic rights for women.

The social reform movement did not radically challenge the existing patriarchal structure of society, nor did it question gender relations. It picked up for reform only those issues that the Britishers were pointing out as evidence of degeneration in the Indian society. Even the women's institutions and organizations that sprang up during this period did not have an independent ideology, but only took off from what the men were stating. This is understandable because it was primarily the wives and sisters of the reformers who had initiated the establishment of these organizations. The direction and content of reform as laid down by the reformers was accepted by the women's organizations without any question. As a result, even when women were speaking for themselves, they were speaking only the language of the men, defined by male parameters (Pande, et. al, 1987: 391).

Women were seen as passive recipients of a more humanitarian treatment to be given by the Western-educated male elite. There was thus an attempt to reform the women rather than reform the social conditions that opposed them. There were no attempts made to alter the power structures and the man–woman relations in the society. This was but natural since the change in the status of woman was being sought without questioning patriarchy itself. Besides seeking reforms through legislation, education was also seen as an important means of changing women's situation

(Forbes, 1981). Women's education, which saw its beginning, now was visualized for creating appropriate wives for the men of the newly emerging Westernized elite (Mazumdar, 1972). The attempt was to create a new Indian woman, truly Indian and yet sufficiently educated and tutored in the nineteenth-century values, to suit the new emerging society. Education for girls was not meant to equip them to be self-sufficient, independent and emancipated or to train them to follow some profession, but instead to become good housewives and mistresses for the home and hearth (Pande et. al, 1987: 393). Thus, the social reform movement had its own paradox: on the one hand, there was a preoccupation with the Western ideas to emulate, assimilate or reject. On the other hand, there was also an element of revivalism, a need to reassert and reinforce a cultural identity distinct from the British colonizers.

Women's roles were also being pushed to a more traditional way of life as a form of backlash to the new ideas colonialism brought to India. Women became emblematic of tradition, and the reworking of tradition came to be largely conducted through debating the rights and status of women in society (Sangari and Vaid, 1989: 90). Consequently, whenever 'Indian' culture was felt to be threatened, an immediate response was the enforcement of more traditional roles for women.

This is not belittling the contributions of the social reform movement. Despite its limitations, it cannot be denied that the social reform movement did help in removing prejudices against women's education and provided a secular space for women in the public realm. The only space available to a woman earlier was in the religious sphere, and in the ancient period, Buddhism and Jainism provided such a space. Nevertheless, women had to choose between religion and domesticity; and if they chose religion, they had to move out of the families by becoming a part of the *Sangha*.

In the medieval period, the *Bhakti* movement declared that God dwells in each individual and that one could attain God through faith. The movement thus provided a space for the downtrodden and marginalized sections of the population, and many women took the opportunity to move out of their daily life of patriarchal control and attain independence (Pande, 2005a: 281–82). For all these women *Bhaktas*, the rejection of the power of the male figure they were tied to in a subordinate relationship became the terrain for struggle, self-assertion and alternative seeking. Yet, the women still had to choose between marriage and a life of domesticity and their love for the supreme God. Many of the women saints in medieval India emerged from an atmosphere of discrimination and oppression where patriarchal values still were held in high regard to chart their own course, emerging in the end as individuals with a mind of their own. All this was only possible due to the space provided by *Bhakti* movement (Pande, 2010: 181).

The social reform movement performed a similar function by providing secular space for women and by addressing the various culturally imposed issues that were crippling them. Raja Ram Mohan Roy argued that *sati* was not supported by *Shastras* and was nothing less than female murder. He also argued against polygamy and for property rights for women. Rabindranath Tagore submitted a memorandum to the Legislative Council for the removal of legal disabilities of remarried Hindu widows and the establishment of girls' schools in every suburb of Calcutta. Keshav Chandra Sen was instrumental in getting the Native Marriage Act passed in 1872, which forbade not only early marriage between boys under the age of 18 years and girls under the age of 14 years but also polygamy, and encouraged widow marriage. Moreover, it allowed inter-caste marriages for those who declared that they did not belong to any recognized faith. Ishwar Chandra Vidyasagar was also very critical of the system of early marriage and supported literacy for women. Soon, many women's organizations also took up these reforms.

Pandita Ramabai's Sharda Sadan (1892) in Poona, Shri Mahipatram Rupram Anathashram in Ahmedabad (1892), Shri Zorastrian Mandal in Bombay (1903), the Maternity and Child Welfare League in Baroda (1914) and the Bhagini Samaj in Poona (1916) were all established with the particular objective of improving the lot of women and removing the various ills in society. These regional organizations were followed by the creation of national organizations such as Women's Indian Association (1917) and the National Council of Women in India (1920). The All India Women's Conference (1926) went on to organize 12 women's conferences till 1937, and the Federation of University Women in India (1920) had the sole objective of stimulating the interests of women in civic and public life and the removal of disabilities of women, whether legal, economic or social and the promotion of social, civil, moral and educational welfare of women and children (Forbes, 2000).

Women also joined the struggle against colonialism. However, while they were encouraged to participate by leaders such as Gandhi, their work in the struggle was mainly an extension of their domestic duties. Very few women were allowed to join the front ranks with men, and the ones who did, spoke of the isolation they felt at times (Kumar, 1993: 4). When Mohandas Karamchand Gandhi came on the political scene, he could draw in a large number of women to the political arena by giving a very broad meaning of *swaraj*. He helped them find dignity in public life and a new place in the national mainstream. Gandhiji's views installed a new confidence among women and a consciousness that they too could fight against oppression.

Gandhiji firmly believed that 'it is good to swim in the waters of tradition, but to sink in them is suicide'. To him, the fight for *swaraj* meant not merely a political awakening but an all-round awakening—social, educational, moral, economic and political and social work. Gandhiji's work was mainly a response and also an answer to finding an Indian path to modernity in a situation where colonialism had to be rooted out and a viable structure had to come in its place. As a result, a large number of women came and joined the civil disobedience movement during the 1930s. Besides Sarojini Naidu and Kamaladevi Chattopadhyay, there were thousands of other women who readily participated in the freedom struggle. In 1931, the Picketing Board was started in collaboration with Bengal Provincial Congress Committee to popularize the home industries, especially the spinning and weaving of khadi. Punjab saw the inauguration of the Civil Disobedience Movement by a procession of 5,000 women at Lahore in 1930 under the leadership of Lado Rani Zutshi and Parvati, the daughter of Lala Lajpat Rai. Durgabai Deshmukh organized the women in Madras to carry forward the policies of the Congress.

The manufacture of salt in defiance of the British laws prohibiting such manufacture had a lot of symbolic value for the women. Here was a very private issue linked to their daily lives in the kitchen, brought to the forefront of the public realm. As a result, a large number of women from the villages also joined Gandhiji at Dandi. Gandhiji firmly believed that by nature women were non-violent, and hence would be more successful in carrying out his programmes of picketing and non-cooperation.

Therefore, when Gandhiji brought India's freedom struggle to the masses, women were very active participants in it. Nehru acknowledges this, and he wrote, 'Though we talk of revolution, political and economic, the greatest revolution in our country is the one that affects the status and living conditions of its women. It was Gandhi, the wonderful man and great revolutionary, who brought a dramatic change among our women, when at his bidding they came out in large numbers from the shelters of their homes to take part in the struggle for India's freedom. Once the old shackles were removed it was no doubt made to make them go back, but they were bound to fail. In his India of dreams, women would enjoy the same rights as men' (Nehru, 1982 [1946]: 363).

Nevertheless, throughout the freedom struggle, the majority of women participated only in supporting roles. The male leadership at this time did not encourage a second line of leadership and women could assume leadership only when the men were in prison. Nehru refers to this in his *Discovery of India*, 'Most of us menfolk were in prison, and then a remarkable thing happened. Our women came to the front and took charge of the struggle. Women had always been there of course, but now there was an upsurge of them, which took not only the British government but also their own menfolk by surprise. Here were these women, of the upper or middle classes leading sheltered lives in their homes, peasant women, working women pouring out in tens and thousands in defiance of government order and police *lathi*. It was not only their display of courage and daring, but what was more surprising was the organizational power they showed.' This was for the first time in Indian history that a large mass of women were mobilized for political purposes in a mass organization.

It was primarily due to the efforts of women and their role in the freedom struggle that women got the right to vote and complete equality in the Constitution of India. Article 15(3) empowers the state to make special provisions for women. A large number of policy documents also followed. Unfortunately, a great gap soon arose between the theoretical status of women and what existed in reality.

The heterogeneity of the Indian experience reveals that just as there are multiple patriarchies, so also are there multiple feminisms.

Hence, feminism in India is not a singular theoretical orientation; it has changed over time in relation to the historical and cultural realities, levels of consciousness and perceptions and actions of individual women and of women as a group. The current widely used definition of feminism states that it is 'an awareness of women's oppression and exploitation in society, at work and within the family, and conscious action by women and men to change this situation' (Bhasin and Khan, 1986).

WOMEN'S MOVEMENT IN POST-INDEPENDENCE PERIOD

Immediately after Independence, India had to deal with a variety of problems. The joy of Independence was tempered by the sadness of Partition, the migration of a large number of people and the outbreak of communal violence in Punjab and Bengal. This was followed by the war in Kashmir, the danger of territorial fragmentation, the dispersion of power among 600 princely states and, last but not the least, the economic dislocation that was to affect women the most. Years of colonial domination had destroyed our indigenous crafts and depleted our natural resources. Industrialization, changing technologies, illiteracy and lack of mobility, all resulted in the inability of women to cope with the new order. Once their labour was regarded as unimportant in the productive market, their role in the family also became marginal, giving them a raw status that became abysmal with the passage of time.

In the first few decades of the post-Independence period, the major concern was the overall economic growth. This was immediately followed by a decade of increased concern for poverty alleviation and equity. Gender issues were subsumed in poverty-related concerns, and there were no specific programmes aimed at women (Women in India, 1985). Women activists during this period were involved in such movements as the anti-price law and famine relief movements and did not start to pick up issues involving their oppression as women until the 1970s. Now increasingly, there has been an emphasis on the promotion of non-governmental, grassroots-level organizations (NGOs) for women's development. Some of these organizations have varied in their scope, objectives and vision, but they have nevertheless provided women avenues for collectively voicing their concerns. These grassroots organizations have questioned the welfare approach to women (wherein women are primarily seen as beneficiaries or recipients of programmes) and instead incorporated an empowering participatory approach. Although questions about the success of these organizations are often raised, it is often seen that women exposed to some amount of mobilization show great potentialities, receptiveness and defining capacities (Banerjee, 1992).

The myth of equality for women was shattered by the path-breaking report, *Towards Equality,* of 1975. The report focused attention on the fact that despite many progressive social legislations and constitutional guarantees, women's status had not improved much. Women continued to have an inferior status in many areas, including the political, economic and social spheres. The report pointed out the sad fact that society had not yet succeeded in framing the required norms and institutions that would enable women to fulfil their multiple roles. The increasing incidence of practices such as dowry indicated a further lowering of the status of women. The report also indicated a process of regression from some of the norms developed during the freedom movement as the concern for women and their problems, which had received an impetus during the freedom movement and had suffered a decline in the past two decades (*Towards Equality,* 1975).

To implement the recommendations of the *Towards Equality* report of 1975, a blueprint of action points and national plan of action for women (1976) suggested measures in the areas of education, health, family planning and nutrition, employment, social welfare and legal status. A separate chapter on 'Women and Development 1980–1985' in the Sixth Five-Year Plan resulted in women being perceived as productive contributors to the national economy. The Seventh Five-Year Plan also had a chapter on 'Socio-economic Programmes for Women' (1985–1989), which moved away from a welfare approach to a more positive developmental one. The Indian Parliament adopted a National Policy on Education in 1986, which too included a chapter on education for women's equality. The National Perspective Plan for Women was released in October 1988, whereas the 2000 SAARC Decade Plan of Action focused on the girl child.

CONTEMPORARY ISSUES OF THE WOMEN'S MOVEMENT

In the decades following Independence, the women's movement has concerned itself with a large number of issues such as dowry, women's work, price rise, land rights, political participation of women, the rights of *Dalit* women and other marginalized women, growing fundamentalism, women's representation in the media and so on. In the process, it has been able to draw a large number of women around three major issues, referred to as the three Gs: the attitude towards the girl child, gender violence and globalization. Women's status in any society is an indicator of its development and progress. The girl child is the woman of tomorrow. Unfortunately, she is by and large neglected by society. Indian culture idolizes boys and dreads the birth of girls. Girl children are breast-fed for a shorter time than their male siblings, and they are also drawn out of school to take care of siblings. The cycle of deprivation and disadvantage is further compounded by early marriage, premature pregnancies and their attended risks. The girl child needs to be empowered to enter the mainstream of economic and social activity (Pande, 2004).

The many forms of violence against women and children are to be understood as gender violence. Until we look at such violence as a developmental and human rights issue and not as a private issue, we will not be able to see the question in its totality. Violence has an economic, social and political cost to society and is not a private affair. Definition of domestic violence in India rests not only upon the nature of relationship between the perpetrator and the victim, but also upon the culturally accepted norms of behaviour. Most of the public discourse equates domestic violence only with dowry deaths. Such an understanding undermines the daily psychological, physical and sexual abuse confronted by women in their day-to-day lives. There appears to be a culture of silence around the issue of domestic violence because of the divide between public and private (Pande, 2005b: 213). The women's struggle against the sale of arrack in Andhra Pradesh had 20 non-political organizations that fought for the scrapping of auctions and bring about a complete ban on its manufacture. Through this movement, women have definitely emerged out winners because they are well aware of their strengths and ability to bring about change in society (Pande, 2005, 215). Most importantly, the anti-arrack agitation is a very good example of the articulation of family violence in public. It showed a feminist way of looking at issues, especially a private issue like family violence and aligning it to a larger issue of state and society. It questioned the notion about domestic violence being private and women not being able to do anything about it (Pande, 2002, 367).

The liberalization of the economy in the wake of globalization in many South Asian countries has vastly diminished traditional livelihood means for the poor. The dominance of rich nations, multinational corporations and international capital over markets, resources and labour in the developing countries through trade, aid and technology transfer has greatly weakened the capacity of nation-states and governments to promote human development and offer protection to the poor people (Pande, 2001: 1). Globalization has also reduced the control of women over resources. It has led to mass displacement; and when both men and women land up in urban slums, it affects the women more due to lack of sanitation and increase of violence. In this process, the knowledge of traditional medicines, herbs and plants has also been destroyed. The rhetoric of globalization promises to remove backwardness through a worldwide exchange of information and the establishment of a cosmopolitan culture; but since the world is based on unequal power relations, in actual practice, these concerns are put on hold, leading to displacement, marginalization and pauperization (Pande, 2007).

Customs, culture and religion are intertwined in a traditional society and change is very slow. The problems that women face at home or within their families in India are uniform regardless of religion, caste or community. Nevertheless, women continue to be governed by a multiplicity of family laws that are detrimental to them due to the political repercussions. Although much is talked about a uniform civil code, no party or political leadership would really attempt this for fear of a backlash since women still have identities built around family and religion and not of citizens of a secular state.

There has been no dearth of documents or policies relating to women. There has been a shift from welfare to development, to integrating women in development, to empowerment. The 73rd and 74th constitutional amendments of 1993, providing for reservation of seats for women in *panchayats* (grassroots-level administrative organizations in the village) and municipalities are a giant stride in the empowerment of women. With 33 per cent reservation for women in rural and urban local bodies, today, 15 years down the line, we have 1.2 million elected women representatives in the institutions of local governance in rural India (Study on Panchayati Raj, 2008). Yet, we are also witness to the hurdles and obstacles placed in passing the Bill providing for reservation in the legislatures and Lok Sabha. The setting up of the National Commission has also helped in creating an environment for the realization of women's equality.

In the post-Independence period, development was the major issue. When the whole debate on development started, there were a number of women who were organizing and mobilizing around the globe for their rights. The development planners and policy-makers did not have any interaction with these groups as they considered feminism as irrelevant to development—a luxury for the better-off women in the industrialized countries. Hence, the first-stage, main-stream development models gave rise to jargons such as 'basic human needs', 'meeting the needs of the poorest of poor' and 'growth with equity'. This phase viewed development as an administrative problem whose solution lay in transferring vast amount of resources and technological innovations from rich to poor countries.

As compensation, the phase that followed stressed the need for integrating women into the development process. Education and employment as a means of income generation became indicators of women's involvement in the development process; but again, a large chunk of rural women were left behind. It was the women's movement that addressed the question of development from a feminist perspective. It has raised important questions on issues of child care, reproductive rights, violence against women, family planning, transfer of technology and rural development and has given the concept of development a new meaning.

If development leads only to an increase in production, then it tends to reinforce and exaggerate the imbalances and inequalities within and in between societies. Development has to be an integral process, with economic, social and cultural aspects leading to the control of one's life situation. Herein comes the concept of empowerment. To conclude, it is the women's movement in India that has been the force behind the long struggle of women's advancement from subordination to gender equality and finally, to women's empowerment. Although a lot needs to be done and still there are several impediments to making this reality available to all Indian women, the women's movement has nevertheless been able to bring women's issues to the centrestage and make them more visible.

REFERENCES

Banerjee, Narayan, 1992, *Grassroots Empowerment*, Mimeograph. New Delhi: Centre for Women's Development Studies.

Bhasin, Kamala and Nighat Said Khan, 1986, *Some Questions on Feminism and Its Relevance in South Asia*. New Delhi: Kali for Women.

Chatterjee, Partha, 1989, 'The Nationalist Resolution of the Women's Question'. In *Recasting Women: Essays in Colonial History*, edited by Kumkum Sangari and Sudesh Vaid, New Delhi: Kali for Women.

DuBois, Ellen Carol, 1997, *Harriot Stanton Blatch and the Winning of Woman Suffrage*. New Haven, CO: Yale University Press. Also see, http://scholar.alexanderstreet.com/pages/viewpage.action?pageId=2259, accessed 27 March 2009.

Forbes, Geraldine, 1981, 'The Indian Women's Movement: A Struggle for Women's Rights or National Liberation?'. In *The Extended Family*, edited by Gail Minault, New Delhi: Chanakya Publications, pp. 49–82.

Forbes, Geraldine, 2000, *Women in Modern India*. Cambridge: Cambridge University Press.

Fraisse, G., 1995, as quoted in Freedman, Jane, 2002, *Feminisms*. New Delhi: Viva Books Private Limited.

Gillis, Stacy, Gillian Howie and Rebecca Munford (Eds.), 2007, *Third Wave Feminism: A Critical Exploration*. Basingstoke: Palgrave Macmillan.

hooks, bell, 2000, *Feminist Theory: From Margins to Center*, 2nd ed. London: Pluto Press.

Kumar, Radha, 1993, *History of Doing, An Illustrated Account of Movements for Women's Rights and Feminism in India, 1800–1900*. New Delhi: Kali for Women.

Mazumdar, Vina, 1972, *Education and Social Change: Three Studies in 19th Century Bengal*. Shimla: Indian Institute of Advanced Study.

Nehru, Jawaharlal, 1982 (1946), *The Discovery of India*. New Delhi: Oxford University Press.

Pande, Rekha, 2001, The Social Costs of Globalization: Restructuring Developing World Economies, *Journal of Asian Women's Studies*, Vol. 10, December, Kitakyushu Forum, Japan. pp.1–14.

Pande, Rekha, 2002. "The Public Face of a Private Domestic Violence", *International Feminist Journal of Politics*. Vol. 4, No. 3, pp.342–367.

Pande, Rekha, 2004, 'The Girl Child in India', *Review of Women's Studies*, XIV(2), July–December: 149–73.

Pande, Rekha, 2005a, *Religious Movements in Medieval India*. New Delhi: Gyan Publishing House.

Pande, Rekha, 2005b, 'Solidarity, Patriarchy and Empowerment: Women's Struggle against Arrack in India'. In *Feminist Politics, Activism and Vision: Local and Global Challenges*, edited by Luciana Ricciutelli, Angela Miles and Margaret M. Mcfadden, New York: Zed Publications, pp. 212–26.

Pande, Rekha, 2007, 'Local and Global Encounters: Gender, Poverty and Globalization in India'. In Development, *Journal of Society for International Development*, Vol. 50, No. 2, Basingstoke: Palgrave Macmillan Ltd., pp. 134–40.

Pande, Rekha, 2010, *Divine Sounds from the Heart, Singing Unfettered in their Own Voices: The Bhakti Movement and its Women Saints (12th to 17th Century)*. New Castle, UK: Cambridge Scholars Publishing.

Pande Rekha and J. Kameshwari, 1987, 'Women's Discourse on Education' (Preliminary Readings of the Speeches Delivered at the Annual Conferences of the Andhra Mahila Sabha (1913 & 1914). In *Proceedings of Indian History Congress*, Goa: PIHC, pp. 390–96.

Panikkar, K.N., 1975, *Presidential Address: Section III, Proceedings of the Indian History Congress*, PIHC, thirty-sixth session, Aligarh.

Phillips, Melanie, 2004, *The Ascent of Woman: A History of the Suffragette Movement and the Ideas Behind It*. London: Abacus.

Pilcher, Jane and Imelda Whelehan, 2004, *50 Key Concepts in Gender Studies*. New Delhi: Sage Publications.

Pollitt, Katha, 1995, *Reasonable Creatures: Essays on Women and Feminism*. New York: Vintage Books.

Rosen, Ruth, 2000, *The World Split Open: How the Modern Women's Movement Changed America*. New York: Viking.

Sangari, Kumkum and Sudesh Vaid (Eds.), 1989, *Recasting Women: Essays in Colonial History*. New Delhi: Kali for Women.

Study on Elected Women Representatives in Panchayati Raj Institutions, 2008, Ministry of Panchayati Raj. New Delhi: Government of India.

Towards Equality, 1975, *Report of the Committee on the Status of Women India*. New Delhi: Government of India, Ministry of Education and Social Welfare.

Women in India – A Country Paper, 1985, Department of Women and Child Development. New Delhi: Ministry of Social Welfare, Government of India.

CHAPTER 2

South African Women's Movements: Thought, Words and Deed – Women in South Africa Organize to Let Their Voices Be Heard

U. Joan Fairhurst

Today, women in South Africa make a point of using celebratory events that take place on 9 August, Women's Day, institutionalized as a public holiday in 1994, to keep alive the notion that gender issues are developmental issues. The role women have played in the country's history has been significant and often tumultuous, yet peacefully effective. To entrench their recognition in society, women have let their voices be heard in ways that could not possibly be ignored. Each year, Women's Day rallies are held country-wide, with assured in-depth media coverage. Particularly significant was the commemorative event of 2006, which represents not only a mirror of the past but also portrays a vision of the future for all South African people who are part of today's ever-growing global village. With reference to this particular occasion, it will be seen that women in contemporary South African society bring together the global and the local in thought, word and deed.

First, the link between the commemorative event of 2006 and the event of 1956 that was celebrated will be explained. Second, a brief overview of the events that led up to the historic action of women on 9 August 1956, and its pre-1994 impact will be given. Third, some thoughts about the effect of the 1956 and 2006 events on contemporary South African society will be shared. Fourth, some evidence of women's achievements in a range of spheres in South African social, political and economic arenas will support the claim that the women of South Africa strive, as they look ahead, to meet the challenges facing a democratic society in the twenty-first century.

THE COMMEMORATIVE EVENT OF 2006

The democratic government of South Africa declared the year 2006 as *The Year of the Women of South Africa* in which a year-long campaign was launched to popularize, promote and recognize women who had, over the years, contributed to the achievement of democracy, whilst simultaneously sending a clear message that, in present-day South Africa, women should be equipped to participate freely and fully in all spheres of life. The theme for the commemoration, *Age of Hope: Through Struggle to Freedom*, captured this vision and guided the planning of events that took place in different parts of the country culminating in the re-enactment of the 1956 Women's March to the Union Buildings in Pretoria on 9 August 2006. Following the re-enactment, the then President, Thabo Mbeki, delivered an address and opened an exhibition depicting the struggles of the women of South Africa. Other prominent speakers also shared their experiences and views, and talented performers presented a cultural programme filled with poetry, song, dance and music. The spin-off of this celebration was seen to be an opportunity to 'mobilize women towards a social movement that would transcend all boundaries and make a difference to the lives of women worldwide' (South Africa DAC, 2006: 1). The celebrations would also mark the ongoing struggle by women in the country for freedom, democracy and equality (Dlamini, 2006).[1]

The initiative was launched on International Women's Day (8 March) of that year, 2006, and supported by the national Department of Arts and Culture, the Western Cape Office of the Premier and the provincial Departments of Cultural Affairs and Sport, Education, the Gender Desk and Youth Commission. Debate took place in the National Assembly and a commemorative tapestry was unveiled at Parliament. People's personal experiences were documented and thoughts expressed in published writings, books,[2] sculptures and other works of art through photographs, drama, storytelling and interviews and anecdotal conversation on stage, screen and radio. A range of social activities took place at the parliamentary, provincial and local levels, under the auspices of non-governmental organizations, business corporations and private enterprises in communities throughout the country, all of which were reported on through national television coverage and articles in newspapers and popular magazines. All events had the same flavour, and women attended these functions *en masse*, with lively yet sincere participation and colourful, vociferous chanting, celebrating the symbolism of the occasion and revealing the strength and determination that have been hallmarks of the many women's overt public demonstrations of purpose since the turn of the century that culminated in the particularly significant event of 1956.

On 9 August 1956, 20,000 women of all ages and from all walks of life, attired in characteristic outfits of infinite variety, came together from the villages and cities irrespective of religious, cultural and political affiliations or dispositions and staged a march on the Union Buildings in Pretoria to protest against the proposed amendments to the Urban Areas Act of 1950 that meant an extension of the pass laws to women. They left bundles of petitions containing more than 100,000 signatures at the Prime Minister's (JG Strydom) office door. Outside the Union Buildings, the women stood silently for 30 minutes, many with their children on their backs. Those who were working for whites as caregivers carried their white charges with them. The women then burst into a song, composed in honour of the occasion, in which the admonishment was loud and clear—'Now you have touched the women, you have struck a rock'. A rock has come to represent women's courage and strength in South Africa. The march 'had the effect of making the people confident and fearless, prepared to defy the laws, to be prepared to go to jail and meet any situation. That was the importance of it. It was the beginning of a new situation, which led even to a person facing the death penalty with confidence, ... You can see that a revolutionary situation was emerging' (Gasa, 2007 a: 207[3]), and it marked a decisive shift in the level, character and activities of the liberation movement led by the ANC[4] towards effective mobilization. The 9 August 1956 March against the carrying of passes bears testimony to the collective strength, determination and unity amongst women of all races and class; the government of the day had banned the march and women defied the ban, and brought the whole country to a standstill (South Africa DAC, 2006: 1; ANC, n.d.).

THE MID-1950s TO THE MID-1990s

This event of 1956 too had been carefully planned under anything but easy circumstances. The driving force behind the action came from women; women leaders and members of women's groups from all over the country as well as women who were ordinary citizens and were no longer prepared to tolerate unacceptable treatment at the hands of political authority. Since the mid-seventeenth century, restrictions were placed on the local inhabitants and slaves that affected their daily lives adversely. The Dutch East India Company established a refreshment station at the south-western tip of the continent of Africa to supply sailing vessels engaged in the spice trade between Europe and Asia, marking the beginning of southern Africa's exposure to the outside world. Many inhabitants moved further away into the interior during the eighteenth and nineteenth centuries; and more settlers arrived, settling mainly on the east coast, a development that gave birth to South Africa's characteristic racial diversity.

Entrenching the difference, the Natives Land Act of 1913 ruled that occupation for the indigenous black[5] people, the Africans, was limited to demarcated ancestral lands; areas not yet annexed by European settlers and amounting to a mere 13 per cent of South Africa's land surface (South Africa Yearbook, 2007/2008: 36) were located in very remote and generally under-resourced rural areas. All land purchases or rental tenancy outside these reserves, later called the homelands, became illegal for black people, and further administrative and legal measures reinforced the division between the white citizens and the black non-citizen (ibid.), thereby affecting every aspect of their lives, particularly employment and residential opportunities.

With the discovery of first diamonds and then gold in the interior of the country, the agricultural heritage changed dramatically, as did the lives of the womenfolk: as it affected where they lived, whom they could marry, where their children would attend school and what they would learn (as education for blacks was deliberately kept at an inferior level). Overseas investors developed mines that led to the growth of towns and cities since the budding industrial set-up needed workers. Men flocked to the fast-growing areas in search of work. But soon their service conditions were such that they were separated from their families, and legal restrictions on their movement were strictly enforced, frequently without compassion: such as the Natives (Urban Areas) Act of 1923 that rigidly put urban segregation in place, and controlled the mobility of black people by means of pass laws.

Numerous other segregationist policies were also put into practice without concern about the people—the Groups Areas Act sanctioned forced removals, prohibited mixed marriages and enforced immorality laws; separate amenities were installed; curfews were imposed; and movement restricted. Simultaneously, various identity documents associated with population registration were being issued.

By the mid-twentieth century, apartheid was firmly in place, seen as 'a continuation, in a more systematic and brutal form, of the segregationist policies of previous governments' (South Africa GCIS, 2007: 38).[6] The pre-1950s South African context was typified by mounting racial tension, and gender discrimination and protests that were ignored never quelled but instead met with more and more restrictions and more severe action to enforce the laws. Personal lives were deeply affected and since, in feminist language, the personal is political, by the mid-1950s when activists took up the cudgels, emotions were running high.

THE PASS LAWS

The Pass laws, in particular, inspired several resistance campaigns (South African History Online, n.d.: 7). Before South Africa's transition to a Union in 1910, protest against colonial laws seemed futile. In March 1912, a group of black and coloured women from the Orange Free State sent a petition against passes signed by 5,000 people to the Prime Minister. After failing to receive a response, six women were sent to meet the Minister of Native Affairs. Again they were ignored; and by May 1913, they decided to pursue more aggressive anti-pass campaigns. On the 28th and 29th of May that year, they resolved to never carry passes again and said, 'We are done with pleading, we now demand!' This passive resistance campaign was met with arrests in Bloemfontein, Jagersfontein and Winburg in the Orange Free State (ibid.)—the main urban centre; an important diamond mining town; and a service centre for a productive farming region, showing the widespread range of impact.

In 1914, the government relaxed Pass laws for women and the resistance campaign ended.

In the settlements of the western part of the Cape Province, especially in the later 1700s, documents restricting the movement of slaves and the indigenous local Khoikhoi people, who lived and worked on farms appropriated by the early European settlers, took the form of permission documents from their employers. In the Eastern Cape in the 1820s, local authorities had to give written permission for British settlers living in Bathurst to travel further afield, which resulted in sixty per cent of the settlers moving to other parts of the country in defiance (ibid.: 1). In the former Transvaal, South Africa's economic heartland favoured with an ever-growing population and agricultural potential, black people were disenfranchised and forced to settle in specific places to provide white farmers with a steady source of labour. In 1866, a Pass law ruled that any black person found outside an allowed residential area without a pass from an employer, magistrate, missionary, field cornet or principal chief could be arrested (ibid.: 2). Even on the early diamond-digging sites, only blacks were forced to carry passes at all times (ibid.). Similarly, on the gold mines of the Witwatersrand (now in Gauteng province dominated by the cities of Pretoria, now Tshawane, and Johannesburg), a pass system was rigorously enforced to keep the men inside their designated areas, as they were housed in compounds and restrictions prevented the workers' families from visiting them. Over the years, the Pass laws continued to remain in place until, in May 1918, black workers embarked on strike action against low wages, poor housing and passes. The Bantu Women's League, precursor of the African National Congress (ANC) Women's League, also led an anti-Pass campaign during this period and pass-burning campaigns were held throughout the country for the entire year of 1930, accompanied by clashes between protesters and the police. These were not happy events, especially for the Indian population and the black people of KwaZulu-Natal.

The constant humiliation and monitoring caused intense anger in black communities. During the war years of 1939–1945, black families began migrating to cities as a result of increased job opportunities, and the grinding poverty they were experiencing in the rural reserves created for them through implementation of the 1913 Land Act. As a result, the urban black population of the country virtually doubled. Administrating Pass laws was costly and difficult because all black people in urban areas had to be checked by authorities. However, despite recommendations from the relevant government department and the Fagan Commission of 1946 to abolish Pass laws as being politically and administratively too expensive, the procedure was merely legally revised.

'Pass Laws inspired a "burning sense of grievance and injustice" in black South Africans' (South African History Online, n.d.: 5).[7] The hated law also forced black South Africans to carry a range of documents, including a photograph, place of birth and employment records, tax payments and criminal records, to suppress freedom of movement; it was illegal to be without a pass, the penalty for which was arrest and jail. A further Act (1956) removed all legal recourse for objecting to the removal of black people from certain residential areas. The Urban Areas Act limited black people to 72 hours in an urban area without permission from a specific municipal officeholder (ibid.: 6). Dissatisfaction among black South Africans grew to unprecedented levels. Popular resistance spread, and after the 1948 elections that ushered in the era of apartheid, strikes and marches began in earnest and police retaliation was brutal. Clashes and repression continued through the following three decades.

Passes gave rise to great protests from women during the 1950s. In 1950, proposed changes to the Urban Areas Act were leaked to the public. The changes involved further restrictions on black women and a more efficient pass system to facilitate this. South African women protested vehemently. The ANC Women's League attracted a huge following with this politicization of black women and declared, 'Our fight is on' (ibid.: 8). When the proposal resurfaced in 1952, protests were launched in all major towns and cities in all provinces—Cape Town, Cato Manor, Port Elizabeth, Oudtshoorn, Stellenbosch, Ixopo and Umzinto. In September 1955, the government announced it would begin issuing passbooks for women in January 1956. This sparked more resistance, and the Federation of South Africa Women (FEDSAW)[8] organized a mass demonstration of more than 2,000 women of all races on 27 October 1955; precipitating a major anti-pass campaign against passes—the 1956 Women's March to the Union Buildings in Pretoria, the country's administrative capital city. The media was awash with news of protest meetings; *The Guardian* daily newspaper regularly carried headlines like 'We will not carry any Passes: African women indignant', 'African women up in arms, mounting opposition to passes for women' and 'Campaign against passes for women gathers force' (ibid.). Faced with such an onslaught, the government decided to abolish passes for women.

On 31 May 1961, the Republic of South Africa (RSA) came into being and the suppression of black South Africans continued unabated. Meanwhile, the country became increasingly isolated from the rest of the world as a result of its apartheid policies. Black resistance soared. The 1970s were marked by turbulence and insecurity as apartheid was met at every turn with popular mobilization despite police response, at the time white male dominated (Shear, 1997: 71).

International outrage grew and events such as the 1976 Soweto riots earned the support of the international community for the cause of freedom in South Africa. The country's relationship with its neighbours also worsened severely as a result of the government's efforts to secure minority white rule by way of manipulating politics beyond its own borders. As the 1980s approached, it was clear that the intense attempts to force development within the homelands and attract people to them, and to control black urbanization, had failed as black people continued to stream into urban areas.

Measures to temper apartheid had to be taken, especially as an economic crisis too was looming. The government granted black workers the right to form unions, but it demanded that all unions, whether registered or not, hand over membership registers to the state. This in effect negated the right to unionize because of the exposure of individuals to state security for surveillance and repression. Black protest escalated, and the then President declared a state of emergency in July 1985 to crush the violence. This too failed, and the initiative was received with international contempt. Efforts to control urban blacks had proven hopeless, and the government repealed the Pass laws on 23 July 1986. It is estimated that since 1800, between 15 and 20 million people had been arrested for violating these laws (South African History Online, n.d.: 8).

By now, apartheid was being attacked globally, and this too was detrimentally impacting the entire country's general economic development. The South Africa of the time, unique and local, was despised by the rest of the world for its policy of racial oppression intensified by race, class and gender discrimination. The effect of the discontent led to the need to organize and through this, to be effective in a situation in which the oppressed were being forced into 'silence'. Protest and resistance were not being effective even though 'women were at the forefront of the Campaign to Defy Unjust Laws' (Gasa, 2007: 209), and even seeking alternatives was not successful socio-politically or economically.

THE ANC WOMEN'S LEAGUE

The ANC was founded, as early as 1912, as a national liberation movement concerned with constitutional protest (South Africa Yearbook, 2007/2008: 36). Women were only allowed to be full members from 1943, and then sought to build their own organization, the ANC Women's League (ANCWL) to engage in mass campaigns. African women had always organized from a mass base[9], as was the case with the Bantu Women's League, formed in 1918 (South African History Online)[10] when women were still only associate members, which fought for the rights of all oppressed people with the upliftment and education of girls as a main focus (Hassim, 2006: 22). However, in 1954, the FEDSAW was formed, bringing together a number of existing women's structured movements whose members were already actively engaged in attempting to improve the daily living circumstances of all people in a country governed by a 'ruthlessly coercive state' (Gasa, 2007: 213)[11] while seeking to assert recognition of their place as women in the public domain. This was reinforced by the ethos and content of the *Women's Charter* that was adopted, denouncing all apartheid legislation.

In their endeavours, the women were not unmindful of cultural practices that discriminated against women; addressing these too as the occasion arose. As Gasa notes, 'From their first entry into the political space, women resisted male domination, acting on their own, representing themselves directly to the Union government and even in their appeals to the empire. ... Of relevance here is the relationship between the private and the public spheres' (ibid.: 215). It is in the former that the mothering function of women is to be accommodated, and in the latter in the political arena; and both these facets are seen to merge and emerge in women's activism in the turbulent times of pre-1994 South African history.

Therefore, in the stormy pre-1994 period, especially from the mid-1980s, when breaking point was being reached in all aspects of South African life—*what were the women doing?* As was happening elsewhere in Africa from the 1990s, women were emerging as visible political actors participating in the generation of policies advancing human rights. The character and nature of women's movements were changing, largely motivated by increasing openness to international norms regarding women's rights and representation and supported by the availability and deployment of resources to advance women. This was being stimulated by the opening up of new opportunities as a result of major societal upheaval (Tripp et al., 2009: ix & 2).

Democratization and political liberalization offered scope for increased mobilization (ibid.: 106), although this did not happen automatically; dealing with barriers and hurdles still required sensitive negotiation and patience. Political activists and organizations were under constant surveillance—and banning orders were strictly enforced with permission to demonstrate against apartheid rule rarely being granted. Although still officially a banned organization, the ANC convened the Malibongwe women's conference to be held in Amsterdam, The Netherlands, in 1990. The conference was attended by South Africans living in exile as well as a wide range of women from South Africa representing various women's organizations.

As it happened two weeks before this meeting, liberation movements were made legal and the release of political prisoners in South Africa was announced. Now the priority was to focus on constitutional negotiations. In 1994, South Africans went to the polls to vote as a democratic society, under an interim Constitution, and the ANC emerged with a 62 per cent majority (South Africa Yearbook, 2007/2008: 41) under the leadership of President Mandela.

POST-1994 CONTEMPORARY SOCIETY

By 1996, South Africa's new, exemplary Constitution was in place; 'one that guaranteed women equality, freedom and security of the person as well as freedom from violence, the right to make decisions concerning reproduction and the right over one's own body' (Tripp et al., 2009: 122) with the significant corollary that, in the event of a conflict, non-discrimination or inequality provisions were to override customary law, a significant breakthrough. Several Acts followed that underlined the credibility being given to women. Of the first, which was contentious on religious grounds, was the Choice on the Termination of Pregnancy that allowed women the right to abortion (1996).

The Commission for Gender Quality Act (1996) was legislated with the aim of ensuring that such gender-sensitive laws were fully implemented. The Film and Publications Act came into force against the degradation of women and children (1996), followed by the Domestic Violence Act, thereby giving legal and institutional protection for victims of domestic abuse (1996). The Labour Relations Act recognizing maternity rights and women's rights against sexual harassment in the workplace and the Employment Equity Act to hire fairly across race, class and disability were two other noteworthy laws.

South Africa fully reflects the reality of the perception that 'Africa is a continent of vast cultural, linguistic, economic, political and ecological diversity' (ibid.: ix) and post-1994, South Africa has been a part of Africa in global context too, having been part of some of its experiences (past and present) and sharing common concerns. Yet, it is different in many respects as it is considerably more urbanized, industrialized and wealthier than its neighbours; gained majority rule recently; it has a large white settler population; and contends with the legacy of an apartheid state (Tripp et al., 2009: 18). Having an autonomous women's movement was a particularly contentious concern, with strong views being held by activists and academics alike. The issue was highly contested at all levels—national, provincial and local—within and beyond the confines of political party debates to the ANCWL, FEDSAW, non-governmental organizations and local grassroots women's groups.

In defining the South African women's movement, the strategic organizational and political considerations of women were named as the primary constituency being mobilized, and the main concerns were the improvement of women's economic standing, political representation, cultural status and legal rights (ibid.: 14). The dominating theme of political discourse was the issue of nationalism; and in South Africa, this constrained the women's movement but many progressive—hence the significance of alliances—and different constituencies were included whose voices heeded. It is to their credit that, during the transition from apartheid to democracy, the women's movement exerted a critical influence on later constitutional changes, influencing party politics and increasing female representation (ibid.: 3)—something that is widely recognized in both government and non-government institutional structures. There has been much scholarly debate on the matter, with diverse opinions being expressed about the effects associated with its status.

Viewpoints on whether democratization has resulted in significant gains for women in contemporary South African society are varied, as is the case worldwide. Waylen[12] feels this is so because of women's long history of mobilization as part of the apartheid movements, hence women activists could intervene, with a variety of political structures of different backgrounds and expertise coming together to creating opportunities for intervention in the negotiations for change. Further, she notes that the triple alliance of women academics, politicians and activists who were able to act strategically in articulating women's interests at critical junctures, and the presence of mechanisms to translate the issues into positive policy outcomes yielded positive results. Hassim[13] (2006) contends that

> the women's movement in South Africa sought associational autonomy but because of its roots in the anti-apartheid movement, it often found itself both energised and constrained by its allegiance to the broader nationalist project. This meant that the women's movement needed to maintain a strong bargaining position to avoid cooptation. It had to negotiate its relationships constantly with the broader anti-apartheid movement and with the African National Congress. The dilemma for the women's movement was how to navigate its alliances with broader political forces while maintaining autonomy to advance women's rights and a feminist agenda.

THE PROGRESSIVE WOMEN'S MOVEMENT

The decision to form a Progressive Women's Movement was taken at a conference in Amsterdam, The Netherlands, in January 1990 (South Africa DAC, 2006). However, after the unbanning of political organizations in 1990, discussions started in earnest to establish an acceptable political dispensation for the country. Initially, women were excluded from taking part in the negotiations. As a result, eighty-one women's groups (Tripp et al., 2009: 65) formed a coalition of women from different political backgrounds and affiliations. Through the National Women's Coalition of South Africa, women were able to take part in the long, but all-embracing negotiation process and to articulate their demands.

The women had drawn up a *Women's Charter for Effective Equality*, based on their *Women's Charter* of 1954, which was presented to the first democratic government under the leadership of President Nelson Rolihlahla Mandela. Significantly, the hopes and aspirations that were raised by women are now contained in the country's Constitution as promulgated in 1996 (South Africa DAC, 2006; ANC, n.d., adapted). The Women's National Coalition that was formed in 1991, and was active in the Constitution-writing process, disintegrated after the adoption of the South African Constitution due to the fact that women began to focus more on party politics once their basic objective of letting their voices be heard had been achieved. However, the ANC and the ANCWL held a view that there was a need for some kind of an organic structure that would specifically take up broader issues of women in post-1994 South African society (ibid.).

Over several years, various discussion papers and resolutions had been developed and adopted, and the formalization of the Progressive Women's Movement took place in 2006. Its key objective was to promote the transformation of South African society into one that is truly non-racial and non-sexist, motivated by the fact that it was felt that the new challenges facing the women of South Africa today could be best dealt with if they acted as a united force; in line with the transformation that was taking place in the country, and in accord with the policies of the South African Development Community (SADC), the New Partnership for Africa's Development (Nepad), the African Union (AU) and the United Nations (UN) (ANC, n.d., adapted).

The objectives of the Progressive Women's Movement were fourfold—to unite the women of South Africa in diversity; to strengthen the relationship between the government and women's organizations; to ensure that the women committed to a women's agenda had their forum; and to fight against the discrimination of women in all spheres of life (ibid.). In line with its vision, the movement would target women who were committed to its grounding principles and who came from different sectors and conditions; representing among others women from rural areas, the business sector, the professional sector, faith-based organizations, workers, young women, women with disabilities, elderly women, workers, unemployed women and women from different political parties (South Africa DAC, 2006).

The stated principles as identified were to fight for the emancipation of women and gender equality, to fight patriarchy, to have a minimum and single platform for action, to develop a coherent and common approach to issues that affect women, to foster good relations in order to shape the development of policy positions, to agree to differ and maintain independence of member organizations but to work towards unity, to provide a support base for all women, to ensure the involvement of women in peace and security processes, to consolidate economic, social, governance and political programmes and to collaborate with other established social movements (ibid.: editorially adapted).

In the economic sphere, the movement sought to pay attention to access to economic resources, credit and information technology, job creation and self-employment. With regard to social transformation, being an issue-based organization, attention would focus on housing, health, land, basic infrastructure, social grants and services and access to education and skills development (ibid.). In the area of governance, the movement would work towards a 50 per cent representation in all governance and decision-making bodies, including those in the business world, while educating women on legislation and policies empowering women and advocating progressive laws that empower women (ibid.). Further, the movement would support and monitor the implementation of international instruments, strengthen relationships with international as well as continental organizations and work towards creating a better Africa and a better world, as well as being committed to transforming South Africa into a prosperous, non-racial, non-sexist, democratic and united country (ibid.; ANC, n.d.).

THE WOMEN'S CHARTER FOR EFFECTIVE EQUALITY

The preamble of the Charter (second draft) that was approved at the Women's National Coalition conference held on 27 February 1994 states:

> As women citizens of South Africa, we are here to claim our rights. We want recognition and respect for the work we do in the home, in the workplace and in the community. We claim full and equal participation in the creation of a non-sexist, non-racist democratic society. We cannot march on one leg or clap with one hand. South Africa is poorer politically, economically and socially for having prevented more than half of its people from fully contributing to its development .... For decades, patriarchy, colonialism, racism and apartheid have subordinated and oppressed women within political, economic and social life .... The development of the potential of all our people, women and men, will enrich and benefit the whole of society. We set out a programme for equality in all spheres of our lives, including the law, the economy, education, development and infrastructure, political and civil life, family life and partnerships, custom, culture and religion, health and the media (Hassim, 2006: 269–70).

The deliberations of the women preparing both these blueprints, the *Women's Charter* of 1954 and the *Women's Charter for Effective Equality*, show that no stone has been left unturned, and that gender issues in true feminist thinking acknowledge human rights by recognizing all aspects of the daily lives of men and women. The Charter provides food for thought for discussions on accommodating diverse opinions and circumstances, for planning research endeavours and for campaigns for setting right what is wrong; stressing that it should address accommodating people from different backgrounds and human conditions, and take action to improve their quality of life. Thinking, networking and action—by thought, word and deed—can be seen as the tripod on which to base successful and peaceful coexistence.

CHALLENGES AND ACHIEVEMENTS

In contemporary South African society, men and women are equally recognized although there are some barriers that have yet to be overcome, and the process of transformation still continues. Where equipped for positions, women serve comfortably and are placed in management positions in the public and private sectors. Women have equal access to educational and employment opportunities and, through the Black Economic Empowerment (BEE) government policy and strategic programmes for its implementation, the empowerment of women figures as a significant priority and specified goal in all sectors of the country's economy. Achievements are escalating but challenges too abound.

In the political arena, women's groups actively draw attention to happenings that are constitutionally unacceptable or not in line with current legislation. Government is also alerted to areas where more should be done with a particular focus on the gender-related aspects of the Millennium Development Goals as set out by the United Nations (2001), especially with regard to poverty alleviation and reduction, education, maternal health, gender equality, child mortality, AIDS and other diseases, as well as ensuring environmental sustainability and developing global development partnerships (Fairhurst, 2009: 8).[14] It is regrettable that the gender budgeting initiative did not succeed largely due to limited resources being made available (Tripp et al., 2009: 5).

Many women serve in parliament and at provincial and local levels despite the constraints they need to address. This is another issue of its own, yet of significance when considering the topic of women in contemporary society as these apply to all women—and men too. Cultural practices in which men are seen as heads and power-holders, with women as subservient to men in the household, can be stumbling blocks to good relationships. The fact that committees are generally male-dominated can put women in an awkward position, as does the common belief that women are by nature reticent and accept that home and family responsibilities are a non-negotiable priority.

Women in leadership, whether in business or government, do not always have their husband's support and face personal, social and financial costs as a result. Yet another constraint is dealing with the perception that spending nights away from home is socially unacceptable behaviour. Apart from social and internal possibilities, international pressures too are placed on the country to ensure that women do participate in political decision-making procedures at regional and sub-regional levels, especially due to obligations to SADC, the AU and the United Nations Economic and Social Council (ECOSOC).

Globally, the call is for a 50/50 quota in all political and decision-making structures as well as at the implementation level, as this creates a platform from which women can influence meaningful change (Zuma, 2009). Women's representation in the total number of 400 seats in the National Assembly has grown from

27.74 per cent (111) in 1994 to 32.75 per cent (131) a decade later; now (2009) standing at 43 per cent (172 seats) (EISA).[15] In this regard, South Africa is faring well, standing third to Rwanda and Sweden, among the 136 countries in the world, with 44.5 per cent women occupying permanent seats in the Lower House and 29.6 per cent in the Upper House, the world average being 18.7 per cent and 17.5 per cent, respectively (Inter-Parliamentary Union, 2009).[16] South Africa has exceeded the situation in Sub-Saharan Africa as evident in having women Speakers of the House, Deputy Presidents, and currently there are fourteen women in the Cabinet in ministerial positions, including correctional services, defence, home affairs, energy international relations and cooperation, mining, public enterprises, science and technology (Zuma, 2009). Eleven serve as deputy ministers, and there are five provincial premiers. The most recent initiative is the establishment of a new Ministry for Women, Children and People with Disabilities (ibid.). Apart from collaborating with the Progressive Women's Movement as a link between government and civil society, this ministry will monitor gender mainstreaming in all areas (ibid.). Women also play leadership roles in political parties and outnumber men as voters. Apart from being clearly visible in the legislature, women also figure prominently in the public service at all levels and increasingly contribute to the work of local authorities.

Table 2.1 *Women in National Parliaments*

World regions	*Single or lower House (%)*	*Upper House or senate (%)*	*Both Houses combined (%)*
Nordic countries	42.5	–	–
Americas	22.4	19.95	22.0
Europe—excluding Nordic countries	21.5	19.4	21.1
Asia	18.5	16.7	18.4
Sub-Saharan Africa	17.6	21.0	18.0
Pacific	13.0	32.6	15.2
Arab States	1.0	7.3	9.4

Source: Women in National Parliaments (as on 30 November 2009) compiled by the *Inter-Parliamentary Union – World and Regional Averages*, http://www.ipu.org/wmn-e/classif.htm, accessed on 29 December 2009.

Access to educational institutions is freely available from an early age, from preschool to the higher education level; and in some cases, more women than men are being awarded further and higher education qualifications. In the social sphere, however, gender relations still tend to be bound to patriarchal conventions in cultural and traditional contexts. However, the application of new family laws has endorsed gender-sensitivity and awareness in contemporary society, and men have been brought on board in women's struggles especially at the community level, with demands for initiatives against the abuse of women and children and domestic violence. In fact, it was recently reported (Kobedi, 2008) that the General Secretary of the South African Men's Forum (Mbuyiselo Botha) agreed with a political analyst (Mohau Pheko) who was quoted as saying 'We would not be having this freedom if it was not for those women ... It is to them that we have to be grateful' when referring to the 1956 March and the 2006 celebrations. Her comment, that is oft quoted in current conversation at women's issues meetings, and which stresses how vitally critical active and continuous engagement is to keep gender on the agenda,[17] was that 'It was the first time that women gave a discerning voice, and ... this voice has enabled us to refuse to be left in the kitchen, to refuse to be pushed down ... to be left out of the political and decision-making areas of our country'. She added, 'The women who took to the street on that day paved the way for women not to allow anybody to stop them from fulfilling their dreams' (ibid.). It is noteworthy that elite women were fairly visible and active in nationalist movements in South Africa (Tripp et al., 2009: 36).

Businesswomen in South Africa are well-organized; and in the formal sector, constant attention is being paid to the needs of women as far as putting into practice the principle of equal pay for equal work, and developing entrepreneurial skills to tap the vast potential that small and medium enterprises offer for self-employment, generally beyond the scope of informal sector activities. South Africa has a disproportionately large percentage of Internet users in Africa (ibid.: 69), and the field of Information Technology affords considerable opportunity for women as employees and entrepreneurs.

Environmental concern is also very much part of contemporary daily life in both urban and rural communities, with litter becoming acutely problematic in under-serviced and crowded settlements. Many women, as members of a group or as individuals, have taken responsibility for attending to this in their own neighbourhoods. Another community feature is that local authorities and interested organizations are encouraging the cultivation of vegetable gardens, mostly for home use but with the possibility of marketing surpluses to increase income. Agricultural technology and skills are being developed and improved methods are being advocated. As a country, South Africa is a signatory to many international and regional conventions and is making an important contribution to present-day scientific debate on environmental issues; in particular, the multifaceted topic of global warming.

CONCLUSION

Over time, changing circumstances have affected the daily experiences of people and women's lives particularly have been affected personally—in the family and household context, in their social world and in the ways in which they have sought to meet their needs to secure a satisfying way of life. In contemporary South African society, women continue to feel the impact of the intertwining of the historical, political, social, economic and environmental influences, irrespective of where they live. Inspiration from the *unity in diversity*[18] theme has driven women in their quest to let their voices be heard, and they have faced challenges with determination, both singularly and collectively. The opportunity to celebrate their significant role in all facets of society arose during the first decade of the twenty-first century and was grasped and planned for with full awareness and recognition of the past. Reflecting on experiences of bygone eras, and focusing on the future, is bound to ensure progress that will lead to a better life for all, with the proviso that gender issues will always figure on the political agenda with a positive spin-off for the social and economic realms. In this chapter, the main features of the commemoration of two significant events 50 years apart have been used to show that through celebration, people of all races, men and women, can purposefully:

- Mobilize, to be active with regards to policies, researching all that has happened and is happening
- Inspire, to carry on and move forward
- Inform, bridging the generation gap and spanning historical time, in the case of South Africa from the seventeenth to the twenty-first centuries, but especially the contemporary phase of 1956–2006

- Organize, bearing in mind the cost, the time and the infrastructure and
- Channel, in that a wide range of emotions come into play when thinking and planning for action to benefit a transforming society thus to bring about the long envisioned ideals of a better life for all.

Bringing together the global and the local as we look ahead is indeed an imperative in the world of today and not only in South Africa as we continue to think, speak and act through our thoughts, words and deeds—thinking, networking and action. The academic and the activist, serving the common cause of promoting women's issues in the interests of justice, equality and tolerance in contemporary society. And there is no doubt that women's agency 'interacts with structural factors to bring about change' (ibid.: 228–29).

NOTES

1. Jordan, Palo, Arts and Culture Minister, cited by Dlamini, 2006.
2. An example of this is the Nomboniso Gasa's edited volume of articles.
3. Sisulu, 2001, cited in Gasa, 2007 a, p. 207.
4. Gasa, 2007, p. 207, who gives a vivid interpretation and captivating enlightening account of the event with insightful feminist analyses of the situation and critique of the work of other scholars. Barnes, 2007, endorses my personal view of the significance of this book as an exposition of past history.
5. Throughout its history, the word 'race' has had a range of political interpretations in South Africa and racial difference has been a sensitive issue on the continent for decades. In this chapter, the black population group refers to 'people of colour' and white to those of Caucasian descent. Early documents spoke of 'Native' when referring to the local inhabitants, the original people of Africa, the Africans. The last (2001) census called for a classification of African, white, coloured and Indian/Asian people (South Africa Yearbook, pp. 2 and 320), but the official Population Register no longer requires this information.
6. South Africa GCIS, 2007, p. 38 referring to colonial rule, Boer Republics, the Union of South Africa (1910) and an Independent Republic (1961) with first democratic elections being held in April 1994.
7. Smit, 1942, cited in South African History Online, n.d., p. 5.
8. ANC membership was not a prerequisite for belonging to FEDSAW.
9. Ginawala, 2006, cited in Gasa, 2007, p. 210.

10. SAHO, accessed 3 January 2010.
11. Wells, 1993, p. 1 cited in Gasa, 2007, p. 213.
12. Waylen, 2007 cited in Tripp et al., 2007, p. 11.
13. Hassim, 2006 in Tripp et al., 2009, pp. 98–99.
14. UNDP 2001 cited in Fairhurst, 2009, p. 8.
15. http://www.eisa.org.za/WEP/souwomenrepresent.htm, accessed 5 November 2009.
16. Inter-Parliamentary Union, 2009.
17. For example, the workshop conducted by Ohadi-Mathews, 2009.
18. South Africa's *'mantra'*, widely popularized at the onset of democracy as a catch-phrase, together with the metaphor slogan of being a 'rainbow nation'. Originally, on the Union of South Africa's coat arms (1910), the motto has been retained, now written in the indigenous Khoisan language meaning 'diverse people unite'.

REFERENCES

African National Congress (ANC), n.d., *A Progressive Women's Movement of South Africa*, http://www.anc.org.za/wl/docs/pwm/progressive.html, accessed on 7 November 2009.

Barnes, Teresa, 2007, *Women in South African History: Basus'iimbokodo, bawel'imilambo/they remove boulders and cross rivers*, edited by Nomboniso Gasa, Cape Town: HSRC Press.

Dlamini, Nozipho, 2006, *South Africa Info*, http://www.southafrica.info/women/womensmarch, accessed on 13 August 2008, http://www.eisa.org.za/WEP/souwomenrepresent.htm

Fairhurst, Joan, 2009, Geography for a Better World; Shared Responsibility, Shared Problems, Opening Address at the 8th Biennial Conference of the Society of South African Geographers held at Centurion 1–3 September 2009, http://www.ssag.org

Gasa, Nomboniso (Ed.), 2007a, *Women in South African History: Basus'iimbokodo, bawel'imilambo/they remove boulders and cross rivers*. Cape Town: HSRC (Human Sciences Research Council) Press.

Gasa, Nomboniso (Ed.), 2007b, 'Feminisms, Motherisms, Patriarchies and Women's Voices in the 1950s'. In *Women in South African History: Basus'iimbokodo, bawel'imilambo/they remove boulders and cross rivers*, Cape Town: HSRC (Human Sciences Research Council) Press, pp. 207–29.

Hassim, Shireen, 2006, *Women's Organizations and Democracy in South Africa: Contesting Authority*. Madison, WI: The University of Wisconsin Press.

International Parliamentary Union (IPU), 2009, *Women in National Parliaments*, http://www.ipu.org/wmn-e/classif.htm, accessed 29 December 2009.

Kobedi, Palesa, 2008, *Interview*, http://www.info.gov.za, accessed on 12 August 2008.

Ohadi-Mathews, Natahsa, 2009, Gender Equality and Government Self-assessment: Best Practice, workshop (CIFAL Atlanta/UNITAR) presented at the 3rd International Conference entitled *'Gender Equality and Economic Development in Africa'*, Hosted by the Ronald Brown Institute for Sub-Saharan Africa (RBI), the University of Pretoria's Institute for Women's and Gender Studies and Georgia State University (USA) at the University of Pretoria 16–18 September 2009.

Shear, Keith, 1997, 'Not Welfare or Uplift Work': White Women, Masculinity and Policing in South Africa'. In *Gendered Colonialisms in African History*, edited by Nancy Rose Hunt, Tessie P. Liu and Jean Quataert, Oxford: Blackwell Publishers Ltd., pp. 71–93.

South African History Online (SAHO), *Imbokodo: The Women – The Rock Women's Struggles in South Africa*, http://www.sahistory.org.za/pages/governence-projects/womens-struggle/orgs-bantu-womens-league.htm, accessed on 16 December 2009; 3 January 2010.

South African History Online, Politics and Governance, Pass Laws in South Africa, http://www.sahistory.org.za/pages/governance-projects/apartheid-repression/pass-laws.htm, accessed on 5 November 2009.

South Africa: Department of Arts and Culture (DAC), 2006, Women Marching for Quality, Peace and Development, an Edited Extract from the 'Base Document' of the Progressive Women's Movement of South Africa (PWMSA), http://www.dac.gov.za/media_releases/21Aug06.htm accessed 5 November 2009.

South Africa: Department of Arts and Culture (DAC), http://www.dac.gov.za/, accessed on 12 August 2008.

South Africa: Government Communication and Information System (GCIS), *South Africa Yearbook 2007/2008*, 15th ed. Pretoria: Government Communication and Information System.

The Progressive Women's Movement, www.anc.org.za/wl/docs/pwm/progressive.html, accessed on 15 August 2008.

Tripp, Aili Mari, Isabel Casimiro, Joy Kwesiga and Alice Mungwa, 2009, *African Women's Movements: Changing Political Landscape*. New York: Cambridge University Press.

Zuma, President J.G., 2009, *Address to the Progressive Women's Movement Dinner, Sandton Convention Centre*, 14 August 2009, http://www.thepresidency.gov.za/president/sp/2009/sp081452.htm, accessed on 5 November 2009.

CHAPTER 3

Women's Movement in the Netherlands, 1870–2009

N.A. Flipsen and Th.P. van der Weide

For most of history, Anonymous was a woman.
—Virginia Woolf

In this contribution, we will highlight in brief the women's movement in The Netherlands in the period 1870–2009. This movement can only be fully appreciated when seen in the context of the overall women's movements in Western countries in the same period.

Where did this still climbing 'gender equality' curve start? To answer that question, we have to go back into history to understand the cause of the chain reaction we are still experiencing. Feminism and women's battles have been, and still are, most complex. We observe that these battles came more or less in three waves, of which the third one is still in progress:

- 1st wave: 1870–1920 (Industrial Revolution)
- 2nd wave: 1965–1985
- 3th wave: 1990s and still ongoing.

For the future, the next wave may be expected, the digital wave.

We start however from the Dutch constitutional law's long-standing provisions for individual rights that emphasize equal rights for men and women. Some of the relevant passages include the following:

Artikel 1: *'Alle mensen worden vrij en gelijk in waardigheid en rechten geboren. Ze zijn begiftigd met verstand en geweten en behoren jegens elkander in een geest van broederschap te gedragen.'*

Artikel 2.1: *'Een ieder heeft aanspraak op alle rechten en vrijheden, in deze verklaring opgesomd, zonder enig onderscheid van welke aard ook, zoals ras, kleur, geslacht, taal, godsdienst, politieke of andere overtuiging, nationale of maatschappelijke afkomst of andere status.'*

Artikel 23.3: *'Een ieder zonder enige achterstelling, heeft recht op gelijk loon voor gelijke arbeid.'*

To give a 'freely translated' sense of the above-mentioned constitutional excerpts, these articles assert that

Section 1: all humans are born equal.
Section 2: each individual is entitled to all rights and freedom, without any differentiation of race, colour, gender, language or religion.
Section 3: each and everyone has the right to equal salary for equal labour.

Moreover, in this paper, we will be using the term 'gender' in accordance with the following description by Elizabeth McGregor and Fabiola Bazi (McGregor and Bazi, 2001):

'Whereas the sex of an individual is biologically determined, gender refers to the socially constructed definition of women and men and the relationship between them. Gender is culture-specific and also varies over time. It determines the conception of tasks, functions and roles attributed to women and men in society, in both public and private life.'

The definition of 'women's movement' is described as follows in the 'Vrouwenlexicon' (1989), a lexicon especially devoted to remarkable women in The Netherlands since 1850:

'For women to strive after societal changes, with the goal to improve the position of women.'

The term 'feminism' originates from the Latin word 'femina', meaning woman. The term was used for the first time around 1800. Feminism came into being in eighteenth century, also known as 'The Age of Enlightenment'. Issues such as rationalism, freedom, equal voting rights and employment of individuals were looked at with more common sense. This way of thinking mainly existed among upper-class liberals, who were very much in favour of the freedom of the individual.

The structure of this article is as follows: in section one, we focus on the first feminist wave in The Netherlands and its impact on society. In section two, we briefly look at the history of women's movements and the second feminist wave. In section three, we go through the third feminist wave and its concerns, finally followed by section 4 with some conclusions.

THE FIRST WAVE

The first wave of feminism in The Netherlands took place in the period 1870–1920, and can be seen to be a consequence of the Industrial Revolution (Berg and Hudson, 1992). Until 1870, Western countries were organized as a traditional society. Around 1870, we see the beginning of the Industrial Revolution, which had a large impact on society in general, but especially on family issues and role pattern. Old structures did not fit well anymore, and a fundamental change was required. The Netherlands followed the same line of development as the surrounding Western European countries.

One effect of the Industrial Revolution was the introduction of the proletarian family with its (nowadays) familiar traditional role patterns (ibid.). Already, in the 19th century, women were striving for equal rights for men and women. In 1919, this led to voting rights for women, which could be seen as a big step forwards. Nevertheless, other issues still needed attention, such as juridical justice and the right to labour for married women. Other important rights were access to higher education, abortion and pregnancy leave (which was later on turned into parental leave).

At first, job opportunities were available for women and equal work was offered in factories. But due to heavy labour, long working hours and unequal payment, women opted out of participation in the labour market. The traditional roles of women as housekeepers and caretakers and men as the income provider became a fact. These role patterns were guaranteed posterity in the post-industrial society. Only a few women would be given the opportunity to penetrate into higher education and school jobs. What's more, the Industrial Revolution also led to a significant increase in population, due to the delayed dropping of the birth rate as a response to a reduced death rate caused by improved conditions. This has been described as the Plateau Model (Roos, 2009; Weide and Flipsen, 2009).

This wave was mainly a protest movement from women coming from the higher societal classes. Their protest was against exclusion for participation in education and labour, peaking with the battle for women's voting rights. Organized women's movements started as early as in 1889 with the creation of the 'Vrije Vrouwen Vereeniging' (Association of Free Women) by Wilhelmina Drucker. In 1919, voting rights were legitimized and the feminist wave tempered gradually. It was an important step forward in history for women's participation in societal issues as well as for gender equality.

Aletta Henriëtte Jacobs (1854–1929) was the symbol for this wave, and acted as a barrier-breaking role model for other women. She was the first woman not only to enter but also to complete a university course in The Netherlands, and the first female physician. She was already different at an early age and did not enjoy the housework that women were supposed to carry out. She would spend her evenings learning several languages from her parents, which was something out of the ordinary for that time. In 1871, she entered the University of Groningen. She became to first woman in The Netherlands to obtain her medical degree in 1876 and her doctoral degree in 1878.

We can see how her entering university and obtaining the right to higher education may have pushed the first feminist wave into society. It is important to recognize this as an important historical moment, which led to many other changes and role models in the years ahead.

During this first wave, parallel to the Industrial Revolution, we observe some interesting changes with regard to the existing labour environments and women's participation in the same. Factory labour introduced itself as an option next to home labour. An explanation for this can be found in the fact that, at that time, war industry was of big importance and women were needed to participate, as work was more than the men could handle on their own. Besides, men were not part of society but forced to go to war. The value of traditional handicraft diminished as it was unpaid labour.

Another reason for feminist actions was the class division, with unequal possibilities for women to develop. Women of the poorer class were forced to labour in the home, unable to search for outside jobs; whereas women belonging to the upper class, having maids, had more support in performing household duties.

They would seek activities outside their homes as they had nothing much to do at home and were often bored.

Married women at that time still did not have any status, not even by law, and choosing education or finding work instead of their daily tasks at home was not yet socially acceptable.

THE SECOND WAVE

The big economic crisis of the 1930s, followed by the Second World War, caused a pause in the women's movement in The Netherlands. Women became in great demand in the industrial world as the men involved themselves in war activities. However, after the war, women were less needed in jobs, and those involved in the war economy started returning to their housework. Women were once again ruled out as far as workplace participation was concerned. The women's movement had been silenced, and the results achieved during the first wave were not followed up on. Instead, there was pressure on the women to devote themselves to their families.

The second feminist wave (1965–1985) started in the *roaring Sixties* and was mainly focused on financial and sexual liberalization for women. The main point was that women claimed independence, especially in decisions regarding their own body. Fighting for the right to abortion became one of the spear points of the, at that time famous and notorious group, 'Dolle Mina' (Mad Mina; Mina is a popular Dutch girl name). Another organization named 'Man, Vrouw, Maatschappij' (Man, Woman and Society) mainly fought for

- equal possibilities for education and income.
- right to the same chances and possibilities for personal development for both men and women.
- breaking the traditional role patterns.

Members of this organization were mostly in their thirties; generally well educated; had married and unmarried status; and were mostly (almost 82%) women.

Other examples of women's liberalization in those years were the rise of some more radical movements such as 'Paarse September' ('Purple September', named after the Palestinian militant organization 'Black September'). They were focused on achieving immediate changes in the traditional role patterns in society. Their method was more or less to create awareness among the suppressed groups in the male-dominated society. Women would participate in discussion groups, talking about central problems and life issues such as work, sexuality, childcare, appearance, and so on. It was not allowed for men to participate as they were seen as the suppressors.

Paarse September and some other like-minded groups were called autonomous women's movements. They were not bound by religion or political backgrounds, and each strived for a particular goal, varying from education for girls to legalization of abortion or equal rights for homosexuals and lesbians. In 1969, another movement within the Dutch Government emerged. They were called 'Rooie Vrouwen' (Red Women) and were able to influence politics from within their party. They were keen on media attention and became well-known for their activities against the stereotyping of women as sex objects or dumb housewives in the media.

Despite feminist issues being put on the political agenda (emancipation, positive action planning, position of girls and migrant women), there was enough reason for further action as just 40 per cent of women were economically independent; meaning their salary was equal to government aid wages. Up to 1985, there still was

- no female representative in the parliament
- only 9 per cent of the full professors in universities were women
- only 4 per cent had board member positions in companies and
- only 10 per cent had any kind of top positions in society

As a policy for improvement, positive discrimination was introduced; giving women first choice in case of equal qualification. This rule was especially applied to governmental positions (Wikepedia, 2009).

THE THIRD WAVE

Unexpectedly, a third feminist wave entered our society in the 1990s, and is still an ongoing process. This wave was more involved with the new streams of women moving into Dutch society. Many of these women come from developing countries and are still living according to their traditional societies.

The most important issues for this wave are as follows:

- The battle for equal remuneration for equal labour.
- Cultural and religious equality for female migrants; for example, those coming from the Caribics, Morocco and Somalia.
- Protesting the non-cooperative family attitudes to young women of other nationalities—mainly Islamic—expressing their own identity.
- Emancipation focused on involvement of men (fathers) and women.
- Streams focused on increasing the choices and possibilities for women.

The position of women in the year 2010 in The Netherlands, regarding work, household, access to education, partnership and equal contribution to the economy, is becoming more and more in balance; and information does not show any significant imbalance between men and women. Many academic masters programmes attract at least as many women as men. Yet, we still see gender-related preferences; in some education programmes, female students are dominant; in others, the male students are dominant. These preferences follow patterns that are considered traditional patterns.

While some people claim the existence of a glass ceiling, others claim that women have a rather different career perspective than men. Nevertheless, career development opportunities are becoming more and more accessible to women. We can therefore infer that some barriers are yet to be overcome, and that these can be mostly traced back to the traditional and deep-rooted ways of thinking, as well as the norms and values of the society we live in.

We can also note that there is significant improvement regarding the issue of equal pay for men and women, which was enforced by a body called the 'Commission Equal Treatment', created in 1994 to enforce this right for all women and to penalize erring employers.

An impact of new technology on society is very apparent and can be seen in EU reports and studies, especially in relation to family structures. For example, the birth rates in the EU are dropping. Some people think this is a consequence of better education and career perspectives for women. We think this will eventually lead to a new wave in women's movements.

CONCLUSIONS

As described in Section 1–3, we conclude that progress has been made towards equality and the equity of men and women. Up to now, this process has already taken a century and is still ongoing. Societal changes as well as human traditions and values seem to need a lot of time, and need to be pushed from various angles. Role models are needed to break barriers and existing thinking patterns, and often changes do not come easily but only come with power and force. For the Western societies, in particular the Dutch society, women have been able to place themselves in all layers including positions of power, the same as men. New technologies are contributing to self-development and women's liberalization. These technologies provide new opportunities for women to engage with society.

REFERENCES

Berg, M. and P. Hudson, 1992, 'Rehabilitating the Industrial Revolution', *The Economic History Review, New Series*, 45(1): 24–50.

Flipsen, N.A. and van der Weide, Th.P., 2009, 'Implementing Gender Issues in ICT', *Africa Education Review*, 6(2): 308–323.

McGregor, E. and F. Bazi, 2001, *Gender Mainstreaming in Science and Technology*. London: Commonwealth Secretariat.

Roos, A.M. de, 2009, 'Modeling Population Dynamics', Institute for Biodiversity and Ecosystem Dynamics, University of Amsterdam.

Weide, Th.P. van der and N.A. Flipsen, 2009, 'Reflections: Engendering ICT Development', *I4D (Gender and ICTs)*, VII, Nr 7 (July–September 2009): 20–21.

Wikipedia, 2009, Version on 17 February 2010, http://nl.wikipedia.org/wiki/Feminisme#cite_note-

CHAPTER 4

Barriers, Breakthroughs and Backlash: The English-Canadian Women's Movement

Shauna Wilton

Canadian women today are more equal to men than women in most other countries. According to the World Economic Forum's *Global Gender Gap Report*, in 2010, Canada ranked twentieth in terms of gender equality (Hausmann et al., 2010). While Canadian women, feminists and others continue to strive for perquisites such as greater wage equality, better maternity and childcare benefits, and improved physical security for women, they have made many advancements over the past 100 years. These progresses can be traced through the different waves of the Canadian women's movement and the ways in which they framed women's issues and mobilization. This chapter explores the English-Canadian women's movement from the beginning of the twentieth century until today, with a focus on women's legal and political issues and advances. The chapter also looks at the treatment of questions of diversity by the various waves of the movement.[1]

Goss and Heaney argued that three main collective action frames exist within the women's movement: maternalism, egalitarianism and feminine expression. Maternalism 'highlights women's roles as mothers, nurturers and caregivers, as well as their differences from men' and 'the belief that women have biological—and perhaps psychological—differences from men' (Goss and Heaney, 2010: 29). The egalitarianism or equality frame emphasizes women's sameness or similarities with men and has been used to justify equal political and civil rights, in addition to equal treatment in the workplace and the public sphere (ibid.: 30). The feminine-expressive frame 'reclaims feminine stereotypes and attire and uses them in a playful, self-parodying way in order to call women to action, rooted in individual empowerment through the reclamation of "Girlie" iconography and unabashed feminine sexual expression' (ibid.: 30).

In different ways and at different times, these three frames have influenced the Canadian women's movement, often resulting in hybrid or multiple calls to action. At the same time, the Canadian women's movement, as with many women's movements across the world, has found it increasingly difficult to speak and act for 'women' due to the diversity of experiences and locations of Canadian women, as both the oppressed and, in some cases, oppressors.

Today, at the beginning of the twenty-first century, the situation of Canadian women is more vulnerable than it has been for many decades, and it is becoming increasingly necessary for feminists and women's organizations to develop frames and calls to action for women who can meet the combined challenges of neoliberalism, neo-conservatism and globalization.

This chapter explores the prevalence of the first two of these frames within the English-Canadian women's movement, as well as the need to develop new frames for the twenty-first century. In doing so, it focuses on the legal and political gains made by the English-Canadian women's movements, as well as the backlash and diminishing benefits of the last few decades.

THE FIRST WAVE: MOTHERS, WIVES AND DAUGHTERS

During the late nineteenth and early twentieth centuries, women began organizing themselves to improve the condition of both women and society in general. This first wave of women's mobilization in Canada is important as it represents the early organizing of women to achieve gender-specific goals (Errington, 1993). Concerned with social issues such as immigration, alcohol abuse, poverty, family life and education, English-Canadian women began advocating for women's right to vote. They argued that by obtaining the right to vote, the unique characteristics and attributes of women, defined through their maternal role in society, would work to the benefit of society as a whole. 'It became increasingly clear ...

that though women's concerns and suggestions for change were often applauded, politicians, legislators and businessmen were not inclined to provide legislative support. [...] The answer, it seemed, lay in getting the vote, so that through women's voice in the democratic process, Canadian society could be saved' (ibid.: 77–8). Although there were serious doubts about giving women the vote—both from women who saw politics as an inappropriate place for ladies and mothers and from men who were concerned both about women's ability to think rationally and the potential for dramatic change to the existing societal power structure—the winning of the vote for most women in Canada in 1918 was a major achievement, as it represented the formal and legal shift of women's activities and influence from the private sphere of home and family to the public sphere of political life.

One example of early women's organizations in Canada is the Imperial Order Daughters of the Empire (IODE), an international organization involving British women in the colonies of the British Empire. Being concerned about the future of British-Canada, they met in church basements, parlours and halls. They developed strategies to assimilate new immigrants, and created the symbols and materials to prepare the nation's children for the duties that accompany citizenship in Canada and the British Empire (Wilton, 2000). During public lectures and in magazines and newspapers, maternal nationalists, such as the IODE, promoted a vision of Canada that aimed at preserving the dominance of British culture, symbols and citizens in Canada (ibid.). Similarly, the National Council of Women of Canada (NCWC) embraced the nationalist goals of British-Canada, arguing that the same skills they used to manage the home could be used to foster the development of the British-Canadian nation (Strong-Boag, 1976; Wilton, 2000).

The women's movement of the time was dominated by middle-class, English-speaking women engaged in issues of social reform. Feminists, such as Nellie McClung, worked to promote women's rights through a framework of maternalism and as mothers of the nation (McClung, 1972). Maternal feminists proposed using the 'private sphere' and characteristics often associated with women, such as nurturing, self-sacrifice and caring, as an alternative to the male-dominated and masculine character of public life. Later feminists, such as Ruddick (2003), argued that maternal values and practices provided a basis for an alternative model of citizenship. She suggested that the skills and values of mothering, such as a commitment to others, self-sacrifice, sharing and connectedness, could potentially replace the masculinist values of the public sphere with an ethic of caring. Di Quinzio similarly argued that the process of raising children shares many similarities with the process of raising citizens, and that their respective practices can potentially inform and benefit each other. At the turn of the twentieth century, the idea of women as mothers of the nation was a compelling one; particularly in the British Empire, where women were seen to exert a specific civilizing influence (see Roberts, 1979; Sheehan, 1986; McClintock, 1997; Stoler, 1997).

The 1929 'Persons Case' was built on the earlier success of the suffrage movement and signifies the end of the first wave of the women's movement in Canada. In this landmark case, the Judicial Committee of the Privy Council (JCPC) in England overruled a decision by the Supreme Court of Canada declaring that women were not legal 'persons' under Canadian constitutional law. The case, brought forward by five Alberta women—Emily Murphy, Nellie McClung, Irene Parlby, Louise McKinney and Henrietta Muir Edwards—aimed to have women declared legal persons so that they could be appointed to positions of power in the public sphere, such as in the Canadian Senate. These five veterans of the first wave of the Canadian women's movement were successful in breaking this legal barrier to women's equality. The decision of the JCPC overruled prior common law which stated that 'women are persons in matters of pains and penalties, but are not persons in matters of rights and privileges' and instead declared that 'the word "persons" in section 24 [of the *British North America Act*] includes members both of the male and female sex' (Library and Archives Canada, n.d.).

Despite the advancements in legal and political equality garnered by the first wave of the Canadian women's movement, these gains were largely the result of efforts of middle-class English-speaking women and largely to their benefit. Although some women utilized a more liberal, equal rights framework, and were concerned with the conditions and issues of working class, poor and immigrant women, the majority of the work was done by and for this relatively privileged group of women. This is evident from the fact that the suffrage movement aimed largely at ensuring that English women got the vote to replace the British men fighting in the First World War, and the fact that men and women of Asian descent did not win the right to vote until 1948, and Aboriginal Peoples until 1960. These ethnic, racial and class-based divisions within the Canadian women's movement became more apparent during the second wave.

THE SECOND WAVE: BUILDING MOMENTUM FOR GENDER EQUALITY

The women's movement in Canada made the most dramatic and obvious gains for women's equality during the second half of the twentieth century. Working in a socio-political culture dominated by rights-based discourses and the emergence and growth of new social movements within the Western world, the second wave of the Canadian women's movement was well positioned to make claims for women and to demand political and legal equality (Black, 1993). However, Jill Vickers argues that despite several decades of apparent inactivity after winning the vote and the Persons Case, there is a direct connection between the first and second waves of the English-Canadian women's movement. The second wave, she asserts, is not just another New Social Movement that emerged within the post-Second World War ideological space created by the new Left, but a continuation, albeit transformed, of the ideas that shaped the first wave, as well as the actions of women in the interwar years (Vickers, 1992).

In 1967, Prime Minister Lester B. Pearson announced the appointment of a Royal Commission on the Status of Women in Canada. As Vickers suggests, the 'credit for the Royal Commission on the Status of Women (RCSW) belongs to the generation of activists—middle-class club women, usually characterized as liberal feminists—who predominated during the long interval between these two waves—the interwave generation' (Campbell, 2009: 53). The Commission is generally seen as the first success of the second wave of the women's movement, and as a blueprint for future activism (Arscott, 2010). The RCSW made its report in 1970, suggesting 167 recommendations. 'Within a few years, one-third of the 122 federal recommendations had been implemented, another third had been implemented in part and still another third remained completely undone' (ibid.). Twenty-five years after the report, almost all of the recommendations had been implemented (ibid.).

Yet, despite the success of the RCSW, its recommendations and influence have also been contested. The Commission and document, as Jane Arscott argues, are ultimately reflections of liberal, egalitarian feminism and speak from the perspective of middle-class, white Canadian women. 'The Report was produced in a setting in which assimilation to one of 'two founding races' was the dominant metaphor for describing the Canadian population. Heteronormativity was rigidly enforced and social change was regarded as a slow process of democratization spanning several centuries, with the mid-twentieth century figuring as the mid-point in that long saga' (ibid.). Thus, the issues of minority women were intentionally excused. This approach is typical of the initial part of the second wave of the women's movement, in which women were essentialized, and gender identity was assumed to override other forms of identity, such as class and race. However, as this chapter discusses further, the idea of the 'universal woman' became seriously contentious by the 1980s.

Despite the ground-breaking nature of the RCSW, there was dissatisfaction over the process, and the final recommendations that 'culminated in April 1972, when hundreds from across the country gathered to form a new non-governmental, activist umbrella organization—known as NAC—the National Action Committee on the Status of Women' (McPhedran, 2006: 7). This was followed the next year by the establishment of the Canadian Advisory Council on the Status of Women (CACSW) by the federal government, which later became the Status of Women Canada.

Status of Women Canada has been the primary government agency responsible for tracking, measuring and promoting women's equality since the 1970s. Their mission is to promote 'equality for women and their full participation in the economic, social and democratic life of Canada' (Status of Women Canada, 2010). Historically, work towards achieving equality for women has advanced through the women's programmes and various funding mechanisms for research that allow for Status of Women to provide information and advice to other government departments and policy-makers, and to fund organizations that provide services for women and act on behalf of women, including groups such as the National Association for Women and the Law and NAC.

The funding and efforts of Status of Women Canada are generally believed to have contributed significantly to the creation of positive policies and legal precedents for women (National Association of Women and the Law, 2006).

The second wave of the women's movement culminated with the activism surrounding the 1982 Constitution of Canada, which included a new *Charter of Rights and Freedoms*. In particular, the efforts of women's groups ensured strong equality guarantees for women in sections 15 and 28. Section 15 guarantees the equality of all Canadians and, significantly, allows for programmes and activities aimed at eliminating the disadvantage of various special groups. Section 28 asserts the primacy of gender equality, stating that all of the rights and freedoms contained in the Charter are guaranteed equally to male and female persons. These two sections provide a strong foundation for the legal claims of women for equality.

Marilou McPhedran argues that 'intensely focused women's activism during negotiations over text yielded substantive amendments in our much heralded constitution. Yet, women's constitutional activism has often been treated as a "sidebar" in mainstream accounts of these formative periods in democratic evolution' (6). The success of the Persons Case and the momentum gained from the RCSW and the newly-formed NAC and Status of Women Canada, combined with the continuing lack of success that women were having in the Canadian courts on issues pertaining to divorce, aboriginal rights, employment and maternity rights under the non-constitutional Bill of Rights, indicated the necessity of constitutional guarantees of equality (McPhedran, 2006: 7–8). In the end, the concerted efforts of thousands of women activists across the country ensured that women's equality stayed on the constitutional agenda, despite repeated efforts to sideline or silence the voices of women within the constitutional process. This success paved the way for women's legal activism, as they used the guarantees in the Charter to fight discrimination through the courts as well as the parliament (see Hein, 2000; Sheldrick, 2004).

CHALLENGES TO THE SECOND WAVE

Beginning during the second wave, and continuing until today, there has been a dramatic increase in the work on identities, and the intersections between different identities, by feminists and other scholars. Among feminists, this work developed out of work on the 'woman question'. Within the feminist movement, both in Canada and elsewhere, conflicts arose surrounding the identities of members. A significant segment felt that it was necessary for members to see themselves first of all as women, and to address the oppression of women before they addressed other types of oppression that women experienced. They felt that fighting against more than one form of oppression would be divisive and would serve to diminish the legitimacy of the women's movement. Other feminists, however, argued that this in itself was oppressive, as it ignored the other identities of women based on ethnicity, class and sexuality, all of which were also sources of oppression and could not be ignored (e.g. Young, 1990). 'The notion of essential feminist interests failed to place women's interests concretely in historical social relation, assumed an essential opposition of interests between men and women and hegemonized the concerns of white often middle-class women' (Anthias, 1991: 34). In the end, essentializing women's interests and identity proved to be more dangerous than addressing the diversity of women and their experiences (Spelman, 1988).

These changes within international feminist theory were reflected in the articulation of the goals and aspirations of the Canadian women's movement. Women's organizations were increasingly forced to explain which women they represented. Questions of race and class started to complicate their demands for gender equality and their ability to organize themselves, particularly given the divide in Canada between English-Canadian, Quebecois and Aboriginal women's organizations. NAC, for example, came under increasing criticism for their inability to represent the Canadian 'woman'. With the rise of neo-liberalism and neo-conservatism in Canada, and with the appearance of anti-feminist groups such as REAL (Realistic, Equal, Active, for Life) Women who utilize a frame of maternalism to refute the claims of equality seekers, the women's movement and its organizations found it increasingly difficult to frame their concerns in a manner that had broad popular appeal.

BACKLASH: NEO-LIBERALISM, NEO-CONSERVATISM AND THE NEED TO REFRAME THE STRUGGLE FOR GENDER EQUALITY

Nancy Fraser argues that 'with the benefit of hindsight, we can now see that the rise of second-wave feminism coincided with a historical shift in the character of capitalism, from the state-organized variant ... to neoliberalism'. Reversing the previous formula, which sought to 'use politics to tame markets, proponents of this new form of capitalism proposed to use markets to tame politics' (107). Ultimately, towards the end of the twentieth century, the feminist critique of androcentric state capitalism was co-opted by neo-liberals and their drive to deconstruct the state welfare system, with negative consequences for both the women's movement and women in general. The focus on recognition, versus redistribution, that has shaped political discourses during the past two decades is evidence that while much of the message of second-wave feminism and the idea of gender equality has been broadly accepted within Western countries, the measures necessary to alleviate women's inequality have failed to materialize (Fraser, 2009). In fact, in Canada, we have actually witnessed the rolling back of state programmes that benefit women.

The rise of neo-liberalism and neo-conservatism in Canada had a dramatic impact on the ability of women, and organizations acting on behalf of women, to influence government policy and priorities. Within the context of several high-profile cases decided in favour of equality guarantees, for example, we see a backlash from Conservative Canada against the so-called 'Charter Canadians' (Knopff and Morton, 2000). These Charter Canadians—women, the disabled, minorities, gays and lesbians—are seen as using the new constitutional equality guarantees to gain advances for their own members at the expense of the 'average' Canadian (ibid.). Instead of being understood as acting in the interests of Canada and Canadians, equality-seeking organizations are become increasingly characterized as self-interested and acting against the interests of Canada.

This rhetoric was popularized by the Reform Party of Canada, which emerged on the national political scene in the late 1980s, gaining power in the 1990s. The Reform Party was a populist party arising from conservative Alberta. Its vision incorporated market liberalism and social conservatism (Patten, 1999: 29), and was one in which all Canadians and provinces would be treated equally, by which they meant that they are treated the same. All citizens would share a common national identity, and ethnic and identity politics become part of the private life, separate from the functioning of the federal government. The growing popularity of this perspective limited the ability of women's groups to make public claims for political measures aimed at reducing inequality and eliminating discrimination; instead, we are all just citizens and our gender 'identity' is a private matter, not a matter deserving political attention. As Sharpe and Braid state:

> The Reformers want a nation at once united and decentralized, a country without public debt where all people are declared equal but no individual receives special help. They believe that women should make their way without affirmative action or any federal program to lift them up. ... There would be no official multiculturalism, sharply limited bilingualism, and no funding for any private group to preserve its identity. (Sharpe and Braid, 1992: 10)

While the Reform Party no longer exists, their ideas continue to shape the politics of the partisan Right in Canada, and were carried forward (albeit perhaps in a more moderate form) by the Alliance Party and now the new Conservative Party of Canada.

In 2006, the new Conservative Party, an amalgamation of the old Progressive Conservative Party, the right wing and populist Reform and Alliance parties led by Stephen Harper, formed a minority government that remains in power at the time of writing. Although the Harper Conservatives had minority governments from 2006-2011, the fragmented and weak nature of Canada's other political parties has enabled his government to make broad changes that significantly undermine the struggle for equality in the country. Many of these changes have a direct impact on the Canadian women's movement and serve to implement the ideology outlined earlier.

Following their election in 2006, the new Conservative government 'declared that the goal of gender equity had been achieved and then purged any reference to gender equality from the mandate of Status of Women Canada' (Brodie and Bakker, 2008: 7). They then proceeded to cut the operating budget of SWC and terminate the Independent Policy Research Fund, which supported 'gender-based policy research' (ibid.: 5). This has 'effectively put an end to the capacity of SWC to generate independent policy research and to assemble external expertise to advocate for women's equality and gender equity inside and outside of the federal government' (ibid.). Moreover, under the new funding guidelines initiated by Stephen Harper's Conservative government upon their election in 2006, Status of Women Canada can no longer fund activities involving law reform, advocacy or research. Instead, funding is to be focused on direct service provision. While funding services for Canadian women is important, the funding of research and advocacy-oriented organizations is arguably essential to the advancement of women's equality in Canada. In the end, the concrete result of the Conservative government's changes in the funding structure of Status of Women Canada is the closure of equality-seeking, advocacy and research-oriented organizations.

On 20 September 2007, for example, the Canadian women's organization, the National Association of Women and the Law (NAWL) closed down its operations. NAWL, a non-profit advocacy organization, had existed for over 30 years, working to promote the equality rights of all women in Canada. Some of NAWL's major successes over the years such as lobbying for the inclusion of gender equality in the Charter of Rights and Freedoms, for changes to the criminal laws surrounding sexual assault, and, more recently, for pay equity in the workplace, have helped to shape the political landscape in Canada and the security of women—economically, politically and socially—within it.

'Cutting the Status of Women departmental budget by 40 per cent, or $5 million, was the first signal that the year-old Conservative government would not take steps to advance women's equality' (Mitchell, 2007). In addition, the government announced that groups that include lobbying as part of their mandate would not be eligible for grants and that 12 of 16 Status of Women offices across the country would be closed (ibid.). This was in addition to the elimination of funding for the Court Challenges Program, which funded Charter challenges launched by marginalized groups that would otherwise be unlikely to afford the legal costs of taking a Charter case to the Supreme Court. These changes in the funding available for women's organizations have severely impacted the ability of women's groups to be outspoken advocates on women's issues. As Judy Rebick, a prominent feminist and activist, notes, 'The decline of a militant feminist movement corresponds with the hegemony of neoliberalism in economics and politics. Women's service groups are under so much pressure to privately raise money to survive that most of them have given up any advocacy function for fear of losing corporate, community, and what's left of government funding' (Rebick, 2010).

In addition to the Harper government's elimination and reduction of funds available for research and advocacy on women's issues in Canada, they also cancelled the Liberals' proposed $5 billion national childcare programme, replacing it with 'a mere $100 a month, taxable dollars, which barely pays for a babysitter on a Saturday night' (Zerbisias, 2010). The 2006 election debate surrounding the national childcare programme demonstrates how the New Right has been able to dismiss the evidence and arguments proposed both by feminists and the Left. The childcare debate became about 'choice' for families and neo-conservative family values, rather than the reality of childcare needs and costs in the country. Brodie and Bakker argued 'that contemporary social policy reforms, while often attributed to the ongoing pressures of economic globalization, the ascendance of neo-liberal thinking in political and policy circles, and broader shifts in the economy, labour markets and social structures, also have been accompanied by the progressive disappearance of the gendered subject, both in discourse and practice' (7). Talking about 'women's issues' in Canada today does not hold a lot of political water (Brodie, 2008; Brodie and Bakker, 2008: 7; Jenson, 2008).

Despite the Conservative declaration that we have achieved gender equality in Canada, there is evidence of women's continuing gender inequality. As an example, Canada lags behind other Western states, at 33rd in the world, in terms of the earnings gap between men and women. 'On average, the estimated earned income for Canadian women is $28,315 compared with $40,000 for men' (Grant, 2010). In addition, the discrepancy tends to occur when women have children, as women without children tend to have more comparable wages to men. 'Women who leave the workforce to have kids tend to experience "an unexplained, but persistent" 3 per cent wage penalty per year of absence' (ibid.). One of the authors of the *Global Gender Gap Report* says 'countries have to adjust for the fact that marriage and motherhood are not at odds with women's advancement in the workplace ... Progress will be achieved when countries seek to reap returns on the investment in health and education of girls and women by finding ways to make marriage and motherhood compatible with the economic participation of women' (World Economic Forum, 2011).

The global research on the economic impact of women's equality demonstrates that 'closing the gender gap provides a basis for a prosperous and competitive society' (ibid.). Yet, as Brodie and Bakker demonstrate in *Where Are the Women*, the continuing attacks on social programmes combined with the cuts in funds available for women's organizations has led to a deterioration in the position of women in Canada over the past decade, particularly those that are most vulnerable. They found, for example, that '38% of families headed by lone-parent mothers lived below the poverty line, compared to 13% of male lone-parent families and 7% of two-parent families. Statistics Canada also reported that, in 2004, females were six times more likely than males to be victims of sexual assault and far more likely to experience criminal harassment, stalking, and spousal abuse' (Brodie and Bakker, 2008: 6). As well, in Canada, the situation of aboriginal women or first-generation immigrant women is generally much worse than the situation of a white, middle-class woman of West European background. Thus, the goals of economic and social equality, as well as physical security for women, are far from achieved.

In addition, while Canadian women rank high in the world in terms of education and participation in the workforce, women are still located in the lower ranks. 'Thirty-six per cent of legislators, senior officials and managers and 57% of professional and technical workers positions are occupied by women' (Hausmann et al., 2010). This inequality is visible among Canada's politicians, where women appear to have hit a glass ceiling. Their relative absence from provincial and federal elected assemblies is likely related to a paucity of informed and vibrant debate on women's issues today (Trimble and Arscott, 2003; Sawer et al., 2006).

CONCLUSION

The continuing inequality of Canadian women, combined with neoliberalism, and the disappearance of the female subject, provides serious challenges for feminism and women's ability to organize in the twenty-first century—how do we frame the struggle for gender equality in this socio-political and economic context? How do we address the differences between women? How do we reconcile the goal of gender equality with various cultural beliefs, values and practices that often underpin or excuse inequality, without advocating intolerance ourselves?

One option is for women's groups to work together with other groups and organizations seeking social change. As Rebick argues:

> The women's movement that emerged from the '60s is a shadow of its former self, focused primarily on service provision, women's studies, and on-line activism. And what is left of the grassroots women's movement is fairly marginalized and without influence at the same time as feminist ideas are so widespread that even a profoundly anti-feminist government like Harper's has to appear to support equality for women. If a new feminism is to emerge as a force, I think it will be as part of the network of movements and groups that are currently battling for social and environmental justice on a global scale (Rebick, 2010).

Fraser, on the other hand, suggests that recent economic crises may weaken the foundations of neo-liberalism, allowing for new forms of social organization. She proposes 'to examine the prospects for reactivating feminism's emancipatory promise in a world that has been rocked by the twin crises of finance capital and US hegemony' (Fraser, 2009). As well, at a global level, the opportunities for women to work together and to learn from other countries and contexts are understudied. By exploring the mechanisms and frames for advancing claims for women's equality within, between and among states, we may find new ways of framing women's concerns that are suitable for the new century. Whichever of the options we choose, the challenges faced by the Canadian women's movement in the past demonstrate the need for new and creative strategies for advancing equality and justice in the future.

END NOTE

1. The Canadian women's movements are a vast topic. This chapter focuses on the English-Canadian movements and on legal and political gains and losses. For information on the Quebec women's movement, see

Micheline Dumont, 'The Origin of the Women's Movement in Quebec', in Constance Backhouse and David H. Flaherty (eds.), *Challenging Times [Electronic Resource]: The Women's Movement in Canada and the United States*. Montreal, Quebec: McGill-Queen's University Press, 1992, pp. 72–89.

Micheline De Sève, 'The Perspectives of Quebec Feminists', in Backhouse and Flaherty (eds.), *Challenging Times [Electronic Resource]*, 1992, pp. 110–116.

For the Aboriginal women's movement, see

Emily Luther, 'Whose "Distinctive Culture"?', *Indigenous Law Journal*, Vol. 8, No. 1, 2010, pp. 27–53.

REFERENCES

Anthias, Floya, 1991, 'Parameters of Difference and Identity and the Problem of Connections – Gender, Ethnicity and Class', *Revue Internationale de Sociologie [International Review of Sociology]*, 1(2): 29–51.

Arscott, Jane, 2010, *'More Explosive Than Any Terrorist's Time Bomb': The RCSW Then and Now', Canadian Political Science Association Annual Conference*. Montreal, QC: Concordia University. 2 June 2010. Web 7 January 2011.

Backhouse, Constance and David H. Flaherty, 1992, *Challenging Times [Electronic Resource]: The Women's Movement in Canada and the United States*. Montreal, QC: McGill-Queen's University Press.

Black, Naomi, 1993, 'The Canadian Women's Movement: The Second Wave.' In *Changing Patterns: Women in Canada*, edited by Sandra Burt, Lorraine Code and L. Dorney, 2nd ed., Toronto, ON: McClelland & Stewart, pp. 151–76.

Brodie, Janine, 2008, 'Putting Gender Back In: Women and Social Policy Reform in Canada'. In *Gendering the Nation-State: Canadian and Comparative Perspectives*, edited by Yasmeen Abu-Laban, Vancouver, BC: UBC Press.

Brodie, Janine and Isabella C. Bakker, 2008, *Where are the Women? [Electronic Resource]: Gender Equity, Budgets and Canadian Public Policy/Janine Brodie and Isabella Bakker*. Ottawa, ON: Canadian Centre for Policy Alternatives/Centre Canadien de Politiques Alternatives.

Campbell, Gail G., 2009, 'Are we Going to do the most Important Things?' Senator Muriel McQueen Fergusson, Feminist Identities, and the Royal Commission on the Status of Women', *Acadiensis*, 38(2): 52–77.

De Sève, Micheline, 1992, 'The Perspectives of Quebec Feminists'. In *Challenging Times [Electronic Resource]: The Women's Movement in Canada and the United States*, edited by Constance Backhouse and David

H. Flaherty, Montreal, QC: McGill-Queen's University Press, pp. 110–16.

DiQuinzio, Patrice, 1995, 'Feminist Theory and the Question of Citizenship: A Response to Dietz' Critique of Maternalism', *Women & Politics [Binghamton]*, 15(3): 23–42.

Dumont, Micheline, 1992, 'The Origin of the Women's Movement in Quebec'. In *Challenging Times [Electronic Resource]: The Women's Movement in Canada and the United States*, edited by Constance Backhouse and David H. Flaherty, Montreal, QC: McGill-Queen's University Press, pp. 72–89.

Errington, Jane, 1993, 'Pioneers and Suffragists'. In *Changing Patterns: Women in Canada*, edited by Sandra Burt, Lorraine Code and L. Dorney, 2nd ed., Toronto: McClelland & Stewart, pp. 59–91.

Fraser, Nancy, 2009, 'Feminism, Capitalism and the Cunning of History', *New Left Review*, 56: 97–117.

Goss, Kristin A. and Michael T. Heaney, 2010, 'Organizing Women as Women: Hybridity and Grassroots Collective Action in the 21st Century', *Perspectives on Politics*, 8(1): 27–52.

Grant, Tavia, 2010, 'Canada Lags in Gender Gap Ranking', *Globe and Mail*. Web. 7 January 2011.

Hausmann, Ricardo, Laura D. Tyson and Saadia Zahidi, 2010, *Global Gender Gap Report 2010*. Geneva, Switzerland: World Economic Forum. 7 January 2010.

Hein, Gregory, 2000, 'Interest Group Litigation and Canadian Democracy'. *Choices IRPP*, 6(2): 1–32.

Jenson, Jane, 2008, 'Citizenship in the Era of 'New Social Risks.' What Happened to Gender Inequalities?' In *Gendering the Nation-State: Canadian and Comparative Perspectives*, edited by Yasmeen Abu-Laban, Vancouver, BC: UBC Press, pp. 185–202.

Knopff, Rainer and F.L. Morton (Eds.), 2000, *The Charter Revolution and the Court Party*. Peterborough, ON: Broadview Press.

Library and Archives Canada, n.d., 'Are Women Persons? The "Persons" Case', *The Archivist*, 119, Web 7 January 2011.

Luther, Emily, 2010, 'Whose "Distinctive Culture"?' *Indigenous Law Journal*, 8(1): 27–53.

McClintock, Anne, 1997, '"No Longer in a Future Heaven": Gender, Race and Nationalism'. In *Dangerous Liasons: Gender, Nations and Postcolonial Perspectives*, edited by Anne McClintock, Aamir Mufti and Ella Shohat, Minneapolis, MN: University of Minnesota Press, pp. 89–112.

McClung, Nellie L., 1972, *In Times Like These*. Toronto, ON: University of Toronto Press.

McPhedran, Marilou, 2006, 'Creating Trialogue: Women's Constitutional Activism in Canada', *Canadian Woman Studies/Les Cahiers de la Femme*, 25(3): 6–17.

Mitchell, Penni, 2007, 'Harper Slams Door to Equality', *Herizons*, 20(4): 9.

National Association of Women and the Law, 2006, 'The History of Status of Women's Canada *Women's Program* and Why it Matters,' *Canadian Feminist Alliance for International Action (FAFIA)*. 10 January 2011.

Patten, Steve, 1999, 'The Reform Party's Re-Imagining of the Canadian Nation', *Journal of Canadian Studies*, 34(1): 27.

Rebick, Judy, 2010, 'New, Stronger Feminism to Renew Fight for Social Justice', *CCPA Monitor*, 17(3): 11.

Roberts, Barbara, 1979, '"A Work of Empire": Canadian Reformers and British Female Immigration'. In *A Not Unreasonable Claim: Women and Reform in Canada, 1880s–1920s*, edited by Linda Kealey, Toronto, ON: Women's Press, pp. 185–201.

Ruddick, Sara, Diane P. Freedman and Olivia Frey, 2003, 'Maternal Thinking'. In *Autobiographical Writing across the Disciplines: A Reader Durham*, Duke University Press, pp. 216–29.

Sawer, Marian, Manon Tremblay and Linda J. Trimble, 2006, *Representing Women in Parliament: A Comparative Study*. London; New York: Routledge.

Sharpe, Sydney and Don Braid, 1992, *Storming Babylon: Preston Manning and the Rise of the Reform Party*. Toronto, ON: Key Porter.

Sheehan, Nancy, 1986, 'Women's Organizations and Educational Issues, 1900–1930', *Canadian Women's Studies*, 7(3): 90–4.

Sheldrick, Byron M., 2004, *Perils and Possibilities: Social Activism and the Law*. Halifax, NS: Fernwood.

Siddiqui, Haroon. 2010. 'How the Harperites are Eroding One of Canada's Foundational Pillars', 10 January. *Toronto Star (Canada)*.

Spelman, Elizabeth V., 1988, *Inessential Woman: Problems of Exclusion in Feminist Thought*, Boston: Beacon Press.

Status of Women Canada, 2010, 'Who are we', *Status of Women Canada*. Web. 14 January 2011.

Stoler, Ann Laura, 1997, 'Making Empire Respectable: The Politics of Race and Sexual Morality in Twentieth-Century Colonial Cultures'. In *Dangerous Liaisons: Gender, Nations and Postcolonial Perspectives*, edited by Anne McClintock, Aamir Mufti and Ella Shohat, Minneapolis, MN: University of Minnesota Press, pp. 344–73.

Strong-Boag, Veronica Jane, 1976, *The Parliament of Women: The National Council of Women of Canada, 1893–1929*. Ottawa, ON: National Museums of Canada.

Trimble, Linda J. and Jane Arscott, 2003, *Still Counting: Women in Politics across Canada*. Peterborough, ON and Orchard Park, NY: Broadview Press.

Vickers, Jill, 1992, 'The Intellectual Origins of the Women's Movements in Canada'. In *Challenging Times [Electronic Resource]: The Women's Movement in Canada and the United States*, edited by Constance Backhouse and David H. Flaherty, Montreal, QC: McGill-Queen's University Press, pp. 39–60.

Wilton, Shauna, 2000, 'Manitoba Women Nurturing the Nation: The Manitoba IODE and Maternal Nationalism, 1913–1920', *Journal of Canadian Studies*, 35(2): 149.

World Economic Forum, 2011, 'Global Gender Gap', *World Economic Forum*. Web. 7 January 2011.

Young, Iris Marion, 1990, *Throwing Like a Girl and Other Essays in Feminist Philosophy and Social Theory*. Bloomington, IN: Indiana University Press.

Zerbisias, Antonia, 2010, 'Canada's Standing Nosedives in Annual Gender Gap Ranking', 24 February. *Toronto Star (Canada)*.

Part II

Caste, Class and Governance

CHAPTER 5

Building Budgets from Below: A Tool for Engendering Economic Governance, Opportunities and Constraint

Indira Mahendravada

The budget is not only a technical instrument for compiling and reporting on government income and expenditure plan, but it is also a declaration of the government's fiscal and financial objectives and its socio-economic priorities. To achieve the three important characteristics of good governance, namely transparency, accountability and participation, engendering the budget process is very important. Earlier, it was assumed that budgets are gender neutral. However, with the emergence of methodologies for Gender Analysis of Budgets and Gender Responsive Budget, it became an acknowledged fact that budgets affect men and women differently. As a result, engendering the budget-making process has become crucial to ensuring inclusiveness of women's concerns.

The Singamma Srinivasan Foundation, with the assistance of United Nations Development Fund for Women (UNIFEM), has identified the budget as an important tool whereby women citizens can participate in, and direct, the fiscal policy. According to them, the budget links economic governance to political governance. The Foundation attempts to make use of the existing system for engendering the process, in contrast to the introduction of several programmes for the empowerment of women. It enables women to determine a gender-responsive fiscal policy.

The project emphasizes the economic empowerment of women, and focuses on encouraging budgets that are prepared with the participation of women. To arrive at a methodology, the Foundation selected two GPs and two Corporations in Karnataka for a pilot project. With several rounds of interactive sessions with key groups, including elected women representatives, local women, policy-makers and academicians, as well as participatory exercises and workshops, the Foundation was able to successfully influence the 2005–2006 budgets.

OBJECTIVE AND METHODOLOGY

The present paper makes an attempt to understand the way the Singamma Srinivasan Foundation went about the process of influencing the budget by providing external inputs to the Elected Women Representatives in Mysore district of Karnataka, paying special attention to the following aspects:

1. Understanding the methodology adopted
2. Identifying the positive and negative aspects of the methodology
3. Identifying the constraints
4. Identifying the additional inputs needed
5. Identifying how the methodology can be replicated

A combination of case studies and participatory interactive method was adopted for qualitative data collection, and an interview schedule was used to collect information about the socio-economic background, knowledge levels and participation levels of the representatives.

GOVERNANCE AND GENDER

Urban governance has to be gender sensitive if it has to be equitable, sustainable and effective. According to the UNDP, a gender-sensitive approach to urban governance has the following two principal objectives:

- Increasing women's participation in human settlement development.
- Fostering gender awareness and competence among both men and women in the political arena and planning practice.

At present, there is very little recognition or knowledge of how men and women contribute to the society in different ways. The differences are more due to social reasons than biological ones. Unless urban governance is gender sensitive, these differences cannot be ironed out. Getting more women into the mainstream public offices and bureaucracy is a vital part of engendering urban governance.

Although there is plenty of debate on conceptualizing good governance, the majority of these ignored the manner in which women are excluded from the governance process (Goetz, 1997). Not only is it necessary to understand how women are excluded from the decision-making process due to the various disadvantages under which they operate, both in public and private domains, it is also essential to find ways and means of integrating them into the system so that the development outcomes will not bypass women. According to Netherlands Ministry of Foreign Affairs (2002), gender-sensitive governance includes the following:

- Participation—equal participation in governance institutions and processes, freedom of association and space for an active women's movement
- Transparency—transparency and gender equity in the allocation of resources
- Legitimacy—legislation for gender equity and the promotion and protection of women's rights
- Effectiveness—ensuring the effectiveness of gender-sensitive policies and institutional structures

The Beijing Platform of Action (1995) recognized the role of women by saying that 'without the active participation of women and the incorporation of women's perspectives in all levels of decision-making, the goals of equality, development and peace cannot be achieved' (UNDP, 1995). However, the situation is far from satisfactory. The impact of gender inequality on governance in the case of South Asian countries was explored under the following themes (Tambiah, 2003), namely:

- Politics and governance: as 'public' activities, and the consequent implications for women

- The state–women interface: in the form of the political participation of women
- Women's perceptions, and experiences, of formal and informal institutions of governance
- The role of civil society (movements, NGOs and people's institutions) in engendering governance

The study revealed that women have to overcome several barriers, including both socio-economic and cultural factors, to take part in the institutions of governance. Moreover, the study also reveals that women elected to local bodies come under the 'moralistic gaze' of society and become targets of character assassination.

Even in a state like Kerala, which ranks high in social indicators, elected women representatives are sexually harassed to 'put them in place', thereby preventing them from participating in the governance process (Panada, 2004). Experiences from Karnataka showed that women were also often compelled to participate in the elections by their male kin; and once elected, they are used as puppets to achieve the latter's private goals.

UNDP's Human Development Report (2000) reveals the gender gap in governance in South Asia. There are only 7 per cent of women in Parliament, 9 per cent in Cabinet, 20 per cent in local government, 9 per cent in civil services and 6 per cent in judiciary.

The most important factor that affects the non-participation of women in the decision-making and governance processes is the private and public divide associated with women and men (Panada, 2004). While women's place is considered to be in the private domain, associated with the household, reproductive work and femininity, the public domain is associated with political authority, public decision-making, productive work and masculinity. According to Panada, the patriarchal structure, comprising egalitarian gender relations and stereotypic attitudes, beliefs and ideologies, prevails in both the public and private domains, thereby contributing to women's subordinate status and their inability to participate in governance. Gender inequality in governance is further complicated by other intersecting hierarchies such as class, caste, ethnicity and religion as well as rural and urban localities.

INTERVENTION STRATEGY

After selecting two wards (ward numbers 3 and 24) based on discussions with local officials, the Foundation organized a preliminary meeting with all the elected women representatives (EWRs) of MCC, where they were sensitized about the need for looking at budgets from a gender perspective, and the role they can play in influencing the budgets. The members were also motivated to prepare an 'ought to budget' by conducting mock sessions. With this exercise, it was found that, given opportunity and training, women are able to participate in the budget process and take care of the socio-economic needs of the local people, even when they are illiterate or ignorant.

SSF in partnership with Janaagraha developed the module, and a network of bureaucrats, NGOs, resource persons, knowledgeable women and SHGs was formed.

The first step was to introduce the concept of budget and its various components to the EWRs, citizens and the authorities. After this, ward-level interactive sessions with local women representatives, SHG members and prominent women were held. At this stage, the group was encouraged to identify local needs and prioritize them. After this, the group also identified the individuals/organizations to initiate action in addition to identifying sources of income as well as ways of raising it. In the second step, these demands were put to the officials/decision-makers concerned in the presence of the EWRs to discuss the feasibility of making changes in the forthcoming budget. The entire exercise was conducted before the preparation of 2005–2006 budget, in order to give the EWRs the opportunity to ensure that the group's priorities get reflected in the budget. The EWRs were also encouraged to prepare a vision statement for their ward.

SOCIO-ECONOMIC PROFILE OF ELECTED WOMEN REPRESENTATIVES

There were 23 women representatives in Mysore City Corporation at that time, the majority of whom were educated up to SSLC/PUC. There were also three uneducated but literate women. The EWRs were a mixture of several castes and political parties. All the women were married and in the age group of 30–45 years, with the majority (80%) being from families with political experience. There were very few first-generation entrants.

According to the women, nearly 50 per cent of them came into governance because of their husbands, who encouraged them to contest. Another 30 per cent of women were promoted by political parties. Only one among the women said that she had contested in elections because she was interested and that it was her own decision. All the women were of the opinion that it was only because of 33 per cent reservation that women were given importance. The majority of the EWRs acknowledged the influence of political parties in their participation and decision-making. According to them, the parties extend a lot of support and, in return, they followed the party high command's ruling in all aspects. Nonetheless, it is important to note that when questioned about influence of politics on governance, the majority of the EWRs acknowledged the fact that party-based governance was not always good, and that for good governance, the representatives should be beyond political parties.

Out of the 23 women representatives, only 50 per cent of them said that they were aware of budget allocations and that they participated in the process. A comparative study of the participation and educational levels indicated that those who are educated and are graduates took more active part, even when some of them were first-generation entrants, when compared with less-educated EWRs. Uneducated women, on the contrary, did not show any interest. According to them, the parties would take care of all that.

OUTCOMES OF THE INTERVENTIONS

Providing inputs for capacity building of EWRs has certainly made an impact on the thinking process, not only of the EWRs, but also other active citizens and women SHG members, as the interactive sessions were held in the wards.

IDENTIFICATION AND PRIORITIZATION OF LOCAL NEEDS

During the workshop, women participated actively and identified several local needs. The important characteristics of these needs were as follows:

- These needs were applicable to all the citizens of that area.
- They were not a priority with the MCC.
- The needs ranged from simple intervention for road safety measures to policy issues such as action on encroachments to government lands, as well as actions needed to increase revenue and reduce the tax burden on citizens.

FROM PASSIVE SPECTATORS TO ACTIVE PARTICIPANTS

Because of their participation in the interactive sessions, and the inputs given by the Foundation, some of the EWRs became active participants in the budget-preparing process. These women understood the need for gender-inclusive budgets. The EWRs were able to influence the following changes during 2005–2006 budget:

- Allocations under integrated women's development project were enhanced from ₹50,000 to ₹1,00,000. This helped in increasing assistance to four women's groups in starting micro-enterprises. Earlier, only two groups were getting assistance.
- Budget allocations for buying sewing machines for economically backward women were enhanced from ₹7 lakhs to 10 lakhs.
- A women's insurance scheme called Rajarajeswari Yojana, offering coverage for diseases such as cancer, was proposed to be taken up by the councillors in their respective wards.
- A new head was created under Nirmala Nagara Yojana under which each local habitat group get a sanction of ₹10,000.
- A proposal to constitute a Women and Child Welfare Committee was introduced in the council session by the EWRs, which was approved provisionally. It was sent to the government for approval to make it a statutory committee on the lines of existing statutory committees such as Tax and Appeal Committee, Health Committee, Works Committee and Audit Committee.

ISSUES EMERGING OUT OF THE INTERVENTIONS

The interventions of the SSF have clearly shown that given proper inputs, women EWRs can play an important role in encouraging gender-inclusive budgets. The initiatives to constitute a statutory committee for women and child welfare at the corporation level are a testimony to this. But there are differences in articulation and participation, which makes it difficult to operationalize the inclusion of women's voices and gender perspective. These include the following:

- Lower literacy levels of women are a real hindrance. Women who can only sign their names do not show much interest. They come into the system due to reservation. Out of the 23 women members in MCC, only 4–5 were graduates and only 20–30 per cent showed interest in the process.
- Multiple roles for women, with very little support systems, prevent them from taking greater responsibilities.
- Dominance of political parties: political parties play an important role in the Indian democratic process. The multi-party system, and loyalty to party requirements, also plays an important role in women's participation.
- The existing process of budget making is often too complicated for these women to understand. Moreover, ward-wise income and expenditure were not maintained and allocations are made based on discussions with the works and finance committees, rather than individual ward representatives.

SUGGESTIONS

The following suggestions emerge from the interventions:

- More training and awareness programmes are needed for the EWRs to ensure their capacity building on subjects such as budget making, studying the revenue and expenditure of their wards, identification of local problems through participatory process and so on. Synergic networks need to be developed among the academicians, researchers and voluntary institutions so that each group's strengths can be put together for better capacity building.
- Ward-wise income and expenditure has to be maintained for easy understanding.
- Information and Communication Technologies (ICTs) can be used effectively for capacity building and information dissemination. Training programmes for the members need to be organized. With the introduction of local languages into ICT

programmes, it will not be difficult for the members to make full use of the technology once they acquire the basic skills.

- Support services in the form of transportation facilities, baby care centres and so on are needed for EWRs to take active part in the governance process and shoulder their responsibilities effectively.
- Training programmes are to be conducted for male officials as well as elected members to gender-sensitize them.

REFERENCES

Goetz, A.M, 1997, 'Introduction: Getting Institutions Right for Women In Development'. In *Getting Institutions Right for Women in Development*, edited by A.M. Goetz, London: Zed Press.

Netherlands Ministry of Foreign Affairs, 2002, *Gender and Governance (Draft)*. The Hague: Netherlands Development Organisation, Annette Evertzen.

Panada, Smitha Mishra, 2004, *Engendering Governance: Issues and Strategies*, Background Theme Paper, Silver Jubilee Symposium on Governance in Development, December 14–19, IRMA.

Tambiah, Y, 2003, *The Impact of Gender Inequality on Governance in Essays on Gender and Governance*. New Delhi: Human Development Research Centre (UNDP).

UNDP, 1995, *Public Sector Management, Governance and Sustainable Human Development*. New York: United Nations Development Programme.

CHAPTER 6

Functionality of the Dominant Ideology of Gender in Traditional Hindu Society: An Enquiry*

Smarak Swain

'Male dominance' is a popular topic among radical feminists. The concept of male dominance is based on the difference between sex and gender. Sex refers to the 'biological division into male and female; gender to the parallel and socially unequal division into femininity and masculinity'.[1] This division is based on society's prevailing dominant ideology. Radical feminists, especially of the Marxist brand, believe that this dominant ideology is a handiwork of upper-caste men and hence results in male dominance over women. They argue that the dominant ideology and resultant norms and values of society are responsible for the sexual division of labour, confining women to the domestic sphere, and also for various social evils such as Sati, widowhood and child marriage.

In short, the feminists portray women in traditional Hindu society as passive, unintelligent and excessively confirming automatons. Women's ability to influence men's decisions and behaviours through attachment,[2] affect, socialization, sexuality and other means of social interaction in group situations are usually not stressed. Take, for instance, the argument of pioneer feminist Ernestine Friedl (Haralambos and Heald, 1980), who argued that men are dominant because they control the exchange

*Another version of this paper was published in *Journal of Alternative Perspectives in the Social Sciences*, Vol. 1, No. 2, 2009, pp. 435–48.

of valued goods beyond the family group. The greater the control of men over resources outside the family, the greater their power. But she did not investigate the amount of influence women have over men.

This article starts with the assumption that women are active and intelligent beings, and goes on to investigate the relative contributions of men and women in traditional Hindu society in the formulation of the dominant ideology of gender. Using this perspective, an attempt is made to understand the functions of the dominant ideology to society at large and women in particular.

Section II presents three discussions to be used later in the article. The first relates to the functions of sexual division of labour in traditional Hindu society, whereas the other two discussions investigate social interaction, power and politics in Indian households. Section III investigates issues such as sexuality, Sati, widowhood and child marriage. Section IV discusses in brief the functionality of dominant ideology.

SEXUAL DIVISION OF LABOUR

Pre-modern India was mired by political instability and frequent wars. It was only after the British colonial rule that a semblance of social stability dawned on Indian soil. It can be safely assumed that life expectancy in pre-colonial India was lower. Major casualties occurred in wars. Risky sea and land voyages by traders and merchants also led to loss of life.

Women perform the crucial role of reproduction, and are thereby instrumental in the survival of society. They also perform expressive roles.[3] Hence, it was not advisable for society to let women work in the army or commerce, facing unpredictability and the vagaries of life outside the family.

Moreover, the upper and middle castes in peasant societies lived on surplus value or at subsistence level ... the sexual division of labour between field and household was convenient. The lower castes worked at below subsistence level; hence, both men and women worked outside the realm of the household.

Due to the above reasons, the sexual division of labour in pre-colonial India was conducive to the survival of society as well as functional for women. It thus started as a favourable arrangement, although later it would become part of the normative system, gaining rigidity in the process.

MOTHER-IN-LAW (*SAAS*)—DAUGHTER-IN-LAW (*BAHU*)—SISTER-IN-LAW (*NANAD*) CYCLE

The ideal-typical household in most of Hindu India is the patrilineal patrilocal joint family. Its actual frequency varies across socio-economic levels, caste groups, occupations and regions (Dube, 1986: 7). Decision-making in joint families is theoretically in the hands of the male patriarch. Social interactions between, and the relative influences of, various members in a joint family can be better understood by an analysis of power and politics within the family.

Power refers to the ability to influence another person's behaviour and decisions. Politics refers to all the activities of an individual to gain power. Here, we shall concentrate on female politics in a joint family. A woman's political manoeuvrings in traditional Hindu society can be broadly divided into three phases:[4]

1. *Nanad*: As a girl when she is in her natal home, unmarried.
2. *Bahu*: When she marries and joins her affinal family.
3. *Saas*: When her son marries and brings a daughter-in-law, the *bahu*. She is now the mother-in-law of the *bahu*.

Attachment between mother and child is common in most cultures. Kakar (1978), however, through his psychoanalytic study of the Indian family, draws attention to the unusually close mother–son bond in Indian society. The man is tied forever to the mother, especially in view of the fact that mother's own longing for love is not satiated in patriarchal, joint families.[5]

The girl child observes the close bond between her mother and her brothers. Partly by identification, and partly by socialization, she starts perceiving her brothers as independent entities and herself as a dependant variable. She perceives men as productive resources and herself as a relative dependant on the resource. When the brother marries and brings in a sister-in-law, she faces a major threat to her own obtainment of resources. Due to a similarity in situation, she finds common cause with her mother. Together, they try to minimize the *bahu*'s zone of influence in the family. Marriage in traditional

India being arranged, she experiences many insecurities in her affinal house post-marriage (as explained later). Due to this, she maintains contact with her natal family even after marriage and takes an active interest in household politics of her natal family.

After marriage, she enters her affinal family with the status of a *bahu*. Owing to the novelty of environment in the new joint family, she has to undergo resocialization. Her resocialization is closely connected to her social interaction with her *saas* (mother-in-law) and *nanad* (sister-in-law).[6] As premarital sex is taboo in traditional Hindu family, the husband becomes vulnerable to her influence in return for sexual gratification. In turn, the *saas*, who had reared her son as an exclusive resource (as explained later), feels insecure. She tries to suppress romantic love between her son and the *bahu* so as to keep the conjugal bond secondary. Her daughter, the *nanad*, helps her in this politics. The *bahu* feels insecure because of attempts at marginalizing her relations with her husband (a perceived productive force). She desperately desires a male child. She considers the birth of a male child (i.e. a productive force) as her foremost achievement. This child is the product of herself and hence an exclusive resource she does not have to share with her *saas* or *nanad*.

After her son marries, she assumes the status of *saas* to the *bahu* who joins her family. At this time, her son exhibits a tendency to move closer to the *bahu*, a stranger who can influence him through her romantic moves. Consequently, she feels threatened by the influence the *bahu* has over her exclusive resource.

'Since sons are a woman's most critical resource, ensuring their life-long loyalty is an enduring preoccupation. Older women have a vested interest in the suppression of romantic love between youngsters to keep the conjugal bond secondary and to claim sons' primary allegiance' (Kandiyoti, 1997: 89–90).

The above is an ideal-typical rendition of politics in a household. Actual incidence depends on the relative capability of the individual players, the *saas* and the *bahu*. Another point to note is that life within the household can be active and far from the alienation of women observed by Leela Dube.[7] Alienation of a player in households may happen when he/she is completely sidelined and dominated, which is an exception rather than the norm.

Men of working age in a family are perceived as productive forces. All relations between them and other members of the family (father, mother, sibling, spouse, etc.) are relations of production. The exact nature of relations of production depends on the nature of social interaction between them. All relations to production try to play politics to maximize their power. Interaction between relations of production is characterized by both cooperation and conflict. The primary conflict, it is to be noted, is between the *saas* and the *bahu*, the mother-in-law and the daughter-in-law, as they share the same workspace and stake claim on the same 'perceived force of production', that is, the son/husband. Further, at the onset of marriage, relations between the mother-in-law and the daughter-in-law are normative and puts them in positions of boss and subordinate. Hence, there is greater chance of conflict.

DECISION-MAKING IN FAMILY

On a theoretical plane, the eldest male member of a patriarchal joint family is the absolute head. The unitary model of family which 'treats the household as a single entity in relation to both consumption and production [and] assumes that all household resources and incomes are pooled and that resources are allocated by an altruistic household head who represents the household's tastes and preferences' (Agarwal, 1997) also supported the above view of joint family. However, this model has fallen into disrepute (ibid.). There are multiple poles in a joint family's decision-making process.

The decisions taken in a family are ultimately a summation of the 'bargaining power' of its various members. The members can be divided as follows:

1. Those with direct control over external resources, like men of the working age group.
2. Those who do not have direct control over external resources, including women, the elderly and children.

Bargaining power of those in the second category depends primarily on the following factors:

1. Attachment
2. Sexuality

3. Fall-back options
4. Strength of socialization of those in first category

The mother–son bond can be associated with attachment and the husband–wife bond with sexuality. It may be noted that when the wife gets well settled in her affinal household, she may develop an attachment with her husband but never of the type a mother and her son develop.

It can be said that a wife's bargaining power is more in nuclear families than in joint families.[8] This is because of the primacy of attachment over sexuality in the dominant ideology of society. Whereas 'the western civilization stresses the sexual role of women as wife, Indian civilization stresses the maternal role as mother'.[9]

From the discussion, it can be inferred that sex ratio in the warring castes in pre-colonial India must have been heavily skewed against women. Trying to investigate this hypothesis, J.M. Datta made an analysis of prescriptions on women in Indological literature dated between 600 BC and AD 300 (1957; 1981). He concluded that there was a shortage of women in this period. The sex ratio may have varied in this period, but never reached equality.

Male casualty in this period was high. In addition, 'females have a biological advantage in survival from the time of conception until old age. This advantage [could have been] reversed by actual discrimination against females' (Das Gupta and Adetunji, 1998) like Sati, social death and child marriage (associated with ill-health and high maternal mortality).

Here, the purpose is to investigate the causality of these crimes. No doubt these social evils are an eventuality of the dominant Hindu ideology. But what led to such an ideology? There are numerous contributing factors and pinning the blame on one causal source is naïve. This article intends to concentrate on one of these factors.

SEXUALITY AND CHILD MARRIAGE

It can be noted in many feminist studies that the dominant ideology has tried to control female sexuality (see Uberoi, 2004) through ideals such as chastity, purity, unselfishness, simplicity and modesty. In the Sanskritic model of conjugal sexual relations, 'sexuality is deemed legitimate only for the production of male offspring to continue the ritual offerings to ancestors: and not, primarily, for the production of pleasure' (ibid.). One wonders why a dominant male would try to suppress female sexuality when it would imply suppression of his sexuality as well.

A contributing cause to the formulation of the Sanskritic model could be women themselves. As discussed in Section II, attachment and sexuality are two major techniques of control women exercise over perceived productive forces (working age group men and young male dependants). Based on the following reasoning:

1. Mother–son attachment is 'special' in India.
2. Mother–son attachment has been glorified in the dominant Sanskritic ideology.
3. Wife is often at a disadvantage in household politics ... she has to undergo resocialization and play against the mother, who is an entrenched power pole.
4. Her control over the male by means of sexuality is deplored in the Sanskritic ideology.

It can be concluded that *saas* has a dominating influence in household politics. On feeling threatened by the *bahu*, she created ideas such as purity and chastity in the local tradition. Due to the *Saas–Bahu–Nanad* cycle, these ideas became pervasive and deep-rooted. The local tradition got universalized and found mention in the dominant ideology.

Child marriage is a logical effect of this stringent definition of purity and chastity. Among other reasons, one could have been the insecurity faced by natal family about the appropriation of productive forces and their perception of an unmarried girl as a liability. In addition, child marriage was functional to members of the affinal family, especially the *saas*, in the sense that resocialization and domination of a child is easier to achieve than that of an adult. In child marriage, the *bahu*'s political career as a *nanad* also got shortened; she could not get sufficient political socialization in her natal family. This would have further eased the *saas*'s domination over her.

SATI AND WIDOW REMARRIAGE

The Sanskrit word *Sati* means a chaste and virtuous wife (Statchbury, 1982). The rationale behind Sati in Hindu ideology can be inferred not from a single perspective but from numerous ways of viewing women in society. First, woman and her sexuality were seen as a temptation to the other-worldly Hindus. The primary goal in the life of a Hindu was to gain *moksha* and renunciation was advocated as the means to gain *moksha*. Since

> woman was, for men, Nature's normal means for the satisfaction of his sexual desire, she became synonymous with Desire. For such philosophies and ideals, which emphasized celibacy, Brahmacharya, and required that one should conserve one's vital fluid and so build up stocks and reserves of energy, woman became an enemy (Lal, quoted in Allen (1982)).

Hence, the sexuality of a woman without a husband had to be kept under control. Problem with this explanation is that

> neither in real life nor in the traditional postulates has Hinduism denied materialism or pursuit of pleasure in life. Emphasis has always been on a healthy combination of the material pursuit, *artha-kama*, with the moral-transcendental goals or *dharma-moksha*. The latter was given a theoretically higher place than the former but in practice, the major pre-occupation of all sections of the Hindus was pursuit of material goals and a robust practical attitude towards life (Singh, 1986: 111).

A second major explanation for Sati is purity.

> Historically, the development of Hindu society has been one of ever-increasing hierarchy—of hierarchy based explicitly on an ideology of a parallel development of institutions concerned with the control of female sexuality ... [whenever] purity is the primary idiom of status differentiation, there is certain to be a major preoccupation with the maintenance of female chastity. This is especially so in India where the purity of the caste is a direct function of the purity of its womenfolk. The male members of the caste are in large measure dependant for their status rating on the purity of their women (Allen, 1982).

This is a plausible explanation. This argument also gets support from the fact that hypergamy (*anuloma*), but not hypogamy, is sanctioned in *Manusmriti*. In other words, a woman is not allowed to marry a person of lower birth but a man is. However, while notions of purity could be a factor, it is neither the only one nor a strong one. If it were, Sati would have been the norm, given the fact that purity was jealously guarded by Hindus. But it was not. Not all upper caste widows were burnt.

A third plausible reason was pointed out by Swami Vivekananda. He observed that a surplus of women in the upper classes gave rise to a practice such as Sati[10] (see Sen, 1985: 18). In a similar vein, Bengali novelist Sarat Chandra Chattopadhyay, who made a historical survey of the oppression to which women were subjected in different societies, traced the low value of females among marital races to their relatively surplus number (ibid.).

A deeper understanding of this view can be had from the many variants of Sati in Indian society:

> Two forms of Sati are enjoined in the Hindu scriptures: *sahamarana or* co-cremation, whereby the widow is burned on her husband's funeral pyre, and *anumarana*, when she is burned after her husband's cremation. There are records of this second type occurring up to thirty-five years after the husband's death. There are also a few cases in which the widow became a Sati, on premonition of her husband's death, if he had been absent for some time (Statchbury, Allen).

If Sati had been a regular ritual based on purity, only *sahamarana* would be practised. A few probable causes of both forms are as follows:

1. That the widow became an economic burden on her affinal family, given the fact that women were seen as unproductive.
2. That she became a claimant for a fresh perceived productive force, thereby intensifying the competition.
3. That her sexuality posed a threat to another woman ... argument here is similar to the one presented in the discussion on sexuality.

If Sati is physical death, widowhood in India (among upper castes) is social death.[11] About widowhood in Hindu ideology, it is said that

> ... a widow was expected either to commit Sati or lead a chaste, austere, ascetic lifestyle. According to Manusmriti ... a widow is supposed to be disfigured: and she is dressed in a plain garment appropriate to a widow. After that, she is expected to remain in perpetual mourning: to give up eating hot foods in order to cool her body (her sexual energy); to avoid auspicious occasions because she is considered inauspicious. (Chen, 1998: 25–6)

In short, this social death guarantees that the woman's sexuality does not become a danger to vulnerable men. As discussed earlier, ascetism and other-worldliness are not practised in severity in India. Hence, men were not averse to female sexuality. Then why would the patriarchal society of India, dominated by men, formulate such a dominant ideology so as to restrict the sexuality of widows?

Uma Chakravarti (1998) gives an explanation. Assuming social death as a patriarchal formulation, she tries to draw a conceptual link with caste system: upper castes restrict their own reproduction in order to reduce pressure on the physical resources under their control, while encouraging the lower castes to reproduce in order to increase the human resources under their control (ibid.).

A problem with this explanation is that Brahmins are also upper castes. Brahmins (who professed occupations of priests, poets, teachers, clerks and ministers) used to depend more on the services they provided to others for livelihood than on physical resources. They therefore had no reason to restrict their own production. Also, widow remarriage was practised among the lower castes not because they were encouraged by upper castes, but because they were socially farthest from the upper castes and the great traditions of Hinduism, besides other reasons (see Sen, 1985).

One plausible causal factor for the treatment meted out to an upper-caste widow is the one discussed earlier for Sati. Both are deaths—one physical and the other social. Both were meted out to widows. Therefore, on a conceptual level, the purpose behind both must be same.

Tŀ. sexual division of labour in traditional Indian society was functional to the society. When it became rigid and a part of the dominant ideology, it became dysfunctional to women's freedom in more than one way. It influenced the psyche and the patterns of social interaction of women. A dysfunctional result of this was the competition and conflict among women over men as perceived forces of production, which contributed to widow-burning, widowhood rituals, child marriage, female infanticide and a value preference for sons. What was *dysfunctional* for the victims was *functional* to other women; also to society, as the sex ratio was aptly balanced, thus not leading to a demand–supply imbalance in the marriage pattern.

If unnatural discrimination against women leading to physical murder, social death or death by poor health had not been there, the consequences would have been either of the two:

1. Practice of polygyny
2. Many girls would have remained unmarried

Polygyny would have intensified the household politics, giving the man greater latitude in decision-making (since his bonds with each woman would have been weaker). Such a situation could also make the *saas* all-powerful and tyrannical. Ultimately, this situation would have denigrated the condition of women further. Another dysfunction could be that polygyny would lead to frequent conflict over succession in joint families.

An excess of unmarried women in their natal families would be a worse consequence. It could lead to widespread prostitution and excessive female labour. Excessive female labour in high castes would have affected *Jajmani* relations of production (although this situation has the potential to break the sexual division of labour and give women the freedom to work beyond the household).

Hence, we see that the alternatives would have been dysfunctional to the society and its institutions, as they existed then. I dare to opine that, on the overall, the dominant ideology was functional to society then, and maintained a stable equilibrium between various social systems.[12]

Hence, we conclude that both men and women have contributed to the formulation of the dominant 'male' ideology of gender in traditional India, while one can debate on the functions and dysfunctions of this ideology over time. Over-emphasizing male dominance in studies of dominant ideology is risky. Women were as active and intelligent then as now. Their role in scripting of the Sanskritic ideology and the functionality of same needs to be studied further.

NOTES

1. Ann Oakley, quoted in *Concise Oxford Dictionary of Sociology*, 1994.
2. In the sense defined by J. Bowlby, 'Attachment and Loss: Retrospect and Prospect', *American Journal of Orthopsychiatry*, Vol. 52, No. 4, 1982, pp. 664–78.
3. Ann Oakley was extremely critical of Parsons' view of the 'expressive function of women' (see Haralambos, 1981). The expressive function is not functionally universal and exceptions do exist; nevertheless, its role in socialization cannot be overlooked.

4. The three phases have been named here after the local names of statuses of: a woman newly inducted into a family by marriage (*bahu*), her mother-in-law (*saas*) and her sisters-in-law in affinal family (*nanad*).
5. Observes Mandelbaum: 'Between mother and son, there is everywhere in India a strong, tender, unchanging, dependable bond ... a mother is respected; motherhood is revered' (1970: 62). Ashis Nandy has defined mother–son relationship in upper-caste society as 'the basic nexus and the ultimate paradigm of human social relationships in India' (1980: 37).
6. The affinal family for a newlywed is close to a total institution for the bride. 'The young wife is at the bottom rung of the hierarchal ladder. She is expected to fit into her new family, learning and adhering to its customs and norms rather than to those of her natal family, and gradually learning to consider this family as her own. She is expected to be extremely submissive and deferent, expressing respect for the female in-laws and her husband in the first few years, and containing almost all her feelings. It is culturally recognized that her husband is more attached to his mother than to her, since the maternal nurturance is viewed as transcending sexual intimacy. Nevertheless, it is understood that he and his wife will gradually become increasingly involved over the years ... her anxiety is much more focused on her mother-in-law to whom she is an outsider, than to her husband' (Ahmed, 2003).
7. By using 'seed and earth' metaphor, Dube states that women are alienated from productive resources because they have no control over production. Leela Dube, 'Seed and Earth: The Symbolism of Biological Reproduction and Sexual Relations of Production', in Leela Dube, Eleanor Leacock and Shirley Ardener (eds.), *Visibility and Power: Essays on Women in Society and Development*. New Delhi: Oxford University Press, 1986.
8. Conjugal bond is weaker than consanguine bond in joint families.
9. Central theme of '*The Indian Ideal of Womanhood*' published by Ramakrishna Mission, referred in Allen (1982).
10. Although this observation of Swami Vivekananda was not based on any empirical evidence.
11. 'Social death' has been used in the context of Hindu widowhood by Chakravarti (1998).
12. Today, the same dominant ideology has become dysfunctional. Son preference as a value has led to a heavily skewed and alarmingly decreasing sex ratio. Sex ratio in India has decreased consistently from 972 in 1901 to 914 in 2011. This can be explained in terms of the

contradictions that come about in the social system when a traditional society modernizes at a fast pace.

REFERENCES

Agarwal, Bina, 1997, *Bargaining and Gender Relations: Within and Beyond the Household,* http://www.binaagarwal.com/downloads/apapers/bagaining_and_gender_relations.pdf, accessed on 10 September 2013.

Ahmed, Imtiaz, 2003, 'Between the Ideal and the Real: Gender Relations within the Indian Joint Family'. In *Family and Gender: Changing Values in Germany and India,* edited by P. Pernau, Imtiaz Ahmed and Helmut Reifeld, New Delhi: Sage Publications.

Allen, Michael, 1982, 'Introduction: The Hindu View of Women'. In *Women in India and Nepal,* edited by Michael Allen and S.N. Mukherjee, Canberra, ACT: Australian National University.

Chakravarti, Uma, 1998, 'Gender, Caste and Labour: The Ideological and Material Structure of Widowhood'. In *Widows in India: Social Neglect and Public Action,* edited by M.A. Chen, New Delhi: Sage Publications.

Chen, Martha Alter (Ed.), 1998, *Widows in India: Social Neglect and Public Action*. New Delhi: Sage Publications.

Das Gupta, Monica and Jacob Adetunji, 1998, 'Women and Mortality'. In *Women in the Third World: An Encyclopedia of Contemporary Issues,* edited by N. Stromquist, New York: Garland Publishing Inc.

Datta, Jatindra Mohan, 1957, 'Variation in Sex Ratio in Bengal during 150 years', *Man in India,* 37(2): 133–48.

Datta, Jatindra Mohan, 1981, 'Was There a Shortage of Women in Ancient India', *Man in India*.

Dube, Leela, 1986, 'Seed and Earth: The Symbolism of Biological Reproduction and Sexual Relations of Production'. In *Visibility and Power: Essays on Women in Society and Development,* edited by Leela Dube, Eleanor Leacock and Shirley Ardener, New Delhi: Oxford University Press.

Haralambos, M. and R.N. Heald, 1980, *Sociology: Themes and Perspectives*. New Delhi: Oxford University Press.

Kakar, Sudhir, 1978, *The Inner World: A Psycho-analytic Study of Childhood and Society in India*. New Delhi: Oxford University Press.

Kandiyoti, Deniz, 1997, 'Bargaining with Patriarchy'. In *The Woman, Gender and Development Reader,* edited by Nalini Viswanathan, Lynn Duggan, Laurie Nisonoff and Nan Wiegersma, New Delhi: Zubaan.

Mandelbaum, David Goodman, 1970, *Society in India, Vol. 1*. Berkeley, CA: University of California Press.

Nandy, Ashis, 1980, *At the Edge of Psychology*. New Delhi: Oxford University Press.

Sen, Ilina, 1985, *Low and Declining Sex Ratio in India (1901–1971): Towards an Explanatory Framework*. Dissertation submitted for Ph.D to the School of Social Sciences, Jawaharlal Nehru University.

Singh, Yogendra, 1986, *Modernization of Indian Tradition*. Jaipur: Rawat Publications.

Statchbury, Elizabeth Leigh, 1982, 'Blood, Fire and Mediation: Human Sacrifice and Widow Burning in Nineteenth Century India'. In *Women in India and Nepal*, edited by Michael Allen and S.N. Mukherjee, Canberra, ACT: Australian National University.

Uberoi, Patricia, 2004, 'The Family in India'. In *Handbook of Indian Sociology*, edited by Veena Das, New Delhi: Oxford University Press.

Part III

Work and Labour

CHAPTER 7

The Feminization of Poverty in Brazil

Leila Bijos

The Brazilian society has showed an increasing strength to overcome social problems and focus on the Millennium Development Goals (MDGs). In this context, characterized by large and well-developed agricultural, mining, manufacturing and service sectors, Brazil's economy outweighs that of all other South American countries and is expanding its presence in world markets. From 2001 to 2003, however, real wages fell and Brazil's economy grew on an average only 2.2 per cent per year, as the country absorbed a series of domestic and international economic shocks. Notwithstanding the setback, the Brazilian commitment has revealed that democratic paths have been followed in terms of human rights trends, carrying out a national action plan that links poverty alleviation to women's rights and universal access to reproductive health.

Based on these guidelines, it has incorporated gender and development (GAD) issues in the Brazilian official agenda, implementing in 2004 the Special Secretariat for Women's Policies. This reveals the government concerns towards population development and the necessity of poverty-reduction strategies; establishing laws and policies as well to protect women's and girl's rights. Many governmental and private institutions have begun to integrate reproductive health services into primary health care, improving facilities, training and expanding access to provide women with better life conditions. To insert women into the development agenda, poverty should be reduced, allowing women to enrol in educational programmes, income generation and regular examinations in health services, breaking the cycle of extreme poverty and promoting social inclusion.

Nutritional and food security budgetary resources have been allocated since 2004 to contribute to the economic and social development of women. Income transfers have been implemented in order to eliminate hunger through *Bolsa Familia* programme launched in October 2003. The benefit is conditioned to the children's school attendance and regular examination in health services. Although the programme encourages positive actions towards breaking the cycle of extreme poverty and towards social inclusion, huge obstacles still exist in the country, endeavouring strong partnerships among governments and civil society for the achievement of the Brazilian objectives.

GENDER AND DEVELOPMENT IN BRAZIL

Women in Latin America have not yet achieved broad political authority or power in the traditional sense of the term. Instead, they have registered specific gains in restricted arenas. They have also managed to promote heightened awareness, among men as well as women, and to advocate some modest policy reforms. They have achieved this success largely through collective organization and mobilization, but most of them have not decided to move on.

During the past two decades of the twentieth century, Latin American citizens have moved into democratic regimes and new human rights trends; but despite these developmental incrementals, a large number of persons still live in absolute poverty. Countries are making real progress in carrying out a bold global action plan that links poverty alleviation to women's rights and universal access to reproductive health.[1]

Based on these guidelines, nearly all developing countries have incorporated GAD issues in their official agenda. This reveals the government concerns towards population development and the necessity of poverty-reduction strategies, establishing also laws and policies to protect women's and girl's rights; and many have begun to integrate reproductive health services into primary health care, improving facilities, training and expanding access.

On discussing globalization and liberalization in the twenty-first century, Latin America presents a real scenario of the suffering and impoverishment of the vulnerable people. To insert women into the development agenda, poverty should be reduced. In this context, as measured by the Gini coefficient, which is the most commonly used indicator of income inequality, income concentration in the country fell by 4 per cent between 2001 and 2004 from 0.93 to 0.9. Although at first sight, this index might seem modest, it represents a substantial reduction in terms of inequality measure; among the seven countries for which there is information on the evolution of income inequality in the 1990s, less than one-fourth have shown inequality reduction rates higher than Brazil's.[2]

In fact, during this period, the average income of the poorest (10%) increased at an annual rate of 7 per cent, whereas the national average income fell by 1 per cent a year. In the period as a whole, the average income of the poorest 20 per cent was some 20 percentage points higher than that of the richest 20 per cent. Therefore, while the perception of the poorest in Brazil was that they were living in a country with a high rate of economic growth, for the richest 20 per cent, the country was going through a period of economic stagnation.

As for the inequality generated by the labour market, the first fundamental aspect to be noticed is wage discrimination based on race and gender. As in nearly all countries in the world, the wages of Brazilian women are much lower than those of men. This differential has remained stable, with a slight rising trend between 2001 and 2004, and therefore has not contributed to the fall in income inequality. Wage differentials by race are also high in Brazil (although much lower than gender differentials); and despite the falls recorded in the past decade, their quantitative importance in explaining the recent fall in income inequality is close to none.[3]

In addition to race and gender discrimination, the labour market can also be a generator of inequalities if it is segmented. With regard to spatial segmentation, possible reductions in high wage differentials between the Units of the Federation (UFs) could be a potential source to explain the fall in income inequality. However, over the past decade, labour markets in the different UFs have not become more integrated, and therefore this aspect has not contributed to reducing the degree of income inequality.[4]

The monthly income rate per capita is the most commonly used parameter to analyze the socio-economic conditions of the population, showing in 2006, ½ minimum North-eastern wage (39 per cent of households), and 32.5 per cent for the North region. South and Southeast regions present lower percentages—12.5 per cent and 13.6 per cent, respectively.[5]

Afro-Brazilian and women represent 42 per cent and 44.5 per cent, respectively, of the Brazilian Economically Active Population (EAP). Summed up, they correspond to 55 million persons or 68 per cent in Brazil; that is, a vast majority: 36 million of blacks of both sexes and almost 19 million white women. Nevertheless, special attention is given to 14 million black women who represent 18 per cent of the Brazilian, who are submitted to a double, or sometimes triple, stigma of discrimination (gender and race, also linked to social discrimination (ILO, 2006: 11)). Life expectancy for white women is 71 years old; 40.7 per cent of Afro-Brazilian black women die before 50 years.[6] In terms of life quality, white men rank 41, white women 69 and Afro-Brazilian men 114, showing the lowest quality-of-life rate (Gender Development Index).

Although Brazil is considered as the fifth largest nation in the world and the largest country in South America, it shows high inequality levels. Economically, Brazil also achieved the eleventh position in the ranking of the countries with the most significant GDP in the world, but the number of excluded people is astonishing (World Bank, 2007).[7] The country passed only 5 per cent of the countries in the inequality ranking. Based on the Monthly Employment Research (Pesquisa Mensal de Emprego—PME, published by the Brazilian Geography and Statistics Institute (IBGE)), it would take at least 20 years for Brazil to achieve a level similar to the countries with the same developement pattern.[8] Brazilian economy has shown a significant growth rate during the past four years, mainly due to the proper execution of the national monetary policy aiming to ensure stability of the internal market and to reduce the effects of the economic risks that can cause negative impacts on the economy prospects. In this context, formal jobs increased in the period 2003–2006, showing a percentage rate of 4.6 million jobs (ILO, 2006). Besides, an increase in the buying power of monthly wages, meaning real gains for the people, is also noticed. In 2005, Brazil reached the total amount of 94 million people, according to the economically active population (EAP).[9] This new scenario presents more women looking for job opportunities, as well as demonstrating their insertion in discussions concerning

GAD, racial inequalities in the country, showing black people discrimination at the workplace. ILO data show 73.3 per cent of white men in the labour market in comparison with 73.4 per cent of black men and 53 per cent of white women compared with 52.7 per cent of black women. Index rates present 30.2 per cent as the total insertion of women in the labour market in Brazil in a period of 10 years (1995–2005).[10] Regarding unemployment, in what way emphasis is put on the level of the economic activity? During the 1990s, unemployment rate increased for both sexes, although for women it presented higher taxes, especially for black women: 8.1 per cent in 1995 and 14.1 per cent in 2005. White men have the lowest unemployment rates: 4.9 per cent in 1995 and 6.3 per cent in 2005.[11]

Sanitation services are found in 70.6 per cent of the total households in the country[12]; but in the North region, a precarious inequality situation shows 12.6 per cent. In the North region, 10.5 per cent counts on sanitation services, Northeast 34.5 per cent, Centre-west 37.2 per cent, Southeast 84 per cent and South 60.6 per cent.[13, 14]

Demography analysis presents a decrease in the percentage of young and an increase in the elderly population. In 2005, the percentage of children from 0 to 9 years was 17.1 per cent; but in 2006, this number decreased to 16.5 per cent. For 40-year-old people, the percentage in 2005 was 31.5 per cent, and there has been an increase to 32.3 per cent in 2006. The same indexes are shown in all regions, but percentages are higher in the South and in the Southeast.[15] The reality shows that the population is getting older for both men and women, due to a decrease in fertility rates (which was 2.1 births per woman and diminished to 2 births in 2006; on the other hand, there has been an increase in life expectation for the Brazilian population). Migration occurs in adults in reproductive age, 37.9 per cent at 18–39 years, and 33.7 per cent at 40–59 years. The absence of jobs in the rural areas and opportunities for a fair income compel people to migrate from the rural areas to the urban centres.

Expectation of life at birth, between 1996 and 2006, presented an increase of 3.5 years—women's situation is more favourable related to men (72.3–75.8 years to women and 65.1–68.7 years to men). Thus, the gross mortality rate decreased from 6.7 per cent in 1996 to 6.2 per cent in 2006.[16] Governmental policies have been implemented aiming at improving the human development goals in the rural sector, and also avoiding the propagation of large-scale slums in the cities, as well as other structural problems such as water pollution, shortage of educational facilities, deterioration of public health and lawlessness.

Geographical factors, such as sparse and irregular rainfall, recurrent drought, poor soils and historically unfavourable economic and social factors were the reasons for the need to have development schemes. Over half of the local population living below poverty lines, and persistent anachronistic political model makes Northeast of Brazil, especially the semi-arid region of Brazil, a highest risk for human security, due to lack of food nutrients, showing an increase in nutritional deficiencies.

Consequently, statistical data reveal that 10.6 per cent of Brazil is located within the semi-arid region, and 12.7 per cent in the hunger polygon. This area encompasses eight states in the western portion of Northeast of Brazil (not including the State of Maranhão). The region also has 85 municipalities in the north of Minas Gerais, afflicted by irregular rainfall and drought seasons. It is within these areas that the greatest risks of food shortages and nutritional insecurity occur, and figuratively speaking, they comprise the cartography of 'hunger'. The decrease in infant mortality rate in that region was the most significant result registered in the country: 37.2 per cent in 2002 and 33.9 per cent in 2004 (MS, SVS, SIM),[17] which shows the implementation of sanitary policies and investments in infrastructure, in health and education sectors in most of the country's urban centres.

MONTHLY WAGE OF EMPLOYED AND ACTIVE POPULATION PER GENDER

Women's major participation in the labour market is registered in four categories that correspond to about 70 per cent of the female working force: general services, 30.7 per cent; agricultural work, 15.7 per cent; administrative jobs, 11.8 per cent; and commerce 11.8 per cent. The major female participation occurred in the Centre-East region, with 36 per cent; in the Northeast region, 26.6 per cent were identified as agricultural jobs; the Southeast region had the most impressive percentage of women in the administrative sector; and commerce absorbed 15.5 per cent in the North region (IBGE, 2007).

Considering the combination of gender-ethnicity, the situation of Afro-Brazilian women is much worse in all fields. Women's average pay still remains 50 per cent of those of men, whereas black women earn 50 per cent of white women's average (ILO, 2005).[18] According to ILO, if the present development rates remain, in a period of 475 years, women will get the same level of income as men (ibid.). Families only consider women as important to do household tasks; consequently, they are not motivated to attend formal classes.

Due to a high rate of AIDS mortality, the Brazilian government implemented antiretroviral (ARV) therapies that are easily available in the market, thus launching in 2004 a universal and free access to drugs. Another indicator to analyze the fight against HIV is the rate of condom use (12.9%) in relation to other contraceptive methods, used by women aged 15–49 years.

In 1981, the first case of AIDS was reported in the country, which required a prompt governmental response to the epidemic that was expanded and strengthened on all battlefronts: prevention, treatment, research, human rights and social organization, as well as ARV therapy and treatment, offering eight countries generic versions at low cost, denominated of Brazilian STD/AIDS Programme. Nowadays, the biggest challenge is to achieve an effective drop in new cases. Notwithstanding, officially, approximately 165 patients are in treatment with 17 ARV medicines distributed for free by the Unified Health System. In 2004, the Brazilian government spent US $260 million on ARV medicines; almost 80 per cent was used to acquire eight kinds of imported medicines. In 2005, about 170,000 people were submitted to the ARV treatment. For 2008, it was estimated that 215,000 people will attend, comprehending an expenditure of US $525 million with imported medicines (Ministry of Health, 2006).[19]

WOMEN VICTIMS OF SEXUAL VIOLENCE

The concepts of oppression, dominance and violence may be among the ways poor people analyze the context of their lives.[20] Among them, priority attention should be given to women and adolescents who are victims of sexual violence, rape, requiring psychological, clinical and gynaecological assistance, due to post-rape pregnancy, prevention of HIV-STDs, prevention of hepatitis B, orientation for adoption of the newborn when the victim desires to do so, legal orientation for the victim and special treatment for the pregnant women who have decided to interrupt the pregnancy. Nowadays, there exist more than 340 women attention services, out of which 100 are hospital services, while 47 are legal abortion services.[21]

Brazilian women have always been subordinated to male power. Authoritarian regimes in the country have a poor record of delivering improvements in living standards, which obliterates women's empowerment. Women lacked a language: they needed to gain control, which would allow them to change their roles in political groups. Even though these Brazilian women felt voiceless in a political context and were unable to express their resentment, they started helping poor and working-class women to articulate their demands for improved urban infrastructure, schools, health care and political participation.

Defining domestic violence in Brazil requires looking at a wide spectrum of issues across communities.[22] They range from rape, beatings and insults faced by women at one end, to husbands not getting their meals on time at the other end. Presently, women are gaining awareness of their rights, as they secure a livelihood, and are becoming less tolerant of irresponsible behaviour by men, acquiring new capabilities and higher skills to face different job opportunities. Nevertheless, there is still a strong code of silence surrounding violence; women are ashamed and sometimes blame themselves for their husbands' wrath. Because of this strong code of silence, it is difficult to gather reliable statistical data. Nowadays, based on the supportive actions of the Brazilian government, of non-governmental organizations, women are being trained and acquiring skills to face abuses, through gender awareness and counselling programmes. The Special Secretariat for Women's Policies eagerly worked on the design and implementation of a National Policy for Facing Violence against Women. With this initiative, the Brazilian government changed the perspective to confront violence against women, recognizing that the State must assume the responsibility for its elimination.

National guidelines on how to provide assistance to women victims of domestic and sexual violence and budget appropriation to construct more shelters for them have been implemented through the National Policy for Facing Violence against Women. Additional proposals for changing the penal code related to rape and for the aggressor have been sent to the Congress, aiming at an appropriate and more just punishment; as well as campaigns drawing attention to human rights. It has the main target to empower women to break up with the perverse cycle of violence they are used to.

Positive results can be accounted for through the implementation of 63 shelter houses, 83 reference centres to take care of women in case of violence, 14 women's public defencive offices, 392 specialized women police stations (DEAM) throughout the country, especially to attend to women victims of violence. Summarizing, there are 160 special agencies in the country, excluding the DEAMs. From this total amount, the Special Secretariat for Women's Policies supported technically and financially 93.12 per cent of the services: 18 in the North region, 23 in the Northeast, 13 in the Centre-West, 77 in the South-East and 18 in the South. US $15 million dollars have been officially allocated in the period of 2003–2006 to provide assistance to women in case of violence. In 2006, 19 reference centres to take care of women in case of violence and 15 shelter houses have been added to the Programme.[23]

Nevertheless, barriers to mainstreaming exist in Brazil, especially concerning violence; it is clearly practised in the Brazilian society regardless of socio-economic strata or ethnical group and can be noticed mostly in family domestic premises. Rape and sexual abuse of children and teenagers by relatives and/or unknowns frequently happen. Involvement in sex industry is a present problem as well. A research initiated in 2006 by the Department of Federal Road Petrol mobilized 1,400 policemen in 26 States and Distrito Federal inclusive, showed 1,819 vulnerable sexual locations in Brazil. The Guardian Angel Operation has the main objective of eradicating the most degrading labour: sexual exploitation of children and teenagers. Health, social assistance, education, responsibility and some legal restrictions on the public have all been developed by the Brazilian government aiming at eliminating this stigma of human rights violations that victimize children and adolescents in Brazil.[24]

Official statistical data show that 820,384 women were victims of domestic violence during 2006, and these women sought help at the Specialized Women Police Stations[25] (DEAMS, 2006), denouncing their partners. A survey by the Perseu Abramo Foundation revealed that in a universe of 2,502 women over 15 years of age, living in 187 municipalities, one out of every five declared that they had suffered some type of violence perpetrated by man. When stimulated by reference to different forms of aggression, 43 per cent of the interviewed women confirmed that they had been victims of gender violence. One-third admitted that they had already suffered some form of physical violence—threat with firearms, aggressions and marital rape. Although some national campaigns have been launched in the country, especially during the month of November 2007, women are still reluctant to denounce domestic violence, due to affective bonds and, in many cases, for lack of alternatives to support themselves and their children, due to economic dependence in relation to their partners. Domestic and intra-family violence against women in Brazil places an enormous burden in terms of loss of productivity and increased use of social services. Although it does not seem to interfere with the ability to get a job, the violence that women are subject to tends to affect their wages and permanence at their jobs, as a result of the physical and psychological problems that undermine their professional performance (World Health Organization Report on Violence, IPEA, 2004).

Although some discrepancies are found, Brazil has never achieved so many developments as in the three previous decades in the recognition and building up of women's rights. The 1988 Brazilian Federal Constitution brought up expressive advances in terms of equality between men and women in the family, education, health, reproductive issues, fighting violence, in the access to labour and security rights.

Before the Magna Carta launch, women had already conquered important victories, beginning in 1932 with the voting law. In 1962, the Statute of the Married Women (Law 4121) conferred women a greater decision power over their lives. In 1977, the Divorce Law (Law 6.515) allowed the breaking off of marriage and allowed women the possibility of a new marriage. In 2005, a series of changes were introduced in the Brazilian Penal Code with Law 11.106. In the past, the 1940 Penal Code was elaborated to and for a patriarchal society, which for years kept women in an inferiority position, confirming the conservative pattern used in the country. With the changes, the women's figure of 'honest woman'—virgins or married—and the adulterous crime have been abolished from the Brazilian Penal Code.

Although changes have been made, there are still tremendous disparities between men and women in terms of basic rights, access to resources, economic opportunities and employment.

'VOICELESS' AND UNEMPLOYED WOMEN

During the past decades, there is an increased awareness that poverty conditions, illiteracy, as well as job opportunities are different for men, women, black and white people. Gender and race are factors that really determine the access to employment.

Latin America has many ethnicities and races, including indigenous peoples, settlers predominantly from the Iberian Peninsula, entrepreneurs (especially from Britain in the nineteenth century), slaves from Africa and, in later times, immigrants from southern Europe (particularly Italians in Argentina and southern Brazil). All these people brought with them social formations that included particular gender relations, but the dominant form was set by the colonizers and reinforced by the Catholic Church.

Brazil is not different from other Latin American countries, where women are members of a group with evident disadvantages, mainly in the labour market, as well as in decision-making processes, to the vulnerability of women concerning domestic violence, or the burden of non-remunerated activities. The official indicators of income, labour, health, education and political representativeness point to unequal power relations and negative resource distribution between the sexes.

Women have been and continue to be underrepresented in the highest spheres of the society and also political power institutions, which confirms their true condition of inequality and poverty. Women's inequalities are higher if we consider their ethnic conditions, once poverty 'feminilization' is a question of race. Poverty is highlighted among black women and descendants of ethnic minorities.

Black women have been throughout history the greatest victims of gender inequalities. Black women are exposed to violence, poverty, discrimination in the labour market, precarious educational and health assistance services—that represents a general life precariousness. For instance, while life expectancy for white women is 71 years, 40.7 per cent of black African-descendent women die before they are 50 years old.[26] The result is evident, linked to these inequalities, as women show a visible feeling of inferiority, lower self-esteem and semi-slavery conditions, which they experience daily.

As a free country and community, we have been wrestling with many of the same racial issues as our parents once did. Still, it is a topic that the media rarely touches. But now, there are compelling reasons to raise the bar and begin reporting on race from all perspectives. Never before has our country been so culturally and racially diverse. It is an opportunity for us to recognize our divisions and embrace our diversity. It is important to rely on the issues of discrimination and prejudice that still exist in our society; among these, the most perplexing one is the oldest, and in some ways today, the newest: the problem of race.

As Brazil steps into the twenty-first century, racial and ethnic mix of our population grows more complex in the grounds of finding the answer to that question, and it becomes a matter of increasing urgency. Focusing on the economic arena (salary and status), we may say that after centuries of colonization, most of the African-Brazilian citizens continue to live below the poverty line. Thus, we consider the issue of poverty as a determinant of race and absence of economic and social participation. We do not foresee any future changes as poverty remains firm in the majority of Brazilian provinces. During the past two decades, the Brazilian people have already made significant progress in the battle to forge a true racial and ethnic melting pot. But we are still far way from declaring victory.

By analyzing the fundamental problems of the most impoverished members of society in Brazil, especially black people, their rights and individual values into collective decisions and the conditions that enable them to enhance their chances of survival and insertion in the capitalist system, we may refer to displacement, as most of indigenous and black African descendants have been taken out of their native lands by oligopolistic groups.

Likewise, once living in urban areas, they become affected by the process of globalization and its corollary, leading to displacement of traditional rites and festivities that are important tools for the transfer of knowledge. Loss of indigenous language, cultural pride and identity are other key factors in this lamentable trend.[27]

By the beginning of the 1980s, after 50 years of institutional construction, implementation and development of policies and programmes, the Brazilian government had proved incapable of finishing social reform alone. It was necessary to get the new social movements and trade unions to structure and give a boost to the social agenda. After the 1982 elections, different kinds of initiatives in the states and towns stood out, creating and launching a new social civil movement in an attempt to make political and social policies more effective.

In the 1990s, new goals suggested the creation of social assistance programmes for the poor and the destitute.[28] The proposed reform of the Brazilian system of social policies did not happen during Fernando Collor's government (1990–1993), although Collor did add the economic and institutional modernization of the country to the political agenda. When it came to social policies, 'the political core or nucleus of that government revealed itself to be extremely conservative, patrimonial and populist'.[29] In addition, the government's resources for social expenses were cut because of the economic adjustment programme; networks of social services were dissociated and all of the food and nutrition programmes that existed until 1990 were extinguished—except for the Programa de Alimentação do Trabalhador (a programme that provides food to workers) and the programme that provides snacks and lunches to schools.

At that time, patronage and the patrimonial system in the management of social policies prevailed. This made the distance between citizens and social services bigger, the result of an incomplete and incompetent neo-liberal modernization by Fernando Collor's government.

During the implementation of the institutional reforms that were a part of the axis of the programme of President Fernando Henrique Cardoso's first government (1995–1998), the goal was to restructure the social contents of democracy in the country, as well as the welfare state. This was based on the objectives of equity and the improvement of social opportunities, including the defence of macro-economic stability, the reform of the government and the stabilization of economic policies. During Cardoso's government, economic stability was the milestone of the success of Plano Real, which created a favourable environment for sustainable growth, generated a real increase in salaries for most Brazilian inhabitants and attracted new productive investments.[30]

To insert minorities into the development agenda, in 2003, the Brazilian government launched the National Agenda for a Decent Job, in partnership with the International Labour Office (ILO). The National Agenda has three main priorities: (i) generating more and better employments, envisaging equality opportunities and treatment; (ii) eradicating slave work and eliminate child work, mainly the worst work conditions for children; and (iii) strengthening tripartite partners, as well as the social dialogue as a means of democratic governance.

The National Programme for Worker Qualification, in effect since 1995, aimed at professional education training regardless of gender. An agreement between the Ministry of Labour and Employment (MTE) and the National Council for Women's Right establishes that at least 30 per cent of all places should be for women trainees. Thus, according to MTE's 2004 report, female inclusion in the Programme was 39.31 per cent: financing resources corresponding to US $11.5 million to attend labour force altogether.

WOMEN'S PARTICIPATION IN LABOUR

Eventually, even when a woman gets a job, it is a temporary one, and that does not ensure household food security. Many poor households face the risk of transitory food insecurity even if, on an average and over several years, their incomes are enough to provide a sustainable standard of living. The question of equity is at the centre of the MDG and it also means a decent labour. For ILO, the Decent Labor Programme means an adequately rewarded job, done in a context of freedom, equity and security, away from any forms of discrimination and capable of offering a dignified life to all citizens.

Gender inequalities arise, therefore, from the socio-cultural and historical constructions that turn sexual differences into discriminations. Such inequalities are expressed in the most varied fields of social relations, beginning in the domestic environment, reaching the world of work, the educational sector, among others. In this context, discrimination leads to poverty and is responsible for several types of vulnerabilities, creating barriers to the advancement of women and groups. The most common form of insertion of black and non-black women in the market labour is through registered employment, which provides them with income generation, inclusive to domestic maids.

During the period from 1999 to 2006, a decrease in unemployment rates in the survey areas has been noticed, which reveals an improvement in the conditions of insertion of women. Analysing inequalities in Brazil, we have to point out that women are the ones who suffer the most as they were not inserted into a framework of economic development. Due to the economic model (liberalism) in Latin America during the first years of this decade, there has been a decrease in salaries for both men and women, independently of sex. This economic constraint has been less severe for women than for men.

Denounces led the Brazilian government to launch in 1997 a Programme to Prevent Slavery, which resulted in the inspection of 129 companies, and a total amount of 808 criminal complaints being filed. Positive results accounted for 27,460 workers who were helped, and 220 others were set free from slavery. 'The Programme of Integrated Actions' was implemented in the States of Pernambuco and Bahia, assisting a total of 28,200 children in 18 towns and cities'.[31]

Reference should also be made to the official programme to remove children from garbage sites in large metropolis where they are sent every day by their parents to collect cans, paper, plastic, petty bottles for selling and with the sales to support their poor families.[32] It is common to see children abandoning their education to reduce household poverty.

FINAL CONSIDERATIONS

Our central hypothesis is that women's social and economic participation emerges as an effort to improve the economic situation of the household, and not as a personal desire to satisfy women's needs as individuals and citizens—or to achieve greater recognition from spouses or other family members. Moreover, this activity takes place within the context of critical gaps—in poverty, gender and place of residence—and with varying implications for heads and non-heads of households.

The main focus of our analysis was targeted to the feminization of poverty in Brazil, showing women's struggle to insert themselves into economic patterns, even without feeling the benefits of public and social policies in their lives. The duality of our analysis highlights a context of women inserted into a modern and globalized world; but in reality, they are not offered the benefits of capitalism.

It is the idea that power is distributed in an unbalanced way between both sexes, leaving women in a subaltern position in any social organization. These subaltern women, ordinary women, see themselves facing big problems presented to them by poverty, unemployment, great migration flows and great responsibility of providing for the family. These are processes of changes that involve the emancipation of women and the rupture of existing traditional ways in their social lives, besides their insertion into a masculine world, of the struggle against power, and the economic system. Women cannot dissociate from the misery caused by the lack of political policies and sometimes by the mental attitudes they suffer from because of lack of attention to the problem of heterogeneity bias.

The lower educational level of poor women, especially heads of households, has negative repercussions for access to 'quality' jobs and, consequently, for their opportunities to achieve economic independence from their partners and to contribute to the economic household, especially if they are black. The potential of this study faces a basic dilemma, that is to destroy the inherited parameters and to try to build very clear theoretical milestones. The theme assumes or takes for granted the analysis of women as social beings, imbued of a lifelong project for the future, full of hopes, expectations and changes. It is the destruction of the notion of domination, the gender *constructo* and of a social capital.

In Brazil, there is a lack of both social and economic opportunities, especially for black people; thus, there is a great internal mobility from the dry lands to the cities. The population suffers from varieties of unfreedom, especially famine that continues to occur in the North and Northeast of the country, denying to millions of inhabitants the basic freedom to survive.

The lower educational level of poor women, especially heads of households, could have negative repercussions for access to 'quality' jobs (i.e. highly remunerated) and, consequently, for their opportunities to achieve economic independence from their partners and to contribute to the economic household. In addition, the large size of families in poor households reduces the amount of time women could devote to income-generating activities. And yet economic participation could allow women to increase their incomes and break this vicious circle of poverty. This could improve the quality of education for children and reduce their reliance on social programmes to satisfy family needs.

NOTES

1. UNFPA State of World Population, 2004, The Cairo Consensus at Ten: Population, Reproductive Health and the Global Effort to End Poverty. New York: UNFPA.
2. IPEA/IBGE, *Brazilian Monitoring Report on the Millennium Development Goals*. Brazil: IPEA, IBGE, 2004.
3. Ibid.
4. On the Recent Fall in income Inequality in Brazil, IPEA, Brasilia: 2007.
5. IBGE, *Síntese de Indicadores Sociais: Uma Análise das Condições de Vida da População Brasileira*. Rio de Janeiro: IBGE, 2007.
6. Moraes, Eunice Léa de. *Relação, gênero e raça na política pública de qualificação social e profissional*, Vol. 1. Brasília: MTE, SPPE.DEQ, 2005, p. 15.
7. The World Bank Annual Report 2007, *Development and the Next Generation*, Washington, DC: The International Bank for Reconstruction and Development, 1 July 2006 to 30 June 30 2007, p. 53.
8. IPEA/IBGE, *Brazilian Monitoring Report on the Millennium Development Goals*, p. 7.
9. PNAD—Pesquisa Nacional por Amostra de Domicílios/Brazilian Geography and Statistics Institute (IBGE), 2005.
10. Ibid.
11. Ibid.
12. Ibid., 2006.
13. Ibid.
14. Ibid.
15. Ibid.

16. Ibid., 2007.
17. MS: Ministério da Saúde (Ministry of Health), SVS: Secretaria de Vigilância em Saúde, SIM: Sistema de Informações sobre Mortalidade (Mortality Information System).
18. ILO, A *Global Alliance against Forced Labour*. Global report under the follow-up to the ILO Declaration on Fundamental Principles and Rights at Work. Report of the Director-General, 2005.
19. Ministry of Health, *National Agenda of Priorities in Health Research*, Secretariat of Science, Technology and Strategic Inputs, Department of Science and Technology, Brasília: Ministério da Saúde, 2006.
20. Bijos, Leila, 2004, *Women and Development: The Regional Microfinance Programme for Women in the Urban Informal Sector: 1980–2002 – A Case Study: Brazil – Bolivia (Doctoral Dissertation)*. Brasilia: University of Brasília, p. 94.
21. Ministry of Health, *National Agenda of Priorities in Health Research*.
22. Bijos, Leila. Summer 2006, 'Gender, Power, Financial Access, and Development in Latin America: Comparing Brazilian and Bolivian Cases', in *Law and Business Review of the Americas*, Vol. 12, No. 3, Texas: Southern Methodist University (SMU) Dedman School of Law, p. 344.
23. *Memória 2003–2006*, Secretaria Especial de Políticas para as Mulheres/ Presidência da República, Brasília: SEPM, Presidência da República, 2006.
24. *Guide for Locating Vulnerably Spots to the Sexual Exploitation of Children and Juvenile Alongside of the Brazilian Highways*, Mapping, 2007, International Labour Office, 2007.
25. Ibid.
26. Statistical data can be found at Fundação SEADE Reports, 2003.
27. Brahy, Nicholas and Tobin, Brendan, 'Protecting and Strengthening Traditional Knowledge Innovation System', *Work in Progress*, Vol. 17, No. 2, Summer 2005, United Nations University, pp. 19–21.
28. Draibe, Sônia M. Paper Presented at Taller Inter-Regional Protección Social en una Era insegura: Un Intercambio Sur-Sur sobre Políticas Sociales Alternativas en Respuesta a la Globalización, Santiago, Chile: Brasil: a Proteção Social Após Vinte anos de Experimentação Reformista, (14–16 May 2002), http://www.comciencia.br/reportagens/ppublicas/pp10.htm.
29. Ibid., pp. 6, 8.
30. Posthuma, Anne Caroline, *Transformações do Emprego no Brasil na Década de 90, in OIT/MTE, Abertura e Ajuste do Mercado de Trabalho no Brasil: Políticas para Conciliar os Desafios de Emprego e Competitividade*, 13 (Anne Posthuma ed., Editora 34 1999).

31. Amadeo, Edward. 'Mercado de Trabalho Brasileiro: Rumos, Desafios e o Papel do Ministério do Trabalho', in *OIT–Brasil–Abertura e ajuste do mercado de trabalho no Brasil, Ministério do Trabalho e Emprego*, Brasília: OIT e Ministério do Trabalho e Emprego; Editora 34, São Paulo, 1999.
32. UNICEF. *Programa Criança no Lixo Nunca Mais*, Brasília: UNICEF, 1999.

REFERENCES

Amadeo, Edward, 1999, 'Mercado de Trabalho Brasileiro: Rumos, Desafios e o Papel do Ministério do Trabalho'. In *OIT – Brasil – Abertura e ajuste no mercado de trabalho no Brasil, Ministério do Trabalho e Emprego*, Brasília: OIT e Ministério do Trabalho e. Emprego, Editora 34, São Paulo.

Bijos, Leila, 2004, *Women and Development: The Regional Microfinance Programme for Women in the Urban Informal Sector: 1980–2002 – A Case Study: Brazil – Bolivia (Doctoral Dissertation)*. Brasilia: University of Brasília.

Bijos, Leila, 2006, 'Gender, Power, Financial Access, and Development in Latin America: Comparing Brazilian and Bolivian Cases'. In *Law and Business Review of the Americas*, Vol. 12, No. 3, Texas: Southern Methodist University (SMU) Dedman School of Law, pp. 341–60.

Brahy, Nicholas and Brendan Tobin, 2005, 'Protecting and Strengthening Traditional Knowledge Innovation System', *Work in Progress*, Vol. 17, No. 2, Summer, pp. 19–21, Tokyo: United Nations University.

Draibe, Sônia M, 2002, *Paper Presented at Taller Inter-Regional Protección Social en una Era insegura: Un Intercambio Sur-Sur sobre Políticas Sociales Alternativas en Respuesta a la Globalización*. Santiago, Chile: Brasil: a Proteção Social Após Vinte anos de Experimentação Reformista, 14–16 May 2002, http://www.comciencia.br/reportagens/ppublicas/pp10.htm, accessed 13 September 2012.

IBGE, 2007, *Síntese de Indicadores Sociais: Uma Análise das Condições de Vida da População Brasileira*. Rio de Janeiro: IBGE, 2007.

ILO, 2005, *A Global Alliance against Forced Labour*. Global report under the follow-up to the ILO Declaration on Fundamental Principles and Rights at Work. Report of the Director-General.

ILO, 2006, *Gênero, Raça, Pobreza e Emprego: O Programa GRPE no Brasil*. Brasília: ILO.

ILO, 2007, *Guide for Locating Vulnerably Spots to the Sexual Exploitation of Children and Juvenile Alongside of the Brazilian Highways*, Mapping, International Labour Office, Brasilia: ILO Office in Brasilia, 2007.

IPEA/IBGE, 2004, *Brazilian Monitoring Report on the Millennium Development Goals*. Brasilia: IPEA, IBGE, 2004.

Ministry of Health, 2006, *National Agenda of Priorities in Health Research*, Secretariat of Science, Technology and Strategic Inputs, Department of Science and Technology, Brasília: Ministério da Saúde.

Moraes, Eunice Léa de. *Relação, gênero e raça na política pública de qualificação social e profissional*, Vol. 1. Brasília: MTE, SPPE.DEQ, 2005.

Posthuma, Anne Caroline, 1999, *Transformações do Emprego no Brasil na Década de 90, in* OIT/MTE, *Abertura e Ajuste do Mercado de Trabalho no Brasíl: Políticas para Conciliar os Desafios de Emprego e Competitividade* (Anne Posthuma ed., Editora 34).

The World Bank Annual Report, 2007, *Development and the Next Generation*. Washington, DC: The International Bank for Reconstruction and Development, 1 July 2006 to 30 June 2007.

UNFPA State of World Population, 2004, *The Cairo Consensus at Ten: Population, Reproductive Health and the Global Effort to End Poverty*. New York: UNFPA.

UNICEF, 1999, *Programa Criança no Lixo Nunca Mais*. Brasília: UNICEF.

CHAPTER 8

Women Entrepreneurs in the Era of Free Enterprise: A Study of the Performance, Problems and Perceptions of Women in Sustaining Business in the Indian Context

Sita Vanka

The primary objective of any country is to achieve rapid, balanced and sustained rate of economic growth. The contemporary era requires that the economic growth and development be supplemented with all-round growth that includes social, political, cultural and other dimensions of development. A major task, therefore, is to stimulate and arouse the people to action aimed at improving their lot by undertaking productive economic activity. Today, this has been the only strategy to bring many into the mainstream of development, as the old model of employment generation in the economy by expanding government and public sector could not payoff the expected results. Thus, the concepts of *self-employment* and *entrepreneurship* have been thought of as viable alternatives to tackle the problem of unemployment in many countries. The creation of an environment that promotes entrepreneurial potential has become an important focal point in every government's policy on development.

INDIAN SCENARIO

India as a developing economy faced similar challenges in the context of its development path. Increasing level of unemployment with subsequent increase in poverty and economic inequality was a common experience in India, as in most parts of Asian countries. The pressure to alleviate these problems has led to an emphasis on creating employment opportunities in India's development planning. The Sixth Five-Year Plan and more particularly the Tenth Five-Year Plan are notable in so far as employment generation initiatives are concerned. Today, there is a strong realization in the Indian economy that economic growth alone, however rapid it is, cannot remove misery and unemployment. For achieving socio-economic justice and national integration, a sound multiphase programme for better utilization of human resource strategy is a necessary task. The experience of the developing world in general and India in particular, of jobless growth in the context of liberalization, privatization and globalization and the rightsizing/downsizing of the public sector has assumed an alarming proportion. Thus, the strategy of employment generation was included as an integral part of the overall strategy of development planning of India.

ENTREPRENEURSHIP

The existence of entrepreneurs and entrepreneurship is probably as old as human activity. The role of entrepreneurship in social and economic development has been recognized only in the recent past. Entrepreneurs have become the objects of curiosity and worthy of scientific curiosity only of late. It is now being increasingly recognized that entrepreneurship is not merely individual economic activity but a phenomenon with crucial social implications. The term has been used in various connotations, which resulted in ambiguity over its meaning and definition. Although no single definition of an entrepreneur is universally accepted and no one profile perfectly fits today's entrepreneur, research provides a sharper focus on the subject.

The association of entrepreneurship and economics has been accepted for quite long—the economists of the eighteenth century introduced, whereas the interest of the economists in the nineteenth century increased till the twentieth century, when the word became synonymous with free enterprise, capitalism and profitable business. For example, Shum Peter (1936) wrote about entrepreneurship and its impact on economic development (Ronstadt, 1984). Whatever the specific activity they are into, entrepreneurs in the twenty-first century are considered the heroes of free enterprise. They have used innovation and creativity to bring out new products and services and have successfully taken the risks associated with their respective ventures.

The International Labour Organization (ILO), the apex world body on Labour issues, describes entrepreneurs as people who have the ability to see and evaluate business opportunities, to gather the necessary resources to take advantage of them and initiate appropriate action to ensure success (ILO, 1982). Whatever may be the definition and thinking on entrepreneurship, entrepreneurs have been considered instrumental in initiating and sustaining socio-economic development. Evidence suggests that countries with more number of entrepreneurs have developed faster as compared with countries with fewer entrepreneurs in society (ILO, 2002). All along, entrepreneurs have identified new opportunities and leveraged them to establish effective forms of organizations across the world. For quite long, it was a male preserve; but in recent years, more women are entering this domain of managing enterprises, both in the developed and the developing world.

WOMEN IN ENTREPRENEURIAL ACTIVITY: THE GLOBAL SCENARIO

By the end of 1999, there were 9.1 million women-owned businesses in the United States. According to the National Foundation for Women Business Owners (NFWBO) a non-profit research and leadership development foundation affiliated to the National Association of Women Business Owners, during the 12-year period from 1987 to 1999, the number of women-owned businesses increased by 103 per cent nationwide, and the employment provided by these firms grew by 320 per cent, whereas sales grew by 436 per cent (NFWBO, 2001). At the end of 1999, women-owned firms represented nearly 40 per cent of all firms in the United States and employed approximately 27.5 million people. In 1996, the Small Business Administration (SBA) reported that the growth in the number of women-owned businesses exceeded the national average in nearly every region of the country, with higher growth occurring in the southern states (Haynes and Helms, 2000). In the United States and Canada, the number of women-owned firms has increased at about twice the national rate. The NFWBO also reported that in 1996, 13 per cent of women business owners in the United States were women of colour. In total that year, there were nearly 1.1 million firms owned by minority-women, employing nearly 1.7 million people and generating more than $184.2 billion in sales. Clearly, the number of women-owned businesses has grown dramatically; and as the results of the NFWBO studies show, the economic impact of women-owned businesses is substantial. The same picture is reflected in Bulgaria, Senegal, Trinidad, Tobago, Bangladesh (ILO, 2002), Hungary (Hisrich and Fuldop, 1993), Poland (Zapalska, 1997) and Australia (Walker, 2000). Thus, the global scenario depicts the emergence and growth of women-owned businesses as an economic force although small in number and small in operations and scale, yet it is a fact that women are beginning to enter the field of entrepreneurship in increasing number.

STATUS OF WOMEN IN INDIA

From the very beginning, Indian women have been managers of the kitchen and dominated the household activities. The impact of this has been so deep that popular perception about women in economic and entrepreneurial activity can only be towards women as in the business of making pickles, *papads*, *masalas* and other household items. This perception is beginning to change with a number of women managing non-traditional enterprises quite successfully. The shifts in policy point to a trend of encouraging women to explore their hidden entrepreneurial potential. Education and rising awareness levels are not only making women increasingly conscious of their existence, rights and work situation, but some of them are also exploring newer avenues of economic participation and development. For this leap towards their betterment, their skill and knowledge, talents and abilities and more importantly a compelling desire and urge to excel are often cited for women taking to entrepreneurship.

The emergence of the women entrepreneur—as one who shows enterprise, has an eye for opportunity, a willingness to take risks, a commercial acumen and who through her enterprise creates substantial employment for others—illustrates a new phenomenon in India. Three decades ago, the women entrepreneur was a species almost unheard of, both policy-wise and in practice. It was only the Industrial Policy Resolution of 1978 that recognized the women entrepreneurs as a special group needing assistance and support in vague terms, and that too as a sequel to the declaration of the International Decade of Women between 1975 and 1985 and the International Conference of Women Entrepreneurs held at Delhi in 1984. In about two decades' time, women entrepreneurs not only entered business in a small way but also ventured into starting and managing large enterprises on professional lines and working hard to sustain and survive in the competing environment. The significance of this phenomenon must be understood not from the increasing number of women participating in commercial ventures, but from the fact that they are entering an arena that was hitherto a male preserve. Academic debate and research led to a re-examination of a woman's role in society and development and to demand measures that would help them realize their full potential and transform their 'reproductive role' into a 'productive role' (White, 1984). The call for *engendering the human development paradigm* at the global level (HDR, 1995) and the year of *empowerment of women* (2000) in India are some examples of recent policy interventions in this direction. Action was initiated on several fronts—education, health, employment, training, etc—by international, national and non-governmental organizations. The result is the conviction among women that it is perhaps the world of entrepreneurship that the recognition and value of women's contribution is the most vital for a better tomorrow (Dhameja, 2002).

WOMEN ENTREPRENEURS IN THE NEW MILLENNIUM

During the past two decades, women have entered the field of entrepreneurship in greatly increasing numbers. By the year 2001, women entrepreneurs had entered many industries and sectors. Many of the earlier obstacles to women's business success have been removed, yet some still remain. Many research questions have been posed, and investigators have examined the economic and social impact of women's business ownership. Finally, scholars of entrepreneurship and small business have studied the influences of and the impact on business ownership by women. The number of research studies has grown since the 1980s, when scholars and policy-makers first cast their attention towards women entrepreneurs.

RESEARCH ON WOMEN ENTREPRENEURSHIP—GLOBAL

The ILO is an organization that promotes the interests and development of women entrepreneurs in its 175 member states. The impetus to focus on women in business came from the report of ILO on *Decent Work* in 1999. The surveys/reports of ILO provide guidance and documentation relating to the development of women entrepreneurship (ILO, 2002). Studies focused on the sectors where women were engaged in business (NFWBO, 2001), reasons for taking up entrepreneurship (Nelson, 1991), predictors of success (Schiller and Crewson, 1997), demographic features (Birley, 1989) and planning the enterprise (Naisbutt, 1985). A developing country such as India evidences a similar picture (Singh, 1993).

RESEARCH GAP AND NEED FOR STUDY

There has been some interesting work on the role of women entrepreneurs in India. Women starting enterprises got a boost with the International Decade of Women between the 1970s and 1980s. Recent studies highlighted comparative studies between business and non-business communities in India. It was found that there is not much of a difference between the business and non-business communities (Gangurde, 2006). Another study in Southern India analysed the institutionally supported and self-supported women entrepreneurs (Manivel, 2005). However, these studies in the Indian context not only reflect the smaller number of studies but also similar studies in different contexts. Contextually, there may be some differences in view of the sociocultural profile of women; but certainly, the problems, performance, reasons for starting business and motivation were found to be similar. A number of studies focused on the urban entrepreneur and more so on the initial phases of the life cycle of the enterprise. Other than the start-up and the growth phase, studies did not focus on sustaining the success of the enterprise and the problems/performance thereof. Success stories/best practices were limited to the male-owned enterprises. Studies on women-owned businesses at best figured in a comparative perspective between male and female or an interesting highlight of the comparative study. The position of the women entrepreneur has been neglected by both the mass media and the academic community. Despite the impressive contribution, women-owned businesses are comparatively understudied in the entrepreneurial domain (Brush and Hisrich, 1998). In particular, studies that systematically analysed the business age, size, strategy, policy, managerial capabilities, business opportunities and analysed their perceptions and opinions on business are nearly absent from the existing literature. Contextually, variations highlighted especially in a developing context such as India are strikingly inadequate (Singh, 1993). Although women in India were late entrants into business, it is all the more saddening to find that this area was not found worth exploring by scholars other than a few and that too women either in academics or practitioners leave the field limited in documentation. This provides for a considerable research gap and need for studies in this direction. Most of the questions relating to the profile, motivation and enterprise data along with the opinions and perceptions of women not only in the start-up but also in sustaining business are left unanswered.

THE STUDY

The Concept

Entrepreneurs as people who have the ability to see and evaluate business opportunities to gather necessary resources to take advantage of them and to initiate appropriate action to ensure success (ILO, 1982) was the concept used for the study.

The conceptual framework for the study was arrived at after incorporating the major constructs previously identified in the entrepreneurship literature in terms of the profile of entrepreneurs (Singh, 1993) and business opportunities (Dhameja, 2002). As can be noted, the entrepreneur in terms of her personality and the enterprise, in terms of its performance and status, determine opinions and perceptions on the issues relating to women in sustaining business (Figure 8.1).

Figure 8.1

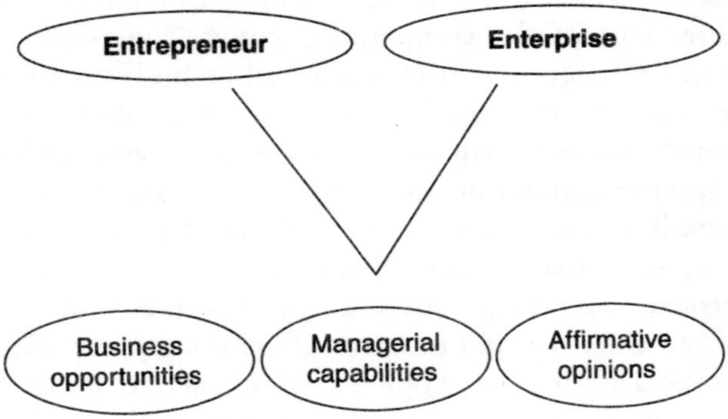

Objectives of the Study

Broadly, the study empirically seeks to examine the entrepreneurial problems and performance of women in sustaining business in Andhra Pradesh. More specifically, it aims at the following aspects:

- Profiling the socio-economic background of women entrepreneurs in sustaining business
- Examining their motivation to start and sustain business
- Highlighting the performance of the enterprise
- Studying the business-related information
- Studying their opinions and perceptions on the reasons that strengthen women in business and in looking for business opportunities
- Identifying their managerial capabilities in sustaining business
- Finding out whether the problems that they face are real or perceptual
- Studying their reaction on the role of women in sustaining business

Scope of the Study

The scope of the study was determined based on the geographical area to be covered, the timeframe within which the businesses were set up, capital/investment committed and managed by women alone in terms of decision-making. Although no sector-specific limits have been identified, all those industries that were women-owned, managed and sustained for more than five years continuously were considered as the enterprises for the study. In a way, although there was no upper limit for the number of years, the minimum enterprise age was determined with the cut-off year of establishment as 2001. All women who decided on their own, spent time on the activities of business and continuously invested in the growth of the firm were other criteria followed in deciding the scope for the study. Andhra Pradesh, an upcoming state in Southern India in terms of the business climate, was the research area for the study.

Research Design

The study is exploratory in nature. Past literature has very little information on similar issues and solutions. This entailed the construction of the conceptual framework based on isolated studies conducted in different contexts. Documentation in the Indian context is much more limited due to the relatively new phenomena of women managing and sustaining business professionally. A lot of qualitative data had to be collected to comprehend the problem and understand the phenomena in the absence of a validated framework. Since the study is aimed at finding out the profile of women entrepreneurs in sustaining business in respect of their traits/characteristics, the enterprise performance in terms of nature of product, nature of unit, level of employees, capital/investment, business-related information and their assertive opinions on the reasons for strengthening women in business, business opportunities, their managerial capabilities, the real/perceptual problems and consistency in their opinions on women in sustaining business—a descriptive research design using the survey method was prepared to capture the relevant data/information.

Data Collection

Data in the nature of both primary and secondary were collected from the respondents. The secondary data are related to the information containing the literature review in journals, books and the information/manuals/websites of the respective enterprises. The primary data were collected from a specifically designed schedule, which was standardized after pretesting on a limited number of sampled respondents. The schedule was designed to elicit the socio-economic profile of the entrepreneur, profile and performance of the enterprise, business-related information, opinions and perceptions on business opportunities, opinion on managerial capabilities in sustaining business, problems in sustaining business and possible solutions and their reaction on certain issues relating to women in sustaining business—work–life balance, skills, support needed, etc.

Tools and Techniques

Two specifically designed schedules—a questionnaire that captured the factual information about the entrepreneurs and the enterprise along with their opinions and perceptions—were specifically given to each of the respondents after taking time from them.

Sample

Women entrepreneurs were identified based on a set criteria. The criteria included the number of people employed, length/period of existence of the enterprise, capital/investment committed and managed by the women alone in terms of decision-making. Thus, the enterprises that were employing more than 10 employees, in existence for more than a five-year period and a capital committed to more than 1 lakh and taking decisions on their own were included in the study. Based on the criteria, a sample of 110 was selected for the study. As many as 87 women entrepreneurs responded for the study with a response rate of 79 per cent. The rest of them were either busy or were not willing to participate in the study.

Data Analysis

Data were analysed using descriptive statistics such as frequencies and percentages for analysing the factual information regarding the entrepreneur and the enterprise and presented using graphs wherever found necessary. The performance dimension was measured in terms of the nature of unit, the nature of product, the nature of employees and the capital/investment by taking the data from the beginning to the current position. To measure the opinion/perception on the *reasons that strengthened women* in business and business opportunities, the respondents were asked to rank them based on the priority given by them. They have been analysed through frequency and percentages arrived at for each of the ranks. In addition, to check their consistency in ranking the reasons that strengthened women in sustaining business, concordance test using Kendall's coefficient of concordance was computed and the value of 'W' was arrived at to examine the association that exists among the rankings of the sampled respondents to each of the reasons identified in the questionnaire. The value of chi-square statistic was also computed to show its significance at 1 per cent level. The opinions and perceptions of women on *business opportunities* have been analysed following the same procedure. Around 15 areas have been identified and included in the questionnaire in terms of business opportunities. To understand the opinion of women on *managerial capabilities* in sustaining business, a 4-point scale was used. The data collected from the respondents were subjected to principal component factor analysis by varimax rotation with Kaizer normalization method by using the criterion that factors with eigen value > 1.00 were retained. Loadings exceeding 0.5 were considered for determining factors. To avoid the crowding of factors, this measure was taken although the literature allows a loading of 0.33 to be the absolute minimum value to be interpreted. This criterion is being used more or less by way of convention (Vasanthi and Rayappan, 2006). The *problems* in sustaining business and the possible solutions to overcome these problems have been grouped and content analysed in a descriptive way. Lastly, *scaling techniques* were used to capture on general women entrepreneurship on a 4-point scale—*strongly agree, agree, disagree* and *strongly disagree*. These four groups were made into two groups—*agree* and *disagree*. The response in terms of the scale provided was recorded. The frequencies and percentage were calculated to highlight the pattern that emerged.

The Results

The data collected are analysed and presented in three sections. While Section 1 presents the socio-economic and motivational profile of the entrepreneur, Section 2 provides the profile and performance of the enterprise. Section 3 highlights an analysis of opinions/perceptions of women in sustaining business.

Section 1: Socio-Economic and Motivational Profile of the Entrepreneur

The study reveals that majority of the women were middle-aged, having education up to Graduation and Postgraduation, were married and had work experience. A significant percentage of them did not have any training and they directly started the enterprise. The few who had training had less than 30 days of training, which was more in the nature of an EDP and supported by the ALEAP or the Government of India in a majority of women. A majority of them planned for a career in entrepreneurship with some who preferred experience, worked as a partner before getting into the career mode. Since the entrepreneurs had previous experience, some of them earned ₹2–3 lakhs annually before starting the enterprise but increased their income substantially with the current income group touching anywhere between ₹ 11 and 60 lakhs. A total of 80.5 per cent of them had an urban background and belonged to the nuclear family (89.7%). In terms of family occupation, very few of their family members had a business background and most of them were in service category. They were self-motivated, but had sufficient family support and leveraging the available opportunity followed by self-identity, enhancing social status and generating employment to others were the motivational factors that helped them sustain in business.

Section 2: Profile and Performance of the Enterprise

The profile reveals that a majority of the enterprises were started around the economic reform process in India in the 1990s, which showed that women nurtured their enterprises and sustained in the dynamic and volatile business environment for quite long. A majority of them also identified the opportunity and started their enterprises from a location other than home. Some of them who started initially from home and moved out to other locations evidenced the growth of the enterprise in size and scale ensuring sustenance of their business. They were sole proprietors in a majority of enterprises, while some of them were partners. Some registered as a private limited company saw the transition from family/partner supported to a professionally managed component. All those women who started their unit in manufacturing grew over time and moved on to large-scale manufacturing. Some of them who were into trading to start with sustained the trading activity and diversified and expanded over time. It is a good sign for women who were into manufacturing also entering trading activity along with manufacturing. The same trend continued in the nature of products too, with women moving into the manufacturing of quality products and offering a wider range to their customers. A good number of women entrepreneurs leveraged the collaboration of ALEAP and COWE with foreign countries and were in business for export only. In the process of scaling up the size of operation, they have generated employment in all the categories—managerial, supervisory and, more particularly, the skilled category because of the knowledge sectors in which they were operating. A majority of them invested substantial amounts, more so in the higher categories of ₹ 11–50 lakhs annually. Similarly, the enterprises had remarkable sales growth in the range of ₹ 11–20 lakhs annually. They also registered higher profits that touched an annualized return of more than ₹ 20 lakhs. They achieved all this by marketing their products at the national and state levels, unlike the way women restricted their entrepreneurial activity to the local area only. A good number of them were in business only for export purposes, proving their success in terms of scale and scope in business. A majority of them advertised their products using cost-effective methods—pamphlets, newspapers, etc. They had invested a good amount of time everyday on business-related issues and took decisious themselves. They could update themselves by attending seminars and business association meetings and also by reading, thus acquiring good skills and knowledge to sustain in business.

Section 3: Opinions and Perceptions

(i) Strengthening Women in Business

A proactive approach, better work–life balance, family support and better success rate among women were the ways which strengthened women in sustaining business. Equal status of women, policy and freedom for women were rated low in order of priority as they thought that it might take some more time given the sociocultural context of India. In sharp contrast to other studies, education of women was assigned the last rank as they perceived that business acumen and experience is more important in sustaining business. The value of chi-square statistic was also computed to show its significance at 1 per cent level. Table 8.1 indicates component-wise average of rankings, W value and X^2 value at 1 per cent level. Thus, there is an association between the rankings and the components, which implies homogeneity in the perception of the group.

(i) Areas of Business Opportunities

The dynamic business environment offers a number of business opportunities for women entrepreneurs. The major highlights of the study have been the low perception of opportunities for women in sustaining business in areas such as electronic/engineering goods and services (47.1%), architect/interior designing (44.8%) and biotech/agrotech, etc. (28.7%), IT (25.3%) and glassware/plastic ware (25.3%). These are all areas that are more

Table 8.1 *Component-wise average of rankings, W value and X^2 value*

S. No.	*Component*	*Average of rankings*	*Deviation square*	
1.	Education of women	6.60	1.29	W
2.	Better success rate among women	4.60	0.74	0.36
3.	Equal status of women	6.36	0.80	
4.	Better recognition to women	6.08	0.38	
5.	Commitment and hard work	4.15	1.72	X^2
6.	Policy encouraging women	8.08	6.87	282*
7.	Better work–life balancing at home	3.33	4.52	
8.	Increased freedom of women	7.99	6.39	*1% level
9.	Proactive women to take up business	3.09	5.61	
10.	Encouragement from family/friends/peers	4.36	1.22	
		Avg. score 5.46	Total 29.55	

or less modern in terms of technology, usage, etc. It is heartening to know the perceptions of women on these areas as they have consistently kept these areas in the lower order of priority (14th rank, 12th rank, 11th rank, 13th rank). It could be understood in relation to the IT industry because of the plenty of opportunities available in terms of wage employment for women. Electronics and engineering goods with an IT component in design and manufacturing is also understandable. But the electronic components industry and the servicing part offer immense opportunity that could be explored by women not only for consumption within India, but also for export potential. Similarly, the purchasing power of the people has increased substantially and designer homes with interior decoration and architect designed are the fashion of the day. Very few wage employment opportunities should provide plenty of entrepreneurial potential for women in this area. Glass and plastics have replaced metals such as brass and aluminium. The range of products that could be explored and the designs at an affordable price is also an area that could be explored by many. Biotechnology/life sciences/pharmaceuticals require investment and a long gestation period. It is but natural for women to keep out of them for business ideas.

Thus, in summary, it could be said that although women preferred the traditional women-dominated areas in terms of business opportunities, it is interesting to note that they have moved from activities that stereotype female imagery. For instance, in apparel, garments and textiles, they have taken up fashion designing and export promotion only. The beauty clinics have gone high tech and the food items have moved away from the kitchen activities to processed foods. A beginning has been made in the modern industries such as IT, health care, etc., which should be the strong areas for women in due course of time.

The concordance test was conducted to find out the association that exists among the rankings of 87 respondents to each of the 15 components given in the study. Table 8.2 highlights the component-wise average of rankings, W value and chi-square value.

(ii) Managerial Capabilities

It's been proved since long that women are the best managers. But this success was restricted to the home front only till recently. Women entered the business scenario and are managing/

sustaining businesses—small and large. The study attempted to elicit the opinions/perceptions of the sampled respondents on 12 such capabilities on a 4-point scale—no skills, some skills, good skills and very good skills.

A *factor analysis* on managerial capabilities was done to resolve the set of variables into new categories known as *factors*. It helped to reduce the complexity of observed variables into new variables, which summarizes the commonality of all the variables. The data

Table 8.2 *Statement showing the component-wise average of rankings*

S. No.	*Component*	*Average of the ranks*	*Deviation square*	
1.	Apparel garments/ textiles	2.02	36.08	
2.	Beauty clinics	3.36	21.84	
3.	Education/school/ preschool	7.68	0.12	W
4.	Baby care/crèche	5.71	5.37	0.71
5.	Food items	3.67	19.04	
6.	Electronic/ engineering goods/ services	12.10	16.59	
7.	Advisory/consultancy	7.41	0.38	
8.	Handicrafts	5.67	5.59	
9.	Health care/medical/ herbal products	6.45	2.50	X^2
10.	Support/ancillary units	6.79	1.53	916*
11.	IT/computer related	10.77	7.51	
12.	Architect/interior designing	11.89	14.86	* 1% level
13.	Biotech/agrotech	11.67	13.23	
14.	Glassware/plastic ware	10.26	4.99	
15.	Others	15.00	48.58	

Overall average ranking 8.03; sum: 198.22

collected from 87 women entrepreneurs were subjected to factor analysis by the principal component factor analysis with varimax rotation by using the criterion that factors with eigen value >1.00 were retained. Loadings exceeding 0.05 were considered for determining factors. The literature on the factor analysis allows a loading of 0.33 to be the minimum value for inclusion. This criterion is being used more or less by way of convention (Vasanthi and Rayappan, 2006). Hence, the set criteria was used to arrive at the factors (Table 8.3).

Table 8.3 highlights the factors, item loadings, eigen value and percentage of variance explained by each factor. The factor analysis yielded three factors accounting for 70.625 per cent of the total variance. Factor 1 consisted of four items and explained 34.007 per cent of total variance. Among the three factors, Factor 1 explains the maximum variance and is most important for women in sustaining business. In Factor 1, *finance* with a loading of 0.883 is the

Table 8.3 *Variable loadings of sustaining business by the varimax rotated principal components (N = 87)*

	Loadings	*Eigen value*	*Variance (in %)*
Factor—1			
1. Finance	0.883		
2. Marketing	0.826	4.081	34.007
3. Training	0.814		
4. Decision-making	0.675		
Factor—2			
1. Technology	0.857		
2. Policy	0.775		
3. Agency support	0.731	3.242	27.018
4. Motivation	0.729		
5. Work–life balance	0.532		
Factor—3			
1. Knowledge	0.750		
2. Worker related	0.715	1.152	9.599
3. Product related	0.652		

most important item. Factor 2 is the next in order of importance. It has five items and explains 27.018 per cent of the total variables. In Factor 2, *technology* with a loading of 0.857 is the important item. Factor 3 consists of three items and explains 9.599 per cent of the total variance and is next in order. Knowledge with a loading of 0.750 is the most important item in this factor. Thus, these new categories in terms of the factors that emerged explain the strategic inputs into business, the skills required in sustaining business and also the inputs essential for women in sustaining business.

(iv) Problems in Sustaining Business

Managing and sustaining business, whether small or large, entails problems.

(v) Suggestions

Women were also asked to provide possible solutions to the problems that they had encountered in business. A number of suggestions were put forth by them as possible solutions; the study reveals that women faced problems in the course of sustaining business. While the problems relating to finance and marketing appear to be *real* and not *perceptual,* these problems were even highlighted by women in terms of the managerial capabilities that they possessed. Marketing and finance were cited by women as areas having *no skills* in these areas (Table 8.4). Studies confirming marketing and finance as a grey area in start-up ventures are also established (Gupta, 1987; Dhameja, 2002). Thus, we can conclude by saying that finance and marketing problems were *really* faced by the women in sustaining business. The other problems in terms of competition, high standards, labour/HRM, risks, etc., do exist and are common in small, medium and large enterprises in these days of competition and performance-driven economies. Hence, these are more *perceptual* in nature rather than *real* considering the context in which the enterprises are placed. Globalization entails competition, high standards, attrition in skilled manpower leading to HR problems, and there is no choice other than to compete to survive and sustain in business through competitive strategies. The suggestions offered by them prove the awareness level of the women entrepreneurs in meeting the challenges. Thus, women should not give up their confidence and commitment to meet these challenges because of their higher awareness levels.

(vi) General Opinions on Women's Issues

The general opinions/perception on issues relating to women in sustaining business was sought on a 4-point scale—strongly agree, agree, strongly disagree and disagree. The responses on the 4-point scale were reduced to two groups--disagree and agree—and calculated in terms of percentages on 19 statements provided in the questionnaire.

There was a *significant trend of agreement* on the role of formal education, knowledge of business and training in sustaining

Table 8.4 *Distribution of sampled respondents by way of problems faced by women entrepreneurs in sustaining business*

Problems	*Count*	*%*
Labour/HRM	17	19.5
Legal/government	6	6.9
Technology	8	9.2
Business contacts	6	6.9
Marketing	46	52.9
Finance	67	77.0
Product	6	6.9
Competition	50	57.5
High standards	26	29.9
Commitment	5	5.7
Customization	6	6.9
Innovation	1	1.1
Family	8	9.2
Quality service	4	4.6
Education	1	1.1
Skill updation	8	9.2
Time management	3	3.4
Sustainability	2	2.3
Customer satisfaction	6	6.9
Risk	12	13.8

business (98.9% each). Similarly, innovation/creativity, networking and worker-related issues fostering women in sustaining business was also significantly agreed too (97.7% each). Support in terms of family, association and women's personality itself in sustaining business was also overwhelmingly agreed as important (96.6% each). Policy support (95.4%), equal success such as male counterparts (93.1%) and inherent advantage of being a woman (88.5 per cent) helping in sustaining business was also agreed upon by many.

Their *disagreement* was also quite vociferous. Women can perform well in a salaried job than in business (86.2%), sustaining business at the cost of home (85.1%), women enter business out of dire need (82.2%) were totally rejected. This proves their confidence in their entrepreneurial ability and work–life balance. They also disagreed on home/children as a prime responsibility of women (60.9%) and maintained that women can perform well in the outside world if the family responsibilities are shared. They also disagreed in terms of raising finances (77.0%) and their marketing skills (74.7%), reinforcing once again that support is essential to sustain in business. Thus, their general opinion was evidence of very strong, confident and affirmative reactions on women-related issues.

CONCLUSION

- The socio-economic profile of the women sustaining business for a longer time period matches with the socio-economic profile of women of all sizes and stages of the life cycle of business.
- It could be said that women nurtured their enterprises and sustained in the dynamic and volatile business environment for quite long.
- In terms of their opinions/perceptions, women were found to be cohesive as a group in terms of business opportunities, managerial capabilities and finding ways to strengthen women in business.
- Their problems were more *perceptual* in nature rather than *real* considering the context in which the enterprises are placed.
- There was a *significant trend of agreement* on the role of formal education, knowledge of business and training in sustaining

business. Their *disagreement* was on women performing well in job than business, compromising home for business and dire need for women to enter business.

The general opinion/perception of women in the contemporary era is a pointer to confidence and assertive tendencies in terms of their personality. This is a welcome step in the right direction as they see gender not as an obstacle to business success, but as an opportunity to continuously prove themselves. In a context like India with family as a major responsibility, business women who wish to succeed must expect to a certain degree to lose honour and respect because they sometimes are also looked at as neglecting family and being too business-minded. More focus on women entrepreneurs in a global context will not only help us find the answers to remaining questions about women business owners, but will also increase our understanding of entrepreneurship in the broadest sense. It is likely that, as we are in the initial years of this millennium, this will be the *century of the entrepreneur* in general and of the *woman entrepreneur* in particular.

REFERENCES

Birley, Sue, 1989, 'Female Entrepreneurs; Are They Really Different?', *Journal of Small Business Management*, 27(1), January.

Brush, C. and R. Hisrich, 1988, 'Women Entrepreneurs Strategic Origins Impact on Growth', *Business Venturing*, 8: 223–42.

Dhameja, S.K., 2002, *Women Entrepreneurs*. New Delhi: Deep & Deep.

Gangurde, S.P., 2006, 'A Comparative Study of Women Entrepreneurs from Business Communities and Non Business Community', Ph.D thesis, University of Pune, Maharashtra (unpublished manuscript).

Gupta, M.C., 1987, *Entreprenurship in SSIs*. New Delhi: Anmol Publication.

Haynes, P.J. and M. Helms, 2000, 'When Bank Loans Launch New Ventures: A Profile of High Growth', *Harvard Business Review*, 75(1): 102–112.

Hisrich, R.D. and G. Fuldop, 1993, 'Women Entrepreneurs in Controlled Economies – A Hungarian Perspective', *Frontiers of Entrepreneurship Research*, MIT, USA.

HDR, 1995, *Human Development Report*. New York: Oxford University Press.

ILO, 1982, *The Practice of Entrepreneurship*. Geneva: ILO.

ILO, 2002, *Developing the Knowledge Base on Women Entrepreneurs*. SEED Program. Geneva: ILO.

Manivel, A., 2005, 'A Comparative Analysis of Institutionally Supported and Self-Supported Women Micro Entrepreneurs in Tiruchirapalli District of Tamil Nadu', Ph.D thesis, Bharatidasan University, Tamil Nadu (unpublished manuscript).

National Foundation for Women Business Owners (NFWBO), 23 April 2001, *Key Facts* and NFWBO fact of the week.

Naisbutt, J., 1985, *The Future of Franchising*. Washington, DC: IFA.

Nelson, B., 1991, 'Small Business Opportunities for Women in Jamaica', *SEDME*, 18(1).

Ronstadt, R.C., 1984, *Entrepreneurship*. Dover: Lord Publishing.

Schiller, B.R. and P. Crewson, 1997, 'Entrepreneurial Origins: A Longitudinal Inquiry', *Economic Enquiry*, 35(3): 523–31.

Shum Peter, J.A., 1936, *Theory of Economic Development*. Cambridge, MA: Harvard University Press.

Singh, K.P., 1993, 'Women Entrepreneurs – Their Profile and Motivation', *The Journal of Entrepreneurship*, 2(1).

Walker, E., 2000, *An Empirical Study of Measures of Success in Micro Businesses*. ICSB, Edith Cowan University.

White, J., 1984, 'The Rise of Female Capitalism', *Business Quarterly*, 49: 137–43.

Zapalska, A.M., 1997, 'A Profile of Women Entrepreneurs and Enterprises in Poland', *Journal of Small Business Management*, 35(4): 76–82.

CHAPTER 9

Women on the Ramp: Bollywood in the Regime of Consumption

Lalit Joshi

This essay is about women, fashion and lifestyle, and its representations in Bollywood. The mystifying experience of being young in the metropolis has recently stirred the fancies of many filmmakers in India, Madhur Bhandarkar's film *Fashion* (2008) being the most explicit statement on the subject.[1] The transformation of urban India into gargantuan manifestations of steel, brick and mortar in the seventies and the eighties was accompanied by the rise of a middle-class which displayed an ever-growing appetite for consumer products, even though economic liberalization and globalization were a few years away. When the Indian economy was finally opened in 1991 under pressure from the International Monetary Fund, it paved the way for the capitalization of the market, the creation and expansion of large consumer retail chains and a phenomenal growth of the information, service and entertainment sectors. Significantly, the beauty and apparel industry that also grew rapidly around this time created a class of (young) middle-class consumers whose numerical strength surpassed a similar class of shoppers in several European countries put together.[2] Also, by a curious conjuncture, the 1990s were marked by successive Indian contestants winning the Miss Universe and Miss World titles, a feat that has not been replicated in the present millennium.[3] This essay explores the complex interplay between the spectacle of redrawing, displaying and consuming the female body and how Bollywood film *Fashion* reworks representation and spectatorship within the cinematic diegesis. The film has been chosen for its critical engagement with the strategies of consumerist seduction and entrapment of women. As a register of the 'contemporary', *Fashion* documents the histories of two small-town models, violated and abused by men from the industry. I have argued that the filmic narrative is not only constructed along gendered lines and spectatorship designed to manipulate male gaze, but gay interludes are thrown in to bring the narrative in sync with the contemporary discourse on sexuality.

FASHION: THE PLOT

Madhur Bhandarkar's[4] film *Fashion* is a compellingly disturbing saga of an ambitious young girl, Meghna Mathur (Priyanka Chopra), who lives with her middle-classs parents in Chandigarh. Meghna aspires to become a supermodel. For this, she must go to Mumbai, the fashion capital of India, despite her father's (Raj Babbar) wishes. But the steadfast support of her mother (Kiran Juneja) ensures Meghna's quiet exit to Mumbai. Temporary residence with her maternal uncle and aunt enables Meghna to peek into the sinister world of fashion and get acquainted with its hidden pleasures and vicarious thrills. A chance meeting with an old gay acquaintance Rohan (Ashwin Mushran) facilitates the process.[5] During one of her auditions, she runs into Manav (Arjan Bajwa), who becomes her friend. Another model who befriends her is Janet (Mugdha Godse). Meghna soon realizes that the industry opens its doors only to those who have been profiled by famous photographers such as Kartik (Rohit Roy). But Kartik is expensive to hire. Meghna will have to raise enough money to meet his expenses. She reluctantly decides to do a lingerie shoot. Despite assurances that the photograph would not be published in the Indian edition, Meghna finds herself on the cover page of a lingerie magazine. Her uncle and aunt are horrified. They throw her out of the house in the dead of the night. Meghna seeks refuge in Manav's apartment.

Meghna struggles against all odds until noticed by the industry. Her mentor is Abhijit Sarin (Arbaaz Khan), the owner of the famous fashion house *Panache*. Meghna knows that it would not be easy for her to dislodge Shonali, the reigning diva of the modelling industry. But her moment of triumph arrives when Abhijit decides to promote her to the number one slot. Success, however, comes with a price tag. Meghna allows herself to be sexually exploited by Abhijit. In return, *Panache* launches her into the highest orbit of popularity. Her photographs now inundate every magazine and television commercial. Once again, Meghna pays the price. Irked by her late nights, her roommate Manav chastises her, bringing their friendship to an abrupt end. This time she takes shelter in an apartment (arranged by Abhijit), which becomes a clandestine hideout for the two lovers. Meanwhile, an estranged Shonali plunges deeply into drugs and has to be admitted to a rehabilitation centre.

When Meghna learns that she is pregnant, she knows it is time to confront Abhijit. But Abhijit acts quickly and ruthlessly by terminating her contract with *Panache*. Shocked and hurt, Meghna is left with no option but to abort the child. A quick turn of events forces her to slide into alcohol and drugs. But the worst is yet to happen. An inebriated Meghna ends up sleeping with a complete stranger in a sleazy bar. Filled with guilt and remorse, Meghna returns to Chandigarh. But Meghna's love for the ramp remains undiminished even when she is in a state of anguish. Her father is quick to realize this. He advises his daughter to return to Mumbai and resume her career in modelling. A year later, Meghna returns to Mumbai only to discover that she has lost her equanimity and confidence. A turning point comes in her life again when she watches a news clipping showing a hapless and vagrant Shonali squatting on the pavement. She brings Shonali home. Rehabilitating Shonali helps Meghna restore her own confidence. But fate ordains otherwise. One day, as she is about to walk the ramp, Meghna is told that Shonali has committed suicide. Meghna refuses to be intimidated by the incident. Narrative closure comes about as we see Meghna on the ramp in Paris.

THE FATAL ENTICEMENTS OF CONSUMERISM

Fashion provides its audience with a strategic entry point into the seductive world of fashion and style. By positioning Meghna as the *sutradhar* (narrator), it also claims to tell the story from her 'point of view'. In fact, women dominate the cinematic space right from the first shot, allowing audiences to easily misread it as a woman-oriented text. However, a significant number of women are cast as immoral, cigarette-puffing, foul-mouthed and alcoholic characters. A complex mode of gendering is reflected in the representation of male characters. There is no strong male protagonist, most men (except Abhijit Sarin and Manav) portrayed as gay/demasculinated. Although this sets *Fashion* apart from other Bollywood films (in that multiple perspectives have been mobilized to address core concerns of glamour and fashion), an irrepressible urge to masquerade as a feminist text dominates the text right till the end.

With global capitalism moving into a new stage of commodity production,[6] the connection between extravagant consumption and insatiability has never been more evident. Consumerism organizes the global domain of commodities and cultural signs in such a way that a game can eventually be played out between what Appadurai has termed 'ethnoscapes' and 'mediascapes'.[7] This is made possible by making people believe that the pursuit of desire through *bhoga* (consumption) can be its only legitimate strategy. In his seminal work on the consumer society, Baudrillard speaks about the 'profusion', 'abundance', 'surplus' and 'spectacle' of commodities that characterize everyday life.[8] Indeed, Baudrillard was among the first to recognize that more than production, it was the phantasmagoria of consumption that needed to be carefully examined and theorized.

Strictly speaking, the humans of the age of affluence are surrounded not so much by other human beings, as they were in all previous ages, but by objects. Their daily dealings are now not so much with their fellow men, but rather—on a rising statistical curve—with the reception of goods and messages.[9]

In addition to inundating human lives with a cornucopia of commodities, consumer culture calls for repeated reinvestments in the body as well as its cartographical alteration. Indeed, with '...the massive rise of the body in consumer culture as a bearer of symbolic value, there is a tendency for people in high modernity to place ever more importance in the body as constitutive of the self'.[10] In a world driven by relentless anxiety, the packaging and promotion of health and fitness programmes centre around the body. In a moving passage, Baudrillard explains how the focus eventually shifted to the woman's body and how it was retrieved from obscurity to be (re)presented as a consumable object:

In the consumer pack, there is a one object finer, more precious and more dizzying than any other—and even more laden with connotations than the automobile. That object is the BODY.

Its 'rediscovery'...its omnipresence (specifically the omnipresence of the female body, in advertising...fashion and mass culture, the hygienic, the dietetic, therapeutic cult which surrounds it, the obsession with youth elegance, virility/femininity treatments and regimes, and the sacrificial practices attaching to it all bear witness to the fact that the body has become an object of salvation. It has literally taken over that moral and ideological function from the soul...For centuries, there was a relentless campaign to convince they had no bodies (though they were never really convinced); today, there is a relentless campaign to convince them of their bodies.[11]

There should be no illusions about Madhur Bhandarkar's film's linkages with the fashion, entertainment and media-marketing industries—the credits reveal it all. Many major brands such as Sunsilk, Kimaya, Reebok, Red FM 93.5, Jimmy Choo, Vogue, La Perla, Minnawale, Epigram advertising and Group M partnered the project. Besides, advertisement guru Prahlad Kakkar and Bollywood celebrities such as Karan Johar, Konkana Sen and Rakshanda Khan make special appearances in the film.

The brand name, which here plays a crucial role, imposes a coherent, collective vision...no longer a sequence of mere objects, but a chain of signifiers, insofar as all of those signifying one another reciprocally as part of a more complex super-object, drawing the consumer into a series of more complex motivations.

Immediately after the credits, the camera cuts into Marine Drive, the filmic trope of modern Mumbai and the media and entertainment capital of India. A pan shot directs the audience's gaze to an array of high-rise buildings dotted with gigantic hoardings before cutting into a juxtaposition of sequences shot inside beauty salons. The rapid montage prepares the audience for the mélange of attractions that are to follow. Several close-ups reveal women applying lipstick, women smoking, women drinking, women's hair being styled, women applying mascara, women's garments being stitched and women being massaged before a fashion show. Because of the use of subtle gay innuendos in the film and the presence of significant women audiences at any given time, it would be reasonable to question the rhetoric of women dressing up to please men. Besides, as Craik cautions, 'other evidence suggests that women primarily dress to please other women. Further, there is no clear pattern as to whose "eyes" women view other women through'.[12]

BIG DREAMS OF SMALL-TOWN GIRL

When the camera cuts into Chandigarh for the first time, the audience gets a glimpse of the purported 'small' town. I prefer the term *qasba* to the small town because of its pre-colonial historicity and lineage. Denotative of being the smallest urban unit of India presiding over a cluster of villages,[13] the *qasba* can also be seen as a register of ambivalences. Geographically and emotionally, the *qasba* lies between the village and the big city. Sometimes, a succession of towns may string the big city with the *qasba,* the *qasba* claiming bonding with all. A *qasba* always yearns to become the big city while tenaciously clinging to its pre-modern/pre-colonial past. The advantage of deploying the term *qasba* is that it helps to explain the resilient character of many Indian towns that can selectively negotiate their pre-colonial and colonial pasts alongside their modern present, without showing visible signs of disjunction.

If Bollywood today has become the habitat of an expanding community of creative directors, actors and musicians, the change can be partly attributed to those whose roots and routes go all the way to the *qasba*. Indeed, the *qasba*-ization of Bollywood had started immediately after the establishment of the film industry in Mumbai. Hardly a decade passed when Bollywood was not flooded with applications from hordes of young men and women belonging to small towns and cities of India. The *qasba* also managed to invade the diegetic space of Bollywood productions because the migrant *qasba* communities wanted to retell their stories of migration and displacement. The fact that Meghna Mathur and Shonali Gujral play *qasba* girls in *Fashion* is a frequent reminder of their small town origins and should make it amply clear that Bollywood's romance with the *qasba* is far from over. Further, Priyanka Chopra who plays Meghna and Kangana Ranaut who plays Shonali in the film are in real life, small-town girls.

There are three shots of Chandigarh. The first shows Meghna inside her dining room. Seated next to her are her father and mother. As the film's *sutradhar,* Meghna begins to speak about her 'big dreams', the phrase being deployed metonymically to invoke images of metropolitan Mumbai and reaffirm her status as a *qasba* girl. The second shot of Chandigarh brings into focus the interiors of Meghna's home and the last shot is of Meghna and her father at the Sukhna lake. Though Chandigarh is not a small town in terms of its material and cultural landscape, Bhandarkar redraws its narrative geography by visual blurring of what Jameson calls '...the appliances and artifacts, the high rises, the object world of late capitalism.'[14] In contrast, the big city, despite the contradictory images of 'temptation, desire and fascination on the hand; fear and terror on the other'[15] it carries, has always lured the small town and its inhabitants. Conspicuous by the far-from-trendy clothes they wear, their faulty English accents, giggly conduct,[16] girls from small-town India nevertheless await their uncertain futures to unfold in corporate India. Indeed, a veteran of beauty pageants succinctly sums up the corporate position by describing the birth of a girl in a small town as an 'unfortunate accident'.[17] Yet, the hope of achieving something in the big city is so reassuring that it makes the future appear less uncertain. All major fashion brands operate from Mumbai, Delhi, Chennai or Bangalore, setting the trends for global, regional and local beauty pageants throughout the country.[18] Finally, it is the beauty pageant that becomes the indexical platform for constructing the image of a truly mobile and liberated young woman:

> In a country like the US...you don't need a beauty pageant to come out of your shell...the environment there has enough and more to liberate young women. In the Indian context, there is very little which allows for a girl to come out and say, 'Hello, I have arrived'...There's almost nothing here except the movies. As I see it, the pageant every year plays a positive role as much as it provides a springboard for a few girls each year, to achieve something.[19]

Even though the fashion industry regularly outsources fabrics, designs and young models from the *qasba*, the brands it creates are well beyond the pecuniary reach of the *qasba*. Whether it is the repackaging of Indian tribal and folk motifs as 'ethnic' or the creation of 'haute' apparel by the industry, the product is essentially designed for the high-end user. Designer Bina Ramani's enterprise is a case in point. Born in India, Ramani spent almost twenty-five years of her life in the United States and Britain, working extensively with leading designers such as Christian Dior and Givanchy, handling fabrics and foreign clients. However, a chance visit to

Delhi in late eighties helped to shift her focus to the Indian market instead. Ramani recalls the experience vividly:

> Coming to India, I recalled the richness of India's traditional heritage. I traveled around a bit and saw the whole place with foreign eyes. Foreigners have always appreciated our wonderful fabrics and our village traditions, but India always neglected them...I developed my own style, quite unique, of using old saris, embroideries, brocades, whatever, and incorporating them into my own design...I have always felt it important to market the Indian image abroad.[20]

It is evident from Ramani's testimony that even when she was dealing with Indian materials, she had her sight fixed on foreign customers. Moreover, if they happened to be Indian, they had to be women of international taste:

> Now women come from Bombay specially to visit my boutique and the fashion is taking off in India too...But I am not concerned to capture the ordinary Indian woman who is mediocre and conventional in her sari. She is not interested in my stuff and, quite frankly, I have no interest in her. The clothes I sell are for people like me, people who lead international lives.[21]

Thus, fashion is all about taste and distinction. *Haute couture* fashion industries must routinely churn out exclusive ensembles for their clientele of rich and discriminating buyers.

In *Fashion,* Meghna's father dreams of his daughter becoming a Chartered Accountant. Like other parents, he too dreads the thought of Meghna's choice of modelling as a career. Such fear is not uncommon among urban middle-class families in India. For example, Miss India 1999, Yukta Mookhey admitted to an interviewer that her parents were initially unhappy with her decision to run for the Miss India contest because of the 'temporary nature of the kind of fame that the pageant brings'.[22] Further, they believed that 'I was too smart for this kind of career...and that I should do something in advertising instead'.[23] But what Mookhey left unstated in her testimony is that more than the 'temporary nature of the fame', parents are haunted by the fear of their daughters sliding into muck and sleaze.

The dramatic changes that urban Indian beauty culture has undergone since the opening of the economy to foreign investment were unmistakable...applicants wore a variety of revealing outfits...the message in many of the professional photographs was that modernity does not wear many clothes.[24]

The tension becomes apparent from the first day of Meghna's arrival in Mumbai. Her maternal uncle's daughter is thrilled at the prospect of having an aspiring model as cousin. But Meghna's aunt is apprehensive that an in-house model might not be a good moral influence on her teenage daughter. Later, as Meghna's professional life becomes more and more demanding; the tension is played out in the open.

URBANITY, MODELLING, COMMODIFICATION

There is no dearth of literature about how fashion constructs subjectivities, regulates social conduct and etiquette and helps negotiate identity along class, gender, race, community, age and culture. Specific styles of dresses, accessories, mannerisms, language and speech, cuisine, dwellings and artefacts of everyday life can mark specific periods of human history. In the era of commodification and mass consumption, a high premium has been placed on visuality, the objective being to encourage entertainment and fashion industries to market desire and fantasy to billions of consumers across the globe. Lifestyle marketing and advertising firms are conscripted to perform this critical function. However, a reverse process is also at work. Homogenization of tastes carries the threat of subverting identity and difference. Therefore, in every historical epoch, there has always been a class of consumers claiming superior penchant and predilection in matters of taste and preference, the present stage of late modernity and globalization being no exception. Baudrillard explains why this occurs:

> you never consume the object in itself (in its use value); you are always manipulating objects (in the broadest sense) as signs which distinguish you either by affiliating you to your own group taken as an ideal reference or by marking you off from your group by reference to a group of higher status.[25]

Fashion is mainly about youth, lifestyle and identity. In India, the study of youth subcultures remains a neglected terrain, while in Europe and North America, youth subcultures have attracted the attention of writers, social theorists and philosophers.[26] However, there is a crucial difference between the two. Indian youth subculture is a recent phenomenon associated with liberalization and globalization and not the product of post-war working class restlessness as was the case with Europe or the anti-war (Vietnam) movement and the United States. For example, in India, there has been nothing comparable to the emergence of (a) punk rock groups (seventies) or the DiY culture (nineties) in Britain or (b) the counterculture movement (seventies) or the punk groups (nineties) in the United States.[27] In other words, unlike youth cultures in Europe and the United States, the youth in India are not known to have evolved strategies of resistance against hegemonic structures of power by recasting group identities in terms of fashion and lifestyle.[28] Bhandarkar's film, therefore, cannot be read as a statement about counterculture.

GAZING AT WOMEN: FASHION IN/AND BOLLYWOOD

Fashion raises pertinent questions about the 'aesthetics of representation and gaze' in Indian cinema. It would be simplistic to declare that the gaze in this film is exclusively androcentric and is constructed to facilitate the 'scopophilic pleasure of looking at women', as Laura Mulvey had once suggested in her essay 'Visual Pleasure and Narrative Cinema' in 1975.[29] In fact, in her later writings, Mulvey had modified her position by pointing out that some films did construct female spectators and there was always a possibility of alternative readings. Her critics such as Mary Ann Doane dismiss Mulvey's strategy of positioning men as 'active' and women as 'passive', and suggest instead that women spectators either have the option of a narcissistic identification with and submission to the feminine form on the screen or of reading and rejecting the screen image as a masquerade.[30] Others such as Jaine Gaines have emphasized the importance of race as a determining factor of gaze (male).[31] Likewise, sexuality (gay/lesbian) has also been cited as a factor.[32] Feminist film theorist Kaja Silverman (The Acoustic Mirror, 1988) argues that more than looking at the image track, there is an urgent need to examine the voices of women (scream, pant, cry, silence) on the soundtrack.[33] But what is missing out in the studies cited here are elaborate surveys of actual responses of male and female cinema audiences to determine their dispositions towards caste, community, gender and sexuality-related issues.

In the case of *Fashion*, it is difficult to argue that the subjectivity of women is constituted by an exclusively heterosexual male gaze. Implicit in the argument of male spectatorship is the absence of active women and queer spectators. This is at odds against the very character of the filmic narrative of *Fashion*, which in some situations seems to be driven by the actions of queer designers. In fact, there are three queer designers in the film, who tend to negotiate sexuality differently from their heterosexual counterparts. At the same time, Rohit's stridently heterosexist utterances and actions often leave behind the impression that he could be a straight queer.[34] Thus, *Fashion* is bound to attract alternative imaginative investments from non-straight spectators and critics as well. *Fashion* also needs to be read against the recent Delhi High Court judgment that suggests an amendment in those sections of the Indian Penal Code that deal with homosexuality.[35] The judgment has been widely applauded by the gay community in India as the sign of eventual recognition of gay identity and rights by the Indian state and society at large.

Recent advances in the gaze theory notwithstanding, the fact that urban public space in India is discernibly male cannot be wished away. In everyday transactions in the public space, women have to negotiate the invasive male gaze by dressing up suitably—the dress for the ramp may be appropriate for specific situations. They also know that even a minor transgression could have dangerous consequences. Models carefully venture out into spaces that have not been secured. The ramp, in contrast, is apparently made to look more secure as the male gaze has been redirected to perform other functions (assessment/grading of participants), in addition to voyeuristic looking. Nonetheless, the complete filtering of fashion shows from public view is becoming increasingly difficult because they hardly remain private events. Many of them are electronically reprocessed and televised for global consumption (Fashion TV, Trendz, etc.). Thus, every fashion event has several sets of audiences—those who watch it in real time and space and others who view its recorded versions in virtual time and space. In the film *Fashion*, we have four major events, seen by small diegetic audiences as well as by millions of cinema and television audiences across the globe.

There is also a need to re-examine the proposition that women on the ramp are hapless victims of male desire. As the recent history of the Indian accomplishments in the Miss World and Miss Universe pageants has clearly demonstrated, success in such events ineluctably has paved the way for triumphant ingress into tinsel town. Other tangible benefits have also followed. For example, being a celebrity means immediate corporate recognition—often a brand ambassador of some product. Moreover, endorsement of a product by a celebrity also prevents quick erasure of the image from public memory. Miss Universe 2000 Lara Dutta recalls her moment of triumph on becoming a celebrity:

> It turned my life upside down! It's a gift, a charming and wonderful gift...It's a very short span of time in which you go through, see and are exposed to so much that it's almost an intensive course that shows you the whole world at once—the glamour, the glitz, as well as the very gritty realities of the issues you work and deal with.[36]

In the case of women celebrities, empowerment is not generally visible along the differential of gender, but it can be felt in terms of their iconic presence in the public domain. As Blum has remarked, 'They represent for us both what we are and what (and where) we long to be.'[37] A fresh approach is therefore required to understand how new media technologies are creating women celebrities without renegotiating the imbricated structures of patriarchy. Also, '... the ways in which women manipulate patriarchal social structures to their own advantage, by actively participating in them', needs to be further explored.[38] A beginning can be made by examining current Indian television soaps and Bollywood films.

But there is a flip side to the narrative of empowerment. In all competitions, losers clearly outnumber the winners. Rarely do losers constitute appropriate script material for the media, unless it is a sensational loser (like the model Shonali in the film) whose story is covered by Page 3 reporters. Gauri Karnik (a contestant in Miss India 2000 who could not make it to the finals) candidly admitted to anthropologist Dewey, 'No one is nice at the pageant. They say everyone is a winner, but it is a lie. We're not sisters, we're competitors. There wasn't too much bitchiness, but there was a lot of competition.'[39] In *Fashion,* the failure to cope with defeat compels Shonali to take the fateful decision of ending her life violently. It is significant to note that Shonali's tragedy is based on a real life incident involving a Delhi model (Geetanjali) in 2007 and which became the focus of much media attention.

MOBILIZING DESIRE

Fashion was released in India when the expansion of multiplexes and high-fidelity technology was already underway and was rapidly spreading into the non-metropolitan hinterland. Viewing coordinates are extremely important to determine the cartographies of modern cinematic reception. For example, where will the film be seen? Will it be in the heart of the city or the suburbia? Pricing of tickets and the distance of cinema halls from neighbourhoods of specific class/community/caste compositions will also determine the ethnographic profile of its audience. Diverse considerations such as these shape the limits to which audiences indulge in fetishist identification with screen images. Mobilizing desire in multiplexes calls for a complex engagement with the senses because it also involves the consumption of corporate merchandise other than the film itself. Entirely different experiences might await the viewer when the film is consumed in a dingy single-screen suburban theatre or seen on television inside a middle-class bedroom. Thus, it is clear that there cannot be a single strategy of reading and experiencing *Fashion*.[40]

Fashion lures its audience by giving them an opportunity to become active stakeholders in the fashion industry. For this, they must begin their journey with Meghna in Mumbai. Their first glimpse of Meghna is with her friend Rohan inside Café Coffee Day. Coffee chains in global India have been successfully marketed as networking hangouts for young urban consumers. They differ vastly from the colonial Coffee Houses both in terms of the décor they offer and the clientele they serve. By locating the protagonist inside Café Coffee Day in the early stages of the narrative, the stage is set for other consumerist attractions that quickly follow.

The first among these is the project of fetishization. The process begins with the transformation of Meghna's unglamorous *salwar kameez* image into a desirable profile. Shomu (whom Rohan addresses as the 'Mother India' of all strugglers) is entrusted with this task. Shomu—the critical link between modelling agencies and aspiring models—is crass and blasphemous, the very opposite of all that Mother India has epitomized in the entire Indian cinematic imagination. The appellation Mother India therefore needs to be read as an inflection. Earlier on, Mother India had always been emblematic of ideal motherhood. But in a regime of consumption, Mother India inverts the normative order. Meghna and Shomu meet again at an audition where the latter proposes that Meghna do a lingerie advertisement to get a break into the industry. Indeed, Shomu emerges as the chief instrumentality through which Meghna's body would eventually be refigured and displayed.

The Rahul Arora show can be interpreted as the event which prepares the audiences for a visual burlesque. A major attraction is Shonali, the showstopper for *Panache*. The auditorium is packed with leading fashion designers, celebrity magazine editors, socialites and the press. Also present is Abhijit Sarin, the owner of *Panache*. As Shonali sashays into the frame, a sensuous song breaks out in the background:

> *Jismon Ka Hai Jalwa*
> *Shohrat Bhi Rahe Jalwa*
> *Maksad Bhi Rahe Jalwa*
> *Ye Jalwa Fashion Ka Ye Jalwa...*
> *(Translation)*
> Bodies are on exhibit
> Let fame be exhibited
> Let intention be exhibited
> This exhibition of fashion, this exhibition...

Jalwa is a word of Arabic origin. Literally meaning exhibition or display, the word has been used in Sufi poetry where poets have sung in praise of God's exhibits. Again, by a clever inflection, the film not only deploys *Jalwa* to literally mean fashion exhibits, but in a sense that contributes to their ultimate valourization. Young, brash, aggressive and foul-mouthed, Shonali is the object of such valourization. A darling of the media, Shonali smokes, drinks, curses and has slipped in and out of relationships. Before the show ends, there are more exhibits for the audience—close-ups of women's bare backs, ankles and calves and clean-shaven chests of men. The camera cuts backstage, inviting and directing the audience's gaze into the dressing room. The dressing room is also the site where Meghna learns why the industry continues to discount her. Meghna's photographs fail to attract the gaze. The panacea is a photo session with Kartik Suri.

In another significant move, a close-up shot exposes the underside of the libidinal economy of global India. As the camera zooms into the front seat of a car, the audience can catch a quick glimpse of Janet and her boyfriend sharing intimate moments. But by the time Janet bids him farewell, she has already forgotten his name. The scene unveils the insidious pleasures of promiscuous existence associated with the lives of models. In another act of unlayering, the camera caressingly worms its way inside a party where predators prowl in search of innocuous victims. We also see Shomu in another role—making models available to prospective clients where they can, in her own words, be served as 'candy'. Meghna is introduced as a famous Bollywood 'item girl'. But before some men can take advantage of her, Janet rescues her. 'The problem with most small-town girls,' Janet tells her, 'is that if a man speaks to them in good English, they are prepared to offer him anything.' Thus, in one brutal stroke, the film unmasks the modus operandi of the flesh traders and their linkages with the fashion industry.

It brings us to the point when Meghna shoots for the lingerie advertisement. As Meghna demurely takes off her gown to expose the lingerie, the camera teasingly violates her body, filling her with a sense of profound guilt and shame. But the model-to-be Meghna is advised to allow the financial considerations to outweigh the emotional. *Fashion*'s celebration of India's post-global sexual economy could tempt us to view the diaphanously draped female body in the film singularly as a corrupting influence of western culture. However, such reading would also imply a disavowal of the legacy of women's representation in Indic art. One of the dominant tropes of ancient and medieval Indian art has undeniably been the 'unclothed, sensual, feminine figure, spanning the spheres of both divine and human representations'.[41] Indian art owes much of its erotic reputation to the disproportionate and sensational propaganda related to the temples of Khajuraho built roughly between the tenth and the eleventh centuries. Guha-Thakurta has suggested that erotic sculptures form only a small percentage of the larger panoply of engravings. She is also critical of the essentialist endorsement that Khajuraho is emblematic of the unrestrained sexuality of Indian culture. In fact, visual representation of the female form in Indian art has either been looked at with intense disavowal (of eroticism/obscenity/nudity) or extreme valourization (of unrepressed sexuality).[42] Actually, both constructs are products of colonialist/orientalist imaginings and both get inflected with contemporary debates about the essential character of India's art and culture. As Charu Gupta has pointed out, in the colonial period, government officials, missionaries and the middle classes were outraged by the increasing visibility of sexuality and eroticism in print and performance—a phenomenon that has been termed 'moral panic'.[43] Also, because there was no consensus about the meaning of the term obscenity and 'extremely divergent material could be classified obscene or indecent' by the government.[44] Many of these trends continued even after Independence, although they have not been the subject of much academic writing and debate. Alongside, there has been little discussion among Indian feminists on the questions of representing women in art and cinema. This is in striking contrast to the enormity of the literature produced about family, law and rights of women in India's colonial and postcolonial histories.[45]

Meghna's capitulation brings her closer to commodification and subsumption. In her maiden appearance in the Nina Mehta show, Meghna is noticed by all celebrity designers, including Abhijit. The camera pans the audience several times to highlight the presence of the Indian designer Rohit Bal lookalike. Also sitting among the audience is the young and famous Bollywood director Karan Johar. In the later sequences of the film, the audience can also witness brief appearances of actor Konkona Sen, adman Prahlad Kakkar and even Bhandarkar himself. More than a strategy for invoking realism, such appearances are contrived to indicate the evident collapse between the screen image and the real world. Perhaps Madhur Bhandarkar's idea of cinematic realism is to juxtapose real-life characters with the filmic. However, as a cinematic device, it serves little purpose. *Fashion,* because of its contemporary signifiers and choice of characters, would have remained a realist enterprise even if Karan Johar, Konkona Sen and Prahlad Kakkar had not made brief appearances in the film.

Meghna's flight from her uncle's home to Manav's apartment marks a bold entry into the metropolitan mode of living. Although hers is not a live-in relationship with Manav, the decision to live under the same roof is an example of how young Indians may eventually redraw their moral boundaries during late modernity. There is yet another declaration of Meghna's ascendancy to celebrity status. The stage for this is set by the events leading to the dismissal of Shonali and the selection of Meghna as the new face of Panache. In an evocative visual, the audience can see a low angle camera panning high rise buildings and finally stopping at a large hoarding carrying Meghna's glowing face, signalling the final act of redemption. A voice-over communicates her heightened sense of individualism. 'The media wants to know everything that I think, wear and eat. I could not have anticipated that this would await me on the road to success'. With this shot, Meghna steps into the treacherous domain of celebrity narcissism. Cashmore argues that such narcissism always emerges from a situation of paradox. Thus, '...the more we are dissatisfied with our looks, the more we tend to idealize or exaggerate the beauty of celebrities...which would tend to heighten our dissatisfaction without reducing our identification'.[46]

Meghna's celebrity status is short-lived. Narrative conflict is precipitated by a series of events—Meghna's brief pregnancy, second homelessness and ouster from Panache. Two quick incidents bring the narrative to a closure. The first is Meghna's interrogation for drunken driving. The incident is flashed on national television and viewed by her anguished parents in Chandigarh. In the second appalling incident, an inebriated Meghna finds herself inside a sleazy bar, sleeping next to a complete stranger. What follows are quick sequences of Meghna's homecoming, a valiant return to Mumbai and Shonali's suicide. The last scene is set in a Paris fashion show where successive mise-en-scenes alternating between the diegetic audiences and Meghna are deployed to proclaim the triumph of the Indian enterprise in the fashion capital of the world.

REVISITING GENDER THROUGH THE LENS

The construction of the Indian woman within the tradition/modernity binary has always been a cause of disquiet. However, in the film industry, where writers, producers, directors and the technical crew are overwhelmingly men, questions of representation and look are decided predominantly by them. Whether it was the woman who had strayed away from her Indian roots (*Andaz*, 1948), the taming of the aberrant woman in *Purab Aur Paschim* (1970) the notorious vamp of the Fifties through the seventies or the avenging woman of the eighties (*Insaaf Ka Tarazu* 1980), *Zakhmi Aurat* (1988) or the promiscuous woman of global India (*Raaz* 2002), *Jism* (2003) and *Murder* (2004)) or the 'courtesan films', a male-dominated industry eventually determines how women need to appear on the screen. It would be naïve to suggest that such representations could be contested had the directorial initiative been be appropriated by women. Even in the films of some women directors such as Mira Nair, Kalpana Lajmi and Deepa Mehta, dissonances are visible between the choice of the subject and its ultimate representation in the diegesis.[47] Thus, even if some women had the power to represent other women, it would be difficult to establish that they could operate entirely outside the powerful structure(s) and discourse of patriarchy, particularly when film budgets burgeon and consumerism becomes a way of life in India. In this sense, representation and spectatorship to a great extent become projects dominated by men in the market.

Fashion unabashedly tells the story of corporeal exhibition in a consumer society. In frame after frame, bodies are displayed, valourized and consumed. Indeed, exhibition and spectacle stimulate consumer desire. In a regime of consumption, the patriarchal gaze can always be mobilized to respond to the call of the market. One way of locating patriarchal presence in the film could be by examining four major events in the life of Meghna about which the film maintains a studied silence. In the first event, when Meghna's father tries to establish the superiority of a career in Accountancy over Modelling, she refuses to argue in her defence. In the second event, Meghna quietly succumbs to Abhijit's perfidy instead of challenging him in a court of law. The terms of contract with Panache had been violated not because of an accidental pregnancy but because Meghna had been carrying Abhijit's child in her womb. The third silence is discernible when Meghna spends one year in solitary atonement in Chandigarh. The audience does not get to hear Meghna's story except indirectly through the point-of-view and the shot/reverse shot. Finally, Abhijit's wife, despite first-hand information about her husband's complicity in Meghna's tragedy, refuses to act against him.

Feminist film theory has generally been animated by questions of women's representation, subjectivity and gaze. But some scholars argue that these are inadequate to explain the ways of looking at the Hindi film narrative. For example, it has been suggested that the image in Hindi cinema is positioned frontally (*darsana*), somewhat in the same way as it is placed in Hindu temples. One consequence of such positioning is that the cinematic discourse enframes and reconstructs *darsana*.[48] Thus, 'the film may mobilize point-of-view codes to represent the subjectivity of the woman; this is done in such a way as to constrain the field of her look by focusing the beloved within a discourse of divinity.'[49] Frontality also ensures that the visual transaction between the spectator and the screen will become bimodal. Both can now see and be seen. Indeed, the *darsana* theory challenges the notion of the camera as an instrument of male voyeurism, but requires more elaboration. We need to know, for example, if the 'look' of men is different when they seek the *darsana* of women from the one which is deployed to see other men? Likewise, how different is the 'look' when women seek the *darsana* of women from the 'look' directed at men? The *darsana* theory also fails to take into account the possible non-binary ways of looking. The critical challenge perhaps is to understand how the gender coordinates are laid out in *Fashion*; but at the same time, the challenge is also to evolve an interpretive template that allows us to conceive the difference without binary opposition. The question therefore is, do Meghna's (Priyanka Chopra) fans identify her as a consumable screen object or do they watch her films to seek a *darsana* of the divinity itself?

In the recent years, 'Indian-ness' has emerged as a contentious issue in politics. Small and aggressive groups claim to speak on behalf of the nation's art and culture. For example, a Hussein painting or a Valentine's Day celebration can rock political emotions of those who have specific constituencies to address. Nonetheless, beauty pageants and fashion shows, with all their contentious signifiers and modes of representation, continue to be organized uninterruptedly. No major incident to vandalize or subvert them has been reported, though earlier on in the eighties, women's organizations did register sporadic protests. With time, ideological resistance to the commodification of women under neo-liberal globalization has lost much of its earlier vigour. Ideological distancing from issues of gendered representation is also symptomatic of new nationalist imaginings. Film scholar M.K. Raghavendra has recently suggested that contemporary cinema allegorizes the nation by identifying a certain community within the diegetic space.[50] If the two major official awards won by *Fashion* in 2009 are any indication, it is tempting to read the event as a celebratory endorsement by the nation-state for being allegorically represented as a community of fashion designers, models and young, aggressive consumers.

NOTES

1. The most acclaimed in this category have been *Dil To Pagal Hai* (1997), *Kal Ho Na Ho* (2003), *Yuva* (2004), *Page 3* (2005), and *Jab We Met* (2007). But it is only *Fashion* that brings together women, fashion and consumption under a single rubric. Priyanka Chopra won the national award for the best actress and Kangana Ranaut for the best supporting actress in 2009.
2. Figures released by the National Council for Applied Economic Research suggest that 35 per cent of the Indian households in 2005 can be classified as middle-class. Out of these, 6 per cent (between 150 and 300 million) classify as middle-class proper (cited in Minna Saavala, *Middle-Class Moralities, Everyday Struggle over Belonging and Prestige in India*. Hyderabad: Orient BlackSwan, 2010, p. 9). For the links between economic liberalization and the new middle-class, see Leela Fernandes, *India's New Middle Class; Democratic Politics in an Era of Economic Reform*, Minneapolis, MN: University of Minnesota Press, 2006.
3. This was in addition to Cricket, Cinema and Information Technology where Indians were making their presence felt globally.
4. A school dropout and the owner of a video library in Mumbai, Madhur Bhandarkar's career in Bollywood began with his debut film *Trishakti* in 1999. This was followed by his much acclaimed works *Chandini Bar* (2001), *Page 3* (2005), *Corporate* (2006), *Traffic Signal* (2007), *Fashion* (2008) and *Jail* (2008). Bhandarkar's films are characterized by strong women characters even when they are not protagonists. His personal life became controversial when model-turned actress Preeti Jain accused him of raping her several times.
5. Positioning Rohit as a gay is definitely tactical. It makes the fashion industry appear less intimidating to unescorted single women. Deploying Rohit as the gay interlocutor also helps the smooth transition of Meghna from a demure small-town girl to metropolitan supermodel. Also, the use of the gay metaphor is Bhandarkar's way to add a touch of realism to the film, the Indian fashion industry being not unknown for its share of gay designers.

6. This stage has been characterized as androcentric, state organized, post-Fordist, transnational and neoliberal capitalism by Nancy Fraser, 'Feminism, Capitalism and the Cunning of History', *New Left Review*, Vol. 56, March–April 2009, p. 99.
7. By ethnoscapes, Appadurai implies a landscape consisting of mobile workers' groups and individuals. Mediascapes connotes production and distribution of images and narratives by modern media to local and transnational consumers (Arjun Appadurai, *Modernity at Large, Cultural Dimensions of Globalization*. New Delhi: Oxford University Press, pp. 33–7).
8. Jean Baudrillard, *The Consumer Society: Myth and Structures*, trans. Chris Turner. London: Sage Publications, 2006, pp. 26–8.
9. Ibid., p. 25.
10. C. Shilling, *The Body and Social Theory*. London: Sage Publications, 2003, p. 2.
11. Baudrillard, *Consumer Society*, p. 27.
12. Jennifer Craik, *The Face of Fashion: Cultural Studies in Fashion*. London: Routledge, 1994, p. 56.
13. The history of the *qasba* has been explored by Ravinder Kumar, *The Social History of Modern India*. Calcutta: Oxford University Press, 1983, pp. 279–82.
14. Fredrick Jameson, 'Postmodernism and Consumer Society', in Hal Foster (ed.), *The Anti-Aesthetic, Essays on Postmodern Culture*, Seattle, WA: Bay Press, p. 117.
15. Joachim Schlör, *Nights in the Big City*. London: Reaktion Books, 1998, p. 10.
16. Susan Dewey, *Making Miss India, Miss World: Constructing Gender, Power and Nation in Postliberalization India*. Syracuse: Syracuse University Press, 2008, p. 80.
17. Ibid., p. 28.
18. Women's magazines like *Femina, Grihashobha, Saheli, Vama* and others help to conjure the image of the elusive beauty who is also a woman of substance. Local newspapers and tabloids vie with each other in routinely reporting fashion events held in educational institutions, including colleges of technology and medicine.
19. This is the text of a conversation between Pradeep Guha, director of the Miss India Contest of 2003, and American anthropologist Susan Dewey. Cited in Dewey, *Making Miss India*, p. 30.
20. Cited in Emma Tarlo, *Clothing Matters: Dress and Identity in India*. New Delhi: Penguin Books India, 1996, p. 296. Incidentally, it was Ramani's initiative that transformed the Hauz Khas village (Delhi) to a major fashion hub in north India. Locating the workshop in the village was a

tactical move indeed. For Ramani and many of her visitors, the village and its residents represented the untainted and the unbroken in the Indian tradition. Visitors to the village could share the unique experience of witnessing craft production in idyllic rural settings. It can be mentioned that romanticizing the village becomes possible 'in situations where people are sufficiently removed from village life to mourn its loss'. (p. 316)

21. Ibid.
22. Dewey, *Making Miss India*, p. 65.
23. Ibid.
24. Ibid., p. 27.
25. Baudrillard, *Consumer Society*, p. 27.
26. For example, see Christine Gledhill (ed.), *Stardom: Industry of Desire*. London: Routledge, 1991; Joke Hermes, *Reading Women's Magazines: An Analysis of Everyday Media Use*. Cambridge: Polity Press, 1995; R. Shields (ed.), *Lifestyle Shopping: The Subject of Consumption*. London: Routledge, 1992; David Muggleton, *Inside Subculture: The Postmodern Meaning of Style*. Oxford: Berg, 2000; J. Ash and E. Wilson (eds.), *Cheap Thrills: A Fashion Reader*. Berkeley and Los Angeles: University of California Press, 1993.
27. Youth movements in the sixties (as well as in the seventies) were internationalist in terms of mobility, activism and ideologically positioned against the state and its structures of authority (Richard Ivon Jobs, 'Youth Movements: Travel Protest, and Europe in 1968', *American Historical Review*, April 2009, pp. 378–89. For youth movements in the '60s (as also in the '70s) being gendered reading of the Counterculture movement in the '60s and the '70s, see Jeremi Suri, 'The Rise and Fall of an International Counterculture, 1960–75', *American Historical Review*, February 2009, pp. 45–67) A rich account of youth radicalism in Britain is found in George McKay (ed.), *DiY Culture, Parties and Protest in Nineties Britain*, New York: Verso, 1998.
28. The notable exception being the mobilization of the urban youth during the Naxalite movement in the 1970s. However, even this mobilization remained confined to select urban pockets in north and eastern India.
29. Reprinted in Bill Nicholls (ed.), *Movies and Methods*, Vol. 2. Calcutta: Seagull, 1993, pp. 303–315.
30. Shohini Chaudhry, *Feminist Film Theorists*. London and New York: Routledge, 2006, p. 41.
31. Ibid.
32. Ibid., p. 43.
33. Ibid., p. 45.

34. For an elaboration of this concept and for diverse approaches to gay and lesbian cinema, see Harry M. Benshoff and Sean Griffin (eds.), *Queer Cinema: The Film Reader*. London and New York: Routledge, 2004.
35. In a landmark judgment on 3 July 2009, the Delhi High Court directed the legislature to amend Section 377 of the Indian Penal Code and decriminalize private consensual sex between adults of the same sex. See timesofindia.indiatimes.com/Delhi-HighCourt...homosexuality/... 4726608.cms
36. Dewey, *Making Miss India*, p. 71.
37. Virginia Blum, *Flesh Wounds: The Culture of Cosmetic Surgery*. Berkeley, CA: University of California Press, 2003, p. 147.
38. Dewey, *Making Miss India*, pp. 5–6.
39. Ibid., p. 75.
40. Ethnographic studies of film audience are still rare in India, fashion being no exception.
41. Tapati Guha-Thakurta, 'What Makes for the "Authentic" Female Nude in Indian Art?', in Shivaji K. Pannikar, Parul Dave Mukherji and Deepti Achar (eds.), *Towards a New Art History: Studies in Indian Art*. New Delhi: D.K. Printworld (P) Ltd., 2003, p. 358. Art historian Susan L. Huntington argues that visibly erotic images actually expressed the 'duality within the universal' and served to protect ordinary people from 'severe psychological or moral damage' (*The Art of Ancient India*. New York: Weather Hill Inc., 1985, p. 400).
42. Ibid., pp. 360–61.
43. Charu Gupta, *Sexuality, Obscenity, Community, Women, Muslims and the Hindu Public in Colonial India*. New Delhi: Permanent Black, 2001, p. 30.
44. Ibid., p. 41.
45. For these debates, see Rochona Majumdar, 'Arguments within Indian Feminism', *Social History*, Vol. 12, No. 4, November 2007, pp. 434–45.
46. Ellis Cashmore, *Celebrity/Culture*. London and New York: Routledge, 2006. An interesting read is Christopher Lasch, *The Culture of Narcissism: American Life in an Age of Diminishing Expectations*. London: Abacus, 1980. In this book, Lasch identifies the seventies as the decade that witnessed the birth of narcissism as heightened individualism in the United States.
47. For example, this is clearly discernible in the figuration of women characters in Nair's *Monsoon Wedding* and *The Namesake*, Deepa Mehta's *Earth* (1998) and *Bollywood/Hollywood* (2002).

48. Ravi Vasudevan, 'The politics of cultural address in a 'transitional cinema': A case study of Indian popular cinema', p. 140. Art historian Partha Mitter has recently observed that women in Indian art are 'represented both as an object of the gaze and as part of the sacred...' (*Indian Art*. New Delhi: Oxford University Press, 2001, p. 77). For an elaborate rendering of the concept of *darsana,* see Diana Eck, *Seeing the Divine Image in India*. Chambersburg, PA: Anima Books, 1981. See also Lawrence A. Babb, 'Glancing Visual Interaction in Hinduism', *Journal of Anthropological Research*, Vol. 37, No. 4, 1981, pp. 387–401.
49. Vasudevan, p. 147.
50. M.K. Raghavendra, *Seduced by the Familiar, Narration and Meaning in Popular Indian Cinema*. New Delhi: Oxford University Press, 2008, p. 297.

CHAPTER 10

Women and the Knowledge Economy: Seizing the Open Moment

M.N. Rajesh

All aspects of human activity that have been fundamentally impacted by the knowledge economy and their forms have been changed; work is one such phenomenon where we see newer forms emerging that were unthinkable just some years ago simply because the knowledge economy had not taken off. One of the best places to illustrate this phenomenon would be to take a glance at the classified columns of any English language newspaper in South or South East Asia and look at the job vacancies (www.timesjobs.com/, http://www.st701.com/). There is a fundamental shift in the way goods and services are produced and delivered—this is the knowledge input, that is, or the knowledge component in the production and delivery of goods and services. Take a simple example of a purchase. Beyond direct payment of cash and purchase of any goods or services, all other forms of payment have to go through electronic networks. Therefore, as direct payment of cash is not possible in many cases, it is done electronically; and therefore instead of humans transferring the vast sums of digital money from one account to another, advanced software programs have replaced humans with deadly accuracy and efficiency in many places, although there are humans ultimately at many ends who are needed to man these machines (Rifkin, 1995: 5).

Similarly, many professions have disappeared or are in the process of rapid transformation, employing a very small number of people than in the earlier phase. A few of them are as follows: the photographic industry—shift from the analog to digital cameras—has led to the elimination of the wet process and the entry of smart software programmes, leading to the decline of the photographic film and rendering large numbers of people working in this industry redundant.

Communications: the entry of the e-mail has led to the death of the teleprinter and large-scale decline in the revenues of the postal department. There are many other sectors and the list can go on and on from very low-tech to cutting-edge hi-tech sectors where there is large-scale unemployment on the one hand and rise of new jobs on the other. Do we explain this phenomenon as a passing phase or the beginning of a new period? Only then can we relate it to the 'woman question' by getting a clear picture of the larger developments.

It would be prudent to give a background to the entire debate on knowledge economy by outlining the basic changes that have created the ideal conditions for the rise of the knowledge worker and then move on to see the mobility of these knowledge workers. Where does this phenomenon happen and what are the mechanisms involved in this process? To begin with, it would be worth quoting Sheikh Zaki Ali Yamani, the oil minister of Saudi Arabia in the 1970s, who once said that 'the Stone Age did not come to an end because we had a lack of stones, and the oil age will not come to an end because we have a lack of oil' (*The Observer*, 2001: 1). Similarly, we are in the middle of a momentous change, that is, the advance of the knowledge economy and here we notice the making of a new geography based on a new divide, that is, the digital divide (Norris, 2001: 72). It is this digital divide that is in one sense crucial for our understanding of the whole process of contemporary gender concerns and provides us with a vantage anchoring point since it encapsulates the larger questions of development and global competitiveness. Three examples would make our understanding easier and provide interconnectedness to the motivational question. As soon as Ronald Reagan was elected as the President of the United States of America, he convened a meeting of futurologists in his office with the agenda of maintaining the United States' great position. Ronald Reagan began by asking those assembled whether the United States would continue to be a great power in the decades to come and one of those present at this meeting was Alvin Toffler, one of the greatest futurologists, and whose reply was that the United States would be a great service economy and this was where the future lay. Reagan immediately quipped whether we would be selling hamburgers and was a bit disapproving of the idea (Eisenhart, 1994: 1). The second incident is about money generated by patents, and here we see that in the knowledge economy, the larger the number of patents, the greater the economic prosperity; in the United States, the per capita generation of patents is 1:2955 per person, whereas for Japan it is in the range of 1:3914 and in the case of India it is 1:10,647,319 and gives a misleading picture that conceals many realities such as the fact that most patents in the United States are generated by ICs, commonly known as Indians and Chinese (Enriquez, 2001: 43). The third example is about Internet connectivity, and it is shown that in South Korea there is a very large penetration of the Internet; that it is almost supplied like water and electricity and every apartment has broadband Internet wired at very low rates, whereas South Korea ranks second and the United States ranks only seventh in the access to broadband Internet (Lewis, 2004: 191). Reading the above three examples, we see that we again return to the start, that is, new ways of making money and this new way is through the new technologies that are broadly called 'digital'. In this world of rapid change, there is instant competitiveness and for a country to maintain supremacy, it has to attract the brightest talent and for the businesses, they have to update themselves with the latest trends. Therefore, for women to get equality in this new setting, the institutional and other structures, that is, the objective conditions, have to be conducive to this end.

In this changed context, commonly referred to as the knowledge economy, we therefore notice that there is a fundamental change in the way money is made in today's world and a singular perusal of the list of the richest people in the world is a singular proof of this phenomenon. Bill Gates, who tops the list with assets of around US $27 billion, would have been unthinkable a few decades ago since the knowledge economy was only in a very marginal and fledgling state then. A table in the much acclaimed book titled *As the Future Catches You* by futurologist Juan Enriquez gives a list of the pre-eminent industries in the United States at the beginning of this century and the second column gives a list of the industries that emerged supreme in the 1960s, whereas the final column is concerned with the 1990s. Tobacco, wood and leather were the main sectors along with railroad in the 1900s and are just not seen in the 1960s where we have steel, automobiles, retailing and construction as the emergent sectors (Enriquez, 2001: 40–3). Surprisingly, there is no linear growth in the coming decades although these companies that have been on the top and have even found newer markets in the emerging economies around the world like the automobile industry and so on. A new category of industries where information is one of the key inputs has emerged in the meantime, and these new knowledge clusters are the main drivers of economic growth presently whose models are being replicated all over the world, and wherever conditions are not ideal for such growth there is outward migration as the host countries allow women to work freely, and thereby contribute to their economy (Ashgarzadeh and Sefa Dei, 2002: 31–6). The same is true of many countries in the south and the loss of our talented women is a national loss.

In South India, we see the Tidel Park in Chennai, hi-tech city in Hyderabad and Bangalore where one can see all the main companies of the world headquartered, such as Microsoft, Google, Adobe, Deloitte and virtually the main players in the Fortune 500 list, along with an endless number of new start-ups and the list is endless and ever growing (Balaji, 1994). This is in fact the first step towards migration towards the United States, since it is in these industries on Indian soil that the work culture and managerial atmosphere of the transnational companies are experienced by the knowledge workers. All these examples show the emergence of hi-tech work as drivers of economic growth in the current economy (Diafzio and Arnowitz, 1996: 52–8).

We have thus seen that this is a new period in world history and to characterize this period as good or bad would be premature for this is where the key lies, in the nature of the things to come. The present period is an open moment in history where there is a possibility for technology to emancipate humanity or enslave a section by the power of capitalist production; that is, the world can either become a techno-paradise or a cyber ghetto—both these extreme futuristic possibilities having technology as a central determinant.

One point to be noted here is that the digital divide is in a sense mirroring the gender divide because it overlaps women who do not have access to the information and skill sets needed in this knowledge economy as they are cut-off 'digitally'.

Having thus outlined the basic contours of the knowledge economy, we see that for the large-scale participation of women at all levels and not just as token representatives or junior partners, there are certain inherent possibilities in the knowledge societies that can be harnessed to this end. In this paper, I outline some of these areas where good beginnings can be made in India. First comes the notion of 'free' knowledge components such as open source and free ware, free online libraries, free training for skill sets and access to information, which is otherwise costly on the one hand; and on the other hand, the high cost leads to the proliferation of software piracy whose turnover in monetary terms is much more than many illegal activities put together. Some of these aspects have already been underlined in a book titled *Information Feudalism* (Drahos and Braithwaite, 2002: 1). As an opposite, the free software for different languages provided by the Indian government has equipped many people with basic skills to operate in this economy at little or no cost, otherwise many of them would be invisible. Second, (not in terms of order or hierarchy but for convenience sake) the knowledge society has its own set of problems and we keep hearing new words such as modern-day slavery, or digital pornography, cyber stalking, cyber harassment, privacy concerns and so on, all of which are detrimental to the progress of women and effective counters to this should also originate from the paradigms of knowledge economy like networking (Lyon, 2004: 2). A strong network of women's voices addressing these concerns would thereby provide a gendered argument and agenda.

We see that current developments such as the cure for cancer, rise of fuel cell car instead of petrol (as this would run on hydrogen), use of genetically engineered organisms for cleaning oil spills and so on, are all based on harnessing these new technologies (Parker, 2006: 1). If one region or country fails to give such facilities, then other regions are eagerly looking to attract such talent as there is a mad race to develop since this is an open moment. A brief survey of the immigration policies of many countries such as Singapore and New Zealand shows that such trends are emergent—the preference for elite high-skilled labour to work in the knowledge economy (Low, 2002: 422). Here too, a successful family is one in which both men and women work and they are knowledge workers that goes on to prove that the loss of one country can be the gain of another in this age (Ashgarzadeh and Sefa Dei, 2002: 31–6).

Having established that this is an open moment, what follows next is an urgency to seize the moment and gender the knowledge economy because this is an open moment where the possibilities for many changes are open, but the fact that the future may soon be colonized and out of bounds is also a looming reality.

The rise of China as the world's second largest economy is not only due to the fact that China has a very large export base centred on manufacturing but also due to the fact that China has emerged as a hi-tech economy (Richard Appelbaum, 2011). While China has emerged as a hi-tech economy, there is a constant media buzz both in the popular press and the academia about the competition between China and India, known as the tussle between the dragon and the elephant. A large majority of publications are engaged in the debate on whether China can continue to sustain its growth rate and the competition of India lies in the advantage of English education competency and also a democratic set-up (Gulati and Fan, 2007). It is clearly evident from a reading of these trends that both these countries want to be early entrants in the knowledge economy and have learnt the lessons of being late entrants in the industrial revolution, that cost them dearly and made them junior partners in a new world system led by the industrial revolution when they lost their status. However, what is absent here in these debates is the wholesale omission of gender as a category in the long-term vision of economic growth of these countries. Along with the growth of India and China, the global order has also seen the evolution of a new term BRICS (Brazil, India, China, Russia and South Africa) signalling that these countries are there to play a key role in the politics and economics of the future as assessed by influential newspapers such as *The Telegraph* (http://www.telegraph.co.uk/finance/comment/liamhalligan/8455805/The-West-has-no-God-given-right-to-be-in-charge-just-ask-the-BRICS.html) and investment houses such as Goldman (http://www2.goldmansachs.com/ideas/brics/index.html). Like China and India, this myopic vision of the future where the omission of gender in the planning is reproduced in the visions of these countries too. This is already evident in the Tiger economies of Asia where the knowledge economy with all aspects of techno-entrepreneurship is seen in full play and a new generation of knowledge workers has emerged in these global cities such as Singapore, Hong Kong and Tokyo. But, here again, one may add the absence of women in the top levels and their visibility at the lower levels (Brooks, 2006: 24–7). How quickly a country can develop is best illustrated by the meteoric rise of South Korea, that was the poorest country in the world in 1953, to one of the most developed economies and also the third largest generator of patents. However, the emergence of South Korea as an advanced knowledge economy has a flip side where we see that there are only 4 per cent of women enrolled in the science education stream (Dahlman and Andersson, 2000: 6).

All the above-mentioned developments signify change at an unprecedented speed that is fundamentally altering the global society and as the case of successful small nations such as South Korea illustrate, the knowledge economy has been understood by the newly-emerging economies as the driver of growth but has also shown that it has bypassed women. A refreshing change comes about in the book titled *The Gendering of the Knowledge Economy* (Walby et al., 2009). However, the focus of the present article is limited to a critique of the knowledge economy and highlighting the urgency of the open moment, which is a critical turning point. This turning point is not highlighted radically since change was slow and therefore adaptation also followed the old organic method. To quote Alvin Toffler, "Because change was slow, he could adapt unconsciously, 'organically.' Today, unconscious adaptation is no longer adequate. Faced with the power to alter the gene, to create new species and to populate the planets or depopulate the earth, man must now assume conscious control of evolution itself. Avoiding future shock as he rides the waves of change, he must master evolution, shaping tomorrow to human need. Instead of rising in revolt against it, he must, from this historic moment on, anticipate and design the future" (Toffler, 1991: 317). This establishes that change is not unidirectional, and therefore an intervention is needed. When we examine this statement in the context of the rise of knowledge economies in the North, East Asian tigers and the BRICS countries, we see that the progression of science and technology and development is not gender neutral but highly biased in favour of a masculine model that excludes women and thus excludes women. However, in the process of getting stabilized, there lies the danger that these biases may become normative, and by then the open moment may well become closed. This example is well illustrated in the shift of the terms from digital divide to information feudalism, suggesting that there is a rapid and renewed encroachment of capitalism into those hitherto free domains. What has to be done lies in the area of policies, planning and delivery, but much more important and urgent is the recognition of the problem and its urgency and by extension bring it on the agenda.

It would not be out of place to quote Toffler again where he says that "yet only rarely does an entire globe-girdling system of power fly apart in this fashion. It is an even rarer moment in history when all the rules of the power game change at once, and the very nature of power is revolutionized. Yet, that is exactly what is happening today. Power, which to a large extent defines us as individuals and as nations, is itself being redefined" (Toffler, 1991: 24). As one of the early prophets of change, Toffler foresaw many elements of the future, but his lack of devoting much space to gender has, however, laid such genealogies where he is invoked without the gender question that ultimately remains an incomplete agenda.

To conclude, we see that this is an open moment in history, a very rare and priceless moment where there are multiple options open and which are getting closed by the minute at lightning speed. Unless there is an urgent attempt to use these spaces, global capitalism will devour them, and therefore action is necessary at all levels and the first step in this direction would be to place this topic on the global agenda. The soft power of the knowledge economy, therefore, has the potential to feminize the workforce as equal partners. To make this possible, this moment has to be addressed and fought with the new weapons at all levels. But what is, however, important is to understand the open nature of this historic context that is still open and offers us directions to steer the course of history. Recognition of this context and the possibilities that it offers and also the speed at which this is being closed is of paramount importance.

In the ultimate analysis, it may be said that as the knowledge economy is reconfiguring the power relations between different regions and countries, the gendering of the knowledge economy will extend this to a massive realignment of global order that would be marked by the gendering of world politics and thus, inaugurate a new era taking full advantage of the open moment.

REFERENCES

Appelbaum, Richard, 2011, *The Chinese Century? Some Foreign Policy Implications of China's Move to High-Tech Innovation* by Ted Tedesco, http://vimeo.com/21611644

Ashgarzadeh, Alireza and George J. Sefa Dei, 2002, 'What is to be Done? A Look at Some Causes and Consequences of the African Brain Drain', *African Issues*, 30(1): 31–6.

Balaji, R., 1994, 'The Formation and Structure of High Technological Industrial Complex in Bangalore'. Unpublished Ph.D dissertation (*The Rise of The Network Society*, Malden, MA: Blackwell Publishers, in Manuel Castells, 2000, reprint). Berkeley, CA: University of California.

Brooks, Ann, 2006, *Gendered Work in Asian Cities: The New Economy and Changing Labour Markets*. Burlington, VT: Ashgate Publishing, Ltd.

Dahlman, Carl J. and Thomas Andersson (Eds.), 2000, 'World Bank, and Organisation for Economic Co-operation and Development'. In *Korea and the Knowledge-Based Economy: Making the Transition*, Paris: OECD Publishing.

Diafzio, William and Stanley Arnowitz, 1996, 'High Technology and Work Tomorrow', *Annals of the American Academy of Political and Social Science*, 544: 52–67.

Drahos, Peter and John Braithwaite, 2002, *Information Feudalism*. London: Earthscan Publications.

Eisenhart, Mary, 1994, 'Alvin and Heidi Toffler on Life and Work in the Information Age', MicroTimes, #118 (3 January), yow.com/marye/tofflers94.html

Enriquez, Juan, 2001, *As the Future Catches You*. New York: Crown Business.

Gulati, Ashok, and Shenggen Fan, 2007, *The Dragon and the Elephant: Agricultural and Rural Reforms in China and India*. Maryland, Johns Hopkins University Press.

Lewis, Peter, 2004, 'Broadband Wonderland', *Fortune*, September 20: 191–98.

Low, Linda, 2002, 'Globalisation and the Political Economy of Singapore's Policy on Foreign Talent and High Skills', *Journal of Education and Work*, 15(4): 421–22.

Lyon, David, 2004, 'New Directions in Theory'. In *The Information Society Reader*, edited by Frank Webster, London: Routledge.

Norris, Pippa, 2001, *Digital Divide*. New York: Cambridge University Press.

Parker, Randall, 2006, 'Eternal Youth, Overpopulation, and Instincts to Reproduce Bioethics Rejuvenation (25 November), www.futurepundit.com

Rifkin, Jeremy, 1995, *The End of Work*. New York: G.P. Putnam's Sons, p. 5.

The Observer, Sunday, 14 January 2001, http://observer.guardian.co.uk/business/story/0,6903,421888,00.html

Toffler, Alvin, 1991, *Powershift: Knowledge, Wealth, and Violence at the Edge of the 21st Century*. New York: Bantam Books.

Walby, Sylvia, Heidi Gottfried, Karin Gottschall and Mari Osawa, 2009, *Gendering the Knowledge Economy: Comparative Perspectives*. New York: Palgrave Macmillan.

Part IV

Violence and Sexual Harassment

CHAPTER 11

Divorced Women in Bangladesh: Socio-Demographic Profile

Neaz Ahmed

Divorce is a universal phenomenon. It is a socially sanctioned arrangement whereby marriage is formally terminated and the family group dissolved (Bertrand, 1967). The practice of divorce is found in most of the societies, but it varies in the conditions that must be met, the sanctions it implies, the frequency with which it is used, the disposition of and responsibility for the care of children, the disposition of family property and effects, the status assigned to divorced persons, and the rituals, procedure and ceremonies that legalize it. The magnitude and trends of divorce may also differ from one society to another and from one religion to another. And also, the perceptions of divorce may not be similar in many countries. For example, in countries such as the United States, Australia and some European countries, the rates of divorce are high compared with other countries.

Like other institutions, marriage is a social institution. Johnson (1970) argued that wherever we look in history or in the contemporary world, whether at civilized people or the most primitive, we find that social life is moulded to a great extent by social institutions such as marriage. There is no society on record, which is without this institution, whatever the cultural pattern may be. The idea of marriage, however, differs from society to society, conditioned always by time and place. As a culturally and socially recognized institution, people almost believe that family and sexual relations should be within legal marriage.

TRENDS OF DIVORCE PHENOMENON

In Asia, the rates of divorce have not been increasing rapidly in many countries due to several reasons. In a country like India, among Hindus, marriage is a sacrament. Although divorce is permitted according to the Hindu Marriage Act 1955, the rate of divorce is increasing slowly. In some cases, divorce is prohibited according to their internal customs and values. But in the Muslim community all over the world, divorce is permitted according to their respective personal and state laws. However, it varies from country to country. The conditions under which divorce is granted vary from painless procedure to long drawn-out, traumatic experiences, etc. In extended family structures, where the individual is surrounded by a large group of kin and his status is well defined and protected, divorce involves little change in regular behaviour and hardly any emotional upheaval. In a society where there is a strong emphasis on attachments within the conjugal family unit, divorce is likely to mean emotional shock, social stigma and economic problems for at least one if not both spouses, as well as for children (Bertrand, 1967).

In Muslim religion, males dominate the females and the religion upholds the husbands. Moreover, the personal laws regulate personal matters such as marriage, divorce, etc. Some laws are against the women and in favour of men. Men are taking advantages by depriving women of their rights. Indeed, it is invariably the law that deprives women. Even after divorce, a woman's identity in society is changed and the societal people call her as "bad woman". They are considered as divorced women. Immediately after divorce, she needs support primarily for sustenance. Who will give this support, if nothing has been provided for by the husband? If parents are not in a position to look after them, where will these women go for fulfilling their basic needs? Apart from physical needs, these women have sexual, social and emotional needs. If the family and society do not look after these women, their problems will remain unabated untill their death.

In Bangladesh, women are mostly dependent on their male counterparts for the fulfilment of basic needs. But the situation of urban women is somewhat different. Due to urban socio-economic conditions, women are working outside their home as paid workers. They interact with other people outside of the family.

Women are acquiring new knowledge, technology and skills. They can determine what is good or bad and have their own likes and dislikes. Traditional norms and customs have been changing substantially. Sometimes, urban women do not bother about the domination by their husbands. As far as divorce is concerned, a husband can divorce his wife at his own will without the intervention of court through the Arbitration Council, but women cannot. Although it has been said that marriage is a civil contract, there is no strict provision for marriage registration. There is also no provision for the maintenance of divorced women. The provision of maintenance is only for minor children of the divorced women. However, in a few cases, divorced women are getting proper maintenance from their spouses. The structure of Bangladeshi family is mostly a joint one. But, urban family is mostly a single one; usually, women can take shelter in their parents' houses. But for these women, shelter is not sufficient when social, psychological and emotional needs are grossly denied.

Divorce is not uniform in character throughout different societies. Bangladesh is not exceptional. In Bangladesh, unfortunately, the family today appears to be a complex and troubled social institution. The marital conflicts and divorce are on the increase in Bangladesh and desertions are common. Marriages are breaking down in a larger number of cases because of various reasons. Sometimes, people ignore the marriage and divorce-related laws. Illegal divorce is more than legal divorce. Divorce is very common, and it is somewhat an easy process in Bangladeshi Muslim society. Due to the easy process, statistics show that women are giving more divorce than men. In view of the easy legal process and not obeying the law, polygamy is taking place in Bangladeshi Muslim community particularly among lower class people. When polygamy is legally permitted, people do not feel ashamed to take an additional wife and many times opt for this.

The above theoretical discussion reveals that the problem of divorce in Bangladesh has different dimensions. There are no uniformities about divorce and marriage laws. The problem of divorce is more acute in Muslim community than others in particular, because divorce is rampant in the Muslim community for trivial and sometimes without any reason. Hence, this study has been thought of to understand the problem of divorced women in Bangladesh.

REVIEW OF RELATED LITERATURE

Literature on divorce and divorce-related issues is enormous in developed countries, particularly in the United States. Over the past three decades, family and family disorganization has become a burning issue all over the world. Efforts are being made at the international level to maintain and protect family life. Despite these, divorce is increasing, and this has become a matter of concern among sociologists and psychologists in Western societies. But, in the least developing countries such as Bangladesh, this aspect has not been given due importance as compared to developed countries. The existing literature is being reviewed here.

Education and age are two important factors which impact the increase and decrease of incidence of divorce. If an educated man marries an educated woman and the age difference is not wide, the chances of incidence of divorce can decline. Shaikh (1998) in his study on social and demographic correlates of divorce in rural Bangladesh by using data from the Demographic Surveillance System in Matlab in Bangladesh for the period from 1974 to 1993 finds that the propensity to divorce in rural Bangladesh declined significantly with an increase in the number of children. It is interesting to note that the relationship between husband and wife's education and the likelihood of divorce was negative and significant. The incidence of divorce declined as the level of education of the husband and wife increased. It is evident that the number of divorce cases was significantly lower among businessmen and agricultural labourers than among farmers. Divorce was higher among 'love matches' than 'arranged' ones. The age difference between husband and wife could influence the incidence of divorce. The number of divorces occurring within the first three years of marriage was significantly higher than in longer duration marriages.

Prior marital status and socio-economic conditions of both parties are considered as a risk for divorce. Divorce can occur in many cases, when both husband and wife have weak economic status, illiteracy and early ages of marriage. Alam et al. (2000) examined the effects of spouses' prior marital status and socio-demographic characteristics on the risk of divorce of 1,762 Muslim marriages recorded in 1982–1983 in Teknaf, Bangladesh. Grooms' prior marital status was characterized into never married, divorced, widowed or polygynous (already cohabiting with one or more wives), and brides' prior marital status was categorized into never married, divorced and widowed. Divorce was recorded by following the marriages prospectively for five years. A longitudinal study design was used. A discrete-time hazard logistic model was used to estimate the effects of spouses' prior marital status and a number of socio-demographic variables on the risk of divorce. Polygynous marriage, remarriage and divorce were found to be common in this traditional Muslim community. The odds of divorce were 2.5 times higher for grooms' polygynous and 1.6 times higher for brides' remarriages compared to their peers' first marriages. The odds of divorce decreased with marriage duration. The grooms' and brides' low socio-economic status, illiteracy and early age at marriage increased the odds of divorce. The odds of divorce were much higher if there was no birth in the preceding six months.

Generally, husbands are more prone to taking initiative of divorce because of the unilateral power of divorcing wives; husbands are taking advantage to divorce their wives. In many cases, divorce is taking place not in a legal way. In that context, Kafi (1982) carried out a study of 359 divorced, separated, abandoned, deserted women in 11 districts of Bangladesh. He found that out of 359 women, 350 were Muslims and 9 were Hindus. A majority (89%) of the divorces had been given by the husbands. Apart froms legal mode of divorce, there was some illegal forms of divorce. Many of the objections, which came from the relations of the husband and wife, were based on their knowledge and experience in the light of traditional 'fatwas', and these objections were not different from that of the religious leaders. It is indicated from the study that men were giving more divorce than women. Here, the researcher has not mentioned the rate of illegal divorce.

Through legal means, rich and middle-class people are taking more divorce initiative than poor people. For a poor man, divorce is nothing to lose, as their life is not ideal value oriented. Ahmed (2001) concluded that divorce was extinct among rich and middle class, although it existed among the poor. For the poor, divorce was easy as there was nothing to receive and nothing to lose at the dissolution of marriage. This was because the large dowry and DOWER payment were rarely made or agreed among them. In most cases, permanent or long separation was chosen rather than actual divorce. Divorce brought a bad name for the family, and the women and her children became a burden if she could not marry again.

Increased divorce rate in Bangladesh can be reduced through women's education. Education can give women empowerment, consciousness and better adjustment with husband and in-laws. Islam and Ahmed (2001) found that while dissolutions due to widowhood were a decreasing trend, the dissolution due to divorce was increasing in the recent past. The resultant effect of these two opposing trends has been a downward trend in the incidence of dissolution due to all causes. Both primary and above primary levels of education significantly reduce the risk of divorce. This implies that efforts should be made by the policy-makers to encourage young women to continue their education to as high as possible.

Peaceful conjugal life can result in a peaceful family and can protect marital breakdown. Rahman (1997) studied marriage, separation and divorce among middle-class families in Dhaka city by randomly selecting 100 married couples. She found that to establish a peaceful conjugal life, some factors such as age, age gap, social consistency between couples, financial solvency, etc., should be considered before marriage. Further, for preventing family disorganization, separation or divorce after marriage, people should be made aware and conscious of creating a peaceful conjugal life. She argued that peaceful conjugal life can prevent separation, family disorganization and divorce.

The empirical studies, which are being reviewed from Bangladesh context, reveal that the phenomenon of divorce has its multidimensional approach. Post-divorce phenomenon is entirely ignored. The aspects which were being explored by the studies were that divorce occurred due to early age of marriage and where there was no child. Although polygamy existed among Bangladeshi Muslims, it was more among higher income groups than higher and middle-class people. Most of the study was conducted in rural areas. In rural areas, illegal divorce was rampant and husbands were giving more divorce than wives. Marriage registration and DOWER were integral part of the marriage. It is seen that many women were not aware of that. Divorce was correlated with many factors such as age, education, occupation, dowry, dower, prior marital status, etc. The causes of divorce were also varied.

RESEARCH METHODOLOGY

There are two broad significances to the study of divorce phenomenon in Bangladesh. One is its legal aspect and another is the socio-psychological aspect. First, in legal aspect, theoretical studies show that the husband can divorce his wife at his own will, but the wife cannot do so. This provision is based on breakdown theory of divorce. But most of the divorce laws are based on the faulty or consent theory of divorce. If either party is at fault, other party can seek a divorce. Thus, there is a limitation of divorce laws among Muslims in Bangladesh as compared with other religions. Second, there is no post-divorce maintenance provision for Muslim divorced women in Bangladesh, which exists in other religions. Third, women's initiative of divorce depends on men's will. If the husband gives power of divorcing to her only, then she can divorce the husband. Otherwise, she has to go to the court for seeking divorce on certain grounds. In the socio-psychological aspect, by considering the easy process of divorce in Bangladesh, what are the conditions of women after divorce? First, how is a divorced woman treated by her kin and non-kin? Second, in what way are they socially attached and adjusted? Third, whether their social status has suffered or not? Fourth, how do divorced women get social support? Fifth, how is their social life when they live without the opposite sex? Sixth, what are the physical and psychological health problems with which they suffer from? Seventh, how do they live, who supports them, when there is no maintenance provision after divorce? To answer these questions, this study has been undertaken to examine the psycho-social and economic conditions of divorced women in Bangladesh (with special reference to Dhaka city).

The aim of the present study is to understand the psycho-social and economic conditions of the divorced women. To achieve this aim, the following objectives have been formulated: (a) to know the socio-economic background of divorced women, (b) to study about the marriage and marital life of divorced women, (c) to analyse the process and procedure of marriage and divorce among the divorced women, (d) to examine the factors leading to divorce, (e) to identify the social reaction towards divorced women, (f) to understand the social adjustment and social relationships of divorced women, (g) to know the social status of divorced women,

(h) to study the social support that the divorced women receive, (i) to explore the social life of divorced women, (j) to understand the psychological conditions of divorced women and to assess the present economic condition of divorced women.

The research design for the present study is a descriptive-diagnostic one, which aims to describe, record, analyse and interpret the conditions that exist. It is also a diagnostic study as the cause and effect are being studied very clearly. Dissolved cases of divorce settled by the Arbitration Council of Dhaka City Corporation and Judicial Family Court of Dhaka District/Metropolitan between 1997 and 2003 up to June constitute the universe of the study.

Non-probability sampling technique has been considered in this study. Among the non-probability sampling techniques, only purposive sampling has been used. There are some government and non-government organizations in Dhaka city of Bangladesh from which divorced women get legal and material assistance apart from Arbitration Council and Judicial Family Court. Sample for this study was drawn from four organizations following certain criterion. They were (a) only Muslim (Sunni) divorced women have been selected for this study, because of divorce not being allowed in the Hindu community; (b) only those who obtained decree from the Arbitration Council and Judicial Family Courts were selected. Illegal divorce cases were excluded for this study. A total of 200 dissolved divorced cases from four organizations have been selected.

Data needed for the study have been collected from both primary and secondary sources. The researcher himself through personal interview has collected the data from the primary sources: the divorced women. Secondary data have been collected from the individual records of the divorced women of the respective institutions. The study consists of five tools: (a) Organizational Record, (b) Interview Schedule, (c) General Health Questionnaire, (d) Alienation Scale, and (e) Case Study. But the data presented in this article have been collected only through interview schedule.

To assess the suitability, efficacy, comprehensibility and applicability of the tools used for data collection, pre-testing was carried out prior to the main study by interviewing 10 divorced women within the geographical area of the study. The data have been analysed by using statistical techniques such as (a) percentages have been calculated for a large number of variables under the study; (b) mean has been applied to determine the relative significance of the individual variables; (c) standard deviation has been applied calculated at some variables, namely age, separation period, duration of marital life and psychological conditions; (d) chi-square test, 't' test and Karl Pearson's coefficient correlation have been computed and applied for hypothesis testing.

OPERATIONAL DEFINITION OF CONCEPTS

Marriage: It has been defined as a culturally approved relationship of one man and one woman or of one man and two or more women (polygyny) in which sexual intercourse is endorsed between the opposite partners, and there is generally an expectation that the children will be born of the union enjoying the full birth status right of their society. In this study, marriage means legal and social relationships according to marriage law.

Divorce: It is the dissolution of marriage. It truly is a complete turn from the way of life the couple had so far (Pothen, 1986). Divorce in the proper and strict sense of the term means complete rupture of the marital bond where the persons divorced returning to their original state of being free to marry. In this study, divorce means legal marital dissolution by decree of divorce generated by Family Court and Arbitration Council.

Divorced Women: It refers to Muslim (Sunni) divorced women who underwent divorce through Arbitration Council and Judicial Family Court.

DATA ANALYSIS AND INTERPRETATION

Age is an important variable in marital disruption. The study reveals that majority (68%) of the divorced women were in the age group of 18–25 years at the time of marriage. But, at present, a majority (60.5%) of them is in the age group of 18–25 years. Zaman (1990), in his study of Kurigram district in Bangladesh, found that 65 per cent of the divorced women were in the age group of 8–13 at the time of marriage. He has studied 20 divorced women, 5 each from four Upazilas in Kurigram district, northern part of Bangladesh. A survey conducted by the Bangladesh Bureau of Statistics (1998) indicates that the highest number of women had been married off in the age group of 15–19 years. Islam and Ahmed (2001), in their study on correlates of marriage dissolution in Bangladesh, involving interviews of 11,236 households found that the number of women aged 30 years or more who were still single was effectively zero. Almost half of them got married before the age of 18 years. Marriage occurs earlier among women growing up in rural areas, earlier among less-educated women than among better-educated women and earlier among Muslim women than among non-Muslim counterparts. They also found that post-pubertal marriages were less likely to end in divorce of those who were married before or at about the same time of their first menstruation. Several studies in Western societies, namely, Menken et al (1981), Mohahan (1953), Shaikh (1998), Burchinal (1965), Glick and Norton (1971), Bumpass and Sweet (1972), Schoen (1975) and Lee (1977) conclude that delayed marriage because of education would increase the capability of normative role performance by increasing mental maturity and thereby decreasing tension in marital life.

The legal age of marriage for girls is 18 years. But the study reveals that 38 (19%) divorced women had been married off before the prescribed age. It indicates that among the divorced women, child marriages were good in number. The earlier studies conducted in Bangladesh context were long ago and were general. The overall age of marriage in Bangladesh is less. Due to conservative

Table 11.1 *Age distribution of the respondents, N = 200*

Age group (in years)	*At present*		*At the time of marriage*	
	Frequency	*%*	*Frequency*	*%*
<15	0	0.0	2	1.0
15–18	24	12.0	38	19.0
18–25	121	60.5	136	68.0
25–35	44	22.0	24	12.0
35–45	11	5.0	0	0.0
Total	200	100.0	200	100.0
Mean + SD	**22.9 + 5.3**		**20.3 + 3.6**	

attitude, acute poverty and giving less importance to the daughters, girls are married off at a lower age. This is especially because parents may think that there is no benefit in investing money on daughters. Daughters have to go to the husbands' houses sooner or later. With this realization, daughters are married off at an early age (Table 11.1).

Education

Table 11.2 indicates that 46.5 per cent of the divorced women were illiterate and secondary-level educated at the time of marriage. Only a few divorced women were graduates and above. Regarding the education of divorced women, Kafi (1982) finds in rural Bangladesh that 70 per cent of the divorced women were illiterate. Similar finding has been reported by Pothen (1986) in Indore, Madhya Pradesh, in a study of urban Hindu divorced women. Her study involving 200 divorced women and their spouses revealed that a vast majority of divorced women (82%) were literate at the time of marriage. Several authors in Western countries, namely Guest (1991), Jones (1981; 1995), Spanier and Glick (1981), conclude that education is directly related to marital happiness and satisfaction, which leads to lower incidence of marital dissolution. Educated men and women

Table 11.2 *Distribution of educational status of the respondents, N = 200*

Level of education	*At present*	*At the time of marriage*		
	Frequency	*%*	*Frequency*	*%*
Illiterate	34	17.0	34	17.0
Primary (i–v)	37	18.5	37	18.5
Secondary (vi–x)	22	11.0	22	11.0
Higher secondary	45	22.5	48	24.0
Diploma holders	9	4.5	10	5.0
Graduate	33	16.5	31	15.5
Postgraduate	16	8.0	16	8.0
Others	3	1.5	2	1.0
Total	**200**	**100.0**	**200**	**100.0**

can adjust with each other very easily. But when there is no formal education and difference in educational attainment is more, personal differences can be aroused in relation to respect and the incidence of marital dissolution can occur. But Houseknecht and Spanier (1980) find contradictory conclusions in Western countries. They conclude that women who began graduate studies after marriage were more likely to divorce or separate than women who began graduate studies before marriage.

In Bangladesh, parents give less importance to the daughter than the son in terms of education. But urban scenario is somewhat different. Urban parents are more conscious about education. As compared with rural areas, urban divorced women are more educated. But it is not more as compared with men. Although after marriage, divorced women do not continue their studies in a large number of cases, certain improvements in education are found in higher secondary, graduation and other levels. Two divorced women improved their education from secondary to graduation. They might have realized that education would bring their livelihood, freedom from dependence on parents. On the whole, it is clear that the educational level of Muslim women was very low as compared to Muslim men.

OCCUPATION

Among the 200 divorced women, a majority of them (71%) had no regular work at the time of marriage. They were mostly housewives and students. Among the working divorced women, higher number was engaged in garment sector. Garment sector is very popular in urban areas, particularly in Dhaka city. Momen (1985) found in six slums in Dhaka city, among 150 divorced and separated women, a majority of the respondents, that is about 60 per cent, had no occupation at all other than being housewives at the time of marriage. Life in a slum is tough, fragile and hard. People come from rural areas to urban areas and take shelter in slums. As compared with other households, slum women work more as they need to survive by themselves. Basically, they are the poorest of the poor class. Pothen (1986) also found that 83.5 per cent of the divorced women had no regular work at the time of marriage. Akhter (2000) argued that in Bangladesh education linked with increased earning power helped strengthen women's position within the family, society and economy. Cherlin (1979) concluded that female employment and marital dissolution were casually related and that the increases in labour force participation had led to higher levels of divorce in advanced societies. Wives' paid work had been ironically associated with a higher probability of divorce. Kenkel (1966) concluded that upper middle occupational level contributed less, middle level proportionately and lower income level much more to divorce cases. Raab and Selznich (1964) maintained that the higher the occupational level, the lower the divorce rate.

Generally, in Bangladeshi society, one finds husband as a breadwinner and wife as a house-maker. In that sense, a majority of the divorced women are unemployed. But after divorce, the situation differs slightly. As many as 10.5 per cent of the divorced women had taken up job, as they were unemployed at the time of marriage. It might be because of their inability to depend on parents that they took a job. This indicates that divorced women not only faced social ostracism but also faced economic dependence.

INCOME

The study shows that divorced women had low income at the time of marriage and even at present. This implies that divorced women had to depend on others for their livelihood. Papanek (1979) argued that women might be able to gain higher independence and a stronger role in decision-making when they earned money independently and consequentially influenced the use of family resources. Women after divorce had no financial support to make a living. For many women, divorce was not expected eventually. Peterson (1989) found that women who divorced at least 10 years ago had significant earnings and income advantages over recently divorced women. Most longitudinal studies in Western societies—Hoffman (1977), Mott and Moore (1978), Corcoran (1979), Espenshade (1979), Moore (1979), Duncan and Hoffman (1985) and Peterson (1989)—indicated that women's economic vulnerability was prolonged for at least five years, unless remarriage occurred and despite dramatic increases in labour participation and hours worked upon separation and divorce. Moore and Waite (1981) found that the risk of divorce increased as wives' relative contributions to total family income increased. Spainer and Glick (1981) maintained that low income was one of the basic reasons for higher probability of teenage marriages ending in divorce. Raab and Selznich (1964) concluded that divorce was a consequence not of poverty but of the social disorganization with which poverty was so closely linked. Low-income families were highly vulnerable not only to divorce but also to other factors, which effectively dissolved the family, viz., desertion and separation.

The overall economic condition of Bangladesh is not encouraging. Moreover, a good number of divorced women are engaged in unskilled labour force such as garment sector and do not have qualifications. As they work in unskilled jobs, the salary of this sector is very low. On the whole, it is indicated that divorce was taking place among low-income people in urban areas of Bangladesh and making them lead a life which they never anticipated.

TYPE OF FAMILY

The study reveals that a higher percentage (84.5%) belonged to single families at present. Similarly, a higher percentage (62.5%) belonged to nuclear families during marital life. The type of family does matter with regard to marital disruption. There is a contradiction whether divorce occurs more in joint families or single families. Sociologists claim that family disorganization is minimum in such larger family units. In the study of Fonseca (1966) in Bombay and Metha (1975) in Delhi, Bombay and Udaipur, among 50 Hindu divorced and separated women (25 each from lower and middle classes), they found that a majority of the cases of family disorganization and dissolution were in joint families. In extended family system, influences from others such as mothers-in-law, sisters-in-law, etc., were more compared with single and nuclear families. Couples in single and nuclear families enjoy more liberty than extended family. Aziz (1979) similarly concluded that in Bangladesh, although the joint family was approved by social tradition, in the study he could not find a single family in which five generations lived together under the same roof. In the study area of North district of Bangladesh, it was rare to find a family in which all nuclear families of three generations lived together under one roof. It was common for sons to separate from their parents within a few years of their marriage. As a result of this

Table 11.3 *Distribution of type of family of the respondents, N = 200*

	At present		*During marital life*	
Family type	*Frequency*	*%*	*Frequency*	*%*
Single*	169	84.5	61	30.5
Nuclear**	29	14.5	125	62.5
Extended***	2	1.0	14	7.0
Total	**200**	**100.0**	**200**	**100.0**

*A couple with or without children

**A couple with or without married children

***Two or more married couples between whom there is usually a link such as parents and unmarried son(s) or daughter(s) or brother–brother, etc.

separation, they started as an elementary family. But Bertrand (1967) concluded that in Western societies, in an extended family structure where the individual was surrounded by a large group of kin, his status was well defined and protected, and divorce had little chance of going through.

In Bangladesh, overall extended family is less compared with single or nuclear family particularly in urban areas, because of accommodation problem, privacy and individualistic tendency of husband and wife. Another reason is employment and overall economic condition. When a person gets a job, he cannot afford a good house and bring parents or other family members. The researcher assumes that due to above circumstances, a majority of the divorced women belonged to single and nuclear families. It indicates that cases of divorce are more among nuclear families than single and extended families. Although extended family is less compared with single and nuclear family forms in Bangladesh, it cannot be a cause of marital dissolution (Table 11.3).

NUMBER OF CHILDREN

It is evident from the study that 82.5 per cent of the divorced women had no children at the time of the study. It indicates that cases of divorce were more among no-children couples. Spanier and Glick (1981) found that the greater the number of children, the lesser the propensity to divorce. Moreover, they found that the sex of the children made a difference in marital stability. Families with at least one son were less likely to divorce than those with all daughters. The livelihood of marital disruption was greater when the marriage involved no children and was least when there were three or more children. Thornton and Freedman (1983) found that approximately 60 per cent of divorced couples had children.

Children can be regarded as a component while taking the divorce decision. Moreover, children can be a burden after divorce, so the couple may not think about divorce. But when there is no child, advantages are more particularly about thinking of remarriage. At the same time, sexes of children are a factor. The husband may expect a son instead of daughter. When repeatedly daughters are born, the husband may decide to marry again for a son and divorce his existing wife/wives. Naturally and culturally, son is valuable than daughter. In this respect, divorce cases are more among no-child and daughters-only couples.

SUGGESTIONS

On the basis of major findings, the following suggestions were recommended:

1. The study reveals that the age of marriage of divorced women was less as compared to other countries such as India. Moreover, some marriages took place before the age prescribed by law. Indeed, child marriages were proportionally more. Due to early age at marriage, women faced a lot of problems in the husbands' house. They might not have prepared for marriage, but they were married. The problem was mainly of adjustment. In Bangladeshi custom, the wife has to please her husband and in-laws as well. Otherwise, she will not be treated well by her husband and in-laws. Education can play a crucial role to make good adjustment with the new environment. On the other hand, the girl should get proper socialization at an early age, which can be a pillar of later life. The problem exists due to child marriage. It is the responsibility of the parents to take appropriate steps to overcome the situation.
2. Parents should change their attitude towards daughters. There should be no discrimination between sons and daughters. Parents also should provide opportunities for proper socialization and personality development, so that they can adjust with any abnormal and untoward situation if it arises. They should

give proper education to their daughters. If girls get education, they will raise their voice in in-laws' house and the age of marriage can be increased.

3. The government should give more and more incentives for girls' education. If educated girls marry educated boys, problems in marital life can be minimized.
4. Under the existing law, among Bangladeshi Muslims, the husband can divorce his wife on his accord will without intervention of court through Arbitration Council, but the wife cannot. Wife can only do so if the husband had given the power of divorcing him on certain conditions or without conditions at the time of marriage registration on registration form. Otherwise, the wife has to go to the court seeking a divorce on certain grounds under the Dissolution of Muslim Marriage Act 1939. There is no equal right of divorce for Bangladeshi Muslim women. Moreover, husbands' unilateral power of divorcing wife and delegation of power to the wife are being misused to some extent. Sometimes, when wives get the power of divorcing husbands, they divorce them without sufficient reasons. And on the husbands' part, they randomly misuse the present existing law. In this situation, in order to protect the marital life, individual right, equal right and social justice, appropriate laws are required, which can give equal protection, and ensure social justice and equal strength. Religious leaders and civil society can play a pivotal role in curbing the problem. People should convince the religious leaders so that unilateral divorce should be/and can be abolished. Civil society can create awareness among people about that. Overall, there is a need for social action so that the government can take some initiative about reforming the law.

CONCLUSION

Divorce is a problem in Bangladesh from both legal and sociological points of view. This problem is not confined only to a specific class. It exists in almost all classes of society, but more so in lower income groups than in higher income groups. The cases of divorce exist in almost all economic and social classes of people in Dhaka city. The overall socio-economic conditions of divorced women are not good. This finding is related to the socio-economic situation in Bangladesh. Divorce is more among women who have no children. Children become a factor in divorce decision. When there is no child, both the parties can take the decision of divorce very easily. Cultural values and family origin play a role in marital adjustment. We live in a society where we need peace, harmony, mutual interaction and understanding. Collective efforts should be made for greater interests of the society even in family life. When family breaks down, everything breaks down. Generally, we believe that divorce is the primary solution of marital conflict, but after divorce, problems are more acute and to a large extent intolerable. Divorced women and their children are becoming vulnerable within our society and face a lot of problems due to their poor socio-economic conditions.

REFERENCES

Ahmed, Shaheen, 2001, 'Marriage Practices in Rural Bangladesh: An Anthropological Overview', *Empowerment: A Journal of Women for Women*, 8: 37–48.

Akhter, Salma, 2000, 'Changing Role and Status of Working Women in Urban Bangladesh: A Study of Dhaka City', *Social Science Review*, 17(1): 223–45.

Alam, Nurul K., Sajal K. Saha and Jeroen K. van Ginneken, 2000, 'Determinants of Divorce in a Traditional Muslim Community in Bangladesh', *Demographic Research*, 3(4): 75–8.

Aziz, Ashraful K.M., 1979, *Kinship in Bangladesh*. Dhaka: International Centre for Diarrhoeal Disease Research.

Bangladesh Bureau of Statistics (BBS), 1998, *Health and Demographic Survey*. Dhaka: Demographic and Health Wing, Ministry of Health and Family Welfare.

Bertrand, Alvin L., 1967, *Basic Sociology*. New York: Appleton-Century-Crofts.

Bumpass, Larry L. and James A. Sweet, 1972, 'Differentials in Marital Instability: 1970', *American Sociological Review*, 37(6): 754–66.

Burchinal, L.G., 1965, 'Trends and Prospects for Young Marriage in the United States', *Journal of Marriage and the Family*, 27(2): 243–54.

Cherlin, Andrew J., 1979, 'Work Life and Marital Dissolution'. In *Divorce and Separation*, edited by G. Levinger and O. Moles, New York: Basic Books.

Corcoran, M., 1979, 'The Economic Consequences of Marital Dissolution for Women in the Middle Years', *Sex Roles*, 5(1): 343–53.

Duncan, G.J, and S.,D. Hoffman.,1985, '*Economic Consequences of Marital Instability. IN Horizontal Equity, Uncertainty and Economic Well-being*, edited by Dravid T. Sweeding, Chicago: Chicago University Press.

Espenshade, T.J., 1979, 'The Economic Consequences of Divorce', *Journal of Marriage and the Family*, 41(2): 615–25.

Fonseca, Mabel, 1966, *Counselling for Marital Happiness*. Bombay: Manaktala.

Glick, P.C. and A.J. Norton, 1971, 'Frequency, Duration and Probability of Marriage and Divorce', *Journal of Marriages and the Family*, 33(1): 307–17.

Guest, Philip, 1991, 'Marital Dissolution and Development in Indonesia', *Working Paper in Demography*. No. 24, Canberra, ACT: Australian National University.

Hoffman, S., 1977, 'Marital Instability and the Economic Status of Women'. *Demography*, 14(2): 67–76.

Houseknecht, S.K. and G.B. Spanier, 1980, 'Marital Disruption and Higher Education among Women in the US', *Sociological Quarterly*, 21(2): 375–90.

Islam, M. Nazrul and Ashraf U. Ahmed, 2001, 'Correlates of Marriage Dissolution in Bangladesh', *Demography India*, 30(2): 245–60.

Johnson, Harry M., 1970, *Sociology: A Systematic Introduction*. Bombay: Allied Publications Private Limited.

Jones, Gravin W., 1981, 'Malay Marriage and Divorce in Peninsular Malaysia', *Three Decades of Change, Population and Development Review*, 7(2): 255–78.

Jones, Gravin W., 1995, *Divorce Trends in Islamic Southeast Asia: Mirror Image of the West?* Paper presented in the Annual Meeting of the Population Association of America, San Francisco, 8 April 1995.

Kafi, Sharif A., 1982, *Divorce*. Dhaka: Bangladesh Development Partnership Centre.

Kenkel, William F., 1966, *The Family in Perspective*. New York: Appleton-Century-Crofts.

Lee, G.R., 1977, 'Age at Marriage and Marital Satisfaction: A Multivariate Analysis with Implications for Marital Instability', *Journal of Marriage and the Family*, 39(2): 493–504.

Menken, J., James Truseel, Debra Stempel and Ozer Babakol, 1981, 'Proportional Hazards Life Table Models: An Illustrative Analysis of Socio-Demographic Influences on Marriage Dissolution in the United States', *Demography*, 18(2): 181–201.

Mehta, Rama, 1975, *Divorce in Hindu Women*. New Delhi: Vikas Publishing House Pvt. Ltd.

Mohahan, T.P., 1953, 'Does Age at Marriage Matter in Divorce'? *Social Forces*, 32(2): 81–7.

Momen, M.A., 1985, *A Study of Marriage, Divorce and Separations among Slum Dwelling Women in Dhaka City*. Dhaka: Bangladesh Society for Enforcement of Human Rights.

Moore, Kristin A. and Linda J. Waite, 1981, 'Marital Dissolution, Early Motherhood, and Early Marriage', *Social Forces*, 60(2): 20–40.

Moore, S.F., 1979, *The Short-Term Effects of Marital Disruption on the Labor Supply Behavior of Young Women*. Columbus, OH: Center of Human Resource, Ohio State University.

Mott, F.L. and S.F., Moore., 1978, 'The Causes and Consequences of Marital Breakdown'. In *Women, Work and Family*, edited by F. Mott, Lexington, MA: Lexington Books.

Papanek, H., 1979, 'Family Status Production Work: The Work and Non-Work of Women', *Signs*, 4(1): 775–81.

Peterson, R.R., 1989, *Women, Work and Divorce*, New York: Albany State University Press.

Pothen, S., 1986, *Divorce: Its Causes and Consequences in Hindu Society*. New Delhi: Vikas Publishing House Pvt. Ltd.

Raab, Earl and Jarger Gertrude Selznich, 1964, *Major Social Problems*. 2nd ed., New York: Harper and Row Publishers.

Rahman, Tania, 1997, 'Marriage, Separation and Divorce among Middle Class Family in Dhaka City', *Social Science Review*, 14(2): 13–28.

Schoen, R., 1975, 'California Divorce Rates by Age at First Marriage and Duration of First Marriage', *Journal of Marriage and the Family*, 37(2): 548–55.

Shaikh, Kashem, 1998, 'The Social and Demographic Correlates of Divorce in Rural Bangladesh', *Asia-Pacific Population Journal*, 13(3): 1–15.

Spanier, Graham B. and Paul C. Glick, 1981, 'Marital Instability in the United States: Some Correlates and Recent Change', *Family Relations*, 38(1): 329–38.

Thornton, Arland and Beborach Freedman, 1983, 'The Changing American Family', *Population Bulletin*, 38(2): 12–20.

Zaman, M.A., 1990, *Why Marriages Break Up? A Study on Divorce in Rural Bangladesh*. Dhaka: US Canada-Bangladesh.

CHAPTER 12

Why Legal Efforts Towards the Abolition of Violence against the Nigerian Women Remain an Illusion: A Case Study of Female Genital Cutting

Olugu Ukpai

Why have legal efforts towards abolishing violence against women such as female genital cutting (FGC) remained an illusion in Nigeria? This article suggests that FGC is not the cause of a problem, but the result of a situation arising out of women's lack of money, power, opportunities and their consequent insecurity, and that gender issues are central to its analysis (Ukpai, 2012: 51). Laws designed to criminalize FGC are unlikely to be effective against the widespread problem of sexual violence in Nigeria because reform is often a top-down process, in which national laws are developed to change rather than to reflect local attitudes (Boyle and Preves, 2000: 707). In addition, anti-FGC laws are designed to regulate rather than to empower women to take independent decisions about their bodies just like their Western counterparts. Martha Nussbaum observes that 'it remains particularly true that women have little legal recourse and may face threat to their freedom, threats or acts of physical violence, or social ostracization for refusing to undergo this harmful traditional practice, or attempting to protect their female children' (Nussbaum, 1998: 119). While lack of legal order obviously perpetuates sexual violence, such as FGC, which takes place in the so-called private spheres, only legal reform programmes designed specifically to empower, reflect the needs, risks and cultural norms pertaining to the grassroots women practitioners of FGC can help curb this social problem.

My argument is informed by Nussbaum's 'functioning capabilities' approach, which offers a cross-cultural account 'that focuses on empowerment and opportunity' in forming human choices (ibid.: 274; 1999; 2000; 2007). Such a perspective seeks to determine what basic principles and adequate measures would be needed to fulfil a life of human dignity. Nussbaum frames these basic principles in terms of capabilities—that is, 'real opportunities based on personal and social circumstances' with which one may, in turn, make choices regarding one's life plan (Nussbaum, 1998: 23–24). It leaves plenty of space for people to determine their life courses once those opportunities are secured for them (Burgess, 1996: 203). Thus, the capability approach is a broad normative framework for the evaluation of individual well-being and social arrangements, the design of laws, policies and proposals about social change in society. This article suggests that those who practice FGC do so because of a lack of central capabilities; they may do so in background and under conditions of intimidation and economic and political inequality. Coercion and consent literature documents that women living in poverty with low education are likely to suffer multiple forms of physical and sexual violence such as FGC (Kalicharan, 1998: 371). The Nigerian-born feminist, Mojubaolu Okome, notes that 'In Nigeria...there is no guaranteed access to social security [for women]' (Okome, 2001). An analysis of FGC must be linked to a consideration of the economic options for women who have undergone FGC and those who carry out the procedure. For this reason, although FGC is an institution that undeniably causes harm to women, and the question of consent is complicated, it is not clear that criminalizing FGC is the best way to remedy the harms. As Jody Freeman puts it, 'The way to empower women is not to punish them for being powerless' (Freeman, 1996: 247).

GAPS IN THE EXISTING SCHOLARSHIP

There has grown up a substantial literature on violence against women such as FGC (Ukpai, Nnaemeka, Efua, Duncan and Herlund). This literature is important because it has created awareness on the negative effects of FGC on women, both short and long term (Dekeseredy and Hinch, 1991; Margaret, 1992; Lee, 1993; Mamdami, 1996; Kameri, 2008; Lincoln, 2011). But it has been, on the whole, very general and unspecific, treating women as a homogenous group, and failing to account for differences across cultures, communities, race and other factors. In the 1980s, the Development Alternatives for Women in a New Era (DAWNE) criticized the Women in Development (WID) approach for its focus on women as a homogenous group. There is an obvious danger in generalizing about violence against women and law within societies that practice FGC because of the diversity of history and culture in which it occurs. Recently published work, such as Farede Banda's classic *Women, Law and Human Rights: An African Perspective*, fails to account for the range of Nigerian women's experiences regarding the impact and position of the law on violence against women, such as FGC, and the gap between law and practice. Banda acknowledged this shortcoming herself when she wrote 'This is not a book about *all women [emphasis mine]* ....It makes no claims to speak for or indeed represent the experiences of all the women of the continent [of Africa]' (Banda, 2005: 10). Second, much of this literature has come from Western scholars, arguably where law has a very specific place in the politics and history of feminist jurisprudence and where feminism has begun to challenge the legal order, especially with reference to law and women's bodies. Referring to the British, but also applicable to other Europeans as well, Dorathy Hammond and Alta Jablow concluded that 'four centuries of writing about Africa have produced a literature which describes not Africa but the British response to it' (Hammond and Jablow, 1970: 197). This underscores the need for an African perspective. Third, and most significant, there is a need for a socio-legal analysis of the practice of FGC to be addressed in order to provide a comprehensive overview of the problem and to challenge sexual violence against women. This is because there is contestation between the law in book and in the actual practice. This hopefully would challenge the parallel black letter law perspective posed in doctrinal analyses that have flooded legal interpretation and analyses.

In 2000, Carl Stychin and Didi Herman observed that '[socio] legal studies of [FGC]...appeared to lag behind [and] much of the work which was produced was centered on the pragmatic use of legal doctrine to achieve progressive legal change' (Stychin and Herman,

2000: VI). The authors called for 'a real diversity of perspectives and approaches ... open to theoretical diversity and innovations' (10). Samia Bano has also noted that 'study that is confined to the private sphere [such as the practice of FGC] is traditionally defined as non-legal and remains largely under-researched' (Bano, 1999: 91). But the veil has been removed, and now the practice of FGC cannot be limited to the private spheres because it has come out in the open, having been carried out in public hospitals, and has been discussed on a talk show on CNN, as well as Oprah Winfrey's show. Rosemary Auchmuty comments that sexuality issues, such as FGC, 'which had once been "private" are now "public", and thus should not be neglected any longer' (Auchmuty, 2007: 119). Broadly, this article is an attempt to bridge the lacunae in scholarship by contributing to the emerging literature on socio-legal analysis of violence against women and law from African perspective.

CONCEPTUALIZING VIOLENCE AGAINST WOMEN

Although the term 'violence against women' has been used to describe widely different behaviours including emotional, sexual and physical assault, murder, genital cutting, stalking, sexual harassment and prostitution, this review will focus specifically on sexual violence with particular interest in FGC. The concept of violence is a universal phenomenon that covers a wide range of ideas, actions and behaviours that cuts across disciplines. Violence against women began to draw attention as a serious social problem in the late 1960s and early 1970s (Renzetti et al., 2001: 25). Francine Pickup points out that it is a relative phenomenon that cut across all divisions of class, race, religion, age, ethnicity and geographical region (Pickup, 2001: 10). Following the way in which the concept of violence relates to issues in a variety of ways, there is no consensus among scholars on its definition.

The Oxford Advanced Learner's Dictionary defines violence as a 'violent behaviour intended to hurt or kill somebody, very strong feeling that is not controlled' (1995). In the field of sociology, it is defined as 'any act carried out with the intention of, or perceived intention of, causing physical pain or injury to another person' (Crowell and Burgess, 1996: 33). But the National Research Council (NRC) limited its definition to 'behaviour by persons that intentionally threatens attempts or actually inflicts harm' (33). While NRC and Oxford Dictionary excluded behaviour that inflicts harm unintentionally, the sociologists cover behaviours that may be unintentional but that are perceived by the victim as intentional (NRC). The cultural relativists have argued that parents who carry out FGC on their daughters do not meant to harm them, but the fact remains that it is perceived as intentional by the victim and should be considered as violence. From the feminists' point of view and UN's declaration statement, violence against women means any act of gender-based violence that results in, or is likely to result in, physical, sexual or psychological harm or suffering to women, including threats of such acts, coercion or arbitrary deprivation of liberty, whether occurring in public or private life (UN). But the feminists' conceptualization of violence against women is in the extreme (Kelly, 1999). Their broad definition recognizes not only physical, sexual and psychological violence but also threats of such harm. The danger in employing a very broad definition is that if the term violence is used to describe practices or norms for which other words already exist, this may result in the power of the term violence against women being diluted.

From the above conceptualization of violence, FGC constitutes sexual- and gender-based violence against women since it is a gender issue. It is carried out on women and girls because of their sex. FGC is a manifestation of institutionalized, historically unequal power relations between men and women, which have led to discrimination against women and the prevention of the full advancement of women. FGC is often done to women to debase them and thus, one of the crucial social mechanisms by which women are forced into a subordinate position compared with men. However, women also have the capacity to victimize and dominate others; estimates are that women account for about half the adults who abuse children in nonsexual ways, and women have enthusiastically supported domination and oppression of different classes and colours of people (Henderson, 1991: 441). She further contends that 'not all men dominate, and it is especially difficult for men who do not dominate to comprehend that they are advantaged in a world that seems to diminish them or oppress them.... Other men do not see themselves as having any power over women at all' (ibid.). Yet, Catherine MacKinnon maintains that although not all men dominate women, men 'as a group benefit from these same arrangements by which women are deprived' (MacKinnon, 1989: 149). She insists that in every race and class, women are reduced to sexual objects; race and class are subsets of male domination and female subordination. 'To be a woman is to occupy a status rather than a "class", women's status is a sex object' (ibid.: 131). In the Nigerian context, Mojubaolu Okome avers that men benefit from domination, a biased 'structural [systemic]...inequality [that] was created from colonial era to benefit men and these structures affect the role of women in contemporary Nigerian society' (Dorkenoo, 1995; Okome, 2001). Nahid Toubia sums it up thus, 'Mutilating of our bodies is a cross-cultural phenomenon that involves comply[ing] with a certain social definition of being a woman' (Toubia, 1995: 235). It is part of global violence and subordination of women in which women's bodies are controlled by a male-dominated social ideology. The battle is, in reality, about power and dominance—about finding a way to justify the abuse of women. The issue is that the silent majority of African women are illiterate, poor rural women, whose lives are still governed by overt patriarchy with built-in complex social mechanisms such as FGC to control their sexuality and reproductive capacity.

THE PHENOMENON OF FGC

FGC, also variously known as female genital mutilation, female genital surgery and female circumcision, is an ancient cultural tradition. The World Health Organization (WHO) defines FGC as 'all procedures involving partial or total removal of the external female genitalia or other injury to the female genital organs for non-medical reasons' (WHO, 2008: 110). FGC falls into four categories, all of which are practised in Nigeria. Type I, *sunna,* is the removal of the prepuce (the tissue protecting the head of the clitoris). Type II, *excision,* involves removing the prepuce and the clitoris together with partial or total excision of the labia minora (the folds of the skin at the opening of the vagina). Type III, *infibulations,* involves the removal of part or all of the external genitalia and stitching the vaginal opening closed (Mgbako et al., 2010: 112). Type IV, *others,* include scarification of the clitoral prepuce, cuts into the clitoris and labia minora as well as into the vagina. Two procedures are mentioned in the literature. They include *angurya* cut that describes the scraping of the tissue around the vaginal opening and *gishiri* cut that is a backward cut into the vagina—an attempt to increase the vaginal outlet to relieve obstructed labour. These are commonly practised in northern parts of Nigeria.

WHO estimates that there are 100–140 million girls and women living today who have been subjected to the practice of FGC, and annually approximately 3 million girls are at risk of undergoing the procedure. Of the 140 million, 130 million live in 28 countries in sub-Saharan Africa. About 6,000 girls undergo the practice of FGC daily, at an approximate rate of one every 15 seconds (Popoola, 2007: 2). In some African countries, nearly 99 per cent of women aged 15–49 have been cut (UNICEF, 2009). Nigeria is ranked amongst five other African countries that account for 75 per cent of all cases of FGC (Conroy, 2009: 110). A recent study carried out in South-Western Nigeria by Byode Popoola indicates that about 60 per cent of the total female population of Nigeria has undergone FGC. But based on my empirical findings in Nigeria, I would argue that the incidence of FGC in Nigeria will probably have been under-reported for several reasons. First, the practitioners do not voluntarily report cases to the government because there is no regulation and mechanism in place for such. Second, for fear of being arrested and prosecuted because FGC has been criminalized in some of the states in Nigeria similar to most African countries (Mgbako et al., 2010: 138). Third, sexual violence against women such as FGC occurs in the rural areas where officials do not have easy access to monitor and evaluate its prevalence due to poor road network. Rural areas are considered tenacious embodiments of deep-rooted cultural beliefs and practice such as FGC (Nnaemeka, 2005). Rural areas have been viewed as 'culturally sensitive ground, embedded with a multitude of traditions, norms and values relating to gender roles and relations, and to status of power in what remain heavily patriarchal social systems' (Ombonga, 2008: 2). Thanks largely to their efforts, clauses prohibiting the practice have been incorporated into a large number of international legal instruments and into the legislation of a growing number of countries including some states in Nigeria, but largely without reflecting the needs, risks and cultural norms of the real rural women practitioners of FGC. This is largely because these rural women practitioners were never consulted during the policy formulation and implementation process.

CONSEQUENCES OF FGC

Women subjected to FGC experience a range of serious short- and long-term health complications (George, 2006). Immediate complications include severe pain, shock, haemorrhage, urine retention and ulceration of the genital region and injury to adjacent tissue (WHO, 2008). Haemorrhage and infection can cause death. Given that the same crude cutting instrument is often used on a succession of girls without intermediary cleaning or sterilization, there is a risk of infection and the transmission of viruses such as HIV (Bennet, 2004; Sarkis, 2004; Beecham, 2010). In order to stop the bleeding during the procedure, 'mixtures of local herbs, earth, cow-dung, ash, or butter' are often rubbed onto the wound, which also leads to infections, tetanus and general septicaemia (Woman Aid Report). But the question that has largely remained unanswered in scholarship is why women practitioners decided to use such crude instruments, 'earth and cow-dung'? Do they have choices?

Long-term health effects include anaemia, the formation of cysts and abscesses, keloid scar formation, difficulty in urinating, urinary incontinence, recurrent bladder and urinary tract infections, menstrual disorders, fistulae and hypersensitivity of the genital area (UNPF). Childbirth can be particularly painful and life-threatening for women who have undergone FGC (UNPF). For example, infections contracted during the original FGC procedure may have ascended to the internal genital and caused vulval adhesions and vaginal scarring that have narrowed or 'completely obliterate[d] the vaginal opening' (UNPF, 2008: 4). Women who have undergone infibulations (stitching shut of the vaginal opening) also suffer a 'direct mechanical barrier to delivery'. (WHO, 2008: 12). These blockages obstruct deliveries, requiring the mother to undergo painful decircumcision. Episiotomies, perineal tears, post-partum haemorrhage, death of the mother during delivery and stillborn or neonatal deaths are also significantly more common among women who have undergone FGC (WHO). Because FGC is a traumatic experience that can leave a lasting mark on the life and mind of the women who have undergone the procedure, psychological, obstetricity and sexual problems are common. In their study of 2006, obstericity was not brought up by Birgitta and Sara Johnsdotte as an important theme in their study about FGC complications among the immigrant Somalian women in the United

Kingdom neither by the informants nor by the health care providers (Coventry Conference Programme, 16). Yet, the largely unanswered question is whether women have any acceptable means of expressing their fears, especially in the rural areas, or suffer in silence. Why women who have undergone such traumatic experience would allows their daughters to experience it? Nussbaum observes that 'it remains particularly true that women have little legal recourse and may face threat to their freedom, threats or acts of physical violence, or social ostracization for refusing to undergo this harmful traditional practice, or attempting to protect their female children' (Nussbaum, 1998: 119). Ellen insists that FGC was conceived by men in some long ago generation as a way of keeping women from having the full measure of their power and freedom and was passed down through the generations by male dominance and the ideologies of patriarchy (Gruenbaum, 2001: 40).

Many reasons are given for the practice of FGC—cultural, religious, and patriarchal. I use patriarchy here to capture men's cultural, economic, political and physical domination and violence devaluation of women such as in the practice of FGC. In the words of Catherine MacKinnon's discussion on patriarchy, it is the power to define 'who does what to whom and gets away with it' (MacKinnon, 1989: 138). FGC is deeply rooted in cultural traditions and is supported nearly equally by men and women in West African countries. Religion is another common justification for the practice of FGC, and many Muslim communities in Africa 'incorporated the cultural practice of female circumcision and made it into a religious requirement' (*New York Times* A: 19). But anti-FC activists have gone so far as to contact respected Islamic religious figures in the Middle East to prove that the Koran does not mandate FGC to be performed on Muslim women (Mgbako et al., 2010: 114).

Whatever justifications, mechanisms and pressures imposed on women to make their body conform to societal expectations, we can explore the real reasons for them only within the context of violence against women. Men use their privileged structural patriarchal power to perpetuate FGC in order to control women's sexual life. FGC represents a continuum of patriarchal repression of female sexuality that has been repressed in a variety of ways in all parts of the world throughout history and up to the present time. These methods vary in scope and in degree, but not in kind. For instance, as recently as 1925 in the United States, a medical association Orificial Surgery Society offered training in clitoridectomy and infibulations '...because of the vast amount of sickness and suffering which could be saved the gentler sex' while in Britain, Dr Charles Meigs 'recommended the application of silver solution to the clitoris of female children who masturbated' (Steinem, 2001: 78).

FGC AND INTERNATIONAL HUMAN RIGHTS INSTRUMENTS

Although organized international organizations against FGC have emerged in the past 25 years, it has also been contended that 'pockets of oppositions had existed for at least a century' (Boyle and Preves, 2000: 707). Early efforts to clamp down on FGC emanated from West with initial debut in the first half of the twentieth century (Bibbings, 1995: 29). For instance, in 1906, the Church of Scotland mobilized against FGC among the Kikuyu of Kenya, but merely succeeded in politicizing the issue rather than reducing (let alone curbing) it (Asma, 1982: 92). Nation-states were not the leading actors in the early campaigns against FGC because, in the early twentieth century, Africa was not organized into nation-states but into a system of territories and protectorates following the Berlin conference. Local representatives of Western colonial powers governed these lands. The colonial powers created parallel judicial systems: one arm applied 'native law' to local disputes and the other arm dealt with 'modern' issues (ibid.). Yet, colonial government actively avoided interfering with local customs to minimize tensions with indigenous population.

The first time the FGC eradication policy was openly discussed outside of Africa was in the late 1930s by the British Parliament (Murray, 1974: 59). The discussion was followed immediately by an informal conclave comprising the wives of British officials in Sudan and educated Sudanese men. While a formal education campaign was launched by the British in Sudan, in 1946, the colonial regime passed a law forbidding the most extreme form of FGC infibulation. However, as with earlier efforts in Kenya, the law merely politicized the issue. This led to the collective and clandestine circumcision of many girls at once as a mark of protest (Asma, 1982: 94–95). On why such laudable policy initiatives failed, Boyle et al argue that international normative influences held sway in creating national policies; they note that 'reform was often a top-down process in which national laws are developed to change rather than to reflect local attitudes' (707). Overall, diffuse, local opposition began to wane in the late 1950s, having had little or no effect on the rates of FGC (Assaad, 1980: 3–6). Only with the globalization of the nation-state system and a rise in international interest in FGC was the practice denounced by some African states. In thinking about reform of family law in African context, and in particular as anti-FGC policies and legislations, there is a need for an approach that involves grassroots participation in the formulation and implementation of policies, an approach that pays attention to people's perception of their normative context and how such perception shapes their attitudes and actions. This would provide a theoretical underpinning that would help in developing a legal framework more in tune with people's lived reality, particularly that of women.

Since the Second World War, there has been a remarkable ideological convergence among nation-states, despite their significant historical and economic differences. Presently, about eighteen African countries have passed legislation criminalizing FGC, some of which include Benin, Burkina Faso, Central African Republic, Côte d'Ivoire, Djbouti, Egypt, Eritrea, Ethiopia, Guinea, Kenya, Niger, Senegal, Tanzania and Togo amongst others (Center for Reproductive Rights, 2008; 2011). While many African nations and grassroots organizations have made great strides in their efforts to abolish FGC, Nigeria lags behind. Nigeria is ranked among five other African countries accounting for 75 per cent of all cases of FGC (Conroy, 2009: 110). Yet, there is no explicit law in Nigeria prohibiting FGC.

The refusal of the Nigerian government to take a stance against FGC makes the issue of FGC particularly difficult to deal with in local practising Nigerian communities. Yet, I contend that the Nigerian parliament would be able to draw upon the existing rights provided in the Nigerian Constitution to draft an anti-FGC law that empowers the women practitioners. Article 17 (3a & e) of the 1979 and 1999 Constitution of the Federal Republic of Nigeria calls upon the state to discourage 'discrimination on account of sex...' and Article 17 (1) guarantees fundamental 'freedom, equality, and justice' (Nigerian Constitution, Article 17). Article

17 (2a) states that 'every citizen shall have equality of rights... before the law' (Nigerian Constitution, Article 17). Article 34 (1a) states that 'no person shall be subject to torture or to inhuman or degrading treatment' (Nigerian Constitution, Article 34). FGC is a gender issue since it is practised exclusively on women and girls; and because only females suffer its harsh consequences, it contributes to discrimination of women in Nigeria. Additionally, Articles 17 (3e), 33 (1) and 35 (1) guarantee the right to 'life, liberty and privacy' of the person, whereas Article 17 (2d) maintains that the 'the sanctity of the human person shall be recognized and human dignity shall be maintained and enhanced' by the state (Nigerian Constitution, Articles 33, 35, 37). FGC is an invasion of personal privacy and can result in the loss of life; the removal of healthy sexual organs is an affront to one's dignity. Last, the Constitution affords special protection to children in Article 17(c) (f), which provides that the state should ensure that the 'health, safety ... of all ... children, young ... are protected against any exploitation whatsoever' (Nigerian Constitution, Article 17). Given FGC's harmful health consequences, the health and safety of girls who undergo FGC is compromised. These articles of the Nigerian Constitution in combination may serve as the basis on which Nigerian anti-FGC advocates could argue that FGC violates currently standing law. In addition, Nigeria could take its model from the 18 African countries that have passed anti-FGC legislations with novel innovations, having learned from the shortcomings of such laws that try to regulate rather than empowering women practitioners. But the enacting of FGC law alone is of limited use. This is because the widespread discrimination against women points to the need for aggressive and autonomous measures geared towards empowering women. Social change requires the demystification of conservative forces, including at times the distorted version of the traditional law.

Supporters of eradication contend that FGC violates the human right to health and bodily integrity and the right to be free from discrimination and violence, both of which are protected by international law (NUTS, 1966; 1989; WHO, 2000; 2006; 2008; UNICEF, 2005; 2006; 2010). Nigeria does not have an explicit law banning FGC or other harmful traditional or religious practices. Nigeria, however, is a party to a number of international human rights conventions, covenants and treaties, which provide a strong basis for the characterization of FGC as a violation of international human rights. Conventions that can be applied to FGC include the Convention on the Elimination of All Forms of Discrimination against Women (hereinafter 'CEDAW'); the Convention on the Rights of the Child (hereinafter 'CRC'); the International Convention on Economic, Social and Cultural Rights (hereinafter 'ICESCR'); and the African Charter on Human and People's Rights (here in after 'Banjul Charter').

Thus, there are sufficient international instruments that Nigeria has ratified unreservedly, which clearly prohibit traditional practices that discriminate against women and harm children. Given FGC's harmful health ramifications against women and the fact that women and girls are FGC's targets, the practice clearly fits within the purview of these conventions. For example, Article 2 of CEDAW directs 'State parties..... (f) to take all appropriate measures, including legislation, to modify or abolish existing laws, regulations, customs and practices which constitute discrimination against women' (Article 2). Article 5 further states—'State parties shall take all appropriate measures: (a) To modify the social and cultural patterns of conduct of men and women, with a view to achieving the elimination of prejudices and customary laws and all other practices which are based on the idea of the inferiority or all other practices which are based on the idea of the inferiority or the superiority of either of the sexes....' (Article 5). More so, Article 24(3) of the CRS states that 'state Parties shall take all effective and appropriate measures with a view to abolishing traditional practices prejudicial to the health of children' (Article 23). Further, Article 19(1) provides that 'State Parties shall take all appropriate legislative, administrative, social, and educational measures to protect the child from all forms of physical or mental violence, injury or abuse' (Article 19). These provisions in both CEDAW and the CRC confer a responsibility upon Nigeria and other signatories to prevent harmful traditional practices such as FGC.

Under the ICESCR, FGC violates the right to health. Article 12(2) of the ICESCR states that '[the steps to be taken by State Parties to the present Covenant to achieve the full realization of [the right to health] shall include those necessary for (a) The provision for the...healthy development of the child' (ICESCR, Article

12). The 'definition of health includes maturity, reproductive, and sexual health' (ICESCR). FGC violates these sections of the ICESCR because it can lead to numerous harmful health effects, and the development of female children to maturity may be compromised (Center for Reproductive Rights, 2008; 2011).

The African (Banjul) Charter on Human and Peoples' Rights includes provisions addressing the right to health (Article 16), right to physical integrity (Articles 4 and 5) and right to non-discrimination (Article 18(3) and Article 28) (African Charter Article 16–18). Currently, Nigeria is a party to the African Charter on the Rights and Welfare of the Child ('African Charter') and the Maputo Protocol to the African Charter on Human and Peoples' Rights on the Rights of Women in Africa ('Maputo Protocol'). Since the African Charter that calls for non-discrimination (Articles 2, 3) and secures the protection of the rights of women as provided for under international human rights instruments has been translated into Nigerian law, Nigerian courts have to rely on it to outlaw FGC in consultation with the real women practitioners (Laws of the Federation of Nigeria, Chapter 10). Although the provisions of the African Charter have been relied on in Nigerian courts, most of the cases dealt with the right to life under past military dictatorships, and there is no jurisprudence relating to gender discrimination (Williams, 2004: 234). The Nigerian legal scholar, Sope Williams, reports that there is no known case where the Nigerian Constitution has challenged human rights violations of women by a private person (ibid.). However, significantly, in *Nemi v The State*, the Supreme Court held that 'since the Charter has become part of our domestic law, the enforcement of its provisions like all our other laws fall within the judicial powers of the courts....' (Para 385). The African Charter on the Rights and Welfare of the Child requires member States of the Organization of Africa Unity ('OAU') to abolish customs and practices harmful to the welfare, dignity, normal growth and development of the child and in particular those customs and practices discriminatory to the child on the grounds of sex or other status (African Charter, 1999). This provision would include FGC as the practice is detrimental to the health and life of a girl child and is a custom that is exclusively performed on females. The Maputo Protocol is one of only two international instruments that explicitly refer to FGC. Article 5 reads that 'States parties shall prohibit and condemn...through legislation measures backed by sanctions, (b) all forms of female genital mutilation, scarification, medicalization and non-para-medicalization of FGC and all other practices in order to eradicate them' (Article 5; Shell-Duncan and Herlund, 2000). But these laws have been ineffective in abolishing FGC because the judiciary has failed to creatively apply them in determining issues relating to violence against the Nigerian women. Also, such programmes and legal reforms have not been developed to reflect the needs and cultural norms of the local women practitioners.

WHY LEGAL EFFORTS REMAIN AN ILLUSION IN CURBING VIOLENCE AGAINST WOMEN: AN EXPLORATION OF THE NIGERIAN LEGAL ENVIRONMENT

The Nigerian women often experience violence and oppression because government tolerates customary and religious practices that adversely affect them. Despite expectations that the early return of democracy in Nigeria would embolden the judiciary to take a progressive stance against cases involving cultural practices and gender equality, an analysis of the court's first decade of gender jurisprudence has proved otherwise. During that period, the judiciary demonstrated failure in addressing the 'woman question' in applying with matters relating to socio-religious and cultural practices against women and girls, especially the practice of FGC (Gerhard, 2001: 95). The Nigerian judiciary has not applied itself to creatively address onerous socio-cultural inequalities under which females labour. Courts and police were reluctant to protect women, and evidence does not exist of any support groups working to protect an unwilling woman or girl against the practice of FGC (Stychin, 1998; Stewart, 2004; Bonthuys, 2008; Igbinovia, 2010).

Why then is the Nigerian government so reluctant to outlaw FGC? How has it got away with ignoring its constitutional and Convention obligations? The answer lies in the Nigerian legal environment. Since the article attempts to explore why the legal efforts have not been effective in abolishing FGC in Nigeria, special attention will be given to the present legal regime and women's status in Nigeria. To this end, I will focus on themes that are of particular relevance to the legal position of women in Nigerian society, namely culture and pluralism. Margaret Owen, a leading figure in the emerging women's legal rights movement, explains that women in African nations are generally the poorest of the poor and the least protected by the law. She further points out that FGC represents a 'social death for women, rubbing them of their status and consigning them to the very margins of society where they suffer the most extreme forms of discrimination and stigma' (Owen, *on line*). Nigeria is one of the African nations alluded to by Owen, and there is a fairly sizeable body of literature that vividly demonstrates that Nigerian women are indeed marginalized and routinely discriminated against by the Nigerian legal regime in a variety of ways.

It has been stated by Henderson that law is not something 'out there' unrelated to culture (Henderson, 1991: 412). Culture encompasses 'the collective beliefs, values, traditions or outlooks... characteristic of particular social populations' (Cotterell, 2004: 4). It influences one's perception of the world. No discussion on violence against women is complete without an analysis on the influence of culture (Cerna and Wallace, 1999: 630). To underscore this point, Arati Rao points out that '[no] social group has suffered greater violation of its human rights in the name of culture than women...' (Rao, 1995: 169). These systems of cultural beliefs and attitudes are reinforced by the law as they are given the force of law, being part of customary law systems. Hence, Roger Cotterell states that law may be viewed as 'culture in the sense of being powerfully shaped by certain cultural assumptions' (4).

These cultural practices such as FGC are gendered (Ukpai, 2010b; 2010c; 2010d; 2010e; 2010f). They are only suffered by women and girls and embedded in unjustifiable socio-cultural attitudes (Ukpai, 2007; 2009; 2010a). These discriminatory practices against women and the cultural prejudices that underpin such practices are not only rife within the traditional society, but have also been institutionalized and legitimized within the official legal system. The Nigerian Constitution provides for the right to personal liberty, equal treatment and non-discrimination (Nigerian Constitution, Article. 39). In the same vein, however, the Constitution protects and preserves Nigerian cultures without stipulating clear principles for resolving internal conflicts that may arise in the pursuit of what many believe to be mutually exclusive goals. In its statement of Fundamental Objectives and Directive

Principles of State Policy, the 1979 Constitution expressly provides that 'the State shall protect and enhance "Nigerian Cultures"' and that 'every citizen shall have equality of rights, obligations and opportunities before the law' (Nigerian Constitution, Article. 21).

The 1989 Constitution of the Federal Republic of Nigeria replaced Section 20 of the 1979 Constitution with the stipulation that 'the State shall protect, preserve and promote the Nigerian cultures that enhance human dignity and are consistent with the fundamental objectives as provided in this chapter' (Nigerian Constitution, Article. 21). Although an improvement over the 1979 Constitution, these provisions have had no beneficiary effect for women for several reasons. First, the 1979 Constitution never went into force and hence is a dead document. Moreover, Section 21 appears in the non-justiciable section of the Constitution and arguably cannot be taken to have conferred substantive rights on anyone (Nigerian Constitution, Section 21, Articles 1, 3).

There is, therefore, tension between protected rights and preserved culture such as FGC that undermines women's rights. And the Nigerian courts have held that customary law (which is largely unwritten and fragmented) is a matter of evidence to be decided on the facts presented before the court in each particular case unless judicial notice has been taken of it (*Romaine v Romaine*). Nigerian courts are yet to develop concrete, equitable standards to guide their interpretations. Much is therefore left to the individual judges (*Adeniyl v. Fagbiyi, Kimdey & Ors. Military Governor of Gongola State; Garba V Lagos State Attorney*, 1991). The standard of 'natural justice, equity, and good conscience' is at best vague and at worst, reflects the views of the dominant powers in the society. During the colonial rule, it reflected the views of the male-dominated judiciary. Prior to independence, judgment depended much on European standards of fairness and good conscience. It can be argued that in post-colonial Nigeria, judgments should reflect values evident in modern constitution democratically passed and accepted and should reflect evolving human rights standards as reflected in major international human rights treaties to which Nigeria is a signatory.

Legal pluralism arising from the co-existence of state law and non-state normative orderings within the Nigerian legal framework contributes to these discriminatory treatments against the Nigerian women, especially in the practice of FGC, that often operates outside the orbit of the legal system. Fifty years after Nigeria attained its independence; its official state legal system continues to conform to this pattern of state law pluralism. The present-day Nigerian legal system may be depicted as a mighty river into which flow the waters from many streams. Ewelukwa has identified six sources of Nigerian Law: Local laws together with English common law, the doctrines of equity and General Application, local legislation, law reports and textbooks on Nigerian law and judicial precedents (Ewelukwa, 2002: 446). The co-existence of these plural bodies of law in the Nigerian legal system has created a complex and confusing legal regime under which women generally are denied adequate legal protection. Andrew Iwobi affirms this assertion when he wrote that 'the versions of indigenous customary law propagated by Nigerian men and applied by the state courts have not only tended to militate against the interests of women [and rights] in general but ... have been manifestly prejudicial [to them]' (Iwobi, 2008: 48).

CONCLUDING ARGUMENTS

Legal Reform and Empowerment Perspective: A Panacea to Ending FGC in Nigeria

In its resolution 63/142, the General Assembly, taking note of the final report of the Commission on Legal Empowerment of the Poor, entitled *Making the Law Work for Everyone*, emphasized the need for legal empowerment of the poor (UN 2). There is the need for a legal reform that will empower the Nigerian women practitioners of FGC to make independent decisions and choices about their bodies. Legal empowerment perspective entails exploring beyond the existence of formal choice and formal opportunity to unveil the practical constraints on formal options for women and under the 'actual conditions under which women live' (Green, 1993: 1261). The empowerment perspective asks whether institution-formulated systems and rules, developed without the involvement of women, can practically serve women, or whether those systems and rules empower only men (ibid.). To date, however, African voices, more especially of the real women practitioners, remain marginal in international discourses and the conception of anti-FGC legislation. Isabella Gunning, for example, who worked on 'anti-FGM' bills in California, discusses her consternation in having experienced the 'glaring absence of input from African women' in developing the legislation (Gunning, 2002: 116). Instead, she observes that several feminists and community organizations, largely white, were consulted or contacted for input and support. It is suggested that a genuine partnership with African women practitioners would, at the very least, lead to more informed legislating.

However, the empowerment perspective does not homogenize the experience of women. It does not assume that the experiences of all women are the same irrespective of class, race and other differences. The empowerment perspective does not necessarily surmise that individual men wish to monopolize power or control the options of women (Nedelsky, 1994; Sen, 1999; Skelton, 2000; Poldermans, 2006). Rather, it treats existing gender relations as generally beyond the control of individuals and as a product of historical forces that benefit men as a group. Within this context, it requires that men and women who want to initiate social change examine the features and numerous traditions of a wide range of public and private institutions such as political, cultural, economic and educational traditions in order to evaluate the role that women play in these institutions and the impact of these institutions on women's lives. A recent study suggests that 'outlawing it by passing anti-FGM legislation [that doesn't reflect the needs, risks and cultural norms of the real women practitioners] can drive the practice underground' (WHO, 2008: 6). In affirmation, a study published in 2000 found that prosecutions had been brought in only four of the 28 countries of Africa and the Middle East where FGM is practised (ibid.: 5–6).

In a research of my own (2011), 97 per cent of the women interviewed in a Nigerian rural community opine that the law would not be useful to them in abolishing FGC. Their notion about law was limited to being arrested, the cost of litigation and going to court and the longevity of court cases that they would not be able to afford (Ukpai, 2011: interview). But when I raised their consciousness, most of them changed their perceptions of the role of the law in abolishing sexual violence against women such as FGC should legal services for them be provided pro-bono. There are no free legal services for women suffering violence in Nigeria. From my findings, for about five decades, these rural Nigerian women have been marginalized, and their opinions have never been sought in policy formulations. If we must end violence against the Nigerian women, an analysis of violence against women such as FGC must directly involve the real practitioners and such policies must be linked to a consideration of the economic empowerment options for women who have undergone FGC and those who carry out the procedure and not criminalizing FGC.

Although feminists have argued persuasively that FGC involves the exploitation of women, but this exploitation is not and cannot be the object of censorship. I suggest that this can successfully be dealt with by employment legislation or laws against criminal assault on women. It would probably help to illuminate the so-called Third-World dimension of violence against women such as FGC and to widen their concern to enlist the harm of economic-cum-sexual violence and exploitation of Third-World women. From my empirical investigations, it is therefore misleading to imply that criminalizing FGC would automatically abolish it or end violence against women. On the contrary, it might make matters worse for women who ply their trade as circumcisers for solely an economic survival reason and at best drive FGC underground or 'encourage a cross-border movement of women from a country where the practice is illegal to a neighbouring country where it is allowed' (WHO, 2008: 6). Feminist historical argument of using criminal law to restrict FCG necessarily has a focus on the interests of women at the consumer end, rather than the production end of the cause. Criminalizing FGC will at best add to the lamination of (legal) violence against women since in most countries where FGM is prevalent, more women than men support the practice (ibid.: 5–6). Although FGC is a clear violation of international human rights; however, there is the need to work with grass-roots communities and participants in the practice of FGC to design and implement such laws to empower them, reflect their needs, risks and cultural norms. This is important if the practice is to be ended in 2015 as prescribed by the United Nations Millennium Declaration Goals. History demonstrates that the Nigerian women have been marginalized in the formulation and implementation of laws and policies that affect their sexuality. More often than not, these women participants in FGC live in the rural areas where researchers seldom enter. The Nigerian *Vanguard Newspaper* of 4 February 2010 insists that we must 'go to communities [rural areas] where it is done, and simultaneously address the issue' (VANGUARD NEWSPAPER, 2010: 4). Similarly, a group of African women researchers argue that the West must accept that it is a problem for African women, and that no change is possible without the conscious participation of African women (Banda, 2005: 213). Social activists and the international community should consider a more grassroots approach in using the law to empower the Nigerian women practitioners of FGC by directly seeking their opinions (Interview, 2011). Unless social activists facilitate strategic feminist litigations by encouraging the courts to conclude that there is a gap between the law on the books and the reality in the field to spur legal reform that will empower the Nigerian women to make independent decisions about their bodies just like their Western counterparts rather than regulating it by the power of the law, violence against them will not only continue but they will remain marginalized, discriminated against and violated.

REFERENCES

Adeniyl v. Fagbiyi, 1993, Vsuits No. E/53/77 AND e/54/77.

African Charter on the Rights and Welfare of the Child. 1999.

African Protocol to the African Charter on Human and Peoples' Rights on the Rights of Women in 2000.

Asma, El Dareer, 1982, *Woman, Why Do You Weep?* London: Zed Press.

Assaad, Bassilli, 1980, 'Female Circumcision in Egypt: Social Implications, Current Research, and Prospects for Change', *Studies in Family Planning*, 11: 3–6.

Auchmuty, Rosemary, 2007, 'Out of the Shadows: Feminist Silence and Liberal Law'. In *Sexuality and the Law: Feminist Engagement*, 2007, edited by Carl Stychin and Vanessa Munro, New York: Routledge-Cavendish.

Banda, Fareda, 2005, *Law and Human Rights: An African Perspective*. Oxford: Hart.

Bano, Samia, 1999, 'Standpoint "Difference" and Feminist Research'. In *Theory and Method in Socio-legal Research*, 2005, edited by Max Travers and Reza Banakar, Oxford: Hart Publishing, pp. 91–111.

Beecham, David (Ed.), 2010, *Is Female Genital Cutting the Obstetric Challenge for Obstetricians, Midwives and Somali Childbearing Women in UK?* Female Genital Mutilation/Cutting (FGM/C) Within the EU, Conference Paper Presented at Westminster Graduate Conference, London

Bennet, Cinnamon, 2004, 'Mainstreaming a Male Perspective into UK Regeneration: The Experience in South Yorkshire'. In *Gender Equality and Men: Learning from Practice*, edited by Ruxton Sandy, London: Oxfam.

Bibbings, Lois, 1995, 'Female Circumcision: Mutilation or Modification?' In *Law and Body Politics: Regulating the Female Body*, edited by Jo Bridgeman and Susan Millns, Aldershot, Hampshire: Dartmouth Publishing Company.

Bonthuys, Elje, 2008, 'Institutional Openness and Resistance to Feminist Arguments: The Example of the South African Constitutional Court', *CJWL*, 20(1): 1–35.

Boyle, Elizabeth Heger and Sharon Preves, 2000, 'National Politics as International Process: The Case of Anti-Female-genital Cutting Laws', *Law and Society Review*, 34(3): 703–38.

Burgess, Ann (Ed.), 1996, *Women in Violent World: Feminist Analyses and Persistent Across 'Europe'*. Edinburgh: Edinburgh University Press.

Center for Reproductive Rights, 2008, *Female Genital Mutilation (FGM): Legal Prohibitions Worldwide*, http://reproductiverights.org/en/document/female-genital-mutilation-fgm-legal-prohibitions-worldwide, accessed 14 October 2013.

Center for Reproductive Rights, 2011 Report, http://reproductiverights.org/sites/crr.civicactions.net/files/documents/AR_2010-11_SPREADS.pdf, accessed 14 October 2013.

Cerna, Christiana and Jennifer Wallace, 1999, 'Women and Culture'. In *Women and International Human Rights*, edited by K.D. Askin and D.M. Koenig, New York: Transnational.

Conroy, Melanie, 2009, 'Refugees Themselves: Asylum Case for Parents of Children at Risk of Female Genital Mutilation', *Harvard Human Rights Journal*, 22(1): 119–31.

Constitution of the Federal Republic of Nigeria, 1979, Lagos, Nigeria.

Constitution of the Federal Republic of Nigeria, 1989, Lagos, Nigeria.

Cotterell, Roger, 2004, 'Law in Culture', *Ratio Juris*, 17(1): 42–70.

Crowell, Nancy and Ann Burgess (Eds.), 1996, *Understanding Violence against Women*. Washington, DC: National Academic Press.

Dekeseredy, Walter and Ronald Hinch, 1991, *Women Abuse: Sociological Perspective. Toronto: Thompson Educational Publishing*. Toronto: Thompson Educational Publishing.

Efua, Dorkenoo, 1994, *Cutting the Rose: Female Genital Mutilation: The Practice and its Prevention*. London: Minority Right Group.

Ewelukwa, Uche, 2002, 'Post-Colonialism, Gender, Customary Injustices: Widows in African Societies', *Human Rights Quarterly*, 24: 424–46.

Fawehinmi v Abacha, Court of Appeal 1996, 5 *Nigeria Law Reports* 739.

Freeman, Jody, 1996, 'The Feminist Debate over Prostitution Reform: Prostitute's Rights Groups, Radical Feminists, and the (Im)possibility of Consent.' In *Applications of Feminist Legal Theory to Women's Lives*, edited by Kelly Weisberg, Philadelphia, PA: Temple University Press, 237–49.

Garba v Lagos State Attorney General, Supreme Court of Nigeria 1991, 7 *Nigeria Law Reports* 739 (1991)

'Georgia: Man Convicted in Daughter's Mutilation', *The New York Times*, 2 November 2006.

Gerhard, Ute, 2001, *Debating Women's Equality: Towards a Feminist Theory of Law from a European Perspective*. New Brunswick, NJ: Rutgers University Press.

Green, Linda, 1993, 'Feminism, Law and Social Change: Some Reflections on Unrealized Possibilities', *Northwestern University Law Review*, 87(4), 23-46.

Gruenbaum, Ellen, 2001, *The Female Circumcision Controversy: An Anthropological Perspective*. Philadelphia, PA: University of Pennsylvania Press.

Gunning, Isabella, 2002, 'Female Genital Surgeries: Eradication Measures at the Western Local Level-A Cautionary Tale'. In *Genital Cutting and Transnational Sisterhood: Disputing U.S. Polemics*, edited by S. James and C. Robertson, Urbana: University of Illinois Press.

Hammond, Dorothy and Alta Jablow, 1970, *The Africa That Never Was*. New York: Twayne.

Henderson, Lynn, 1991, 'Law's Patriarchy', *Law and Society Review*, 25(2): 411–44.

Hornby, Albert Sidney, 1995, *Oxford Advanced Learners Dictionary*. Oxford: Oxford University Press.

Igbinovia, Josephine, 2010, *Female Circumcision Encourages Promiscuity and Polygamy in Men, Says Osarenren*. Vanguard Newpsper, Ibadan: Nigeria

Iwobi, Andrew, 2008, 'No Cause for Merriment: The Position of Widows under Nigerian Law', *Canadian Journal of Women and Law*, 20(1): 37–86.

Kalicharan, Seth, Ernestine Williams, Charsey Cherry, Lisa Belcher and Dena Nachimson, 1998, 'Sexual Coercion, Domestic Violence, and Negotiating Condom Use among Low-Income African American Women', *Journal of Women's Health*, 7(3), 99-119

Kameri-Mbote, Patricia and Nkatha Kabira, 2008, 'Separating the Baby from the Bath Water: Women's Rights and the Politics of Constitutional-Making in Kenya', *East African Journal of Peace and Human Rights*, 14(1), 1-43.

Kelly, Liz, 1999. 'Violence Against Women: A Policy of Neglect or a Neglect of Policy?' In *New Agendas for Women*, edited by Sylvia Walby, London: Macmillan.

Kimdey and Ors, 1988, *Military Governor of Gongola State*. Nigerian Court of Appeal.

Lee, Raymond, 1993, *Doing Research on Sensitive Topics*. London: Routledge.

Lincoln, Ryan, 2011, 'Recent Developments, Rule of Law for Whom?: Strengthening the Rule of Law as a Solution to Sexual Violence in the

Democratic Republic of the Congo', *Berkeley Journal of Gender, Law and Justice*, 26: 139–67.

MacKinnon, Catherine, 1989, *Toward a Feminist Theory of the State*. Cambridge, MA: Harvard University Press.

Mamdami, Mahmood, 1996, *Citizen and Subjects: Contemporary Africa and the Legacy of Colonialism*. Princeton: Princeton University Press.

Margaret, Schular (Ed.), 1992, *Freedom from Violence: Women's Strategies from around the World*. New York: PACT Communications.

Mgbako, Chi, Meghna Saxena, Anna Cave, Nasim Farjad and Helen Shin, 2010, 'Penetrating the Silence in Sierra Leone: A Blueprint for the Eradication of Female Genital Mutilation', *Harvard Human Rights Journal*, 23: 111–40.

Murray, Margaret, 1974, *The Kikuyu Female Circumcision Controversy, with Special Reference to the Church Missionary Society's Sphere of Influence*. University of California.

Nedelsky, Jennifer, 1994, 'The Practical Possibilities of Feminist Theory', *Northwestern University Law Review*, 87(4), 81- 101.

Nnaemeka, Obioma (Ed.), 2005, *Female Circumcision and the Politics of Knowledge: African Women in Imperialist Discourses*. London and Westport, CT: Praeger.

Nussbaum, Martha, 1998, 'Capabilities and Human Rights', *Fordham Law Review*, 166(2),234- 258.

———, 1999, *Sex and Social Justice*. London: Oxford University Press.

———, 2000, *Women and Human Development*. Cambridge: Cambridge University Press.

———, 2007, 'Human Rights and Human Capabilities: Twentieth Anniversary Reflections', *Harvard Human Rights Journal*, 20, 1-23.

Okome, Mojubaolu, 2001, 'Domestic, Regional, and International Protection of Nigerian Women against Discrimination: Constraints and Possibilities', *African Studies Quarterly*, 6(3), available at http://web.africa.ufl.edu/asq/v6/v6i3.pdf, this article was not paginated.

Ombonga, Mary, 2008, *Understanding Experience of Girls in a Centre of Excellence in Kajiado District, Kenya: An Exploratory Case Study*. Michigan State University. A Ph.D dissertation submitted to the Department of Education.

Owen, Margaret 'Widows in Third World Nations', *Encyclopedia of Death and Dying*, available online at http://www.deathreference.com/Vi-Z/Widows-in-Third-World-Nations.html#b, accessed 14 October 2013.

Pickup, Francine, 2001, *Ending Violence against Women, a Challenge for Development and Humanitarian Work*. Oxford: Oxfam GB.

Poldermans, Sophie, 2006, 'Combating Female Genital Mutilation in Europe: A Comparative Analysis of Legislative and Preventive Tools in the Netherlands, France, the United Kingdom and Australia', *European Master Degree in Human Rights and Democratisation,* Master Degree thesis submitted to the University of Southern Denmark, Department of Law.

Popoola, Bayode, 2007, 'A Study of the Prevalence of Female Genital Mutilation and Parents' Attitudes among the Yorubas of Western Nigeria', *African Journal for Physical Health Education, Recreation and Dance,* 13: 17–31.

Protocol to the African Charter on Human and Peoples' Rights on the Rights of Women in Africa, 2011, available at http://www.africa-union.org/root/au/Documents/Treaties/Text/Protocol%20on%20the%20Rights%20of%20Women.pdf, accessed 14 October 2013.

Rao, Arati, 1995, 'The Politics of Gender and Culture International Human Rights Discourse'. In *Women's Rights Human Rights International Feminist Perspectives,* edited by Julie Peters and Andrea Wolper, New York: Routledge.

Registered Trustees of the Constitutional Rights Project v President of Nigeria, Supreme Court of Nigeria, 1992, 2 Nig. Wkly. L. R 98.

Renzetti, Claire, Jeffrey Edleson and Raquel Kennedy Bergen, 2001, *Source Book on Violence Against Women.* London and New Delhi: Sage Publications.

Report, National Research Council, 1996, *Prevention and Understanding of Violence* Ibadan: Nigeria.

Sarkis, Marianne, 2004, *The Female Genital Cutting Education and Networking Project, Female Genital Cutting (FGC): An Introduction,* http://www.fgm-network.org/intro/fgmintro.html, accessed 5 May 2012.

Sen, Amartya, 1999, *Development as Freedom.* New York: Knopf.

Shell-Duncan, B. and Y. Herlund (Ed.), 2000, *Female Circumcision in Africa: Culture, Controversy and Change.* London: Lynne.

Skelton, Ann, 2010, 'Girl's Socio-Economic Rights in South Africa', *South African Journal on Human Rights,* 26(1): 141–63.

Steinem, Gloria, 2001, *Outrageous Acts and Everyday Rebellions,* 2nd ed. New York: Holt Paperbacks.

Stewart, Ann, 2004, 'Entitlement, Pluralism and Gender Justice in Sub-Saharan Africa'. In *Remaking Law in Africa: Transnationalism, Persons and Rights,* edited by Murison Jude, Griffiths Anne and King Kenneth, Edinburgh: Centre of African Studies, 195–213.

Canadian Association of African Studies, 1972, 'Women: The Neglected Human Resource for African Development', *Canadian Journal of African Studies,* 6(2): 359–70.

Stychin, Carl, 1998, *A Nation by Rights: National Cultures, Sexual Identity Politics, and the Discourses of Rights.* Philadelphia, PA: Temple University Press.

Stychin, Carl and Didi Herman, 2000, *Sexuality in the Legal Arena*. London: The Athlone.

Toubia, Nahid, 1995, 'Female Genital Mutilation'. In *Women's Rights are Human Rights: International Perspectives*, edited by Julie Peters and Andrea Wolper, New York and London: Routledge.

Toubia, Nahid and Anika Rahman, 2000, *Female Genital Mutilation: A Guide to Laws and Policies Worldwide*. London and New York: Zed Books.

Ukpai, Olugu, 2007, *Separating Sand from the Mud: Re-Examining Gender Inequalities in Nigeria: Exploring the Impacts and Attitudes of Men towards Female Genital Cutting*. Ann Arbor: Halifax.

———, 2009, *Men's Perspectives on Female Genital Cutting in South-eastern Nigeria: From Another Point of View*. Germany: VDM Verlag Dr. Müller.

———, 2010a, 'Degree as Minimum Requirement for Elective Offices: Bulwark of Discrimination Against Women', *New Nigerian Newspaper*.

———, 2010b, *Female Genital Cutting (FGC) in the Company of Men: A Guide to Current Debate: De-Theorizing Hegemonic Ideology of African Men towards the Practice of FGC*. Germany: Lambert.

———, 2010c, 'Is It A Crime To Be Born A Woman?' *Nigerian Master Web*.

———, 2010d, 'Proposed Elective Office Qualification: A Discrimination against Women', *Nigerian Tribune*, 3 March 2010.

———, 2010e, 'Proposed University Degree Minimum Requirement for Elective Offices: A Bulwark of Discrimination Against Nigeria Women', *Nigerian Master Web*.

———, 2010f, 'Women and Family, Re: Childlessness and Broken Home', *New Nigerian Newspaper*.

———, 2011, *Interview with Rural Igbo Women Practitioners of FGC in South Eastern Nigeria*, a Ph. D field work carried out between October 2010 and January 2011, in file with the author.

———, 'Blacklisting of Nigeria as the New Den of Terrorists? Deconstructing US Imperialist Hegemony on the Botched December 2009 Bombing of an American Airliner by a Nigerian National: Perspective of a Nigerian Student in the UK', *Ìrìnkèrindò: A Journal of AfricanMigration*, 5, available at http://www.africamigration.com/Issue%205/Opinion/HTML/Olugu%20Ukpai%20-%20Blacklisting%20of%20Nigeria.htm, accessed 14 October 2013, the article was not paginated.

———, 2012, 'Crossing The Rubicon: Criminalizing Female Genital Cutting in Nigeria: Rediscovering Human Rights Perspectives', Emerging Ph.D dissertation, School of Law, University of Reading, in file with the author.

UNICEF, 2005, *Female Genital Mutilation/Cutting: A Statistical Exploration*, available at http://www.unicef.org/publications/files/FGM-C_final_10_October.pdf, accessed, 14 October 2013.

———, 2006, *Child Protection Information Sheet: Female Genital Mutilation/Cutting*, available at http://www.unicef.org/publications/files/Child_Protection_Information_Sheets.pdf, accessed October 14, 2013.

———, 2009, *Legal Empowerment of the Poor and Eradication of Poverty*. UN: "Legal Empowerment of the Poor and Eradication of Poverty", 64th Session of the General Assembly (2nd Committee) Special Event, 16 October 2009, available at http://www.un.org/en/ga/second/64/1610summary.pdf, accessed October 14, 2013.

———, 2010, *Recommendations of the Forum on Minority Issues at Its Third Session, on Minorities and Effective Participation in Economic Life*. UN, available at http://www.ohchr.org/EN/HRBodies/HRC/Minority/Pages/ForumIndex.aspx, accessed, 14 October 2013.

United Nations Declaration on the Elimination of All Violence against Women, 1993, UN A/RES/48/104, 85th plenary meeting, available at http://www.un.org/documents/ga/res/48/a48r104.htm, accessed 14 October 2013.

United Nations Population Fund (UNPF), 2008, 'Frequently Asked Questions on Female Genital Mutilation/Cutting', http://www.unfpa.org/gender/practices2.htm, accessed 5 May 2012.

UNTS, 1966, *International Covenant on Economic, Social, and Cultural Rights*, 933, available at http://www1.umn.edu/humanrts/instree/b2esc.htm, accessed, 14 October 2013.

———, 1989, *Convention on the Rights of the Child*, 1577, available at http://www.hivlawandpolicy.org/resources/convention-rights-child-1577-unts-3, accessed, 14 October 2013.

WHO, 2000, 'A Systemic Review of the Health Complications of Female Genital Mutilation Including Sequelae in Childbirth', available at http://www.who.int/reproductivehealth/topics/fgm/fgm_systematic_review_consequences/en/, accessed, 14 October 2013.

———, 2006, # 74, *Progress in Sexual and Reproductive Health Research*, available at http://who.int/hrp/publications/progress74.pdf

———, 2008 (Updated, February 2013), *Female Genital Cutting/Mutilation*, available at http://www.who.int/mediacentre/factsheets/fs241/en/, accessed 14 October 2013.

Williams, Sope, 2004, 'Nigeria, Its Women and International Law: Beyond Rhetoric', *Human Rights Review*, 4(2): 229–55.

CHAPTER 13

Nowhere Girls: A Profile of Sex-Trafficking in Mekong Sub-Region

Lipi Ghosh

Trafficking in women and children has been the subject of several international conventions and declarations and receives considerable publicity in mass media. This problem has become serious in the Asia and Pacific region, especially in Asian countries and Mekong region. However, it remains a subject that needs to be investigated in a scientific manner, especially in this Mekong Basin area. Therefore, the aim and scope of this paper is to focus on promoting information gathering and reinforcing information about trafficking in women and children. It also includes information about the current situation of trafficking in women and children in Mekong Basis region and the casual factors. It aims at presenting national laws and policies of the region (key laws and policies directly or indirectly having an impact on the trafficking) and finally the paper attempts to formulate recommendations concerning the issue.

It is a fact that without a clear understanding and definition of what constitutes trafficking in women and children, it is not possible to develop a strong legal basis for the prosecution and investigation of traffickers, as this trafficking covers a wide variety of situations. Therefore, to have a good definition of trafficking in women and children, it is necessary to look at the issue and have an explicit and coherent policy to combat this evil.

Trafficking in women covers all acts involved in the recruitment and/or transpiration of persons within and/or across national borders (of course, illegal actions) for such works or services as forces labour and marriage, debt bondage, slavery and other inhuman works. Trafficking for sexual exploitation is a form of trafficking that gets considerable attention, but it should be remembered that trafficking does not only mean trafficking for prostitution. Trafficking for the purposes of marital exploitation, bonded labour and work under slave-like conditions also exists.

Sex tourism is the reverse of trafficking. In this case, clients travel from other countries, and there are several small private agencies involved in operating sex tours. At the beginning, the victims follow the route of other villager and go to work as domestic helpers in other places. There are young women who are recruited to work outside their community with the promise of highly paid jobs either in factories or in restaurants, usually in urban areas.

Most victims of this pattern of trafficking are young women who are unaware of the problems and unable to defend themselves. Some young women, before departure, are sexually abused by traffickers. This pattern is also prevailing among women and children who migrate to work in sex-related jobs in cities and then in receiving countries. Their largest concern is the condition of work and the amount of remuneration. Although women are experienced in the trade and aware of the problem, still many of them become victims of unscrupulous traffickers. In fact, trafficking in women has resulted in serious consequences for the society. Many women experience suffering as their body and dignity are trampled upon, and some of them have committed suicide. Many families have been broken and the society is unstable.

Consequences of trafficking in women are tremendous. Obviously, trafficking in women has brought ruinous consequences for families and the society. When a woman is deceived and sold, her family loses a member. The children are separated from their mother, the husband loses his wife and the parents lose their daughter. The act of forcing women and children to practice prostitution to gain profits is a cynical violation of human rights, robbing from the victims their happiness and confidence in life.

Prostitution goes hand in hand with trafficking in women, and such evils cause serious harmful consequences to them. Obviously, using a woman's body and dignity to gain profit is a cynical violation of human rights. This is really an exploitation of women, considering them as goods. Trafficking in women is a fellow traveller of prostitution, and they are closely linked with corruption, deceit and coercion (to gain more money). Most of its victims lose their belief in life. Trafficking in women is a fellow threat to family's happiness. Because trafficking in women is a fellow traveller of prostitution, many of its victims will also be victims of AIDS. Prostitution is a dangerous source of disease transmission, influencing the coming generations. Many families have been broken and the society is unstable.

TRAFFICKING IN MEKONG REGION

Trafficking in women and children in Mekong sub-region has taken on a wider magnitude in recent years. This is particularly true of the cross-border trafficking that has been taking place in the Greater Mekong Area. In a report of the former UN Special Rapporteur on the Sale of Children, Child Prostitution and Child Pornography, it is noted that the high proportion of child prostitutes in Thailand has been aggravated by the arrival of children lured and trafficked from countries such as Vietnam, Cambodia, China, the Lao People's Democratic Republic and Myanmar. More recent studies also indicate that countries in the Mekong subregion are faced with the problem of both internal and cross-border trafficking. 'The countries are often concurrently origin countries, transit countries and destination countries. There is not only trafficking within the region, but across the continents.'

ACROSS THE BORDER TRAFFICKING ROUTES IN THE MEKONG REGION

The Burmese–Thai Routes

Burmese girls are trafficked into Thailand through two main channels: one is through the upper part and the other is through the lower part of the borderline between the two countries. The northern channel includes mainly the Tachileik–Mae Sai border and the Myawaddy–Mae Sot border checkpoints. The main southern channel is the Kawthaung–Ranong border checkpoint. As for the northern channel, most of the girls trafficked are those of minority groups or hill tribes such as Akha, Lahu and Tai. These girls are sent to sex entertainment outlets in several provinces throughout Thailand.

In the South, Indian Burmese girls and girls coming from southern Burmese states are mostly trafficked to work as prostitutes in Thailand's southern province of Ranong before being sent to other parts of Thailand or to Malaysia. Other important cross-border trafficking points are along the Thai–Burmese border: the Three Pagodas' Pass in Kanchanaburi Province and Mae Hon Song.[1]

THE CAMBODIAN–THAI ROUTE

From Cambodia to Thailand, the two main trafficking locations are the open transit points of Poipet in Banteey Meanchey Province and the Island of Koh Kong facing the town of Kompong Som. In Kon Kong, the girls are trafficked through the Head Lech checkpoint to Klong Yai, Trat Province, in Thailand (survey done by Krousar Thmey Organisation, Phnom Penh, 3 May 1995). From Poipet, the girls are being conveyed to the Thai town of Aranyaprathet (Migration, Women and Children: Prostitution and Sex Trafficking).[2]

THE CHINESE–THAI ROUTE

The Chinese girls rescued from brothels in Thailand by CPCR were all coming from Yunnan Province in south-western China (mostly from Sipsong Panna and autonomous zone), and were native of ethnic minorities.[3] From China, the girls are trafficked to Mong-Hpien, Muang-Yang and Mongla in the Shan State of Burma. From there, they would either stop at Keng Tung, or directly go south through the Shan State until they reached the Tachileik-Mae Sai border checkpoint. Once brought through the border, in the Mae Sai District, Chiang Rai Province, the Chinese girls are sent anywhere, depending on the demand of procurers. Most Chinese girls trafficked into Thailand, are not employed in Chiang Rai[4], mainly because they are more valuable in provinces frequented by Chinese tourists, because the trafficking of Chinese girls is more profitable if sold to Chinese customers and also because the customers complain they cannot communicate with them. Many of them are sent to work in larger cities such as Chiang Mai, Bangkok, Korat or South border provinces in Ranong, Songkla or Sungai Kolok,[5] where many Chinese-speaking sex tourists from Malaysia and Singapore make day trips. In September 1994, an anonymous employee at an entertainment venue in Chiang Rai confided in journalists from *The*

Nation that since police began taking action against child prostitution, the procurers decided to send them to the southern provinces, such as Songkhla.[6]

THE LAOTIAN–THAI ROUTE

Most of the Laotian girls are trafficked into Thailand either through Vientiane Province, through Bokeo Province further north-west or through southern provinces. From Vientiane Province, Laotian girls are trafficked to Nong Khai Province and Ubon Ratchatani's Khemarat, Chanuman and Khong Chiam districts as well as Mukdaharn Province in Thailand. Once across the border, the girls are sent to north-eastern cities, such as Udon Thani and Korat. Although there are no open transit points from the Vientiane Province area (a special transit pass is requested by the customs officials), the Lao girls are easily trafficked illegally across the Mekong River which forms the Thai–Lao border. Bokeo Province in Laos is also the gateway for border crossing to Thai Province of Chiang Rai and to Shan State of Burma. Bokeo Province has five districts with four of these situated on the banks of the Mekong River. Ton Phueng District is opposite to Chiang Saen District in Chiang Rai Province and also shares a border with Burma to the west. Both Laos and Thailand have signed an agreement to allow unlimited number of people to cross the border. Bokeo Province's immigration regulations are not the same as in Vientiane as permission is given for people from other provinces also to cross into Thailand. The trafficking of children between Laos and Thailand was also reported from the Laotian southern provinces to Ubon Ratchatani's Chong Mek village in Phibun District in Thailand,[7] that being the routes of trafficking, and it is interesting to study the case studies of trafficking in different places of Mekong Region.

CASE STUDY OF CAMBODIA

More and more Cambodian women are nowadays leaving their villages in search for work in Thailand. The economic needs at home, bad family situation, the promises of the recruiter and optimistic accounts of returnees are important factors influencing women to make the decision to leave their village and make the journey to Thailand. The high demand for women as workers, prostitutes, beggars and so on together with the perceived wealth in Thailand are important pull factors. Within this flow of women to Thailand, some have gone voluntarily and ended up in the situation pictured to them before they left their homes. Others, however, were deceived or forced to work under miserable circumstances.

Over the past year, the phenomenon of trafficking has received growing attention in Cambodia. International organizations, non-governmental organizations as well as the Royal Government of Cambodia have conducted surveys, held seminars, developed strategies, adopted a trafficking law and set up shelters in order to deal with the problem of trafficking. Thus far, the prime focus of these studies, strategies and shelters has been women and children trafficked into prostitution within Cambodia. A study has been carried out by Annuska Derks and Group to provide more information on the phenomenon of trafficking of women and children to Thailand not only for the purpose of prostitution, but also for begging or work in construction, fisheries and domestic work. Their study focuses primarily on the recruitment process, although the follow-up phases of transportation, employment situation and possibly arrest and return have not been neglected.[8] The research team consisted of Mrs Lim Sidedine. Mr Lor Monirith and was led by Annuska Derks, M.A. The research started in Phnom Penh, collecting information and documentation from organizations and persons working on trafficking issues and interviewing women in shelters in Phnom Penh. Then followed field trips to Battambang, Banteay Meanchey, Koh Kong and Prey Veng.

Studies on trafficking of women in Cambodia have thus far focused primarily on trafficking for prostitution. Prostitution and the problems related to it have received increasing attention. Prostitution is not a recent phenomenon in Cambodia. However, the increase of this practice in recent years has followed periods in which prostitution was banned—under the Khmer Rouge regime—or strictly controlled under the Vietnamese-backed socialist regime. Only after the economic liberalization and opening up of the country, and especially with the arrival of UNTAC, did Cambodia see an explosive growth in prostitution. Although the extent of prostitution has decreased after UNTAC left, studies have indicated that problems related to it, like the number of young girls in prostitution, the number of trafficked women and HIV/AIDS infection rates among prostitutes have risen.[9]

Most information available on trafficking in contemporary Cambodia relates to women and girls trafficked for prostitution inside the country. Although it is hard to get reliable data on trafficking and prostitution, surveys of 1993–1994 conducted by Vigilance and CWDA indicated that about half of the women and girls were sold into prostitution, mostly by parents or other relatives.[10]

Many of the reports written on trafficking and prostitution focus on the involvement of parents or other relatives in trafficking of young women in prostitution. This leads to the question on how is it possible that parents are involved in the trafficking of their own daughter? Why is it not problematic for these parents to bring their daughter into prostitution or any other bonded labour situation? Usually, poverty is given as the main reason to these questions. The Situation Report on Trafficking and Prostitution of Children states that 'poor families are by definition more susceptible to promises of jobs for their young daughters, often desperate enough to sell their daughters or other relatives to pay of a debt'.[11] However, important economic reasons alone cannot explain the involvement of parents in this practice. There are several factors coming together with the economic factors that make it possible for parents to let their daughters into prostitution in order to relieve poverty.

In Thailand, the problem of trafficking of young women for prostitution has existed much longer and on a much bigger scale than in Cambodia. Much more research has been done in order to find out the causes and cultural background of this phenomenon. Marjorie Muecke spent several extended periods of time since 1972 conducting fieldwork in the northern part of Thailand. She writes about the 'cultural continuity of prostitution', which also explains why it is possible for parents to be involved in bringing their daughters in bonded prostitution. The economic rewards of contemporary prostitution have enabled young women to support not only urban-based profiteers who control prostitution but also more importantly from a cultural perspective, to remit funds home to their families and villages of origin. Prostitution today is accomplishing what food vending did for the young women's mothers: both of these otherwise disparate endeavours have the effect of conserving norms by which women support the family, village and other basic institutions in Thai society.[12]

As in Thailand, also in Cambodia, prostitution has become an important possible activity through which daughter can fulfil expectations of providing financial support for the family. Parents will allow their daughters to work temporarily as prostitutes to pay back the money borrowed from the *maeban* (brothel owner) through which the family can relieve their financial burden. Women who work as prostitutes recognize their role in providing financial support for their families. One prostitute working in Prey Veng explained she is the second daughter among nine children. Her parents are construction workers, but cannot earn enough to support the whole family. She decided she would agree with her parents to work as a prostitute:

... because I saw the people who work here have money and they have new clothes. They can help their parents ... I cannot save money for myself, because my mother comes every time to take it. She takes 40,000 or 50,000 riel.

It is difficult to tell how extensive the network of recruiters and brothel owners is for the recruitment of women for commercial sex work in Thailand. Although it has become apparent that several layers of people are involved in the process, they do not seem to be part of one huge criminal network that extends its web throughout the country. There are many recruiters, usually women, who follow each other up. They are each individually related to different *maeban* in Cambodia and Thailand. Those with connections in Thailand will persuade women to go to Thailand, saying that it is easier to earn money there. The most beautiful girls, who are brought to work in border towns, are likely to continue to Thailand. A *maeban* in Koh Kong explained:

> The *maeban* who takes the prostitute girls (to Thailand) are mostly women. She tells the girls that she will bring them to Thailand for work. But when they arrive, she takes them to a Thai *maeban*. The Thai *maeban* pays 5,000 baht for each girl. The girls have to work till they have earned twice their price. Then the *maeban* sells them again. This way they continue to pass the prostitute from *maeban* to *maeban*.[13]

Although the recruitment process of women and children into prostitution follows similar lines, crossing the border involves more organization with regard to transportation, relations with corrupt officials and more bribes to pay. Risks are higher for those involved in cross-border trafficking.[14]

Recruiters and receivers of trafficked women and children will therefore demand higher profits for their activities. According to a police official in Banteay Meanchey, the girls sold to Thailand are mostly very young, below 13 years old. In Thailand, they can be sold to a customer for 20,000 baht for one week. But not all these girls stay in Thailand, some are sold even further. A police official in Battambang explained that it is difficult to find the children who are trafficked to Thailand because the big traffickers do not keep them in brothels. They bring them to other countries, such as Hong Kong, Singapore, Europe and so on.

As long as the trafficking of women and children for prostitution is profitable for those individuals involved, it will be hard to stop the practice. Besides, the lack of attention by, and also the involvement of police, border officials and military makes continuance of the practice of cross-border trafficking possible. A police official in Banteay Meanchey commented on the problem of child trafficking:

> It is impossible for us to solve the problem. Our armed forces are involved in this. They secretly transport children in their personal cars and reach the border of Thailand. They cross by the two main gates O'Prick and O Ta Chang. After the parents find out their children have disappeared, they come to complain to us. But we cannot take action when we only know that a child is inside some car going to Thailand.[15]

A police official in Battambang explained why it is easy nowadays to cross the border for traffickers:

> Before, the trafficking of human beings across the border was a rare problem, not like it is now. After the civil war, the Cambodian people lack education, they are poor, so they are inclined to do anything illegal... There are a lot of robeang ways, these are small, illegal ways to cross the border. Some belong to Pol Pot soldiers, some to the government army. But the problem is, do we work for the government, or do we work for ourselves...? Only if our policemen are really neutral and have good morals, can we defeat the problem of trafficking.[16]

There are several places and opportunities to cross the border. Most often, the women are led through Poipet in Banteay Meanchey Province and Koh Kong. The main border gates are open for Cambodians and Thai alike, who want to cross the border for one day. At the border station, they can receive a paper for 10 baht, which allows them to cross the border for 24 hours. Some traffickers will act as though they are accompanying the women or girls for *dai leeng* in Thailand, but without planning to come back, within a day. Besides the main ways, there are several smaller crossing points, without or with little border control. Some of them require a long trip through the mountains. In Koh Kong, the border with Thailand can be crossed relatively easily by boat, especially at night.

According to one police official in Battambang, crossing the border is not difficult for traffickers; but in meetings with the Thai and Khmer border police, the problem of how to combat the trafficking of women and children was discussed. He remarked that

> when someone enters Cambodia, the Khmer police control, when someone enters Thailand, the Thai police control. But now the traffickers choose small ways in the forest to enter and exit. In the meeting, we talked about how to do our work seriously, so we can catch the traffickers. But we have to know whether the police themselves serve the government or themselves.[17]

There are several issues related to trafficking for prostitution. The political factor is related to the will and ability of the government and other political institutions to address the problem of commercial sexual exploitation and trafficking of women and children.[18] In a report on sexual exploitation and trafficking in Cambodia, several of the flaws that exist in this political sphere are mentioned. Most importantly, these flaws consist of the insufficient dissemination and implementation of the Law on Suppression of Abduction. Trafficking and Exploitation of Human Beings (which states that 'anyone who entices a human being, whether male or female, minor or adult, of whatever nationality, whether by persuasion, promises of money or jewellery, or by any other method, and irrespective of whether the individual concerned agrees or does not agree, or by compulsion, threats or use of stupefacient or sedative drugs, for the purpose of abducting and selling the person or making them into a prostitute, that person shall be sentenced to imprisonment of 15 to 20 years. Person receiving shall be subject to the same punishment as the perpetuator'). Person colluding shall include those who provide money or other means for committing of the offence. Means of transport, equipment and property used during the committing of the offence shall be confiscated as State property.[19] The weak structures of the state hinder active involvement of the police in the combat of trafficking and proper border controls. The lack of attention from police authorities and customs officials, and especially their supposed involvement in the flesh trade, is in turn caused by problems such as lack of instruction, low salary and lack of means to combat the people who are involved.

The social factors involved in the existence of trafficking for prostitution are less visible and require a deeper understanding of Cambodian society and culture. Often mentioned are the fragmentation and disruption of families, the traumas, mistrust among neighbours and weakening of community spirit caused by the experiences of the past decades of war, oppression and border camp-life. Traditional values are said to have been lost, which together with poverty have caused growing family problems such as divorce, alcoholism, death or desertion of a parent. This, in turn, leads to weakening ties between child and parent resulting in the child's being sold, running away from home or leaving (with a recruiter) to look for work.[20]

In a paper addressing sexual exploitation from a gender point of view, one of the causes mentioned is the 'systematic undervaluation of females in terms of "property" or ability to earn in the market'.[21] These relate to the cultural values regarding the role and status of women and men. In a vigilance report on women trafficking and child prostitution, it is stated that 'in the context of this [Cambodian] culture, women are generally viewed as sex objects, and women are particularly taught to accept their roles as housewives, submissive to the law of the male world'.[22] Although this is a generally held view, in reality the role of cultural values regarding gender relations and sexual exploitation are much more complex.

Without entering into discussion about the myths and realities of gender roles in Cambodia, it does make sense to question why the rapid growth of female prostitution and trafficking is not considered culturally problematic for Cambodians. Permitting a daughter to go for work far from her village, as a prostitute or any other economic activity through which she can help support her family, seems to be a contradiction to the so-called traditional Khmer ideals. According to these ideals, a young woman needs to be protected and cannot leave her house too far without the company of her relatives. The venerable Mnichenda remarked on this:

> In our society, we have to take care that our daughters be good daughters. A good daughter from the Khmer point of view does not go far from home. As the Khmer saying goes 'Do not keep a good dessert for tomorrow; do not allow a woman to go far' ... Our society gives value to virginity of women. It is not like Europe or America, where they don't care about daughters who go away. But Khmer men love virgins and if parents do not allow their daughters to go to study far from home, we cannot blame them, because they know their daughters will lose their future if they lose their virginity.[23]

As in any society or culture at any time, present-day Cambodia has to deal with these conflicting ideals. Ledgerwood states that 'on the one hand daughters are supposed to be protected, on the other, the teenage daughter must bicycle all the way to the city and sell her goods in order to support the family'.[24] Changing circumstances, opportunities and practices have forced women to undertake all kinds of employment, even far away from their own family. The need to support the family financially has left young women with no other choice but to leave their home village and enter jobs that are not considered to be respectable, like prostitution. Although this may not be in accordance with some ideals held in Khmer culture, as the young woman is far from her protected home as well as losing her virginity, the young woman can fulfil the obligation to support her family. There is a saying in Khmer: *koun proh cencem kmein baan kaa, koun srey touh ci'e sampheng swechey kaa kut mdey dai*—a son does not feel responsible to take care of his parents, whereas a daughter, even when she works as a prostitute, will still think of her mother. As a prostitute explained:

> In general, for Khmer children, the sons do not take care of their families very much. The girls are mainly responsible to support their family. People think that for the boys, all responsibility for their family will be finished after he gets married. For the girls, even if they become prostitutes, they will always take care of their family.[25]

Like Thailand, Cambodia is also predominately a Therevada Buddhist society, although with different specific Cambodian adaptations. According to an elderly *doun chii* [nun] at a pagoda in Battambang, the power of *Karma*, or the working of 'impersonal causation', directs one's life. She explained, regarding the role of sons and daughters in the family, that 'it is true that when we are of old age, our daughter takes more care for us than our son. However, it depends also on our *Karma*, the fruits of our deeds in the past'. According to the head *doun chii,* one has to realize that:

> [I]n Buddhism, we know that we do not need to be angry with someone else about what he or she did to us. If we encounter suffering, we cannot blame someone else. It is the power of our *Karma*... I don't know clearly about the problem of trafficking of women for prostitution. This is also the power of *Karma* which gives bad medicine to a woman which causes her to be sold ... It is our *Karma,* our actions in the past, that make us do bad things... It is our *Karma* and even if we go away, we will still get it... That is why we have to do good actions.[26]

The results of *Karma* can be influenced and merit can be earned by performing good deeds, such as taking good care of one's parents or by supporting the pagoda. As such, the intention of giving is important and will be accepted. The venerable Monichenda noticed that it is the deed that is important:

> Buddhism assures women that although they are prostitutes, they can construct a pagoda. And now there are many pagodas which were constructed with money from prostitutes. Buddha never prohibited prostitutes from using their money to construct a pagoda. I think that is not a wrong thing for these women to do.[27]

This does not mean that Buddha supports the practice of prostitution. However, there exists a liberal stance within Buddhism not to moralize and interfere in one's 'immoral' activities, which allows the acceptance of someone's (good) intentions of giving, without moralizing about the source. This stance, combined with a discrepancy between the ideals in Buddhist spirituality and the reality of practice of some Buddhists, has led to many diverse and even contradictory interpretations concerning the 'Buddhist view' on prostitution.

The psychological perspective or trafficking for commercial sex is discussed in a report of the Physicians for Human Rights.[28] They write that sexual violation, shame, betrayal of trust, separation from the family, fears and depressions make a deep impact on the women's and girls' lives. The bad stigma of being a prostitute can somehow be paid off through offering at the pagoda and through being able to help relieve their families' financial problems. Still, the fact that a woman has already lost her virginity, and therefore is considered *koue* [broken] may make it difficult to return to the life she had before. Being *koue* already, she might decide to stay in prostitution, thereby furthering the possibility of trafficking to other brothels within the country or across the border to Thailand.

Trafficking for prostitution is related to various issues, which within the limited amount of time for this survey could not all be extensively addressed. The economic, political, social, cultural and psychological factors each play a role in the existence and prevalence of this phenomenon. Therefore, neither a particular factor can be held solely responsible, nor will a solution for only one of the inter-related problems terminate its existence. In order to develop meaningful prevention measures, it is important to get a deeper insight into these issues and how they are related to one another.

CASE STUDY OF VIETNAM

Vietnamese men, women and girls are trafficked for sexual and labour exploitation in Cambodia, the People's Republic of China (PRC), Thailand, Hong Kong, Macau, Malaysia, Taiwan, South Korea, the United Kingdom and the Czech Republic for commercial sexual exploitation.[29] Women and men are trafficked for forced labour at factories and construction or as domestic servants. Vietnamese trafficking victims are recruited through fraudulent marriages, false promises of employment, licensed and unlicensed migrant labour recruiting agencies. Many Vietnamese women and girls are trafficked through Dong Tham, An Giang and Kien Giang to Cambodia for sexual exploitation. In 2004, Cambodian police estimated that more than 50,000 girls were in brothels through Cambodia, many of whom were Vietnamese. The World Human Rights Organization and UNICEF estimate that one-third of the prostitutes in Cambodia are under the age of 18, the majority of whom are Vietnamese.[30]

Causes of women trafficking from Vietnam are many. In other words, there are many causes of this evil. In recent years, although Vietnam has recorded a high economic growth rate, it is basically not out of poverty. Unemployment still threatens many people. The need for jobs is increasing, and women are easily deceived by promises to find jobs by traders who in fact sell them into prostitution. Because of the development of the multi-sector commodity economy, the differentiation between the rich and the poor is increasing. A number of poor people try to earn money by all means, including illegal ones such as prostitution, whereas the rich want to spend their surplus money. They spare no money in entertainment, and traders do not mind laws. Another cause is the low educational standard of many women, who are unaware of their rights and dignity, and who do not react when being sold abroad. The degradation of morality and life-style of part of the population is also an important cause leading to the trading in women. Individualism and money are pushing them to emulate one another in earning money by all means, including inhuman acts. Women's dignity and body are considered as kind of goods to be sold for profit.

An important cause of this evil is the imbalance between Chinese men and women. Many Chinese men do not have enough money to marry and they prefer to buy Vietnamese women.[31] Vietnamese women are also recruited through fraudulent marriages. The Vietnamese Government estimates that approximately 10 per cent of the women in arranged marriages with Chinese men may have become trafficking victims. Many women are raped and abused by their husbands and in-laws. In some cases, they are sold off to other men.[32]

There are many causes of human trafficking in Vietnam. UNICEF argues that the causes are poverty, little education, lack of awareness of trafficking, family conflict, the demand of Chinese men for wives and the open, shared and difficult-to-police border between the two countries.[33] The UN Inter-Agency Project on Human Trafficking argues that many of the causes are socio-economic, such as difficulty in finding employment in rural and remote areas, lack of awareness and low education level.[34]

CASE STUDY OF LAOS

There are three types of trafficking in Laos: domestic trafficking for prostitution, cross-border trafficking for prostitution in Thailand and cross-border trafficking for slave labour in Thailand.[35]

Domestic trafficking for prostitution is from rural villages to the cities. Thousands of rural villages are moving from subsistence farming to migrant wage labour in urban areas such as in Vientiane. Periodically, the police investigate and raid prostitution establishments. But regardless of the strict law enforcement, prostitution still operates in night clubs, hotels, guest houses and restaurants. When disadvantaged and poorly educated girls from rural villages migrate to urban areas in search of employment, they are easily lured into bar work, and eventually into making a living from commercial sex. Foreign male tourists are known to be particularly fond of Lao young girls due to the misguided belief that they are less likely to have AIDS. School curriculums lack prevention courses on sexually transmitted diseases and the use of condoms.

The second form of trafficking is the cross-border trafficking for prostitution in Thailand. In 1994, four agents were arrested for recruiting girls in Vientiane. In one case, 'uniformed people' went to villages in Bokeo Province and offered money to ethnic minority families in exchange for their children's labour in factories. The children ended up in brothels in Chiang Rai Province, Thailand. Officials in Savanakhet Province reported that more than 15,000 of their youth sought employment in Thailand in 1995. Most left the country illegally, and an increasing number of them appeared to be young girls under 15 years of age.

Cross-border trafficking for slave labour in Thailand is the third form of trafficking from Laos. The children are then forced to work without pay as factory workers, as servants in private homes and as waitresses in restaurants and night clubs, in order to 'repay their debts or fees'. Some children have to do hard labour without rest and are frequently beaten up by their 'owners'.

The Government of Lao PDR took momentous steps towards setting a legal framework and indicators for progress on the rights of children and their families. In 1990, the Government of Lao PDR signed the Convention on the Elimination of all forms of Discrimination against Women (CEDAW). In 1991, Lao PDR also became a member of the United Nations Convention on the Rights of the Child (CRC) which guarantees for every child from birth to 18 years of age the right to survival, development, protection and participation.

There are no known cases of slave labour in Lao PDR. There have been attempts of trafficking children to neighbouring Thailand. Prostitution exists in urban areas such as Vientiane municipality and some rural villages.[36]

Victims of prostitution are sometimes victimized twice by the legal process when arrested as illegal immigrants into Thailand, many of whom can disappear without a trace. In one instance, three young Lao female suspects were detained in Rayong Province, Thailand, in the same prison cell with male criminals who had gang-raped them for three consecutive days. None of the offenders was prosecuted for rape.

Some parents are not adequately caring for their children. In some rural areas, parents encourage their children to work at home, in the field or elsewhere in order to support the family rather than go to school. This leads the children to have low educational level, lack of vocational skills, low self-esteem and eventually poverty, making them economically vulnerable to the traffickers and crime syndicates. In one instance, entire families left their rural village to beg in the cities.

Foreign investment and economic growth affect employment rate and indirectly affect the prospect for trafficking in women for the reason that they create more jobs and reduce the likelihood for young women to seek such high-risk jobs overseas.[37]

Lao PDR is still a poor developing country and does not have the resources to effectively suppress such international trafficking. Improving poverty level in rural areas would help reduce the tide of economic migration to urban areas and overseas, but development of the economic infrastructure is moving forward at a slow, but steady pace.

Keeping close surveillance of the 1,730-km national border with Thailand to prevent illegal border crossing is challenging. Encouraging rural villagers not to migrate to the cities is difficult if employment opportunities are unavailable for them near their local villages. Measures to change such villagers' behaviour must be comprehensive.

The Government of Lao PDR condemns the trading, abducting, procuring, seducing and smuggling of women for the ultimate goal of sexual exploitation of slave labour and seeks to punish those who operate, finance, facilitate, support and benefit from such criminal activities. Lao PDR's membership to the Conventions on the Elimination of all forms of Discrimination against Women (CEDAW) and the Convention on the Rights of the Child, combined with the 1991 National Constitution, the Penal Code, Labour Law and civil codes, firmly placed children's and women's rights in the first comprehensive legal framework in the nation's history.

The government also signed the Declaration and Plan of Action of the World Summit for Children in 1991. Subsequently, it set up the National Commission for Mothers and Children (NCMC), which drew up the first National Programme of Action for Children (NPA).[38]

Prostitution and pornography are outlawed in Lao PDR. The police periodically raid prostitution rings. Night clubs are allowed to open up until midnight in Vientiane Municipality, but were recently banned in Champasak Province. Punishment is 5–15 years of imprisonment for trading or abduction of humans, 3–5 years for pimps, brothel owners and traffickers, and 3 months to 1 year for prostitution. Rape of young girls aged 15 to 18 is punishable by 5–10 years of imprisonment, whereas rape of girls below the age of 15 is punishable by 7–15 years of imprisonment. Re-education or detention camps for prostitution and juvenile delinquency seem to have only limited success, as some offenders continue to make several repeated offences.

Despite the strict laws, however, prostitutes are still found not only in night clubs, hotels and restaurants in urban areas but also in some rural ethnic villages. Many rural villagers decided to give up farming in pursuit of better opportunities and a better life in urban areas such as in Vientiane or even in cities across the Mekong River in Thailand. Some rural young girls who seek jobs in hotels, night clubs and restaurants have been forced into prostitution by owners seeking more profit.

Lao PDR currently has no law that exclusively addresses the issue of trafficking in women. Articles 92, 119, 122 and 123 of Lao Penal Law specify various degrees of punishment for offences that relate to trafficking activities, but none of the Articles specifies any definition of the term 'trafficking'. Articles 2, 4, 33 and 34 also restrict certain labour activities for women and protect the rights of women.[39]

CASE STUDY OF CHINA

General figures on the number of Chinese women in the sex trade outside of China are very difficult to determine. A high-level Chinese official said that in 1991, a year in which the trafficking of Chinese women rose significantly, approximately 3,000 women went missing from Yunnan. Some of these women were deceived into the sex trade, but others slipped out of Yunnan to work in other occupations. Still others used Thailand as a transit point to enter a third country. The number of women trafficked into the Thai sex trade probably ranged between 500 and 1,500.[40]

The crime of trafficking in women and children in China was rampant before liberation. After the founding of the People's Republic of China in 1949 and under the leadership of the Chinese Communist Party (CCP), the Chinese police organs relying on the mobilization of the people redressed and smashed such crimes and as a result, such crimes were eliminated for good by the 1950s–1960s.

Such crimes staged a comeback however in the early 1970s, beginning from the remote and mountainous villages where the poverty-stricken women attempted to marry out and malefactors profited in trafficking by taking advantage of those women. For the present, the crime is restricted to the rural areas within China. Most victims are female villagers and children and the majority of purchasers too are peasants.

Causes of the crime are manifold. These are the upsurge of the tide of commercial economy and illegal profits drive malefactors to engage in such inhuman crimes. Regional imbalance in economical development and unequal distribution of property and wealth drive massive women to flow from poor native countryside to wealthy areas though marriage, employment or business. These village women are innocent and naive in self-defence and in the absence of moral and legal media for match-making and improper labour market, they are likely to fall prey to human traffickers. Sex disproportion in remote countrysides plus feudal remnants and arranged and trafficked marriage—colossal betrothal dowry requested often exceeds the purchase of wife—brought into existence an extensive market of the purchase of wives. On the other hand, with little legal abiding concept, peasants take it for granted to 'buy a wife with money' instead of considering it an offence. Besides, certain grassroots administrators are feeble and incoherent and are indifferent to trafficking in women and children. Some of them are even partial to the purchaser of a wife under the belief of beneficial match-making.

It is important to note that there have been several crackdowns on human traffickers and punishment to human purchasers.

The crime of human trafficking is marked by obvious localization in that victims flow in and out only in localized areas. In view of the geo-environment and economic development, most women are trafficked out from poor and remote regions in south-western areas as Guizhou, Yunnan and Guangxi, whereas the purchase provinces are in mid and northern China. The crime is rampant in underdeveloped areas in rural than urban areas. Most women trafficked were forced to marry and were used as tools of child production. In recent years, certain human traffickers operated in collusion with offenders who harbour beauty parlours and 'roadside hostel' and force the trafficked victims to prostitution.[41]

Most crimes are organized in groups—streamlined in abduction, escort, reception, delivery and sale and linked in a long chain of operations. Offenders operate under front names and in transient localities that render it difficult for the police during investigation. Most crimes are accomplished at illegal labour markets, railway stations and wharfs in cities and townships. The offenders use forged ID cards, employment certificates and lure native girls in their trap by promise of employment and business. Worthy of notice female traffickers are also in heavy proportion that render them more deception.[42]

Recent years even saw offenders in and outside China operate in collusion for trafficking women abroad in the name of tourism and business. The girls are trafficked from Yunnan borders to Thailand via Myanmar to local syndicates for prostitution. In 1995 and 1996 alone, the Thai police and charity institutions repatriated up to a hundred girls back to China.[43]

Early in 1978, comrade Deng Xiaoping as leader of China indicated that 'it is absolutely necessary to smash human traffickers with fanfare and momentum'. In the past decade, in view of the gravity of the crime involving the traffic in women and children, five meetings have been held nationwide sponsored by the central government to deploy campaigns targeted at the crimes of abduction and trafficking in women and children. Party and government leaders Jiang Zemin, Li Peng, Qiao Shi and Li Ruihuan made important instructions on the occasion. With a view to further promotion to the cause of women and children affairs in China, China promulgated in 1992 and 1995 the 'Programme for the Development of Women Affairs in China' and the '1995–2000

Programme for the Development of Women Affairs in China', which called 'to effectively prohibit the violent aggression and trafficking of women and to stop the illegal activities of prostitution and whoring by the end of this century'.[44]

CASE STUDY OF BURMA

In 1994, the Thai Ministry of Labour and Social Welfare announced that registration of Burmese migrant workers would be commenced in 10 provinces along the Thai-Burmese border. Already, in 1992 and again in 1993, authorities in Mae Sot, Tak Province (opposite Myawaddy in Burma's Karen State), had issued work permits to approximately 10,000 Burmese illegal immigrants for whom their Thai employers had provided guarantees.

As of June 1995, 27,603 Burmese registered immigrant workers who received ID cards were living in Mae Sot, Mae Ramad and Phrop Phra districts in Tak Province. Burmese immigrant workers who were registered in Thailand presently are in 36 districts of 9 provinces bordering Burma, which include Chiang Rai, Chiang Mai, Mae Hong Son, Tak, Kanchanaburi, Ratchaburi, Prachuab Khiri, Chumphon and Ranong, out of 100,356 registered Burmese immigrant workers received identification cards. The Burmese workers' registration implies that the Thai authorities provide them with working permits. The conditions announced in 1994 by the Ministry of Labour and Social Welfare under which Burmese migrant workers are permitted to work in Thailand border provinces were as follows:

- those who entered the country after 9 March 1976 are eligible to apply.
- that migrant workers are employed only when Thai workers are not available.
- that employers act as guarantor for the migrant workers and pay them at least the basic minimum wage.
- that employers pay a 3,000 baht guarantee for end.... Worker to the provincial immigration office, and that the employer pays a 1,000 baht fee per worker to the local Labour and Social Welfare Office. (Deadline to Register Workers, *Bangkok Post*, 27 July 1995)
- that a registration fee of 100 baht be paid by the applicant in order to receive an ID card and a work permit.

Illegal Burmese immigrants who failed to apply for a temporary work permit will be deported. Although Thai authorities are taking some measures to provide illegal immigrants some opportunities to obtain work permits in Thailand, the procedures for illegal workers are relatively complicated for them. As of 21 August 1995, the deadline date for submitting applications, the Tak local employment office said that only 30 Burmese workers had submitted their application, out of almost 30,000 Burmese workers believed to be in the province. This prompted the local administration office to postpone the deadline. In fact, many employers claimed the guarantee deposit is much too high, therefore the Tak chamber of commerce has proposed recently that the Interior Ministry and the Labour and Social Welfare Ministry lower the amount to 1,000 baht per worker and allow businessmen to employ Karen refugees from the border camps.[45] Further, Thai labour law is rarely upheld in favour of workers' rights, especially in an area of unorganized and un-unionized labour such as in the case of Burmese migrant workers. The minimum wage is rarely paid to unskilled Thai workers in rural areas, let alone to migrant Burmese workers. Thai official sources estimate that there are currently between 300,000 and 400,000 Burmese immigrants working both legally and illegally in Thailand, and other sources reported there were about 160,000 Burmese refugees in 22 'refugee/shelter' camps and about 200,000 other illegal Burmese workers in Thailand.[46]

In her study on Burmese women in Thai brothels, Hnin Hnin Pyne identified three kinds of 'choices': 'Voluntary indicates that the woman, prostitute-to-be, approaches the owner manager of a sex establishment herself; bonded implies the involvement of parents or guardians, who receive money from an agent or owner for giving their daughter; and involuntary conveys the use of deception and coercion of the women by an agent or owner/manager.'[47] But Hnin Hnin Pyne adds that voluntary prostitution shall not imply free choice. A girl's decision to become a prostitute must be understood in a political, economic and social context. Interviews with victims of child prostitution in Thai NGO shelters also raised attention to the issue, and revealed that 'many of the girls when asked if they knew they would be working in prostitution before they came to Thailand, said, "Yes." But when asked what they understood prostitution to be, we would get responses such as "wearing Western clothes in a restaurant". Likewise, when asked if they were able to leave the brothels freely, many initially said, "Yes." But asked if in fact they have ever tried to leave, almost all said they had not dared to do so because they had no money or because they feared being arrested or sold to another brothel. When asked if they could refuse clients, again, the answer was almost unanimously, "Yes." Yet asked to give specific examples, most could not, and it turned out that refusal was almost unheard of because the women and girls feared repercussions from the brothel owner and pimps.'[48]

A recent survey done by Images Asia[49] on 50 Burmese prostitutes revealed that the trend had somewhat changed in the way Burmese women entered prostitution in Thailand. The prostitutes interviewed by the NGO in brothels and in hospitals all claimed to be over 18 years of age, but some results of the survey may be applied to Burmese prostitutes rescued from a brothel in Thailand, who had been forced to work in slavery-like conditions and these women had been trafficked into Thailand. The survey done by Images Asia in 1995 reveals that many Burmese women came voluntarily to Thailand to work as commercial sex workers (CSW), and a few of them were actually trafficked into Thailand. Yet, the survey focused on women only and not on children, who remain a major target for traffickers. These Burmese women are both and illegal forced prostitutes. Most women interviewed by Images Asia said they did not expect the working conditions to be as difficult, and several revealed, that they did not have a good understanding of what prostitution really meant and what were the health consequences and risks involved.

Thus, an overview of the study reveals that there are cultural, familial, economic and historical reasons behind the decision of children to work in sex-establishments. In Thailand and its neighbouring countries, children are expected to support their parents, obey their wishes and show them gratitude and respect, whatever the difficulties imposed by the prevailing situation. Many children who migrate to work hard in difficult and in dangerous situations feel that they should not go home 'empty-handed' due to the traditional responsibility to look after their parents. As a matter of fact, 'prostitution is often perceived as possessing economic value for the country's development, as in the case of sex tourism, and fulfilling a traditional role of daughters who are caretakers of the family and community'.[50]

If they can, they will send remittances to their families in order to pay for survival. Theravada Buddhism conveys similar teaching. The Theravada or 'small vehicle' Buddhism found in Burma, Cambodia, Laos and Thailand encourages young women and girls to feel responsible for helping their families financially. Theravada Buddhism rejects the notion that women and girls can reach enlightenment. Thus, contrary to the Buddha's teachings, only men are encouraged to become monks and to pursue the spiritual life. The initiation to monastic life, therefore, is a way for a boy to show gratitude and pay respect to his parents and the burden to raise money for his family will be far less important than for his sister, who can only gain merit by working to raise money for her poverty-stricken family. This is another reason why many girls feel that they must make sacrifices for the benefit of their families, villages and their own *karma*.

WHY IN THAILAND?

Thus, women and girls from all countries of Mekong region are trafficked into Thailand. Of them, Burmese are the most significant foreign nationality found to be working in brothels in Thailand. Chinese girls from the Yunnan Province are the next most significant group. The Human Rights Watch team estimated that in 1993, at least 10,000 Burmese women and girls entered Thailand to work as prostitutes annually, and therefore the total number of them working in the sex industry in Thailand should conservatively range between 20,000 and 30,000. In October 1993, the Democrat MP for Chiang Ma, Narong Niymtha, said he witnessed the smuggling of girls at Chiang Rai's Mae Sai District opposite Tachileik in Burma, where the girls, whose nationalities were unknown, were brought by a pick-up truck from Tachileik through the official checkpoint into Chang Rai District. He estimated that at least 150 young girls were smuggled through Tachileik every week.[51] This figure implies that nearly 8,000 Burmese and Chinese girls are smuggled every year into Thailand from the northern Tachileik–Mae Sai border checkpoint alone. The Chinese police in Yunnan reported in 1992 that more than 5,000 girls left the province for Thailand each year.[52]

Apart from Burmese and Chinese girls, several Laotian and Cambodian girls have been rescued from Thai brothels. Currently,

Krousar Thmey, a Cambodian NGO, estimates that about 20–30 children per week are trafficked to Thailand, which is equivalent to an annual flow of between 1,040 and 1,560 children leaving Cambodia to Thailand. Efforts to come up with specific figures on the number of Lao women and girls either working in or rescued from the Thai sex industry have, thus far, been unsuccessful, as the Laotian people speak a language very similar to the Thai language.

The crucial question is why Thailand is the trafficker's destination? A few reasons could be identified by this present researcher. One important reason is that regarding foreign asylum seekers and refugees, the Thai government has yet to adopt a consistent or humanitarian response towards foreign (non-Thai) girls who survived forced prostitution. The position of the Thai government vis-à-vis foreign women who have been trafficked to Thailand and forced into prostitution is that they are illegal immigrants, and that they must not be permitted to stay in Thailand. In Ranong Province, the inconsistencies of the Thai government have been particularly appalling. In one article, Ranong chief inspector Police Lieutenant Colonel Sudchai Yanrat claimed that it would be easy for the police to actively weed out illegal immigrants and foreign prostitutes, but such a campaign could ruin the fragile economy of Ranong, which depends strongly on Burmese labourers.[53]

Thai government in the past clearly viewed sex entertainment as a stimulant for economic growth. In 1992, the UN Commission on Human Rights adopted a Programme of Action for the Prevention of the Trafficking and the Sale of Children, Child Prostitution and Child Pornography saying in part that 'special attention should be paid to the problem of sex tourism. Legal and other measures should be taken to prevent and combat sex tourism, both in countries from which the customers come and those to which they go. Marketing tourism through the enticement of sex with children should be penalized on the same level as procurement'.[54]

Tourism became an increasingly profitable industry in Thailand from the early 1970s onwards. In the late 1980s, this industry was the major source of foreign exchange, surpassing exports such as rice and textiles. The rapid development of the sex industry has played a significant role in this tourist boom. The public sector also has its own share of responsibility in the 'wild' development of the sex industry in Thailand. Hnin Hnim Pyne quotes Thanh-Dam

Troung:[55] 'The campaigns abroad to promote tourism focus on (i) the open sexuality of Thai women as shaped by local norms and the market; (ii) the submissive nature of Thai women as satisfying the need for a man to dominate; (iii) poverty as a justification (the clients are helping out these prostitutes support themselves and their families). Local campaigns stressed female sexuality as playing a critical role in the country's development and growth.'[56]

Prostitution flourished in Thailand during the Vietnam War. from 1964 to 1976, as 50,000 soldiers were based in Thailand while about 700,000 came annually for 'Rest and Recreation'. After twenty-five years, although the American presence ended, the booming tourism industry continued to sustain a portion of the sex industry in Thailand. Over the past three decades, the number of international tourist arrivals has seen an almost constant annual increase. Tourism arrivals jumped from 1 million in 1973 to 2 million in 1981 and from 4 million in 1988 to 5 million in 1990. Along with the growth of this industry, many government officials did encourage the development of the entertainment industry as a means of enticing more tourists.[57]

The development of the tourism industry has expanded with the organization of 'sex tours' arranged for foreign tourists. Foreign customers can select girls and boys from a book of photographs presented by agencies in their home countries, who will be provided once the customers arrive in Thailand.[58] In 1990 and in 1991, the number of tourist arrivals reached 5.3 and 5.1 million, respectively, of whom more than 65 per cent were unaccompanied males.[59] A German survey published by the German Health Ministry in 1995 revealed that in 1990, about 30 per cent or 50,000 of the German tourists who came to Thailand came only for sex entertainment purpose.[60] The Tourism Authority of Thailand (TAT) aims at 6.7 million tourist arrivals in 1995, a growth rate of 8.65 per cent over 1994.

According to the Tourist Authority of Thailand, the average Malaysian visit generates about 1,300 baht compared with the 25,000 baht spent by the average Japanese visitor, because most of the Malaysian visits are simply day trips across the border. Malaysians will remain the largest visitor group, expected to represent more than 1 million in 1996, followed by the Japanese market. The government support for tourism has been more direct in some instances, as government officials have often encouraged the opening of sexual-oriented entertainment establishments in order to increase tourism. In March 1993, the Governor of Songkhla was reported as supporting the idea that prostitutes be prevented from returning home during the Thai New Year period 'Songkhran' and instead be made to participate in the annual Songkhran parade because 'their participation would make the procession more colourful [...] I think they will attract foreign tourists'.[61] Since 1993, the Thai government has not changed its tourism policy, although several NGOs suggest that the government should establish strict guidelines for attracting tourists in Thailand and encourage ecological tourism and cultural tourism.

However, the existence of the sex industry should not be exclusively linked to international tourism, as the local Thai demand for sex entertainment, although less obvious, constitutes the bulk of sex services. Most clients of prostitutes in Thailand are Thai men. As Hnin Hnin Pyne notes that although the local side of the sex industry is less obvious, it is far more prevalent than sex tourism.[62] A study done by USAID in 1990 revealed that 75 per cent of Thai men have had sex with a prostitute and 48 per cent experienced their first sexual intercourse with a prostitute. In context of impressive growth of HIV/AIDS disease in Thailand, it is doubtful that men's behaviour in Thailand has changed much in the past 4–5 years.[63]

LAW SITUATION OF THAILAND AND TRAFFICKING IN THE REGION

It is pertinent to discuss the law situation in the region and most specifically in Thailand, which aims to combat trafficking. Existing legislative safeguards against human trafficking are somehow not very clear. There is some confusion caused by conflicting and contradictory laws contained in three 'sets' of the Thai legislation on child trafficking and prostitution. The first is the Trafficking in Women and Girls Act (Anti-Trafficking Act) which was passed in 1928. The second 'set' is made up of two laws: the Suppression of Prostitution Act of 1960 and the Entertainment Places Act of 1966, both of which are, like the Anti-Trafficking Act, outdated. The third 'set' of legislation is made up of several articles within the Thai Penal Code of 1956 and of the Thai Immigration Act of 1979.[64]

Thailand has acceded to two international legal instruments, the Convention of Elimination of All Forms of Discrimination against Women (CEDAW) and the Convention on the Rights of the Child (CRC). The other international laws pertaining to children's rights and trafficking are recognized by the international community as being customary international law; and although the Kingdom has not acceded to these instruments, it is obliged to respect and apply them.

Thai Legal Instruments demand discussion of some important Acts. The first remarkable Act is *The Trafficking in Women and Girls Act (Anti-Trafficking Act) of 1928*. This anti-trafficking Act was passed in 1928 as a result of the perceived numbers of foreign nationals in Thai brothels. It prohibits trafficking in women and girls. In Section 4, any person who brings women or girls into Thailand for the purpose of having sexual intercourse with other persons, and any person who is involved illegally in the trading of women and girls in Thailand for such purpose, will be liable to not more than seven years of imprisonment and/or a fine of not more than 1,000 baht. Section 7 states that women and girls, who have been trafficked in Thailand, will be exempted from imprisonment and/or fines. Before being deported from Thailand, however, Section 6 specifies that the victims must be sent to a state reform house for 30 days, a period that can be extended by a judge. The anti-trafficking law also requires Thai authorities to arrange and shoulder the cost of the victims' repatriation to their country of origin.[65]

The Suppression of Prostitution Act of 1960 is another important Act. The Suppression of Prostitution Act (Prostitution Prohibited Act) was passed in 1960 in part because of great pressure from the United Nations that was campaigning at that time for the abolition of prostitution.[66] The Act replaced the Contagious Diseases Prevention Act of 1908, which aimed at controlling prostitution. The new law of 1960 was intended to eliminate prostitution[67] by making it an illegal activity. It applies sweeping measures against all forms of prostitution—adult or child, male or female—without distinction. Under this law, male and female prostitution and anyone else who is involved in arranging and/or profiting from the Act are liable to punishment.

Section 5 states that prostitution soliciting in streets and public shall invite imprisonment of not over three months and/or a fine of not more than 1,000 baht. Section 6 states that prostitutes selling sexual services in brothels shall face jail term of not more than six months and/or a fine of not more than 2,000 baht. Section 7 provides a similar penalty for those prostitutes who sell sexual services to customers of similar gender. According to Section 8, procures shall face a jail sentence of not more than three months and/or a fine of not more than 1,000 baht. Section 9 states that brothel managers and pimps shall face imprisonment for not more than one year and/or a fine of not more than 4,000 baht, and Section 10 provides that brothel or sex establishment owners shall face imprisonment for not more than six months and/or a fine of not more than 2,000 baht.

Under Section 11–16, in order to reform convicted prostitutes, they can be provided with medical treatment and sent to an assistance centre where they can receive vocational training for a period not exceeding one year from the day the person has satisfied the sentence of the court. It the person tries to flee the centre, penalty includes imprisonment for not more than three months or a fine of 1,000 baht or both. It empowers the Director General of Public Welfare to issue disciplinary and work regulations for assisted persons, and to punish those breaking the rules by (i) a maximum 15 days' confinement or by (ii) the exemption or reduction of benefits or facilities provided by the assistance centre.

The Entertainment Places Act of 1966 is another remarkable legal instrument. The Entertainment Places Act of 1966 was designed to pave the way for brothels to be legalized in the guise of massage parlours, bars, night-clubs, tea houses and so on. Its enactment occurred within the context of a national policy to increase state revenue from the 'rest and recreation' activities of US armed forces stationed in Vietnam. According to Section 3, 'Entertainment Places' are established which provide baths, massage or steam bath services with women attending to male customers. Dance establishments, bars and other establishments where dance shows are performed are also defined as entertainment places under Section 3 of the Act. According to Section 4, these places are only allowed to operate under licence obtained from the local police stations. The use of licensed establishments for prostitution is illegal. The Act, under Section 16, sets a minimum age of 18 years for women working in these establishments. The penalty against the owner of an establishment that employs women under the age of 18 is absurdly light—just 2,000 baht (Section 27). The Entertainment Places Act empowers the police to close a place in which commercial sex is offered. It also provides for the Social Welfare Department to send prostitutes to rehabilitation centres where they are to receive vocational training.

The Penal Code of 1956 is also another strong legal instrument. The Thai Penal Code was adopted in November 1956. Under the Penal Code, prostitution is not illegal, but the procurement for the purpose of prostitution is. The Penal Code assigns more severe penalties to this offence than those contained in the Prostitution Prohibition Act. Sections 276, 277, 278, 279, 282, 283 and 286[68] are far more specific and provide harsh punishment for abuses against girls forced into prostitution. Penalties increase if either offence is committed against girls under 18 years of age and again if committed against girls under 15 years of age.

Section 276 penalizes forced sexual intercourse with a woman 'who is not wife, against her will, by threatening her by nay means whatever [...]' and the punishment shall be of 4–20 years' imprisonment and a fine of 8000–40,000 baht. The minimum jail penalty is increased to at least 15 years and the minimum fine increased to at least 30,000 baht if this sexual offence is committed under the threat of a gun or explosive or with 'the participation of persons in the nature of destroying the women'; such offence could also lead to life imprisonment.

Section 277 makes sexual intercourse with a girl under the age of 15 statutory rape, even if it is committed with her consent. The punishments laid down are imprisonment of 4–20 years and a fine of 8,000–40,000 baht. Similar to Section 276, if the offence is committed by participation of persons in the nature of destroying the girl, or if it is committed under the threat of a gun or explosive, such will be punished with life imprisonment. Also, Section 277 increases the minimum jail penalty and fine to 15 years and 30,000 baht, respectively, if the offences described in Sections 276 and 277 cause grievous bodily harm to the victim.

Sections 278 and 279 penalize indecent acts committed on a person over 15 years of age and not over 15 years of age, respectively. Indecent acts committed by means of threat or other act of violence, such as taking advantage of a person, unable to resist or causing such person to mistake him for another person deserves penalties of not more than 10 years jail and/or a fine not exceeding 20,000 baht. For the offences described in Sections 276, 277, 278 and 279, if they cause death to the victim, the offender shall be punished with death or imprisonment for life.

Section 282 refers to the offence of procurement for sexual purposes and stipulates that anybody who 'in order to gratify the sexual desire of another person, procures, seduces or takes away for indecent act, whether [...] such offence are committed in the different countries or not, shall be punished with imprisonment of 1 to 10 years and a fine of 2000 to 20,000 baht. [...] If the commission of the offence [...] is occurred to the girl or woman not yet over 18 years of age, the offender shall be punished with jail term of 3 to 15 years and a fine of 6000 to 30,000 baht. If the commission of the offence [...] is occurred to the girl not yet over 15 years of age, the offender shall be punished with imprisonment of 5 to 20 years and a fine of 10,000 to 40,000 baht', and anybody who supports such commission of offence is liable to the same punishments.

Section 283 punishes any person who undertakes to persuade for the purpose of obscene acts, using deceitful means such as threats, violence or coercion with imprisonment from 5 to 20 years and a fine from 10,000 to 40,000 baht, whether the various acts are committed in different countries or not. If the offence is committed on a person not yet over 18 years of age, the minimum imprisonment sentence will be 7 years and the minimum fine 14,000 baht, and if the offence is committed to a person not yet over 15 years of age, the minimum jail sentence will be 10 years and the minimum fine 20,000 baht. This Section also provides for life imprisonment and death penalty.

Section 286 suggests punishments of 7–20 years in jail or life imprisonment and fines of between 14,000 and 40,000 baht or life imprisonment for pimps who under this article are classified together with procurers.[69]

Title XI of the Penal Code refers to child trafficking as offences against liberty and reputation. Section 309 punishes persons who compel others to act under threat of injury to life, body, liberty and reputation. Section 310 refers to the illegality of forced confinement and detention. If such offence causes death or grievous bodily harm, the offender shall be punished as provided in Sections 290, 297 and 298, which provide for jail sentence of 6 months to 20 years depending on the seriousness of the offence. Section 312 penalizes trade in human beings for slave-like exploitation and Section

317 refers to child abduction for lucre or indecent purposes, and imposes a penalty of 5–20 years' jail and a fine of 10,000–40,000 baht. In Section 318, persons who dishonestly buy, dispose or accept a minor taken away from her/his parents or guardians against the will of such minor will receive similar penalties to the abductor. Finally, under Section 320, any person who sends a person out of the kingdom by means of threat, violence or undue influence shall face a jail term of 2–10 years and/or a fine of 14,000–20,000 baht.

The Thai Immigration Act of 1979 is also an important Act to be discussed. The Thai Immigration Act, as amended in 1980, forbids the illegal entry into Thailand and punishes such offence by detention of up to 10 years and fines of up to 100,000 baht. Among the persons to be denied entry under Section 12 are those not in possession of valid travel documents, those without means of subsistence, those seeking work as unskilled labourers, those who have engaged in prostitution, trading in girls, drug trafficking or other immoral activities. Any person who 'brings or takes an alien into the Kingdom [...] shall be imprisoned for not more than 10 years and fined not more than 100,000 baht'. It also provides that any person who is aware of an alien illegal entry into Thailand, but 'despite such knowledge provides accommodations, hiding place or assistance [...] shall be imprisoned for a period of not more than 5 years and fined not more than 50,000 baht'.[70] An exception is made regarding persons from neighbouring countries who do not hold valid travel documents but who enter Thailand with permission. Section 13(2) states that 'citizens of the countries having common borders with Thailand [can] temporarily cross the border in compliance with the mutual agreement made between Thailand and those countries'.

Now the question is why and how prostitution and trafficking are rampant within such an intensive legal system. In fact, a few significant weaknesses of the Thai legal framework can be discussed in this context. The weakness of the current legal framework for dealing with trafficking and prostitution has raised concerns within the legislature and among several governmental organizations and national or international non-governmental organizations (NGOs). The Anti-Trafficking Act needs serious reform since it does not prohibit trafficking in boys, nor does it address the selling of Thai women and girls outside of Thailand. Also, trafficking victims are remanded to a penal reform institution for not less than 30 days. In the Prostitution Prohibition Act, the customer is not liable to punishment while the penalties on procurers and brothel owners are extremely light with a maximum jail sentence of 1 year and a maximum fine of 4,000 baht. Penalties are lighter than those under the Penal Code. The definition of 'places of prostitution' is far too vague and thus difficult to enforce. In addition, the law does not distinguish between voluntary prostitution and forced prostitution, since according to the Prostitution Prohibition Act, even a person who was lured or forced into prostitution is liable to imprisonment and/or a fine. Not only are the sanctions against abusers too light, there are several inconsistencies and contradictions between these four legal instruments. The Penal Code severely penalizes persons who have intercourse with minors, yet the Prostitution Prohibition Act omits to do so. The Anti-Trafficking Act exempts women or girls trafficked into prostitution from imprisonment or fines, whereas the Prostitution Prohibition Act makes no such exemption. Further, the Prostitution Prohibition Act clearly undertakes discrimination against trafficked prostitutes.[71]

In fact, fear of the exploding AIDS pandemic in Thailand in the late 1980s resulted in the emergence of a political debate regarding prostitution and trafficking. The Seventh National Economic and Social Development Plan of 1992–1996 includes the Children and Youth Development Plan (the 'Plan'), which enumerates some negative aspects of the impressive economic growth Thailand has experienced during the past 15 years. Child Prostitution and child sexual abuse are among the several child abuses listed by the Plan, which explains the causes of such abuse as due to children being 'influenced by improper social values with regard to consumption and sexual relationship. Many are forced or misled to serve business interests or the [sex] entertainment industry. Law enforcement, as well as measures to protect, prevent, guard and supervise children [...] are not efficient.'[72]

Chuan Leekpai, the former Prime Minister, who was in office from September 1992 to July 1995, has long been associated with efforts to improve the education and health of children, and consequently one of his administration's major stated goals was to bring an end to child trafficking and prostitution. In order to prevent and eradicate child prostitution and trafficking in Thailand, the Chuan administration boasted of two goals: (i) one was to improve formal and informal education opportunities and to provide vocational training under the Public Welfare Department. Among the policies formulated in the Children and Youth Development Plan to promote child development are (a) the extension of compulsory education from 6–9 years for in-school children aged 6–14 in order to develop their knowledge and basic skills, (b) the acceleration of occupational training for out-of-school youth in 14–25 age group, and (c) the acceleration of prevention [...] and rehabilitation programmes for Children in Especially Difficult Circumstances (CEDC), [...]) and scholarship in poor rural areas under the Ministry of Education. (ii) The other was to eliminate prostitution of girls under 18 years of age. Advised by Dr Saisuree Chutikul.[73]

Chuan Leekpai announced in November 1992 to provincial governors that he intended to put an end to child trafficking and forced prostitution. This campaign was aggressively supported by the Minister of Interior, General Chavalit Yongchaiyudh, who declared he wanted the closure of all brothels within two months. The Prime Minister himself did make a distinction between voluntary child prostitution and forced child prostitution, and made it clear to the public that he would not attempt to eradicate prostitution in general. Chuan Leekpai even recognized and condemned the involvement of government officials in such abuse.[74]

Following the Prime Minister's announcement in November 1992, a sex worker in the southern town of Songkhla came to the town hall seeking protection as she was convinced that pimps and/or police were going to kill her. She was denied protection and a short time later was killed in the town hall itself. The government response to the public outcry was a major crackdown on brothels, with many brothels going underground for several months. However, the action of the Chuan Leekpai administration proved ineffective in reducing child prostitution. The newly-elected coalition government led by Prime Minister Banham Silpa-archa (Chart Thai Party) that came to power on 2 July 1995 presented the cabinet's polices on 26 July 1995. Although the policy regarding 'children in difficult circumstances' was expressed in quite a vague manner, the government declared that it will take action against child prostitution and trafficking.

Although the laws' inconsistencies and contradictions contribute in some ways to the defeat of the Thai government to eradicate trafficking and/or prostitution, the government's failure to combat prostitution lies more in the non-enforcement of the most obvious prohibitions.[75] The Entertainment Places Act has clearly never been enforced. Many sex establishments operate without any licences and provide sex services. The main articles of the Thai Penal Code relating to prostitution and trafficking are also rarely enforced.[76] For example, Article 27, which is the only current legislation relating to clients of sex workers, has never been enforced. An indication of the lack of interest of law enforcement authorities in reducing prostitution is that it has become customary for most officers to apply the legislation that is the most lenient on the abuses, that is, the Prostitution Prohibition Act of 1960.[77]

The Anand Panyarachum administration established an anti-prostitution task force unit within the Crime Suppression Division (CSD). At the time, the unit's supervision was under the CSD Deputy Commander Police Colonel Bancha Jarujareet, second in charge of the CSD. The task force's duty was to raid every brothel in the country that had prostituted children detained against their will. Even though the unit was understaffed with only six police personnel and one vehicle, under the command of Pol Col Bancha, the unit was very active and collaborated well with CPCR. Rescue operation was often organized following investigation of forced child prostitution by CPCR and other local NGOs. When underage prostitution were found in brothels, the unit would send them to NGOs' emergency shelter where the girls were given counselling, medical and psychological assistance, vocational training, before being repatriated to their homes, whether in Thailand, Burma, China or Laos. The anti-prostitution task force, however, was plagued from its beginning. The understaffing was mainly due to a lack of financial support and a lack of collaboration and assistance from the local police was often reported.

Under the following Chuan Leekpai administration, the Crime Suppression Division's task force unit, which had previously the authority to override local police deal with forced and child prostitution directly, was weakened. In late 1992, the CSD's anti-prostitution task was disbanded in favour of a new CSD unit named 'Co-ordination Centre for the Prevention and Suppression of Child Prostitutes and Child Labour Abuse'. The mandate of this new section is to maintain a database on brothels and to carry our raids and rescue operations in cooperation with other local police units. Local police units, however, are often accused by local activists and Thai officials themselves of being involved directly or indirectly in the sex trade.[78] The new unit focused on public information through the editing of posters and booklets, inviting the public to contact the unit in case of alleged child abuses.

Although the Anti-Trafficking Act of 1928 forbids the imprisonment or fine of women or girls who are trafficked into Thailand, the Thai policy has been to instead apply the Prostitution Prohibition Act. Indeed, the Chuan Leekpai administration continued to allow discriminatory practice by the Thai police[79], who continue to arrest female victims of such abuse, thus infringing the Convention on the Elimination of All Forms of Discrimination against Women (CEDAW) ratified in 1985.[80] The Crime Suppression Division Police in Thailand have conducted many raids on brothels throughout Thailand in which Thai, non-Thai minority and foreign girls[81] from bordering countries have been simply transferred from detention in a brothel to detention in a police station, army barracks or detention centre such as Ban Kretakern, the Women's Detention Centre in Pakkred, Bangkok. Unfortunately, due to high levels of corruption,[82] girls who have been 'released' from forced prostitution have at times been released from detention and sent back to the brothels after the owner arrived at the police station to pay their 'fines'.[83] In addition, it is easy for those responsible for the trafficking and abuse of girls forced into prostitution to avoid imprisonment or to gain early release; in fact, they are imprisoned by paying bribes to police and prison officials.[84]

The corruption of many Thai officials has often been criticized, not only by the media or NGOs, but very often by Thai officials themselves.[85] The active or passive participation of Thai officials (customs officials, local police, etc.) has been one of the major reasons for the growth in child trafficking in Thailand. The lack of rights for illegal workers and the collusion between Thai trafficking syndicates, police and immigration officers is a major contributing factor to the increase in child trafficking in recent years.[86] But the usual penalty applied to officials implicated in trafficking, and brothel protection rackets is usually very low. For example, police officials are usually transferred to another posting if found guilty of such offences.

The government also failed to push for the arrest of the agents, brothel owners, recruiters or clients involved in child trafficking, prostitution and associated violations.[87] The brothel raids that occurred from 1991 onwards did involve the arrest of pimps and brothel owners, but these efforts were extremely limited. When the arrests took place, a new case reached the courts and offenders were sentenced. Following the brothel raid that took place in Ranong in June 1992, during which 33 Burmese women and girls were rescued, the police arrested two guards and two members of the brothel owner's family, but the brothel owner escaped. Another five brothel raids in Ranong in July 1992 involved 79 Burmese women and girls and led to the arrest of two brothel owners only, but all the others escaped. In July 1993, a raid in Muang District, Kanchanburi Province, involved the arrest of 32 Burmese girls and women, but the pimps and brothel owners escaped again.[88]

In many cases, however, when agents, pimps or brothel owners have been arrested, they have usually been charged under the Prostitution Prohibition Act that carries lighter penalties than those provided under the Penal Code.[89] Colonel Surasak Suttharom pointed out that both the revision of the Prostitution Prohibition Act and the enforcement of the law by the police were crucial, but most important too was the need to place pressure on the judicial system to prosecute cases and not allow them to be settled out of court.

According to CPCR, who filed several cases of lawsuit against child prostitution, legal actions in child prostitution cases take a long period of time. Some cases, which happened in 1991, were still under preliminary court or under the process of investigation of witnesses of the complainant in 1993.[90] For cases of child prostitution that are reported all over the country, hearings take place at local courts where the crime takes place. The gap of time between one hearing to another could last months. And if the witnesses do not live in the same provinces or districts, it would take even longer. In order to shorten for consideration the cases by courts, CPCR has exercised an important role. When cases involved foreign children, their absence during the trial greatly affected the nature of the lawsuit, and often it has not been possible for CPCR to quicken legal procedures, even though foreign child victims were involved.

Unfortunately, little information is available on the number of brothel owners, pimps, women and children arrested under the Prostitution Prohibition Act, the Entertainment Places Act, the Anti-Trafficking Act and under the Penal Code. In response to the increasing number of children being victim of sexual abuses, prostitution, trafficking and other criminal activities, the Office of the Attorney General in Bangkok established the Child Rights Protection Committee in August 1995. The Committee has several objectives: to work for the protection of children's rights according to Thai and the international legal instruments and to promote judicial co-operation with other countries. Currently, as the establishment of the Committee is very recent, the team is doing some research on the issue of child rights abuses in Thailand.

Given the complexities of the issue, policymakers and lawmakers from the six countries of the Mekong sub-region examined the extent to which laws and policies exist to prevent and remedy the problem of trafficking in women and children.

Key issues discussed are quite significant. First, all six countries of the Mekong sub-regions are parties to two international treaties which contain provisions that can be used against trafficking in women and children, such as the advocacy of laws and law enforcement. In addition, they have all participated in adopting a variety of international declarations and programmes of action which have an impact on the issue. This indicates that the framework for needed action is present. However, the problem lies in poor implementation of all the international standards. Second, in all countries in the Mekong sub-region, there are laws which can be used to counter the trafficking of women and children. Again, most of these laws are poorly implemented. Often, migration laws are applied, leading to the punishment of trafficking victims as illegal migrants. Law enforcement has also failed in dealing with the perpetrators of trafficking. Third, cross-border cooperation at bilateral and sub-regional levels is mostly carried out informally and in an ad hoc manner. Even where there are already existing policies and mechanisms that could be used to stem the tide of trafficking in the regional context, they have not been used to the maximum extent.

All the Mekong region countries agreed to:

1. use a working definition of trafficking in pursuing cases of trafficking victims.

2. make use of existing legislation to protect victims of trafficking and not to punish them as illegal migrants.
3. promote an inter-disciplinary approach to law enforcement that will cover not only protection but repatriation, rehabilitation as well as reintegration of trafficking victims.
4. establish national mechanisms, e.g. National Committee/Task Force on Trafficking.
5. develop Plan of Action to combat trafficking in women and children. The plan of Action sets timeframes as well as targets.
6. organize consultations for the establishment of bilateral and sub-regional forms of cooperation.
7. promote information exchange and networking between government and non-governmental organizations.
8. convening of another regional consultation by the year 2000.

There are some additional Coordinated Mekong Ministerial Initiatives against Trafficking (COMMIT Process). COMMIT MoU signed by the six GMS countries to fight against human trafficking. Sub-Regional Plan of Action has been developed to turn the policy commitment into practice. National Plan of Action that is in line with the Regional Plan of Action has also been developed/amended. UN, international and civil society organizations have formed 'partnership' to support the government implementation. Annual review and planning meetings among senior officials of the six countries also prescribed some additional recommendations: promulgation of laws to cover not only in-country trafficking but also cross-border situations. It wants the coverage of not only trafficking but also forced labour and slavery-like situations, and finally it speaks for promotion of formal bilateral and multilateral forms of cooperation.

Therefore, in the long run, one can observe that there are still several challenges to improve the situation in Mekong region. First, resources are limited to address this complex issue. We can understand how national laws and procedures prevent effective cooperation in victim identification process, investigation and prosecutorial process (e.g. Mutual Legal Assistance law). Causes at the source and communities are also difficult to address (e.g. poverty, lack of employment opportunities). Data collection remains unsystematic and incomplete. To date, trafficking interventions have generally targeted almost everybody other than those who benefit most from the trafficking crime—the exploiters. No single organization can deal with global problems such as human trafficking, but whether cooperative responses or inter-agency strategies can facilitate a more effective response still remains to be seen. However, given that human trafficking is currently being addressed by a myriad of UN agencies, national and international NGOs, inter-governmental organizations and governments, a greater understanding of past and current experiences is critical if future strategies are to involve effective cooperative relationships among organizations at national, regional and global levels.

NOTES

1. *Trafficking and Forced Prostitution of Burmese Women in Thailand,* by Chris McMahon, Bangkok: ECPAT. Information Centre, October 1994 and *A Modern Form of Slavery: Trafficking of Burmese Women and Girls into Brothels in Thailand,* by *Asia Watch and Women's Rights Project, Human Rights Watch New York,* 1993.
2. A Compilation of Current Reports from Cambodia, presented by the CCPCR and CWDA and Krousar Thmey, July 1995.
3. *Far Eastern Economic Review,* 9 September 1993, p. 36.
4. *Thai Border a Haven for Illegal Immigrant Trade,* interview with Chiang Rai, Governor, Khamron Booncherd, *The Nation,* 7 September 1994.
5. Silent Suffering, *The Nation,* 6 July 1992.
6. *Thai Border,* 1994.
7. Report by Michael Harrow of Help the Children Association in Ubon Ratchatani, May 1995.
8. Annuska Derks, *Trafficking of Cambodian Women and Children to Thailand.* Phnom Penh: IOM International Organization for Migration and Centre for Advanced Study, 1997, p. 3.
9. Ibid., p. 7.
10. *The Trafficking and Prostitution of Children in Cambodia: A Situation Report.* Phnom Penh: UNICEF, 1995.
11. Ibid., p. 17.
12. Marjorie Muecke, 'Mother Sold Food, Daughter Sells Her Body: The Cultural Continuity of Prostitution', *Social Science, Bangkok,* No. 7, 1992, p. 891.
13. *Trafficking and Prostitution,* p. 17.
14. Jasmine Caye, *Preliminary Survey on Regional Child Trafficking for Prostitution in Thailand.* Thailand: CPCR, 1995.

15. Derks, *Trafficking of Cambodian*, op.cit., pp. 16–17.
16. Ibid., p. 17.
17. Ibid.
18. *The Role of Community Education in the Prevention of Commercial Sexual Exploitation of Children*. Thailand: ECPAT, 2000.
19. National Assembly, 'Commission on Human Rights and Reception of Complaints', *Report on the Problem of Sexual Exploitation and Trafficking in Cambodia*. Phnom Penh, 1997, p. 20.
20. *Trafficking and Prostitution*, p. 18.
21. WEDO, *Root Causes: A Gender Approach to Child Sexual Exploitation*. Stockholm: World Congress against Commercial Sexual Exploitation of Children, 1996, p. 12.
22. Human Rights Vigilance of Cambodia, *Report on Sex Trafficking of Women and Children*. Phnom Penh, 1996, p. 3.
23. See Annuska Derks, 'Perspective on Gender in Cambodia: Myths and Realities', *Cambodia Report*. Cambodia Development Resource Institute, Phnom Penh, Vol. II, No. 3, November–December 1996.
24. Judy Ledgerwood, *Analysis of the Situation of Women and Cambodia: Research on Women in Khmer Society*. Cambodia: UNICEF, 1992, p. 5.
25. Derks, *Trafficking of Cambodian*, p. 21.
26. Ibid., p. 27.
27. Ibid., p. 23.
28. Physicians for Human Rights, *Commercial Sexual Exploitation of Women and Children in Cambodia, Personal Narrative: A Psychological Perspective*. Boston, 1996.
29. US Department of State Trafficking in Persons Report, 2007 in http://www.humantrafficking.org/countries/vietnam, accessed 26 February 2010.
30. East Meets West Foundation, ADAPT Program Research, The Face of Human Trafficking in http://www.humantrafficking.org/countries/vietnam, accessed 26 February 2010.
31. Nguyen Phong Hoa, *Vietnam, Illegal Labour Movements, Trafficking in Women and Children*. Hanoi: Vietnam Lawyer's Association, 25–28 November 1997, p. 8.
32. UNICEF: The Children in Vietnam in http://www.humantrafficking.org/countries/vietnam, accessed 26 February 2010.
33. Ibid.
34. UNIAP: Vietnam Overview in http://www.humantrafficking.org/countries/vietnam, accessed 26 February 2010.

35. Anonymous, Lao People's Democratic Republic, *The Situation of Trafficking in Women*. Vientiane, November 1997, p. 4.
36. Ibid., p. 6.
37. Ibid., p. 8.
38. Ibid., p. 10.
39. Ibid., p. 12.
40. Vorasakdi Mahatdhanobol, *Chinese Women in the Thai Sex Trade*, translated by Aaron Stern, edited by Pornpimon Trichot. Bangkok: Chinese Studies Centre, Asian Research Centre for Migration Institute of Asian Studies, Chulalongkorn University with support from International Organisation for Migration (IOM), The Centre for the Protection of Children's Right Foundation, 2007, p. 78.
41. Zhang Weihang, Zhu Yantao, Fang Yuzhu, 'Abduction and Trafficking of Women in China: Status Quo of the Crime and Counter-measures', Regional Conference on 'Illegal Labour Movements: The Case of Trafficking in Women and Children', Southeast Asian Fund for Institutional and Legal Development through the Canadian International Development Agency, United Nations International Children's Fund, Child Rights Asianet, Center for Asian Legal Studies—University of British Columbia and the Mekong Region Law Center in Co-Operation with the National Commission on Women's Affairs of Thailand; Bangkok, 25–28 November 1997, pp. 2–3.
42. Ibid.
43. Ibid., p. 6.
44. Ibid.
45. *Illegal Burmese Workers Get Deadline on Permits, Bangkok Post*, 28 August 1995.
46. Mr. Wallaee, Chairman of the Karen Refugees Committee, reported to *The Nation* that the number of Karen refugees had increased from 50,000 to 120,000 since the end of 1994; Burmese Refugees Here Top 160,000, *The Nation* 27 July 1995; *Move to Curb Conduct of Burmese Immigrants, The Bangkok Post*, 20 June 1995.
47. Hnin Hnin Pyne, *AIDS and Prostitution in Thailand: Case Study of Burmese Prostitutes in Ranong*, May 1992, p. 2.
48. *Human Rights Watch*, p. 2.
49. *Images Asia, Burmese Women Sex Workers in Thailand*. Paper prepared for the NGO Forum on Women: Beijing, 30 August 1995 to 8 September 1995; Images Asia is a Thai NGO based in Chiang Mai.
50. Pyne, *AIDS and Prostitution in Thailand*, op.cit., p. 19.

51. *Procuring Girls for Sex Trade Commit, Bangkok Post,* 14 October 1993.
52. Kritaya Archavanitkul, *Situation Analysis of Trafficking of Girls and Child Prostitution Policy in Thailand.* Taipei: Consultation on Child Trafficking, 1–3 June 1994.
53. *Ranong's Constructive Engagement Poses Big Dilemna, Bangkok Post,* 13 September 1992.
54. Vitit Muntarbhorn, *Countering the Spread of Child Sexploitation, Bangkok Post,* 5 December 1994.
55. Pyne, *AIDS and Prostitution in Thailand,* p. 17.
56. Truong Thanh-Dam, 'The Dynamics of Sex Tourism', *Development and Change,* Vol. 14, 1990, pp. 533–53.
57. Ron O'Grady, *The Child and Tourist,* ECPAT, Bangkok 1992, p. 97.
58. Ibid., pp. 56–7.
59. Wathinee Boonchalaksi and Philip Guest, *Prostitution in Thailand,* Institute for Population and Social Research, Mahidol University, Bangkok, 1994, p. 15.
60. *AIDS, Sex und Tourismus, Ergebnisse eine Befragung Deutscher Urlauber und Sex Touristen.* German Health Ministry, 1995.
61. Boonchalaksi and Guest, *Prostitution in Thailand,* op.cit., p. 17.
62. Pyne, *AIDS and Prostitution in Thailand,* p. 19.
63. *Thai's Attitudes and Behaviours Regarding AIDS,* sponsored by USAID, June 1990.
64. Some of this report is copied from *Mc Mahon, Trafficking and Forced.*
65. Kobkun Rayanakom, *The Trafficking in Women and Girls Act of 1928; Study on Laws Relating to Prostitution and Traffic in Women.* Foundation for Woman, Bangkok, 1993, p. 11.
66. Boonchalaksi and Guest, *Prostitution in Thailand,* op.cit.
67. In the Prostitution Prohibition Act, the word 'prostitution' is defined as an act promiscuously rendering sexual services for remuneration.
68. *The Penal Code of Thailand,* 1956. *Book II: Specific Offences,* Title IX, Sections 277–86, and Vitit Muntarborn, *The Legal System of Thailand.* The Law Association for Asia and the Western Pacific, Los Angeles, 1981, p. 24.
69. *Archaic Prostitution Act must go, The Nation,* 9 November 1992.
70. Immigration Act, *Government Gazzette,* Vol. 96, Part 28, Special Issue, 1979, p. 45.
71. The Prostitution Prohibition Act penalizes the prostitutes, who are predominantly female, but exempts their male clients. While the law

criminalizes female 'promiscuity', and seeks to reform such behaviour (Penal Code, Sections 11–16), the legal system tolerates similar behaviour in males and makes no provision for their reform.

72. Children and Youth Development Plan During the Seventh National Economic and Social Development Plan 1992–1996, Published by the National Youth Bureau, Office of the Prime Minister.

73. Saisuree Chutikul was Minister in the Office of the Prime Minister Anand Panyarachun, for Women, Children Youth, Education and Social Development. She later became advisor to the PMs, Chuan Leekpai and Banham, for women and children issues. *Chuan Demands End to Child Exploitation, Bangkok Post,* 3 November 1992; *Chavalit Wants All Brothels Closed, Bangkok Post,* 7 November 1992; *PM Gives himself 3 Months Deadline to Curb Child Sex, The Nation,* 14 November 1992.

74. *Chuan Declares All-Out War on Child Prostitution, The Nation,* 28 September 1993.

75. *Human Rights Watch,* p. 27.

76. Mc Mahon, *Trafficking and Forced,* p. 24.

77. *Archaic Prostitution Act must go, The Nation,* 9 November 1992.

78. *Human Rights Watch,* p. 37.

79. For additional details regarding Burmese children, refer to *Human Rights Watch,* p. 84.

80. *Convention on the Elimination of all Forms of Discrimination against Women.* Part I, Article 2, and Part IV, Article 15.

81. *Statistics of the Centre for Protection of Children's Rights.* CPCR, Bangkok, 1994.

82. *Human Rights Watch,* pp. 75–82.

83. *Bangkok Post* reports in February 1992.

84. Interview with friends of women representative in March 1993.

85. *Thai Border,* 1994.

86. For more details, refer to *Human Rights Watch,* pp. 75–82.

87. *Chuan's War on Sexploitation Seen as a Failure, Bangkok Post,* 2 April 1993.

88. *Human Rights Watch,* p. 82; *Police Save 79 Burmese Women from Five Brothels, The Nation,* 9 July 1992.

89. Vitit Muntarbhom, *A Scourge in Our Midst, Bangkok Post,* 13 November 1992; *Chuan's War on Sexploitation Seen as a Failure, Bangkok Post,* 2 April 1993.

90. Report on CPCR's activities in 1993.

CHAPTER 14

Stalking in Andhra Pradesh and Intervention Strategies

B. Ratna Kumari

The year, 2010 is an important time to reflect on progress, as it marks the 15th anniversary of the adoption of the Beijing Declaration and Platform for Action at 4th World Conference on Women (1995) and the 10th anniversary of Security Council Resolution 1325 (2000) on women, peace and security (UNIFEM, 2010). Even though there is development and progress, why are women not enjoying peace and security in their life? Answer should be the prevalence of violence against women across the globe. Stalking is another new form of violence against women in this millennium.

It is common to hear mothers tutoring their young daughters to be wary of strangers who might trail them. Young working women who stay alone in metro cities prove to be soft targets to be stalked. Even older women encounter such behaviour while walking or jogging or even shopping. The security for women on roads either during day or night time has become a great problem due to various stalkers. Girls who are pursuing a university degree or intermediate education may be stalked by a fellow student. A woman belonging to any age group is susceptible to it. It has been seen in many cases that before committing a sexual offense or launching a physical attack, the criminal stalks the victim. In recent incidents, it has been noticed that the stalker might fling acid on the face of the victim or brutally kill with a knife or sword by cutting the neck head or sometimes rape the girl and murder her or threaten her parents or even kill the parents of the girl in order to take revenge of some sort.

Since the 1990s, there has been an increasing concern about violence against women and the girl child in both developed and developing countries. Violence of any kind has a detrimental impact on the economy of a country through increased disability, medical costs and loss of labour hours. However, because women bear the brunt of domestic violence, they disproportionately bear the health and psychological burdens as well. Despite the existence of a number of legislations for providing protection to women, crime against women and the girl child has increased.

Various socio-economic and political developmental programmes such as education, employment, training and skills upgradation for women have created more opportunities to the new generation women to go for any job, especially information and communications technology (ICT) jobs, corporate and service sector in flexible shifts. When we take comfort with the advancement of women in our country on one side, gender violence in terms of domestic violence, family violence and stalking become a great challenge for women's empowerment. Thus, the act of stalking have killed many young women for the past decade and caused both parents and family members great suffering. Hence, stalking gives a great challenge in the post-modern century for the women empowerment in India in general and in Andhra Pradesh in particular. A research study (Ratna, 2010) and experiences of ICTs sector reveal that there is an increasing rate of incidence of stalking of women in India and in particular, Andhra Pradesh. Even though the Government of India has enacted Protection from Domestic Violence against Women Act (2005) and a good number of support measures were taken, the crime rate against women is increasing gradually with new forms. Hence, there is a need to study the 'Reasons for stalking in Andhra Pradesh and Intervention Strategies' to curb this evil from the society.

DEFINITION AND MEANING OF STALKING

Stalking is any repeated conduct directed specifically at another person which causes the person (or a member of that person's family or household) to fear his/her safety. Such conduct includes following another person and acts that threaten or intimidate another person through fear of bodily injury or death of self or members of that person's family or household or an offense being committed against that person's property. Stalking refers to a harassing or threatening behaviour that is engaged in repeatedly and silently. Stalking can happen in person, through the mail, e-mail, over the phone, acid attacks, stabbing, emotional blackmail during dating or other avenues. It may occur in any combination of students, faculty and staff including student to student (or) peer harassment and in any gender combination. In this connection, the present study has made an attempt to understand the levels of knowledge of university students on stalking problems in Andhra Pradesh and to sensitize them so as to prevent this ghastly act.

Stalking first attracted widespread public concern when in 1989 a young actress named Rebecca Shaeffer, who was living in California, was shot dead by an obsessed fan who had stalked her for three years. The case drew extensive media coverage and revealed how widespread the problem of stalking was to both celebrity and non-celebrity victims. Until the enactment of anti-stalking laws, police had little power to arrest someone who behaved in a threatening but legal way. Even when the suspect had followed his victim, sent her hate mail or behaved in a threatening manner, the police were without legal recourse. Law enforcement could not take action until the suspect himself first acted on his threats and assaulted or injured the victim. Stalking is any repeated conduct directed specifically at another person that causes that person (or a member of that person's family or household) to fear his/her safety. Such conduct includes following another person and acts that threaten or intimidate another person through the fear of bodily injury or death of self or members of that person's family or household or an offence being committed against that person's property.

- Repeated pattern of harassing behaviours
- Intention to frighten, intimidate or terrorize a particular victim
- Men and women are the perpetrators

CLASSIFICATION OF STALKING

Psychologists often classify individuals who stalk into two categories: psychotic and non-psychotic. Many stalkers have pre-existing psychotic disorders such as delusional disorder, schizo-affective disorder or schizophrenia. Most stalkers are non-psychotic and may exhibit disorders or neuroses such as major depression, adjustment disorder or substance dependence, as well as a variety of Axis II personality disorders, such as antisocial, avoidant, borderline, dependent, narcissistic or paranoia. Some of the symptoms of 'obsession' over a person are part of obsessive compulsive personality disorder. The non-psychotic stalkers' pursuit of victims can be influenced by various psychological factors, including anger and hostility, projection of blame, obsession, dependency, minimization and denial, and jealousy. Conversely, as is more commonly the case, the stalkers have no sympathetic feelings towards the victim, but simply a longing that cannot be fulfilled due to either their personality or their society's norms.

SIX TYPES OF STALKERS

- **Rejected stalkers** pursue their victims in order to reverse, correct or avenge a rejection (e.g. divorce, separation, termination).
- **Resentful stalkers** pursue a vendetta because of a sense of grievance against the victims—motivated mainly by the desire to frighten and distress the victim.
- **Intimacy seekers** seek to establish an intimate, loving relationship with their victim. To them, the victim is a long-sought-after soul mate, and they were 'meant' to be together.
- **Incompetent suitors,** despite poor social or courting skills, have a fixation; or in some case, a sense of entitlement to an intimate relationship with those who have attracted their amorous interest. Their victims are most often already in a dating relationship with someone else.
- **Predatory stalkers** spy on the victim in order to prepare and plan an attack—usually sexual—on the victim.
- **Cyberstalkers** using the Internet or electronic means to harass.

MOTIVATING FACTORS OF STALKING

The motivations for stalking are many. They include the desire for contact and control, obsession, jealousy and anger and stem from the real or imagined relationship between the victim and the stalker. The stalker may feel intense attraction or extreme hatred. Many stalkers stop their activity when confronted by police intervention, but many do not. The more troublesome stalker may exhibit a personality disorder, such as obsessive-compulsive behaviour, which leads him or her to devote an inordinate amount of time to writing notes and letters to the intended target, tracking the victim's movements or travelling in an attempt to achieve an encounter.

PSYCHOLOGY OF STALKERS

Individuals characterized as stalkers pursue and attempt to insert themselves or control the lives of others. Motives vary from perceived relations or friendship or predatory advances. Stalking consists of a series of actions that in themselves can be legal, such as calling on the phone, sending gifts or sending emails. However, the number and extent of which are identified as criminal activity such as harassment and invasion of privacy.

The majority of stalkers are non-violent. Stalkers may use threats and violence to force their victim to compromise, such as vandalism, routing through bins and property damage. Physical and sexual attacks are less common. Stalkers motives are formed from psychopathic tendencies, however often misclassified by media and public perception as sociopathic due to their ability to present themselves as normal. Similarly, the ego of the stalker is a core element, rather than sexual instinct.

ADVERSE EFFECTS ON STALKING VICTIMS

Stalking can be a terrifying experience for victims, placing them at risk of psychological trauma and physical harm. Common emotional consequences include depression, anxiety, loss of self-esteem, shame, hopelessness and a sense of vulnerability that can persist long after the stalking ends. It is common for victims to blame themselves, especially if the stalking results from an established relationship with the stalker. Give stalking is comparatively rare, criticism from families and friends for choosing such a partner may compound the issue. Disruptions in daily life necessary to escape the stalker, including changes in employment, residence and phone numbers, may take a toll on the victim's well-being and lead to a sense of isolation. Stalking is a form of mental assault, in which the perpetrator repeatedly, unwontedly and disruptively breaks into the life-world of the victim, with whom they have no relationship (or no longer have). Moreover, the separated acts that make up the intrusion cannot by themselves cause the mental abuse, but do taken together (cumulative effect).

VICTIMS AND PERPETRATORS OF STALKING

In general, stalking victims are women from all walks of life, and most of them are trying to end a relationship with a man, often one who has been abusive. The persons involved may be married or divorced or may have been sexual partners. In other cases, the stalker and the victim may know one another casually or be associated in an informal or formal way. For example, they may have had one or two dates or talked briefly but were not sexual partners, or they may be co-workers or former co-workers. In a small number of situations, the stalker and the victim do not know one another. Cases involving celebrities and other public figures usually fall into this category. Generally, girl child, adolescent girls, home managers (married women) and single women are victims and the perpetrators are unknown persons, intimated persons, relatives, peer group or classmates of those being stalked.

STALKER TYPOLOGIES

The typology can be viewed as a continuum based on the dimension of the degree of relationship of the Stalker to the Victim (*Stranger vs Non-Stranger*) and dimension of Mental Health Issues (*Delusional vs Non-Delusional)*.

Simple Obsessional

Most common typologies are prior relationship, perception of mistreatment on the part of offender, personality disorder and short duration volatility.

Love Obsessional

No prior relationship, usually known through media, delusional disorders common, long duration and offenders mostly male.

Erotomanic

Delusional disorder, no prior relationship, long duration and offenders mostly male.

False Victimization Syndrome

Victim becomes suspect, fictitious, rare, attention and/or attempt to re-establish existing relationship primary motives.

FALSE CLAIM OF STALKING

Cultural misnomers around this issue have led to false claims being reported for the purposes of an attention or false criminal damage, which in some cases are due to the supposed victim having psychological problems of their own. In 1999, Pathe, Mullen and Purcell said that popular interest in stalking was promoting false claims. In 2004, Sheridan and Blaauw said that they estimated that 11.5 per cent if claims in a sample of 357 reported claims of stalking were false. One worry is that false claims may in part be due to misidentification on the part of the victim; yet similarly high-profile cases have shown how pressure to act can result in case collapses or false imprisonment of innocent people.

STALKING NEXUS GENDER STUDIES

The majority of reported stalkers are male, although it is believed due to public perception that more female stalkers go unreported. The demographic characteristic and psychiatric status of male and female stalkers do not differ, except that male stalkers are more likely to have a history of criminal offences and substance abuse. The duration of the time invested in stalking and the frequency of associated violence are equivalent between male and female stalkers. Women are more likely to target someone they have known—such as a professional contact—and rarely target strangers. Women often target other women, whereas men generally stalk women only.

STATISTICS IN ANDHRA PRADESH WITH RESPECT TO STALKING ON WOMEN

Violence is the most serious violation of all basic rights that a woman suffers in her own home at the hands of members within her own family or outside of the home. The manifold problems associated with violence have been systematically exposed by data and in-depth work undertaken by several people in the women's movement of

India. Indeed a number of recent studies such as National Family Health Survey (NFHS) and National Crimes Record Bureau have identified the home as the first site of violence against women and girl children. Violence may take many forms and can mean threats, intimidation, manipulation, kidnapping, dowry harassment, murders, torture, isolation, keeping a woman without money locked in, deprived of food and abusing children in various ways to frighten her or enforce compliance. Thus, violence is never restricted to a single incident and it becomes more frequent and more severe over time. The violence may continue for many years on women.

AN OVERVIEW OF THE STATISTICS OF STALKING AND OTHER CRIMES AGAINST WOMEN

One of the most serious impediments to women's development is the phenomenon of continuing and increasing violence against them. Needless to say, this constitutes a serious violation of women's human rights. For women, violence is a phenomenon that starts at conception and carries on through their entire life span. Gender violence manifests itself in various forms—female foeticide and infanticide; sexual abuse; incest, molestation; sexual harassment and assault at home, workplace and on streets; marital rape; domestic violence in the form of wife assault; women battering; and stalking.

The concept of equality between male and female is enshrined in the Constitution of India. Of course, the preamble of the Constitution, which is the supreme law of the land, seeks to secure to its citizens including womenfolk, justice—social, economic and political, liberty of thought, expression, belief, faith and worship, equality of states and dignity of the individual. The difference in treatment between men and women by the state is totally prohibited by the Constitution of India. But, the equality of state guaranteed by the Constitution is only a myth to millions of women for whom life is stalked by various kinds of violence.

REASONS FOR VIOLENCE AGAINST WOMEN IN INDIA

In India, women are prone to violence by their own family members in the house or by outside people at the working spots, on ways to go to workplace and sometimes at the net centres also. Ferguson (1984: 95) writes 'women are not powerless because they are feminine; rather, they are feminine because they are powerless, because it is a way of dealing with the requirements of subordination'. However, the culture, gender and power are, therefore, intimately bound up with each other in organizations as well as in society. Why does the male dominate the women in various spheres of women's life cycle? This is because of the following:

- The pervasiveness with which gender and culture permeate language, thought, social structures and organizational facts.
- The elusiveness of their definition in relation/contrast to a difficult concept 'nature'.
- The ambiguity between gender assumptions, rules, values and beliefs in the society, without forgetting that gender is a pervasive symbol of the power relation. Therefore, gender is socially produced by processes in which organizations actively participate and by which these organizations are shaped; practices make gender in that they produce and reproduce social relations and material culture and the artefacts that sustain them (Gherardi, 1995: 18).

Again, these gender processes are concrete organizational activities, both material and ideological, whereby advantage, disadvantage, exploitation and control, action and emotion, meaning and identity are patterned through in terms of a distinction between male and female (Acker, 1990: 146). Thus, the culture conveys into organizational analysis subjectivity, emotionality, ambiguity and sexuality; all these themes associated with the symbolism of the female in its fundamental psychological ambivalence.

In other words, the field of studies which falls under the umbrella terms of 'culture' can be depicted as a monster with five heads, which are connected to a body in which they find unity and a common life source (Alvesson and Berg, 1992: 93) has classified the above five approaches to organizational culture as follows:

- *The head as culture,* that is, culture as one of many organization variables: culture as a system of values and beliefs, which links with a deeper level of basic assumptions shared by the members of an organization; cultural cognitivism that regards the system of cognitions and shared forms of knowledge; cultural artefacts that relate to unitary symbol systems unique to an organization and that function as 'culture-bearing milieux'.

- *The head as meaning construction,* which possesses two eyes swivelling between organizations as shared meanings or as constructions and deconstructions of meaning.
- *The head as ideology,* which considers what positions or actions are correct, what behaviour or attitude is legitimate. This head has two ways of thinking ideology: (i) neutrally, as a specific philosophical system, that is, the corporate ideology of an organization; (ii) pejoratively, as political ideology that legitimates the interests of dominant groups
- *The head as psychodynamics,* which considers the way in which the culture phenomenon is related to unconscious and primitive aspects of human behaviour. This head has two eyes that look at shared fantasies and the organizational members' projections of their inner impulses and contradictions, and at the archetypes made manifests in the myths, rituals or other 'cultural blinders' inherent in the unconscious of organizations.
- *The head as symbolism,* which generates a symbolic picture of the organization. This head also has two eyes: one to see the particularism of symbols and the other to see their universalism.

Again, these five approaches create the question of gender bias and discrimination in the society. In turn, it leads to violence or crimes against women. One of the most serious impediments to women's development is the phenomenon of continuing and increasing violence against them. Needless to say, this constitutes a serious violation of women's human rights. Violence against women is one of the most significant, yet little understood and acknowledged factor instrumental in the phenomenon of marginalization of women in the development processes. Gender violence manifests itself in various forms: female foeticide and infanticide, sexual abuse, incest, molestation, sexual harassment at work and on the streets, marital rape, domestic violence in the form of wife assault and woman battering. In some places, there exists a unique culture—specific forms of violence against women such as female genital mutilation in some African countries and harassment/murder/beating for dowry in India. Of all the forms of violence that women face, domestic violence remains the least reported and largely suppressed.

Violence against women began to draw attention as a serious social problem in the late 1960s and early 1970s. Since then, the term 'violence against women' (VAW) has been used to describe a variety of different behaviours including emotional, sexual and physical assault, murder, genital mutilation, stalking, sexual harassment and prostitution (Crowell and Burgess, 1996). Explanations for VAW have developed within a wide variety of disciplines including sociology, psychology, law, public health, social work and women's studies. Consequently, there are a number of competing theories, each with different implications for policies aimed at eliminating the problem. Social learning theory, more often termed as the *intergenerational transmission of violence* is learned in the context of socialization in the family, the primary agent of socialization (Straus et al., 1980; Kalmuss, 1984; O'Leary, 1988).

Bandura (1978) suggested that violence can be learned from three primary sources, such as family, culture and subculture and media. Walker (1984) used the term of 'learned helplessness' of women lead to violence against women. Hence, both micro- and macro-oriented theories that explain about sociocultural issues, especially the ideology of submission, patriarchy, hierocracy and other characteristics of perpetrator and victim. However, the trend has moved towards the development of multidimensional theories of violence which take into account the social structural factors as well as individual characteristics.

The present study has made an attempt to study the details of crime against women in India in general and with some other states in comparison with Andhra Pradesh and Visakhapatnam city in particular.

STATISTICAL PROFILE OF CRIMES AGAINST WOMEN

According to the estimations of National Crime Report Bureau (NCRB, 2007), the incidence of crimes against women in Andhra Pradesh are as given in following Tables.

It is evident from Table 14.1 that the incidence rate of violence against women in India has increased gradually from 545 rape cases in the year 2004 to 1,020 cases in the year 2008. The number of dowry deaths has also increased from 53 during the year 2004 to 149 in 2008. Regarding rape cases, dowry deaths and murders, the incidence rate has increased tremendously, and gives an alarm for protection of these vulnerable victims.

Table 14.1 *Details of violence against women in India during 2004–2008*

June—December	*2004*	*2005*	*2006*	*2007*	*2008*
Rape cases	545	898	1006	1026	1020
Dowry deaths	53	114	118	142	149
Murders	344	651	728	875	597
Total	**942**	**1663**	**1852**	**2043**	**1746**

Source: 1. National Crime Report Bureau (NCRB)
2. Streevada Patrika *Bhoomika*, Vol. 5, 12 October 2009

Table 14.2 *Details of crimes against women in some states of India during 2004–2008*

Crimes	*Andhra Pradesh*	*Uttar Pradesh*	*Madhya Pradesh*	*Bihar*	*Rajasthan*
Dowry deaths	613	2076	742	1172	–
Kidnapping cases	2097	4478	–	2530	–
Torture	4406	–	6772	–	–
Harassment by their husbands/ family members	11,335	7650	–	–	8170
Sexual harassment	2411	2714	762	–	–

Source: 1. National Crime Report Bureau (NCRB)
2. Streevada Patrika *Bhoomika*, Vol. 5, 12 October 2009

Table 14.2 gives details about crimes against women in some states of India during 2004–2008. Among Andhra Pradesh, Uttar Pradesh, Madhya Pradesh, Bihar and Rajasthan, the rate of harassment by their husbands/family member is much more in Andhra Pradesh (11,335 cases) and Rajasthan (8,170 cases), whereas Uttar Pradesh (7,650 cases) follows in the next ranking. Regarding dowry deaths, Uttar Pradesh stood first (2,076) and Bihar follows next (172). Regarding the crime of torture cases Madhya Pradesh occupied first while Andhra Pradesh is in second place. If we analyse micro-level statistics, we can understand how, many women suffer and even undergo brutal death by violence and stalking (see Table 14.3 for more details). It inferences that the cases of violence are on the rise while a new form of stalking is also gradually increasing.

Here, stalking includes not only the offences by unknown persons but also threats by own people in various forms.

A study was conducted to provide data about the perceptions and attitudes of the people towards stalking.

Table 14.3 *Violence against women during 2005–2009 in Visakhapatnam*

Crimes	*2005*	*2006*	*2007*	*2008*	*2009 (up to May)*
Murders	15	12	10	7	4
Dowry deaths	2	1	2	12	7
Tortures	392	394	47	28	16
Harassments for dowry (498A cases)	27	33	525	492	175
Rape cases	28	21	24	27	10
Kidnapping	21	23	26	28	16
Stalking	41	69	97	83	38
Illegal marriage cases	4	14	12	–	–

Source: 1. Data taken from Mahila Action Committee Report from 2005 to 2007

2. Data taken from *Enadu*, Regional Telugu Newspaper, 2007 and 2008

PURPOSE OF THE STUDY

To better understand the broader context of violence in which stalking occurs, the Centre for Women's Studies has conducted a survey of stalking problem for obtaining the opinion of the student community towards this problem. The purpose of the study was to explore University students' awareness and experiences of stalking and to suggest the coping strategies to manage the problems and challenges of stalking.

RESEARCH SETTING

Andhra Pradesh is unique in several respects. Some of these unique features are as follows:

- Its history of social movements
- It was one of the few states which adopted green revolution

- Development of participatory institutions including self-help groups
- Its remarkable progress in technical education
- Its innovative poverty alleviation strategies
- Its distinctive demographic experience
- The State was at the forefront in economic reforms

Above all, the experience of Andhra Pradesh with these unique features raises several far-reaching issues on the strategies to be followed in improving human development. However, the State has to focus on 'inclusive growth' as there is still a considerable degree of poverty, inadequate human development and significant regional, social and gender disparities and problems in delivery system. As a result, the State has the highest incidence of violence against women in terms of total crimes, both private (with in the household or domestic) and public. The violence rate (i.e. crime incidents per lakh women) for 2005 in Andhra Pradesh was about 36, the highest among the major Indian states, and the contribution of the state to the total crimes against women in India was the highest at 13 per cent. Moreover, the violence rate has increased, especially during the past decade (i.e. 1995–2005) with indication of even a further rise in future (Human Development Report, Andhra Pradesh, 2007). Among the crimes against women, stalking is one of the horrible acts that requires preventive and interventionist strategies to curb this ghastly act.

OBJECTIVES

The present study has made an attempt to study the following objectives:

- To recommend countermeasures to stalking and classification of stalking and types of stalkers
- To review the statistics of stalking and other crimes against women with respect to women in Andhra Pradesh
- To analyse the perceptions and attitudes of the students in Andhra University consisting of Colleges of Arts and Commerce, Science, Engineering and Technology to understand their levels of knowledge about stalking

- To study the success and failure in case studies of women stalkers in Andhra Pradesh
- To suggest remedial measures and intervention strategies taken by Dr Durgabai Deshmukh Centre for Women's Studies in Andhra University to control the stalking of women in Andhra Pradesh

METHODOLOGY

The present study is based on primary and secondary sources. We have collected data from nearly 750 students of Andhra University. The research study examines the attitudes and perceptions of the students regarding stalking. With regard to stalking, the survey has collected data on 'the prevalence of stalking among students', awareness regarding the stalking problem; the experience of stalking victims, students' response and opinion about stalking. The researcher has interviewed with the students directly and collected opinions from the NSS students and other professionals from psychology and journalism. The researcher has consolidated the statistics on stalking which was happened in the State to view the dimension of this problem and sensitize the policy makers, governance, researchers, NGOs and the student community.

SAMPLE AND DATA COLLECTION

Primary data are collected from the students of Andhra University studying in various university colleges pursuing different courses. For convenience, the students are grouped into categories such as arts, science, engineering and technical. Since, the perceptions, approach and attitudes of the students are different from one

Table 14.4 *Percentage distribution of respondents according to the courses in Andhra University*

S. No.	*Courses*	*Frequency*	*Percentage (%)*
1	Science	353	46.8
2	Arts	369	48.9
3	Engineering/Technical	34	4.1
	Total	756	100.0

Source: Field study

discipline to another; we have collected data using random sample method on students belonging to various courses in the university. The study further discussed the stalking aspects such as causes for stalking, students' attitudes and perceptions about stalking and interventionist and coping strategies to curtail the problem. Further, the present study has collected secondary data for the details of women victims of stalking from newspapers and other electronic and mass media.

PERCENTAGE DISTRIBUTION OF RESPONDENTS ACCORDING TO THE COURSES IN ANDHRA UNIVERSITY

In our study, majority of the students belonged to Arts and Science groups, that is, 48.9 per cent and 46.8 per cent, respectively. The percentage of respondents from engineering and technical courses were very low, that is, 4.1 per cent and below (Table 14.4). One reasons for this was the non-availability of the students because of examinations. Moreover, the students studying arts courses responded better than the other students because the students having social science background are more capable of viewing the societal problems in different ways and find out solutions to the problems.

PERCENTAGE DISTRIBUTION OF RESPONDENTS SEX-WISE

Some of the case studies on stalking revealed the fact that perpetrators are not absolutely known to victims, but in one way or the other they were having intimacy or interaction with the victim before they were attacked. For instance, in case of Lakshmi Prasanna who was snubbed by Srinivas in her classroom itself, revealed that both of them were known to each other earlier. Therefore, if we want to know the causes for attacks and the situations that encouraged them to commit the offence, one should get the opinion from both the male and female. Hence, we collected data from both male and female students of Andhra University. From this data it was noticed that the female respondents constituted more than male, that is, 62.1 per cent and 37.9 per cent, respectively. Perhaps the reason is victims are more often women and hence female students responded to the problem immediately rather than male students.

DISTRIBUTION OF RESPONDENTS ACCORDING TO AREA-WISE FAMILY BACKGROUND AND THEIR PARENT'S OCCUPATION

Since family background influences the mode of thought among the students, an attempt was made in order to know the perceptions of the respondents belonging to different family backgrounds. Majority of the respondents have come from rural areas, that is, 58.5 per cent and the respondents belonging to urban areas constitute 41.5 per cent. Most of their fathers are working as agricultural labour (36.6%), and some are government employees (24%) and some are businessmen (13.5%). A few are working as private employees (7.7%) and others are engaged in self-employment. Whereas, most of their mothers are home managers (82.6%), only a few are working as government employees (1.2%) and few are engaged in self-employment.

DISTRIBUTION OF SIBLINGS OF THE RESPONDENTS

We selected the respondents who have siblings because they might have had experience of stalking problems sometime or the other. In fact, they are the right persons to give suggestions. In our study, most of the respondents have either sisters or brothers, that is, 35.2 per cent and 33.5 per cent, respectively. Some respondents have both brothers and sisters, that is, 27.7 per cent. The study revealed that majority of respondent's brothers and sisters are studying, that is, 71.4 per cent and some are engaged in work (12.9%). A few are engaged in both studies and work, that is, 8.8 per cent. Most of them are college going and studying in the University, that is, 39.4 per cent and 34.3 per cent, respectively. As the sequences of incidents relating to stalking are happening in the society and the victims exclusively belonged to the student's community, students are well aware about the problem. It was found that nearly 86.1 per cent of the respondents have heard about stalking problems. Of course, some people are not aware of the problem at all, that is, 13.9 per cent.

The studies revealed the fact that the possibility of stalking is more in case of the college going students. It is made clear that 29 per cent of either the respondents or their sisters are stalked by others by sending messages through mobile or mail. Of course, most of them have not experienced this personally, but they have come to know of the problem through media or through their friends.

PERCENTAGE DISTRIBUTION OF RESPONDENTS' AWARENESS ABOUT STALKING INCIDENTS

We have also collected data in order to know whether the students are following the sequence of incidents on stalking and whether they are considering the problem seriously or not. Around 57.4 per cent of them were aware of the recent incident (i.e. on 18 September 2009 in Rajahmundry, Rajesh attacked Anusha with a knife and killed her parents when they condemned the attack), whereas 42.6 per cent of them had not known about the issue, which tells us that they had not considered the problem seriously.

PERCENTAGE DISTRIBUTION OF THE KNOWN FORMS OF STALKING BY THE RESPONDENTS

Most of the respondents knew about the problem in the form of acid attacks (32.7%). Some respondents experienced personally, or they came to know the problem through the experience of their friends (16.1%), some respondents came to know the incidents of stalking in the form of threatening on roads (4.9%), killing of parents (4.5%), brutally killing of the person (2.2%) and damaging

Table 14.5 *Percentage distribution of the known forms of stalking by the respondents*

S. No.	*Forms of stalking*	*Frequency*	*Percentage (%)*
1	By stabbing with sword	36	4.9
2	Through acid attack	247	33.7
3	Brutal killing	17	2.3
4	Damaging the property	12	1.1
5	Killing parents	34	4.6
6	Threatening on roads	37	5.1
7	Following silently	121	16.5
8	No response	250	33.1
	Total	756	100.0

Source: Field study

of property (1.1%). Majority of the respondents did not know the problem (30.7%) because of lack of awareness about the problem (Table 14.5).

PERCENTAGE DISTRIBUTION OF RESPONDENTS' PREFERENCE TO AVOID THE STALKING PROBLEM

An attempt was made to know how they would respond to the problem of stalking in their real life. Most of the respondents prefer to inform their parents (25.7%) and some prefer to inform their friends (24.7%). Only a few respondents prefer to approach the police (16.4%), whereas some people avoid the situations by ignoring the problem altogether.

FORMS OF STALKING EXPERIENCED BY THE RESPONDENTS

Stalking can take place in any form such as sending messages through mobile, through mailing and following the victim silently and so on. An attempt was made to know how the stalkers cause nuisance to others. In recent years as the usage of mobile phones and internet has been increasing and the people are misutilizing the facilities, that is, by sending unwanted messages through mobile and mailing through the Internet. Respondents were asked whether they had ever been stalked by any one. Result from the study shows that about 19.6 per cent stalking cases happened by sending messages, through mobile and the Internet. It was also found that some stalkers followed silently (13.9%) and some are hunting them wherever they go (12.6%). A few cases are included in writing of filthy words on walls (4%).

The study also revealed the causes for stalking. The advanced communication facilities such as mobiles and Internet offer new opportunities for cyber stalking. Most of the respondents are of the opinion that giving mobile number to others (31.7%) and taking it from friends (14.4%) and giving e-mail ID to unknown persons (13.2%) and by knowing user name of some persons (2.1%) may cause stalking. In recent years, both electronic and print media have become responsible for stalking (13.3%). Some of the respondents felt that family relationship (2.9%) and broken families (1.6%) impact the socialization of children are also indirectly causing stalking.

It is a general opinion that stalking is inhuman, uncivilized and brutal which abstracts one's own freedom. Most of the respondents feel that the activities of stalker are inhuman (34.6%), uncivilized (24.2%) and brutal (26.8%). The problem of stalking could be arrested if the targeted persons inform their parents or others, before they are attacked by the perpetrators. In this regard students' opinions are collected to know in what way they will respond to stalking issues. It can be noted that most of the respondents gave preference to talking to their parents (31.8%). And some preferred to bring the issues to light (15.4%). Some preferred to call for help through youth associations (13.1%) and calling youth friendly network (12.4%). A few are of the opinion that by talking with the stalker on behalf of the victim the problem could be solved (8.9%).

We have collected the suggestions from the respondents on how the stalkers could be punished. Majority of the respondents suggested that they should be punished in public (42.8%). Nearly, 34.4 per cent suggested that through counselling the attitude of the stalker can be changed. Nearly, 10.2 per cent of respondents suggested that stalkers should be sentenced to death. A few of them specified that the stalker must be life imprisoned (7.6%).

CASE STUDIES—VICTIMS OF STALKING: AFTERMATH

There is not just life after an acid attack, there is even achievement. That is what Anuradha and Pranitha have shown.

ANURADHA

The first heinous crime was in the form of stalking on Anuradha. She was the first acid attack victim of the state in Hyderabad. She was a B.Sc (Agriculture) student in 1997 when she lost her left eye in an attack by another student. After suffering for a long time, she is now working as a Bio technologist. She also received compensation from the Home Minister, Smt Sabitha Indra Reddy at a conference on 'Women and Child Concerns' in Hyderabad on 3 July 2009. This was the successful case study of Anuradha. Behind this, episode there are a lot of tears, trauma, agony, pain and sorrow, which was experienced by her and her family members. It shows her strong confidence, perseverance and persistant hard work to climb the highest steps in her life. We are appreciating her personality, and companies' support to give placement and moral support of her parents to keep her journey in a successful way.

T. PRANITHA
Repeated cases of acid attacks in Andhra Pradesh form a part of disturbing trend of rising stalking attacks and crimes against women. Pranitha (22 December 2008) and her friend Swapnika were both final year B.Tech students of Kakatiya Institute of Technology and Science (KITS) in Warrangal. They were chased and attacked with acid by three young men in Warangal town. Swapnika suffered over 50 per cent burns and fought for three weeks before her end came. But Pranitha kept on fighting through different surgeries, but the doctors say her ordeal is far from over as she will have to undergo a few more surgeries to reconstruct her face.

Showing exceptional courage, Pranitha passed her final year B.Tech exams with distinction scoring 82 per cent. On her success, Pranitha told that 'I was not in a position to even hold or open the book, flip the page and I would just read with my eyes.' Her achievement has brought a smile back on her mother's face. Her mother Subhasini in her words 'Today we are happy but what we lived through, nobody can or should live through. We have lived through hell.'

Recently, Pranitha has been appreciated and awarded for her sincere, hard work, intelligence and strong confidence by our honourable President Ms Prathiba Patil. We are appreciating her strong mind and soul to fight against stalking havoc and she stands as a role model for the people who are depressed, suppressed and oppressed by this stalking disaster. She was already promised by the IT companies to give a jole appointment. The State Government of Andhra Pradesh has promised that the case study should be integrated in the academic curriculum and syllabus. Once again, we are appreciating the great success achieved by Pranitha in spite of her hardships, pain, agony, trauma and turmoil she has undergone through this stalking incident.

PREVENTATIVE MEASURES

- Never give your name, phone number or address to anyone over the Internet. The person you give the information might be ok, but others can get the information just as easily.

- Vary the times, places and the duration you exercise; the routes you take to and from school, work and home. Stalkers pick up on people's everyday routines.
- Maintain an unlisted phone number. It costs less than your life.
- Have a computer user name that does not tell people too much about yourself.
- Pay attention to obsessive or possessive behaviours in those you date.
- When you break up with someone, make a clean break, do not lead anyone on.

Suggestions if you believe you are being stalked:

- Tell someone you trust and contact the proper services (i.e. the police).
- Document everything the alleged stalker does: gifts, letters, e-mail messages, phone messages, pictures of vandalism and so on.
- Restrict your registration information and change your PIN number.
- Sever all ties with the person you think is stalking you.
- Treat any threats as legitimate and inform law enforcement authority immediately.
- Make sure your door has a dead bolt, and change locks if all keys cannot be accounted for.
- Carry a cell phone at all times.
- Tell your apartment management what is happening and provide them with a picture of suspect.
- Tell your teachers/parents/heads/chief wardens or well-wishers about the alleged stalker and his/her misbehaviour.
- Stalking is illegal and a violation of Andhra University Policy. If you believe you are being stalked, call for assistance from the helping agencies such as women protection cell, counselling centre from women's studies, family courts and police stations in general, and NGOs who are working for this cause.

CONCLUSION

In this study, we considered the perceptions and attitudes of the students towards stalking. It can be noted that the students of social sciences responded better than the other students because the students having social science background are more capable of viewing the societal problems in different ways and find solutions to the problems. Since the victims are more often women, and hence female students responded to the problem immediately rather than male students. Since attitudes and perceptions are greatly influenced by the socio-economic conditions of the people, hence an attempt was made in order to know the perceptions of the respondents belonging to different family backgrounds. It is noticed that though majority of the respondents have come from rural areas and from agriculturist families they are also aware about the problem.

The study also revealed the opinion of the respondents having siblings and studying at college and university levels. They responded well and expressed their views and opinions about the stalking problems. Of course, most of them have not experienced it personally, but they have come to know of the problem through media or through their friends. The study also examined the levels of awareness about the stalking problems. As the sequence of incidents relating to stalking is happening in the society and the victims exclusively belonged to the student's community, students are well aware about the problem. The study revealed the fact that the possibility of stalking is more in case of the college-going students. It is clear that either the respondents or their sisters are stalked by others by sending messages through mobile or mail.

The study also pointed out that most of the students are not following the sequence of incidents on stalking because they are not considering the problem seriously. Generally, stalking takes place in the form of acid attacks, brutal killing, threatening on roads, stabbing with sword and following silently on the roads. Most of the respondents have known the problem in the form of acid attacks. Some respondents have come to know of the problem through the experience of their friends. Majority of respondents do not know the problem because of lack of awareness about the problem.

The study also revealed the respondents preference of actions to avoid the stalking problem. Most of the respondents prefer to inform their parents or friends. Only a few respondents prefer to approach the police, whereas some people avoid the situation by ignoring the problem. Stalking can takes place in any form, such as sending messages through mobile, through mailing and following silently. In recent years as the usage of mobile phones and the Internet has been increasing and people are misutilizing the facilities by sending unwanted messages through mobile and mailing through the Internet. Result from the study show that most of the stalking cases happened by sending messages through mobile and the Internet.

The study also revealed the views of the respondents about the causes for stalking. The respondents opined that the advanced communication facilities offer new opportunities for cyber stalking. Most of the respondents are of the opinion that giving ones mobile number to others or taking it from friends and giving e-mail ID to unknown persons or by knowing username of some persons may cause stalking. Some of the respondents felt that the family relationship and broken families that impact the socialization of children are also indirectly causing stalking. Most of the respondents feel that the activities of stalkers are inhuman, uncivilized and brutal.

The problem of stalking could be arrested if the targeted persons inform their parents or others, before they are attacked by the perpetrators. It is noticed that most of the respondents gave preference to talking to their parents and some preferred to call for help through youth associations and calling youth-friendly network. A few are of the opinion that by talking with the stalker on behalf of the victim the problem could be solved. The study also considered the suggestions of the respondents on how the stalkers could be punished. Majority of the respondents suggested that they should be punished in public. Some of the respondents opined that through counselling, the attitude of the stalker can be changed.

REFERENCES

Acker, J., 1990, 'Hierarchies, Jobs, Bodies: A Theory of Gendered Organization', *Gender and Society*, 4: 139–58.

Alvesson, M. and P.O. Berg, 1992, *Corporate Culture and Organizational Symbolism*. Berlin: de Gruyter.

Bandura, A., 1978, *Social Learning Theory of Aggression*. Englewood Cliffs, NJ: Prentice Hall.

Crowell ,Nancy A. and Ann W. Burgess,(editors) 1996, *Understanding Violence Against Women,* National Research Council, National Academy Press, Washington, D.C.

De Keseredy, W.S. and L. MacLeod, 1997, *Women Abuse: A Sociological Story*. Toronto, ON: Harcourt Brace.

Ferguson, Kathy E. 1984, *The Feminist Case Against Bureaucracy*, Philadelphia: Temple University Press.

Gherardi, Silvia, 1995, *Gender, Symbolism and Organizational Cultures*. New Delhi: Sage Publications.

Gross, Linda, 2000, *Surviving a Stalker: Everything you Need to know to Keep Yourself Safe*. New York: Marlowe & Company.

Kalmuss, D., 1984, 'The Intergenerational Transmission of Marital Aggression', *Journal of Marriage and the Family*, 46: 11–19.

National Crime Report Bureau (NCRB), 2007. Ministry of Home Affairs, http://ncrb.nic.in/cii2007/home.htm, accessed 15 September 2013.

O'Leary, K.D., 1988, 'Physical Aggression Between Spouses: A Social Learning Theory Perspective'. In *Hand Book of Family Violence, V.B. Van Hasselt,* R.L. Morrison, A.S. Bellack, and M. Hersen (editors), New York: Plenum, pp. 31–56.

Straus, M.A., R.J. Gelles and S. Steinmetz, 1980, *Behind Closed Doors: Violence in the American Family*. Garden City, NJ: Anchor Press.

Walker, L.E., 1984, *The Battered Woman Syndrome*. New York: Springer.

CHAPTER 15

Desertion of Married Women by Non-Resident Indians: Problems and Challenges

R. Jayasree

Violence against women has always remained a part of patriarchal value system combined with the societal mechanism by which women are forced into a subordinate position. Thus, it can be said that basically it is a manifestation of unequal power relation. This violence may take place at various levels, that is, within the family, at workplace, at public places and even in the state/judicial custody. While the basic reason for violence against women is their lower status in a male-dominated society educationally, economically, politically and socially, there are other factors too. The increasing criminalization of society, media images of violence, poor enforcement of legal provision, unabashed and rising incidents of alcoholism and addiction along with erosion of traditional values have all added to it.

The Government of India has enacted many laws to safeguard the interests of women in India. This has helped to strengthening the woman's position at the workplace. However, ironically, their status in their matrimonial homes has deteriorated as there has been no just and effective legal remedy to guarantee their physical safety, mental stability, financial and economical welfare, and custody of children.

Indian women remain marginalized in decision-making by a variety of processes that begin at a very early age within the family.

Women have very little say in decisions affecting their own lives, even after marriage. For most Indian women, marriage itself is not a matter of choice. Only a small minority, even among educated women from well off families, has had any role in deciding when and to whom they will get married. Thus, even in the twenty-first century, women continue to be burdened by their very womanhood. They continue to be suppressed, subordinated and discriminated in numerous ways, and are relegated to second-class citizens.

Desertion of married women by their non-resident Indian (NRI) husband is an emergent, unique form of violence against women. The problem of women being deserted by their NRI husbands is particularly significant in many progressive states in India such as Punjab, Andhra Pradesh, Haryana, Delhi, Kerala, Gujarat and Maharashtra. These states have more number of NRI populations. Although desertion of women has been an issue of the forum of women activists and NGOs for the past few decades, their concern is only for the deserted and destitute women belonging to the downtrodden. However, the issues of NRI-deserted women are of recent origin and because of its sensitive nature and family influence, no concentrated efforts have been taken. Moreover, these women do not speak about the violence/crimes they have been subjected to because of the social stigma attached to the divorced/deserted women. Besides, they want to protect their family. Hence, the majority of the deserted cases were not exposed.

DEFINITION OF NON-RESIDENT INDIAN

An NRI is an Indian citizen who has migrated to another country. Other terms with the same meaning are overseas Indian and expatriate Indian. For tax and other official purpose, the Government of India considers any Indian national away from India for more than 180 days in a year as an NRI. In common usage, this often includes Indian-born individuals who have taken the citizenship of other countries.

In simple terms, an NRI is a person who is not resident in India. It does not, however, follow that a person's residential status keeps changing whenever he/she goes abroad and irrespective of the duration of his/her journey outside India. For a proper appreciation of the term 'NRI', therefore, one has to turn to Section 2 (p) of Foreign Exchange Regulation Act (FERA). FERA defines an NRI as an Indian citizen who stays abroad for employment, business or vacation or any other purpose in circumstances indicating an indefinite period of stay outside India.

Other examples of NRI are Indian citizens working abroad on assignments with foreign government/government agencies or international/regional agencies such as the United Nations Organisation (UNO) (including its affiliates), the International Monetary Fund (IMF), the International Bank for Reconstruction and Development (IBRD), the World Health Organisation (WHO), and so on. Officials of the Central and State Governments and Public Sector Undertakings deputed abroad on temporary posting are also regarded as NRIs.

Thus, Indian citizens who proceed abroad for higher studies, short business visits, training, medical treatment, and so on. are treated as resident in India even during their temporary absence from the country. NRIs become residents of the country only when they return to India for permanent stay. They continue to remain NRIs on their visits to the country during vacations.

DESERTION

Desertion means to abandon, leave or runaway. Deserted women are a group of women who have been abandoned or left out by their husbands after marriage without any time limitation. The period of marital life among the deserted women varies from a few days to many years. The reasons for desertion are many. However, the most important reason for desertion of women irrespective of their socio-economic, religious and cultural status are the extramarital relationship or bigamy of their husbands. Moreover, demand of excess dowry after marriage and ill treatment of wives without any reason also leads to desertion.

While analysing the 'Desertion of Married Women', it is appropriate to highlight the laws related to desertion by Sagar Chand Jain in his book *The Law Relating to Marriage and Divorce* (1986). Desertion means the intentional permanent forsaking and abandonment of one spouse by the other without the other's consent and without reasonable cause. It is a total repudiation of the obligation of marriage. In view of the large variety of circumstance and modes of life involved, the courts have discouraged attempts at defining desertion, there being no general principle to all cases.

Desertion is not the withdrawal from a place but from a state of things, for what the law seeks to enforce as the recognition and discharge of the common obligations of the married state, the state of things may usually be termed, for short, the home. There can be desertion without previous cohabitation by the parties, or without the marriage having been consummated. The person who actually withdraws from cohabitation is not necessarily the deserting party. The fact that a husband makes an allowance to a wife whom he has abandoned is no answer to a charge of desertion. The offence of desertion is a course of conduct that exists independently of its duration, but as a ground for divorce it must exist for a period of at least two years immediately preceding the presentation of the petition or where the offence appears as a cross-charge of the answer. Desertion as a ground of divorce differs from the statutory ground of adultery and cruelty in that the offence founding the cause of action of desertion is not complete, but is inchoate, until the suit is instituted. Desertion is a continuing offence.

For the offence of desertion, so far as the deserting spouse is concerned, two essential conditions must be there, namely (1) factum of separation and (2) the intention to bring cohabitation permanently to an end (animus deserendi). Similarly, two elements are essential so far as the deserted spouse is concerned: (1) the absence of consent and (2) the absence of conduct giving reasonable cause to the spouse leaving the matrimonial home to form the necessary intention aforesaid. Desertion is a matter of inference to be drawn from the facts and circumstances of each case. The inference may be drawn from certain facts that may not, in another case, be capable of leading to the same inference; that is, the facts have to be viewed as to the purpose that is revealed by those acts or by conduct and expression of intention, both interior and subsequent to the actual acts of separation. If, in fact, there has been a separation, the essential question always is whether that act could be attributable to an animus deserendi. The offence of desertion commences when the fact of separation and the animus deserendi coexist. But it is not necessary that they should commence at the same time. The de facto separation may have commenced without the necessary animus, or it may be that the separation and the animus deserendi coincide at this point of time; for example, when the separating spouse abandons the matrimonial home with the intention, expressed or implied, of bringing cohabitation permanently to a close.

NRI DESERTION-RELATED VIOLENCE

The menace of NRI grooms deserting their legally wedded wives is rampant in India irrespective of regional, religious, caste and other socio-economic background. Instances of desertion and domestic violence against women married to NRIs are on the rise, according to the Delhi Commission for Women (DCW). According to the then Chairperson of DCW, Kiran Walia, 'It does not matter whether the women are from progressive, educated families or from lower middle class ones; domestic violence is all pervasive and is on the rise among NRI mates.'

The opinion of the then DIG of Police, Hyderabad, Ms Anjana Sinha, was also the same. According to her, more than 500 NRI cases were registered in her office (Women's Protection Cell, Hyderabad) within a period of seven months in 2004, ever since she took over charge.

In the above context, Shri Harbhajan Singh Mann speaks up for brides dumped by NRIs in Punjab. Mann said, 'Police stations in Punjab were flooded with complaints of fraud by NRI husbands who lured women with the promise of a luxurious life abroad in exchange for a handsome dowry from their families but abandoned them within days or months.' According to Sardar B.S. Ramoowalia, former MP and Social Activist from Punjab, 'Indian women were financially and physically exploited by NRI grooms, and ironically, the victims have no laws to protect them.' He said Punjab Police had instructed their men to help such aggrieved women; but unless a proper law was enacted, justice could not be delivered. He also said the marriages of NRI grooms and Indian brides had become an organized business, run much like a mafia. In his opinion, matrimonial advertisements in vernacular newspapers seeking NRI grooms are mostly bogus.

Violence against women by NRIs in the United States has been exposed by Manavi, an NGO working for South Asian Women's problem in the United States and is quite shocking. According to them, there are several cases when a couple gets married in India, then comes to the United States—the wife experiences domestic violence—on the pretext of a vacation or something like that, the husband takes the wife to India and then leaves her there, while he alone comes back to the United States. In such a situation, the wife cannot come back to the United States if her H-4 Visa has expired in the meantime or the husband has not filed for her Green

Card. This way, the woman becomes completely helpless. Because of the stigma attached to divorce (separation), her living in India becomes difficult, but she cannot go to the United States either.

DESERTION OF MUSLIM WOMEN BY ARABS

Altholugh desertion of married women by NRI is rampant in states like Punjab, Andhra Pradesh and Kerala, the desertion of Muslim women by Arabs is a special feature in Andhra Pradesh and to some extent in Kerala. Since Muslim Personal Law permits polygamy for men, and as per Islam religion marriage is a contract, thousands of Muslim girls/women become victims of desertion.

In the State of Andhra Pradesh, especially in the old city of Hyderabad, hundreds of poor Muslim adolescent girls are the victims of Arab marriages. During the recent past, UAE nationals marrying girls from Hyderabad has become a regular feature. These marriages have some historical background. It was evident that during the 1930s, the Nizams had a good relationship with Arabs. Accordingly, many Arabs came to Hyderabad as military officers and started marital relationship with Muslim girls (*Deccan Chronicle*, 5 September 2004). Often, poor Muslim girls are virtually sold by their parents to the Arabs. In such marriages, the parents of the girls get a bulk amount as Mehar from the Arabs. Besides, one or more brothers of the girl get jobs in the Gulf countries.

MAGNITUDE OF THE PROBLEM OF NRI DESERTION

Andhra Pradesh, which is presently gaining importance in global market especially in the field of Information Technology, sends a large number of men from India to foreign countries. Many of them lure innocent brides from Andhra Pradesh informing falsely that they work in established companies. Only after marriage do the bride's family realize that they have been cheated.

The motives of marrying off the girl to an NRI boy were numerous. Marriage was considered a favourite ticket abroad not only for the girl herself, but also for the rest of the family. With the strict clamping of immigration rules, the old route to prosperity and citizenship in the affluent countries had become tougher. The modus operandi of NRI men would be to come to India after a working stint in the United States or Europe and to display ostentatiously their affluence and offer to marry local girls who could bring large dowries. Often, a holiday visit to their native village holds the promise of a temporary liaison with a village belle for the duration of their visit, besides a handsome dowry.

Ex-party divorces are also common among the NRI marriages. Here, the boy would obtain divorce from foreign countries, where the brides got no opportunity to defend themselves. Due to the lack of evidences and absence of respondents in the court, the petitioner takes a long period to get justice. The delay in settlement of cases adversely affected the life of deserted women by depriving them of their prime years.

Generally, at no stage do parents of the girl try to enquire about the NRI grooms, their previous marital status, profession, work place, income, and so on. The parents of the girl ignore the formalities such as verifying the credentials of the prospective bridegroom or taking the precaution of getting the marriage registered. These marriages usually take place within a short time period.

Majority of the victims thus never had a chance to go abroad along with their husband. This is due to their lack of knowledge about the procedures and formalities that they are required to fulfil to go abroad. They were either duped by their NRI husbands or by some professional lawyers who cheat them by charging thousands to lakhs of rupees in the name of arranging visa for their daughters. The ignorant victims and their families become prey to these professionals without any fruitful results. They become helpless and remain under a lot of debt for ever. The girls usually were forced to stay with their in-laws where they had to bear all harassment in the form of dowry demands, sexual harassment by male members in the family, beatings, torture, and so on.

If an NRI husband somehow happened to send sponsorship to his wife, it was withdrawn at the last moment on some pretext, thus disabling her from getting immigration. This again became the ground for NRI husbands to demand heavy cash from girl's parents to send sponsorship papers for their wives. If the wife by any chance succeeded in joining her husband abroad, her stay was either made miserable there or her stay was wilfully cut short. She was brought back home to India on some pretext, and deprived of her passport and other documents, leaving her a helpless victim. She was badly abused by her in-laws and became vulnerable to sexual harassment in the private sphere of her in-laws' home.

This trend shows that usually girls and her parents do not seek any legal advice or counselling after desertion. They keep on waiting for compromise or reconciliation. Girls themselves are not willing to take any legal action against their husbands with the hope that one fine day she will manage to fly abroad along with him. The social pressures also force them to keep quiet in this regard. They never disclose in society about his unwillingness to take his wife along.

Another major problem faced by the victims and their parents is the non-registration of FIR when complaints are lodged by victimized girls. Instead, they are confronted with the insensitive attitude of police and insulting behaviour, the attitude that obstruct them from having an easy access to police. The in-laws take every measure so that FIR could not be lodged. Either action is not taken to register the FIR or the registration is inordinately delayed. Sometimes, police also starts harassing the victimized girl by commenting that she had 'loose character' and by asking sexual favours. Some respondents also complained that they get threats from the police officials not to lodge an FIR against her husband and in-laws.

The complaints were routinely referred to the district women's crime cell where obstructive attitude usually resulted in insulting behaviour and harassment. The insensitivity among the police force to the issue makes the victims more vulnerable. Further, whenever an accused NRI husband or his parents named in FIR visited their hometown, no step was taken to arrest them or impound their passports. The Look Out Notice by concerned immigration authorities was usually not sent in time, thus facilitating the accused persons to escape abroad.

In most of these cases, the girl's parents become helpless as they had already paid a huge amount of dowry for the marriage and were usually in debt. Being deserted, deceived and left without any idea of their own identity, women had to bear the brunt of the effect of desertion. Nevertheless, all of them may not get the support of their family to express their grievances and fight for their rights legally.

Due to the sensitive nature of the problem and silent sufferings of the Indian women, there are no statistics of domestic violence against Indian women in the United States, because not much formal attention has been paid to the South Asian community. However, in this regard the services rendered by Manavi, Sakhi and other organizations helping victims of domestic violence in South Asian community in the United States is to be appreciated for their advocacy and supportive services.

- Sonia Munshi, Programme Director for Manavi, a South Asian Women's Organization, located in New Jersey. 'We can try to quantify this problem only by looking at individual case load from individual agencies. At Manavi, for example, we get over 300 calls each year from women who are experiencing some form of violence'.
- Daya, another international organization working for South Asian victims of violence and abuse in Texas, tried to find out reasons for the abuse and violence. According to them, the culture and the traditional upbringing of the boys inculcated a superiority feeling and a right to get what they wanted even when it meant using violence to get it. Besides, the process of immigration and acculturation can put additional stress on a relationship. The pressures of 'making it' in the United States, coupled with easy access to alcohol and the absence of extended family support, may exacerbate a potentially violent relationship.
- According to Soma Dixit, even women want to get out of such untoward relationships, but are held back due to immigration issues. The spouses of H-1 Visa holders, who are given H-4 Visas, have no right to employment; they do not have a social security number and no independent immigration status.

H-4 Visa holders have to live under the control of their spouse. According to Shivali Shah, an attorney offering legal counsel to distressed women, 'often husbands will mislead their wives by saying that they have filed for permanent residency card and women hoping for a green card will continue the relationship' (*The Hindu*, 28 November 2004).

Generally, H-4 women and their families are under the impression that coercion and violence are part of only the lower classes. The parents believe that since their daughters have higher education and the grooms have good jobs in the United States, the marriage would be peaceful and joyful. The recent study conducted in the United States by Shivali Shah on H-4 Visa holders found that most women are Indian by birth or descent. Most are college-educated, upper middle class and English speakers with ambitions of good career. Most women had arranged or semi-arranged marriages. Their husband earned $50,000–$110,000. None of the women had their own assets or income source. One woman had ₹30,000 saved from their work in India—a pittance in dollars.

In the above context, it is appropriate to highlight few case studies of women who were deserted by their NRI husbands.

CASE STUDIES OF NRI-DESERTED WOMEN FROM ANDHRA PRADESH

Case Study 1

Ragini (all names have been changed to protect their privacy) aged 26 years, residing at Hyderabad, has been deserted by her husband Ramu, who was working as software engineer in the United States. Decree of divorce has been granted. Her marriage was solemnized as per Hindu customs and rituals with Ramu during 1998 at Ati, Chittoor district of AP. The marriage was arranged within a week because the bridegroom had to leave immediately. At the time of engagement, the bridegroom party demanded a dowry of ₹10 lakh. Which, after negotiations, came down to a cash of ₹4 lakh in addition to gold worth ₹3 lakh and silver and other articles worth ₹1 lakh. At the time of marriage, Ramu introduced one of his girlfriends who accompanied him from the United States to attend his marriage.

After marriage, within a week the boy had to leave. Before that, he demanded a house, which her parents wanted to give her. Documents were made in both husband and wife's name. That house cost around ₹10 lakh. Then, immediately he changed his stand and demanded her to transfer the house in his name alone; otherwise, he said he would not take her to the United States.

He used to go around and stay with his girlfriend. Although the respondent got shocked by this behaviour, she did not reveal it to her parents. She thought he will change after the departure of that lady. Meanwhile, her in-laws also started harassing her by asking the details of her parents' property. And they began demanding more money. They demanded another ₹1 lakh to take her to the United States. This demand was also fulfilled by her parents and he took her to America after a month.

Before their departure, the so-called girlfriend of her husband reached America, and she was awaiting his arrival. There Ragini faced all cruelty and harassment from her husband. She was treated as a servant. He was enjoying life with the other lady as husband and wife. She could not reveal this to anyone, not even to her parents because she was isolated and had no contact with the outside world.

She was totally depressed and silently suffered the torture. Meanwhile, one day her in-laws called her in the absence of her husband; thus she revealed the facts and his connection with the other lady. They took it very lightly and said they knew their relation even before marriage and this is quite common in the United States. She was astonished by the words of her in-laws, and only then she came to know that her husband was already married and this marriage was only for dowry. He wanted to invest the amount in his business in the United States. Again, he was demanding another ₹3 lakh to invest in his business with his girlfriend.

The respondent and her parents were not willing to deposit anything, because they became aware of the intentions of the boy. She filed a criminal petition against him in the family court. The copy of the case was served to him through the embassy. In the first trial due to the absence of the party, the case was prolonged.

The girl stayed with the boy only for 21/2 months in America. After that, she was deserted and there was no question of a reunion. She filed a case for divorce and hoped he will be punished under criminal procedures, and will be forced to return all her property. She suggested that when the parents give dowry, there should be a clear account and some valid documents should be made. They should not simply pay the amount. It should be given in the name of the girl.

Case Study 2

Radhika, the only daughter of her parents, is from a Hindu Brahmin family and has completed her MCA. She was very good in her studies, and socially active. After completing her MCA she was looking for a good job. In the meantime this marriage proposal was made by one of her relatives. The bridegroom party also approached her family for alliance. The boy was an engineer working in the United States. Without any second thoughts or enquiry, her father agreed for the alliance. The boy's family demanded ₹5 lakh along with gold and silver articles. But her father said, they could give only ₹3 lakh and 20 tolas of gold as dowry. After negotiations, the bridegroom's party agreed for marriage. She was also fully convinced for this marriage because she thought after marriage she could go to the United States and get some job there because she had an MCA degree.

The marriage was performed on 9 May 2004 in Secunderabad under Hindu religious rituals. Since it was a Brahmin marriage, they had to follow many rituals and formalities. The registration formalities were also done in the presence of the Registrar. At the time of marriage, 20 tolas of gold, silver articles and furniture worth ₹2 lakh was given. Besides, his sister and mother gave a list of items and articles that were needed at the time of marriage. When she was brought near the mandapam, the bridegroom and his parents started demanding another ₹2 lakh in cash. He refused to tie the matrimonial knot until they gave ₹2 lakh. But her father was not able to arrange the money immediately. He requested for some time, but the groom did not agree. Without getting another ₹2 lakh, they did not want to tie the matrimonial knot and take her to their residence. The bridegroom and his family members left the marriage hall.

On the day after of the marriage, she appeared at Mahila police station, Begumpet, and registered a criminal case against her in-laws. This incident left her and her parents shattered. Her father even went to the bridegroom's house and requested them again, but they did not even allow him to enter their house.

They waited for a year thinking that the boy will change his mind and come back. But it was of no use. Finally, her relatives and parents decided to file divorce case against her husband, though she had not had a marital life. Her marriage was registered, and hence she had to get a divorce. She filed the case at AP Women's Commission, Secunderabad, on June 2002. After a year of waiting, she decided to take up a job and accordingly she joined a software company in Chennai. She got all moral support from her parents and they advised her to forget all the past and lead a happy life. She frequently visits her parents and she wants to continue her job in Chennai.

Her case is in Mahila Lok Adalat, but has not been settled due to the absence of her in-laws and husband. She suggests taking serious steps to settle the case soon, which will help to reduce the tension of her parents. Her suggestion is that one should not blindly believe the NRIs. Without making thorough enquiry about their whereabouts parents should not fix marriage. Besides, the government should punish such men or imprison them for dowry harassment.

Case Study 3

The victim, a Christian aged about 30 years, belongs to a middle-class family. Her husband, aged 35 years, is a resident of Charlotte, USA. Their marriage was performed in 2006 as per Christian rites and customs. He is a software engineer. She got married at the age of 25 years. As per the demands of the bridegroom's parents at the time of marriage, the girl's parents gave an amount of ₹3,00,000 in cash, ₹2,00,000 worth household articles, ₹2,00,000 worth gold ornaments and ₹1,00,000 for other miscellaneous expenditure. Her parents have only one daughter and two sons. Since the boy was from the United States, the girl's parents were happy and they did not have any second thoughts when the proposal came through a marriage broker. Moreover, the boy had only 15 days time, therefore without further enquiry they fixed the marriage in a hurry. After marriage, he left for the United States and promised her visa immediately. Accordingly after three months, she got her visa and joined him in the United States. She got a Green card in November 2008 in the United States.

After three months, her husband started harassing and ill-treating her. He used to beat her mercilessly, and demanded more dowry from her parents. He became an alcoholic and began having affairs with other women. He did not show any interest in her and threatened to divorce her. The harassment increased, and he did not allow her to talk with her parents over phone.

Meanwhile, for a period of one year her husband lost his job; during that period her parents helped him financially. Again, after he got job, he started ill-treating her and totally isolated her from the rest of the world. He would lock her in a room and bring other ladies to his house and have relationship with them. She tolerated all the harassment and torture caused by him in the hope that he will change and repent and treat her well. But all attempts were futile. She was very much afraid of him and his family members. This harassment continued, and once he beat her and kicked her out of his life. Having no other alternative, she was forced to come back to India. Then, her parents and other relatives informed the in-laws about his behaviour. His parents supported their son and unnecessarily blamed her and abused her with vulgar and filthy language and bluntly refused her. Her parents tried to convince them to settle the matter, but his parents openly declared that their son is not willing to continue relations with her as his wife. He wanted to get a divorce. She decided to file a case against him for divorce and maintenance under Christian marriage law. Accordingly, she filed the case in the Vijayawada family court. The case is under trial.

The respondent and her parents had a strong view that the government should take proper measure to punish the offenders in NRI cases. Parents should think twice before finalizing marriages of girls with NRIs. They should have a complete enquiry about their status abroad, character and employment details, and so on. She had the opinion that a special cell must be established in India to check the NRI harassment.

Case Study 4

Laila, aged 26 years, from a lower middle-class family, educated to primary level got married in 2004. Her father is a pensioner, and she has four sisters and one brother. The marriage was arranged through a broker and performed as per Muslim law. Her husband aged 30 years is working in Muscat. At the time of marriage, her parents gave a cash amount of ₹ 1,50,000 and valuable articles, and spent an amount of ₹ 1,00,000 for marriage arrangements.

After 2 months of marriage, her husband left for Muscat leaving her behind with his parents, where she was harassed by them to the extent that she was compelled to starve most of the days. She had no contact with her husband, nor did her husband try to find about her well-being. For nearly two years and seven months, she stayed in his house and was harassed. After that, she was unable to bear the harassment and went to her father's house. Since then, she is living with her parents without any maintenance from her husband's side.

After leaving the house, she informed her husband about the harassment and her pitiable condition and requested him to make arrangements for her maintenance. He turned a deaf ear and did not even reply to a single letter of the respondent. She also sent a fax message to his employer but received no response. She tried all efforts to get maintenance from her husband, but it was of no use. He was earning nearly ₹ 30,000 per month and had sufficient means to pay maintenance to her. However, he was wilfully avoiding her and trying to get married to some other lady. When she came to know about his new marriage, she filed a case in the family court in

Hyderabad for her maintenance and divorce. She claimed ₹ 10,000 for her maintenance from him per month from 2005 onwards. The case is under trial.

She said that if she stays with her parents, they would compel her to marry someone who will be an older person, in all probability an Arab Sheikh who is willing to pay. She is not interested to get married again. She wishes to live independently. She needs some security for her future life. According to her, the government should take necessary action to get speedy judgement in such cases and adequate maintenance from the husband. She is very much against the Triple Talaq in Muslim law. Most of the Muslims practice polygamy and desert many poor women. She has strong views about change in the Muslim personal law.

Case Study 5

Ms. Ganga was working in a bank. She got married very late, at the age of 35 years with a man working in Dubai, through newspaper advertisement. He gave false information that he was working as a computer engineer. He also belonged to Hyderabad. Within a month after marriage, she resigned from her job and they left for Dubai. He did not demand any dowry for marriage, but her parents spent on all expenditure and gave ₹ 5 lakh to the boy towards marriage expenditure. After reaching there, she came to know that she had been cheated and that he did not have a permanent job. There, he forced her to work and she got a job in Muscat. She worked for nearly one year, while he was living in Dubai without any job, rather on her salary. He would take all her salary and enjoyed life lavishly. Ganga was staying alone and working in Muscat. She was forced to send money, otherwise he would threaten her life. She came to know that he was enjoying life with other women in Dubai which upset her.

After a year, she informed everything to her parents. They were very upset and asked her to come back to India immediately. She returned to India and filed a case for divorce. Finally, after a year she got divorce. She was finding it difficult to Cope up with her life. Her father was a source of support for her, Who advised her to rejoin her job. She became very depressed when she lost her father after 6 months. Now her friends and family are giving her moral support through counselling and trying to help her to come out of her mental distress.

She felt that parents should thoroughly enquire about the boy before taking any decision in order to avoid fraud and being cheated. Law should be stringent to punish the cheaters. Counselling must be provided for women in distress. For poor deserted women, government should provide some provision of maintenance.

Case Study 6

Ms. Begum, 35 years old, belongs to a poor Muslim family of five children. Her father died recently. She is illiterate and can only sign her name. At the age of 14 she got married to a 37-year-old Iranian through a broker. Because of poverty, her parents literally sold her to this old Sheikh for ₹7,000 and two tolas of gold without doing any enquiry about him. He was working as an attendant for the Diwan of Doha city. The marriage was performed according to the Muslim Sunnah-ul-Zamal religious rituals. The marriage was also registered in 1983 at Andhra Pradesh Wakf Board, Hyderabad, under Andhra Pradesh Government letter No 2074/wakfs/69–29, dated 7 July 1973 under Indian law.

After the marriage, she stayed with her husband for two months at her residence. He used to give money for all their expenses during his stay. After two months, he left for Doha and promised her that he will arrange her visa shortly. It took nearly seven years for getting her visa. In the meantime, he visited India thrice. He wrote letters and called over phone. When he visited India, he would give ₹2,000–3,000 to meet her expenses.

After 7 years, her father arranged her passport and her husband sent visa for her and she went to Doha. After few days of stay in Doha, she was sent to Iran where her in-laws were living. Then only she came to know that he was an Iranian and she was his third wife; the other two of them had died due to ill health. He did not have any children as he was impotent. As soon as she reached Iran, he changed her nationality from Indian to Iranian by taking her signature and she got the Iranian passport.

After two weeks' stay in Iran, they returned to Doha and he started ill-treating her physically and mentally for no reason. He forced her to have sex even when she was not well. He also suspected her fidelity and blamed her that she had illegal contact with his friends. Very often, he brought his friends home for dinner. If anyone talked to her, he would suspect her, beat her and abuse her after they left the place. Sometimes, he would lock her up in a room and give food only at night. She was not allowed to talk to her parents or anyone else over there. She requested him to send her back to India for seeing her parents. Meanwhile, her father died due to ill health. She cried a lot but to no avail. He said, if she wanted to go from there, she had to go to Iran to serve his family and brothers, but she would not be sent back to India. Whenever she asked to be sent to India, he would beat her. In the meantime, she lost two of her sisters due to ill health.

In August 2003, she received a telegram from her uncle that her mother was sick and she wants to see her daughter. Then too, he refused to send her to India. He warned her about asking repeatedly to go to India. Finally, she went on fast for 4 days without food. She said she wanted to go to India otherwise she will die. Finally, he agreed to send her to India with 45 days' visiting visa to see her mother. She was given ₹ 7,000 for her expenses.

After her father's death her mother was working as maid servant in 3–4 houses for her survival. After reaching Hyderabad, she felt very happy and shared her 14 years of imprisonment abroad and the story of her sufferings. She felt that she was free from that jail and from the clutches of the cruelty of her husband. As per the advice of her relatives, she lodged a complaint in the office of the Commissioner of Police, Hyderabad, on 24 September 2003, and decided not to return to her husband's place and also to get back her Indian nationality. She could not tolerate the ill-treatment of her husband any more, and decided to get 'khula' divorce. She got the triple talaq in September 2003. A Quasi pronounced the talaq in the presence of two more persons.

She is now living with her mother engaged in preparing safety pins and paper covers. They get around ₹ 30 per day. Her relatives helped her in filing case and complaints. Now, she is a divorcee as per Muslim law and has to follow the Iddath period. She is again trying to get her Indian citizenship, for which she has already approached the authorities. She has approached the embassy office and submitted an application and complaints to the Iranian Embassy. She has also approached the Qatar Consulate-General, New Delhi, through correspondence to declare her an Indian citizen and to communicate the acceptance of her divorce as per Mohammedan law.

Finally, on 19 February 2004, she put up a case in the family court, Civil Court, Hyderabad, for dissolution of her marriage.

Thus far, she did not receive any direct communication from her husband though he had completed divorce as per Mohammedan law. As she has not received any written document, she approached the honourable court for protecting her from her husband by passing a decree for dissolution of marriage. The court also sent him notices. The first 'peshi' was also completed, but her husband did not attend, nor responded. The case was adjourned to June 2004. She has not received any financial support or maintenance from her husband till date. She felt that for illiterate and poor people, the government should provide legal support and also provide some counselling and education to cope with such kind of situations. She also suggested that the government should take proper measures to control the Arab marriages and not allow them to marry from India. Muslim personal law also should not allow the men to marry as many times as they wish. She also requested to be given some skill training to get some income for her survival.

SUGGESTIONS

- Registration of FIRs should be made mandatory in cases of desertion. It should also be ensured that no name of any accused is deleted from the FIR. Arrests of all accused persons named in the FIR should be effected without delay. Filing of *challans* in the court should be expedited as per Clause 20(1) (B) of Hindu Marriage Act, and it should be ensured that no FIR is ordinarily quashed.
- The accused NRI groom named in the FIR is a 'proclaimed offender', and if he is holding an Indian Passport, the Indian Missions abroad should be empowered to impound his passport and send him back to face legal proceedings in the concerned court in India.
- The Indian Government should enter into bilateral agreement with countries having large Indian diasporas to take criminal action against offenders on the basis of reciprocity, especially section 44A of CPC and Section 3 of Maintenance Orders Enforcement Act of 1921. Such agreement would enable recognition and enforcement of foreign divorce decrees, maintenance orders, child custody and other foreign orders. This will help women who are oppressed in the name of 'Arabi Kalyanam'.

- Matrimonial Property Arrangement at the time of marriage or after the marriage should be made compulsory and should be registered to help protect the property rights of deserted women. It has been reported, for example, that laws relating to maintenance allowance of deserted women were being flouted indiscriminately. It would, therefore, be necessary to enter the name of NRI-married woman in the ownership record of ancestral property of the husband within the country. This could help check NRI cheating and in initiating action against the NRI in case of fraudulent behaviour and will offer an economic support to the deserted bride.
- Ex-parte divorces taken by NRIs from courts abroad should not be recognized as legally binding in India.
- Counselling centres in police stations should provide support to the victims. There should be a provision of legal aid cell in all district headquarters to provide information regarding matters related to dowry, divorce, maintenance, child custody, etc. They should also provide information with regard to visa, passport and other statutory needs for staying abroad.
- Police and judiciary needs to be sensitized towards this serious social issue of desertion of married women by NRIs. This would go a long way in providing support and humanitarian treatment to victims and ensure speedy judgements of such cases of violence against women.

From the above evidences, it has been observed that desertion of NRI-married women in India and the victims of domestic violence by the husband in the United States and other countries need immediate attention from policy makers, governments and legislations to protect their rights.

REFERENCE

Jain, Sagar Chand. 1986. *The Law Relating to Marriage and Divorce.* New Delhi: Surjeet Book Depot.

CHAPTER 16

Perceptions and Institutional Responses to Sexual Harassment: A Study of Central Kerala

Rebecca John

Through this paper, I wish to problematize what is popularly known as the 'Kerala Model of Development' in relation to gender equality by arguing that the statistical optimism about the status of women in Kerala belies the everyday experience of violence women face. I explore this problem by looking at people's perceptions about sexual harassment of women and girls in public spaces and the various redressal mechanisms the state has created and its effectiveness.

In the context of Kerala, there is a need to interrogate women's educational attainments and access to other resources in the context of entrenched patriarchal social structures especially the family. It is more so in the light of visible evils like the spread of dowry system, the spread of visible fundamentalist phenomenon of Muslim women wearing purdah, degrading depiction of women in mass media especially in the popular 'cinemas' of the time and the kind of reporting seen in popular print media (especially a ploy to increase their circulation, which makes one wonder how it is different from the so-called 'yellow magazines'), the growing number of violence against women in the form of rape and sexual harassment (eve teasing) in both domestic and public places. Crimes against women are occurring in Kerala with an alarming regularity. The Economic Review 2004 released in February 2005 by the Kerala Government says that atrocities against women increased by 300 per cent from 1991 to 2001. The State is rocked by what is dubbed in popular media as 'sex scandal' every now and then involving top politicians, businessmen, media tycoons and the social elite, making it difficult for the culprits to be booked under law as the case gets scuttled at the level of enquiry itself.

Kerala has been considered relatively free from the conventional restrictions against women's education and employment, or women owning property. This has been associated with early twentieth-century social reforms, which widened access to education across genders and the matrilineal forms of family that sanctioned women's right to property. On the flipside, these social and legal reforms changed the existing scenario in favour of a society more grounded in patriarchal norms and values. Patriarchal structure is associated with systemic legitimation of violence against women. Given the high literacy levels of Kerala, there is better crime reporting than other states, although it is still difficult for people to report cases of sexual harassment due to constraints of time, resources (stigma and fear associated with reporting), effort and legal procedure. In contrast, the more heinous crimes get reported according to the official statistics.[1] Hence, I chose to study the issue of sexual harassment in public places to deconstruct the popular notions regarding the status of women in Kerala.

DEFINITION AND LEGAL SAFEGUARDS

The all-pervasive and widespread form of violence called sexual harassment by feminists has become such an integral part of a woman's life that it even defines her everyday life—so much so that sexual harassment has become routinized or even naturalized through practices of what Foucault called 'normalization'. So common is the malady that most women themselves fail to recognize it as a problem and treat it as normal. Others over the years have developed internal coping mechanisms. Although women feel distressed by their experience, few can put a finger to the humiliation. The phenomenon of sexual harassment, until recently, eluded a definition, a label or a name.

The existing Indian legislation recognized three forms of sexual assault against women: rape, molestation and eve-teasing. Eve-teasing is the closest concept to sexual harassment one can find (a reminder of the colonial law that continues into the present times), but it was commonly and popularly defined as verbal or gestural teasing only, with no physical contact.

However, the harassment that women experience often includes physical actions such as touching, grabbing of breasts or 'accidental' jostling against them. This is probably one of the few crimes that are committed in broad daylight and among many crimes perpetrated on women that are completely ignored by the police and the public. The most troubling aspect of the discourse on eve-teasing is that it is deployed in explaining violence in public places such as buses, parks, streets or any other crowded area by single men or groups of men. Further the term 'eve-teasing' trivializes the whole experience and also conjures up the image of the woman as the seductress. In addition, eve-teasing is viewed by the police as benignly as the term implies. Molestation, according to police records, is much more common than rape, but it is generally regarded as eve-teasing and rarely punished (Anagol-McGinn, 1994; Kumar, 1995; Thomas and Kitzinger, 1999; Baxi, 2001). Therefore, feminist discourses in India named eve-teasing as a form of perfidious sexual harassment.

The Indian Penal Code (1860), which contains laws for punishment of offences committed within India, lacks specific provisions to deal with instances of sexual harassment of women. The sections in the IPC that defines Sexual Harassment also does so within the framework of 'modesty' and 'obscenity' such as Section 294 (obscene acts and songs), Section 354 (assault or criminal force to woman with intent to outrage her modesty) and Section 509 (word, gesture or act intended to insult the modesty of a woman).

The constitution guarantees certain provisions for the protection of women which in most cases has not been upheld. The constitution guarantees not only equality to women, but also directs the state to adopt positive discrimination in favour of women for neutralizing the socio-economic, educational and political disadvantages faced by them (Fundamental Rights).

Following the Bhanwari Devi gang rape case for the first time, the law recognized sexual harassment as a violation of human rights and the focus of violence got shifted from a criminal wrong committed by an individual to systemic discriminatory conduct that needs redressal and prevention. The Vishaka Judgment[2] defined sexual harassment stating that sexual harassment includes such unwelcome sexually determined behaviour (whether directly or by implication) as follows:

1. Physical contact and advances that include 'accidentally' brushing against a woman's body, unwelcome touching, hugging and leaning over, sexual assault, stalking or any other physical conduct which is unwelcome.
2. A demand or request for sexual favours.
3. Sexually coloured remarks including obscene phone calls, wolf whistles, and so on.
4. Showing pornography that includes display of pornographic pictures on the walls.
5. Any other unwelcome physical, verbal or non-verbal conduct of sexual nature which could be leering, inappropriate invitations, obscene phone calls, and so on, which is unwelcome.

All employers or persons in charge of workplaces whether in public or private sector were also asked to take preventive steps. Rules and regulations were to be publicized prohibiting sexual harassment and it was to be the responsibility of the employer to provide appropriate work conditions to ensure that the environment is not hostile towards woman employee. Further a Complaint Committee was to be constituted, which is to be headed by a woman and not less than half of its members should be women, and to prevent the possibility of any pressure or influence from senior levels, such Complaints Committee was to involve a third party, either an NGO or another body that is familiar with the issue of sexual harassment. The Supreme Court also called upon the Central/State Governments to consider adopting measures including legislation to ensure that the guidelines laid down in the Vishaka Judgment are observed.

Further, the Supreme Court in Apparel Export Promotion Council vs. A.K.Chopra[3] stated that:

- Sexual harassment can take place even if there is no physical contact.
- Witness or documentary evidence is not always necessary to prove a sexual abuse charge.

These judgements have further clarified and expanded the narrow definition and understanding of sexual harassment.

As a step to deal with sexual harassment at the workplace, the National Human Rights Commission convened a meeting on 25 April 2001 to consider how universities and educational institutions could implement the guidelines and norms prescribed by the Supreme Court in the Vishaka Judgment. In the meeting, it was decided that the University Grants Commission (UGC) would write to the various Vice Chancellors of all Central Universities informing them that they were bound by the Judgment to set-up Complaints Committees and the Vice Chancellor was to keep the UGC informed about the working of such Committees, failing which appropriate action was to be taken against them. Setting up a complaints mechanism was also made as a pre-condition for granting assistance to all aided and affiliated schools by the Central Board of Secondary Education (CBSE). Both the UGC and the CBSE were also requested to instruct all educational institutions to make periodic reviews of the action taken by them in respect of setting up of the complaints mechanism. Following this, the UGC made it a mandatory criterion under National Accreditation Advisory Council (NAAC)[4] to give accreditation for colleges, whereas the CBSE through various letters[5] sent out to all schools aided and affiliated to them urging them to take immediate steps to curb sexual harassment of the female teachers/other female employees and the girl students. Further, a clause was also added in the CBSE affiliation by laws that the schools have to comply with the norms prescribed by the Supreme Court in the Vishaka Judgment failing which the schools can be disaffiliated.[6]

It is with this background that I conducted my study in two districts of central Kerala—Ernakulam and Kottayam.[7]

NAMING THE PROBLEM

MacKinnon has argued that sexual harassment is 'sufficiently pervasive as to be nearly invisible, contained by internalized and structural forms of power, it has been nearly inaudible tacitly, it has been acceptable and taboo; acceptable for men to do, taboo for women to confront, even to themselves'(MacKinnon, 1979).

Sexual harassment is a new name describing an old problem. The past decade has seen a remarkable growth in awareness of sexual harassment at work, leading to a widespread recognition that it is a problem that must be addressed. The fact is that women learn to expect sexual jibes and jokes and unwanted physical advances as part of life, because the experience of sexual harassment in public spaces is an aspect of a permissive form of urban governance since gender and its articulation with caste and class is socially constructed. Women have always found their own means for coping with sexual harassment either by laughing it off, ignoring it or telling the harasser to shove off. It is only in recent years that sexual harassment is not seen as an act of individual deviancy, rather it has been conceptualized as a form of structural violence against women.

To support my argument, through the questionnaires, hypothetical situations were given to the respondents as a tool to find out their understanding of the term sexual harassment. These situations were all too familiar ones to the type experienced by the women in their daily lives. For example, while a woman is travelling in a bus, a man keeps staring at her and groups of men whistling or passing comments at a woman. The options given to the respondents were to identify whether the said incidents fall under sexual harassment, eve-teasing or any other and if yes, to specify.

It may be noted that both these situations do not involve physical touch. And these forms of public harassment have been categorized as eve-teasing by the larger public which has led the respondents to call it eve teasing and not sexual harassment. This categorization is evident when it comes to the other situations where physical touch of some kind was involved, be it someone rubbing against a woman while travelling in a bus or a man rubbing against a woman's back while in a theatre or the like where majority of the respondents have identified it as sexual harassment for the simple reason that it involves physical contact.

The point to be noted in this regard was that in most cases, women fear to respond as it would lead to her being ostracized and no other woman coming to the victim's rescue. In fact, it is school students who are most affected by the so-called 'Social Stigma' or 'Societal Education' in this regard as they also get initiated into a world of silence over sexual harassment. One of the girl students who witnessed sexual harassment of an adult woman narrated how the conductor fondled the breast of a middle-aged woman passenger in the bus, and yet the woman did not even look at him. Young girls witness adult's silent acceptance of sexual harassment and this acts as a norm for girls to imitate when they face harassment. The young girl who sees it also understands that she is not to react.

During the focus group discussion I had with youngsters, it was evident that women resent the sexualization of their bodies and one of the most common ways is for men to stare at women's breast–the shame, embarrassment and anger that this form of harassment evokes was palpable when a woman in the group said 'the male gaze is always fixated at the breasts of a woman, the visible sign of a woman's femininity, the signal of her sexuality'. We live in a culture that objectifies the woman as a whole and breasts in particular that freezes the 'masters'' (to be read as men) gaze. Hence, what we find is that women tolerate visual forms of sexual harassment, until these forms of harassment cross a limit that comes to be encoded as 'indecent'. Sexualized gaze is then seen as 'normal' to the social understanding of masculinity. Therefore, if one ignores 'eve teasing' in Kerala, there is no need to wonder why. There are women who said that it is a daily happening issue that they have learned to live with that they do not find anything odd in it. As one of the respondents rightly put it, 'it's a normal behaviour'. Both women and men have this normalized gaze as part of their daily routine that they do not find anything amiss. In fact, they might find something odd if there is no gaze.

Another problem area, which is in another respect a positive development, was that all my young respondents reported that they feel free to discuss their problems with their parents. However, they also said that their parents often told them to avoid certain places or certain people or not to 'attract' other men. The teachers also found it difficult to fill out my questionnaires, as it was very troubling for them to answer certain questions that they found too personal. It seemed that the teachers (women) whom I interviewed held perceptions of sexuality and violence that relegated speech about sexuality and sexual harassment to the personal realm–hence, maintaining the dichotomy between the private and the public–wherein sexual harassment remains a personal problem that must not contaminate the public space and academia, nor be identified as a social problem affecting women and girls.

Hypothetical situation six in the questionnaire was more to do with sexual harassment at the workplace where a teacher/classmate/colleague makes sexual innuendos towards a woman that makes her uncomfortable and how one would react to it. This case would directly come under the purview of the Vishaka Guidelines. Apart from the male respondents, majority of them acknowledged it as sexual harassment.

Except for the boys, the percentage of respondents who would react in such a situation is abysmally low with vast majority taking to the recourse of not reacting at all, or to a smaller extent informing the authorities, that too knowing fully well that there will be no action taken. Women in general agreed that they are scared to complain because it is pointless to complain against a man to another man; and in most cases, the women victim would be a student and the perpetrator, a professor of a higher reputation, and moreover he could also reduce their grades. The political pressure that gets exerted in such cases along with pressure from other faculty on the students is also high. And it was also interesting to note that all the women students were of the opinion that the men from their college or university would never harass them. With regard to girl students, again the same story got repeated. This is due to the notions of brotherhood as emphasized under patriarchy whereby men, especially classmates, are seen as the protectors of the women/girls in class. They are the big brothers.[8]

PUBLIC PERCEPTION

All the respondents were further asked whether in their opinion there was an increase in cases of sexual harassment in the past 10 years; and if yes, why did they think there was an increase especially since Kerala is hailed as the state that distinguishes itself from the other states in India with regard to women's development. The responses clearly show that undoubtedly there is an increase in cases of sexual harassment in Kerala in the past 10 years. In all categories of the respondents, over 90 per cent have said there is an increase, the percentage being more among men and boys.

This led to the next question as to what in the perception of my respondents were the reasons for the increase in sexual harassment. This did throw up interesting reasons such as social stigma associated with woman when they report such cases which was largely identified by girls; break-up of joint family; lack of self-control; influence of media, which again is a reason cited by many; dressing of women in such a way as to provoke men; women's increased public participation; unemployment or lack of financial security; and the like.

Education was itself pointed out as a reason for increase in sexual harassment. Respondents felt that education is now oriented towards getting more grades and has become job-oriented. Kerala has been hailed as the state that has achieved the highest literacy rates among women, but this education system itself has been pointed out as the biggest bane for women. Today's education does not create socially aware citizens but rather a self-centered person. 'Social responsibility has been compromised for personal benefit. There is a conceptual change in the meaning of education with education now meaning job creation' according to Jyothi Narayanan (Sthreevedi District Representative, Ernakulam),[9] an after-effect of privatization of education starting 1957, opposing the system proposed by the Left Front Government which had envisioned more State-run schools and colleges. As an after-effect of globalization, 'government is seen withdrawing itself from the role of the main service provider of public utilities, social welfare no longer being a priority for the state', said Jyothi.

Other aspects of globalization were also cited as reasons for increase in sexual harassment; for example, boys pointed technological advance as a reason for increase in cases of sexual harassment as this led to easy availability of pornography. Globalization was also seen to herald in a new kind of consumer culture, whereby everything was seen as an object to be purchased or used. The minds of the people have been infiltrated with the idea of making profits and in this mentality everything is seen as an object. Hence, women are seen as sex objects. There is a growing tendency for commodification of people. Influence of Western culture was one of the few reasons that were identified by all. Boys, women and men have also identified weak law and order as a major problem that has led to increase of sexual harassment.

The same question was also posed to some other persons whom I had interviewed. According to Dr Shamim Aliyar (two times chairperson of Gender Justice Committee at Cochin University of Science and Technology),[10] the increase in cases of sexual harassment is mainly due to the objectification of women, the fact that women are seen as sex objects coupled with the fact that more and more women are entering public sphere and men do feel threatened. 'It is a power game where men try to show their superiority over women in one way or the other, with sexually harassing the women being easier as women are soft targets'. She also opined that men who are jobless literally often inflict the not-so-severe sexual harassments. This leads to the question of increasing unemployment rates in Kerala with some men also identifying this as a reason.

If there is such an increase of sexual harassment in public spaces, one obviously would ponder as to how girls and women negotiate this everyday reality.

NEGOTIATING PUBLIC SPACES: SCHOOL CHILDREN

In most literature on public spaces, we find that the very category of the 'public' is constituted as an adult category. By this, I mean that the experiential everyday realities of children negotiating public spaces remain invisible, even in literatures on public spaces (see Massey, 1994; Kitchin, 2002; Martin et al., 2003). This absence is also marked in research conducted on sexual harassment in public places (see Jagori's Audit Report on Sexual Harassment in Delhi, 2006). However, the negotiation of the public space in relation to roads, parks, markets or schools remains central to children's lives. I begin my discussion on space by remarking on how this negotiation alters over time in order to negotiate the perceived increase in sexual harassment in public places.

I begin the discussion on how public spaces are constituted by an observation. An important aspect that came to my notice was the increase in school buses plying on the roads with all the schools having increased their fleet to take all the students of the school, with schools sticking to the exact timings with no extra-curricular activities or even extra classes for students. If not the school bus, parents drop and pick up their children in their private vehicles or other means of transportation that was arranged for the students. This way schools assure parents that their child is safe from rising sexual harassment cases in public transportation, if they are sent to that particular school. A phenomenon that is new and something that was absent when I was a student in the same district 10 years ago, when almost all students used to rely on public transportation for their travel to and from school. Although the reasons for increased privatization of travelling might be more complex, it is one of the means through which parents and the school authorities have tried to address the problem of sexual harassment in public places without addressing the cause of it. My opinion through the conversations that I had with teachers, school authorities and my own memories of growing up is that, the 'dangers' of public spaces are negotiated by parents by ensuring that children are secure within the home and the school.

All schools follow strict disciplining after Standard 6 with both girls and boys sitting separately in the same class be it even in the library, a suggestion mooted by the parents. The students are not allowed to interact freely with the opposite sex even in the corridors of the schools during recess time since they are always under the gaze of the authorities who are disciplining them. This is not to say that the perceptions of how spaces are gendered outside the school or the home do not fold within the school. The technique of segregation is deployed here to regulate girls and boys, the analytic reminiscent of 'governing at a distance' from Cooper's (1998) account.

NEGOTIATING PUBLIC SPACE: ADULT WOMAN

This raises the question where exactly women are harassed the most. With respect to girls, there was 100 per cent unanimity when all of them identified bus and roadside as the place where they have been harassed. When it came to women respondents, the answers varied.

These figures point to the fact that women are less harassed in parks, but in the case of Kerala, this does not mean that parks are safe, but that parks are monitored. The public parks in both the districts are under surveillance and one has to pay an entrance fee to enter. Though the fee is minimal, the question of whether it is public park raises a question. Apart from this, apartments have their own play areas that are strictly for the apartment owners (Table 16.1).

Why are so-called 'public parks' regulated? According to the municipal authorities, these parks had become the playground of 'anti-social' elements and 'respectable' families feared going to parks. Therefore, to attract more people to the park, there was a need to renovate the park. The fee charged is the user fee that is used for its maintenance. Now, like the official pointed, there are more people in the park of a certain class. A public place has been cordoned off or restricted for certain class of people. The symbolic representation of urban parks as orderly spaces facilitated the inclusion of 'respectable' women. This is a way of making a certain kind of public look like the public. This idea of governance, which invests in a public that it looks like the public, may be contrasted to the experience of the public place as an embodied space. Herein, I wish to elicit the experiences of women who filled out my questionnaires to mark out the public spaces they feel safer in.

There were some interesting responses in this regard gleaned from interviews with individual women. One woman said that any place is safe provided women have the courage to go alone, thereby repudiating the idea that certain public spaces must be closed off to women. Another woman said that women are not safe anywhere including their own home. Hence, whether a public space looks like one is predicated on the model of the domestic as a bounded space, the latter however does not preclude sexual danger. There was another response which was interesting, for according to her, a woman is safe inside a religious place not outside it alluding to the increase in number of sexual harassment cases in religious places. But the fact remains that you are safe in a religious place – religion playing an important aspect in the life of an average Malayalee.

Table 16.1 *Women's responses to places of harassment*

Places	*Percentage*
Roadside	35
Bus stop	30
Market	9
Parks	2
Bus/train	38
Theatre	10
Neighbourhood	2
All places	11
No place	25

REDRESSAL MECHANISMS

Violence against women has been inherited through the various social dictums and practices over centuries, but the modern state has also developed various institutions as a redressal mechanism to deal with this issue. The state instead of addressing the underlying cause of the issue have time and again invented such institutions to maintain the status quo, that is, power relations among men and women. The present study also tried to gauge the effectiveness and defectiveness of these redressal mechanisms in operation.

Schools do not implement Vishaka Judgment though there has been a directive from the CBSE since Sexual Harassment of children is not seen as an appropriate category to introduce into their universe even though children experience sexual harassment. They generally prefer to turn a blind towards the truth.

WOMEN'S CELL AND GENDER JUSTICE COMMITTEES

There is a common perception that sexual harassment amounts to involvement of physical contact, whereas any other kinds of harassment which does not involve physical contact is eve-teasing, those that leads to mental or emotional disturbance. The Women's Cell and Gender Justice Committees prevailing in the campuses of these two districts—which not being the initiatives of the students or staff concerned but a result of a government order or an UGC directive—in the wake of the Vishaka Judgment also confirm with these common perceptions prevailing in campuses. These universities and colleges do not even have a University Policy on Sexual Harassment, and there is no procedure followed in cases. Ample proof of this is the fact that none of the respondents have heard of the Vishaka Judgment.

I found that violence against women does not define the programmes of the Women's Cell. Rather, women students are seen as potential housewives rather than working women in the future since the programme privileges certain activities that complete women's femininity as good homemakers. In one of the colleges that I visited, this cell acts as training ground to 'how to become a better housewife', with women students being taught driving, cooking, stitching, etc. and also given counseling sessions – a kind of finishing school. The same college also had a Gender Justice Committee again as part of an UGC Guideline[11] which had a male faculty as the Chairperson of the Committee, violating the guidelines[12] given by the Vishaka Judgment. Further, in Kalady University a case was registered against the Vice Chancellor of the University; the NGO representative in the Committee hearing the case proceedings was none other than a Panchayat member with the same political affiliation as the accused, violating the rules laid down by the Vishaka Judgment, and further they did not follow the rule that half the members have to be women. The case only had token representation of women. Recently a year ago when a case came up in Cochin University against a faculty, I was told that the Administration along with the Staff Association rallied behind the faculty, leading finally to his acquittal, and the concerned students who raised the issue with the administration being given warnings due to which they are even scared to talk to anyone, leading my attempts to talk to them, let alone contacting them, going futile. The Committees are nominated with no elected representatives finding place in such Committees, which raises the question of lack of accountability. It was also interesting to note that after the much known SME ragging (rape) case,[13] MG University still does not have a functioning Gender Justice/Sensitization Committee and the student representatives on campus felt that there is no need for such committees since the Union is there on campus to deal with all students' issues, be it even sexual harassment.[14]

AWARENESS REGARDING SEXUAL HARASSMENT COMMITTEES IN THE WORKPLACE

Since there were committees existing in the educational space to assess their functioning, I further asked my respondents about the existing laws if any to deal with sexual harassment and whether they are aware of the existence of Sexual Harassment Committees in their institutions.

As mentioned earlier none of the schools have set up such committees although there has been a CBSE directive in this regard. Hence none of the students were aware of the Vishaka Judgment, especially the girls. A majority of both boys and girls were also not aware of the fact that sexual harassment is a punishable offence legally.The responses elicited from the women and men should be seen in the light of the fact that all colleges and universities that I visited have a Gender Justice Committees existing though maybe not in the same name. Among women who said they have heard of Vishaka Judgment were also mostly lawyers or law students. More than 70 per cent of women and men were not aware of any laws regarding neither sexual harassment nor the fact that there is a gender justice committee existing in the institution. Hence it is apparent that the impact of Vishaka Judgment is negligible when we talk of the level of implementation.

POLICE

None of the girls had ever seeked the help of the police, whereas in the case of the women, 84 per cent said they have never seeked the help of the police and 16 per cent said they have but only 10 per cent said the police have come to their help in such cases. The police on the other hand said that the people never give correct information so they find it difficult to take action. Sreesanth, S.P. Kottayam District[15], was of the opinion that 'people should not call up and say there are eve-teasers in the area', and while probing further they would refuse to give their identity or the locality. In such cases it becomes difficult to nab the person. If this is the police version, a respondent from Ernakulam district had an incident to recall where when she and her friend called the police when they were harassed in a theatre, the police's response was 'why did you girls come alone? You should have come with some men'. The police immediately put the blame on the women. During the course of my fieldwork, I had experienced a situation where a drunkard passed sexual comments at my mother and the policeman was a silent spectator. When I complained to him, his response was 'my duty time is over'. When police are irresponsible or not protecting victims, which victim would inform the police? There were many a respondent who said they do not feel comfortable approaching the police. The police force in Kerala is seen by the average Malayalee as a 'threat force'. This threat perception was also seen in the people's lack of awareness regarding the nearest police Station in their locality, exception being the political activists who have visited one for obviously different reasons. About 89 per cent of girls and 85 per cent of the women said they are not aware of any police station in their locality.

Finally, I asked what the respondents thought was the possible solution to this problem or what they thought need to be done to address sexual harassment in a more successful manner (Table 16.2).

According to Jyoti Narayan,[16] if the 'police intervenes in a stricter manner some issues can be solved', but what is seen as of now in Kerala is the fact that the police is very 'insensitive when it comes to women's issues and problems and behave in a gender biased manner'. Most of these issues need 'immediate redressal', but as of now there is no such mechanism. In this regard, all government institutions have been a dismal failure. According to her, there is a need for segregation of demands, and 'those which require speedy disbursal have to be dealt with in a time bound manner'.

Table 16.2 *How to address sexual harassment*

	Girls (%)	*Boys (%)*	*Women (%)*	*Men (%)*
Women's groups should be active	55	28	35	27
NGOs should sensitise men and women	22	14	12	6
Police should be more active	22	56	27	21
Need for laws and its implemenatation	66	56	28	4
All of the above	11	28	31	33
Don't know			12	15

CONCLUSION

The above analysis reveals to a larger extent the general public discourse regarding sexual harassment in Kerala. There is a presence of indifference to gender issues, and this is more evident in the case of sexual harassment in public places since this is a behaviour that has been normalized by both men and women. There exists an ambivalent understanding of what constitutes sexual harassment which is often encoded by the category of eve-teasing.

An important aspect ingrained in women's mind from childhood is that men are their protectors, and the real oxymoron is that women are sexually harassed/eve-teased by men and these men are also seen as their protectors. This shows how the discourse of kinship is assumed to give women immunity from sexual harassment—which belies their everyday experience—making it harder for them to name such violations as injuries. The idea that strangers sexually harass women informs this perception that women students wait to be harassed by teachers or students or friend.

As part of socialization, there exist various cultural perceptions about how women should be treated and how they should respond to the treatment. In most cultures, women are taught to adhere to man's dominance to show respect, where resisting against male power structure is considered to be a deviant behaviour. This socialization process starts at childhood which affects sexual harassment as an adult discourse. This calls for immediate restructuring of socialization processes by the institutions of socialization such as family, education and the like.

NOTES

1. NCRB data.
2. 1997 VII AD S.C. 53 Vishaka vs State of Rajasthan.
3. 1999(1) SCC 759.
4. For NAAC accreditation one of the criteria to be fulfilled is the setting up of Women's Cell www.ugc.ac.in.
5. Letter No. I/ 14(60)/2004/ dated 16 February 2004.
6. www.cbse.nic.in : CBSE Bye Laws pp. 17 and 20.
7. This study included both primary and secondary data collection. Data were collected through questionnaires consisting of both close-ended and open-ended questions administered to the common public who was chosen using the simple random sampling method from among the identified universe, that is, the two districts of Kottayam and Ernakulam. Questionnaires were administered to both women and men from different social backgrounds and age groups. These data were further corroborated where necessary through structured and unstructured interviews of concerned officials and the common public. The secondary data included analysis of publications of the government or that of various institutions, books, magazines and newspapers and reports prepared by research scholars. I also looked at the relevant laws and appellate judgements.

   My target group included school children above the age of 13 years, college students and students of three central universities in the two districts, namely, Sree Sankaracharya University, Kalady; Cochin University of Science and Technology, Cochin; and Mahatma Gandhi University, Kottayam. Girideepam Bethany School, Kottayam, was taken up in the school category. In the college category, BCM College and Baselious College, both in Kottayam and St Theresa's College and Maharajas College in Cochin were taken for my study. There was no particular reason behind choosing certain college over the other. A known women's college and a coed college nearby was chosen according to my convenience.
8. See *The Hindu*, 16 July 2007, for an advertisement against sexual harassment by Delhi Police where they call upon men to protect woman from eve-teasing.
9. Interviewed on 27 March 2007 at Ernakulam.
10. Interviewed on 20 March 2007 at CUSAT, Cohin University of Science and Technology.

11. For NAAC accreditation, one of the criteria to be fulfilled is the setting up of Women's Cell; www.ugc.ac.in.
12. In Vishaka vs. State of Rajasthan (1997 VII AD S.C 53), the Supreme Court laid down the guidelines to set up a Complaints Committee to be headed by a woman and not less than half of its members should be women.
13. In October 2005, a first semester B.Sc Nursing student of School of Medical Education Kottayam under the MG University was gang-raped in the pretext of ragging. There was an attempt by the college authorities as well as the Kottayam Medical College doctors to hush up the case. The chargesheets were finally filed on 19 January 2006.
14. According to Vishaka Judgment, sexual violence including rape does not come under the purview of such Committees.
15. At a police–public Interface at Kottayam East Police Station.
16. Interviewed on 27 March 2007 at Ernakulam.

REFERENCES

Anagol-McGinn, Padma. 1994. 'Sexual Harassment in India: A Case Study of Eve-teasing in Historical Perspective'. In: *Rethinking Sexual Harassment*. edited by Clare Brant and Yun Lee Too. London: Pluto Press. pp. 220–34.

Baxi, Pratiksha. 2001. 'Sexual Harassment'. *Seminar*. 504–5.

Cooper, Davina. 1998. *Governing Out of Order: Space. Law and the Politics of Belonging*. London: Rivers Oram Press.

Kitchin, Rob. 2002. 'Sexing the City'. *City*. 205–218.

Kumar, Rachel. 1995. *Emerging Trends in Female Unemployment in Kerala: A Quantitative Analysis*. Thiruvananthapuram: International Congress on Kerala Studies, pp. 73–4.

MacKinnon, Catherine A. 1979. *Sexual Harrassment of Working Women: A Case of Sex Discrimination*. New Haven, CT: Yale University Press.

Martin Deobarh, Eugene McCann, and Mark Purcell. 2003. 'Space, Scale, Governance, and Representation: Contemporary Geographical Perspectives on Urban Politics and Policy'. *Journal of Urban Affairs*, 113–21.

Massey, Doreen. 1994. *Space, Place and Gender*. Minneapolis, MN: University of Minnesota Press.

Thomas, Alison M. and Celia, Kitzinger. 1999. *Sexual Harrassment: Contemporary Feminist Perspective*. Springer.

Wharton, Amy S. 2005. *The Sociology of Gender: An Introduction to Theory and Research*. Oxford: Blackwell Publishers.

Part V

Marginality and Health Issues

CHAPTER 17

Politics of Gender: Issues and Challenges of Muslim Women in India

K.M. Ziyauddin

Gender is everywhere. Gender is a key ingredient for individual and group life, social relations and culture. Gender is political in the sense that societies are ordered according to a certain pattern of gender behaviour and gender power relations. Gender politics comprising the ongoing construction of the social gender relations within which individual and groups act in all spheres of societies. There are many actors who are engaged in gender politics. Among these are social movements that challenge the dominant gender order. The women's movement in India took off in the 1920s, building on the nineteenth-century social reform movement. The women's movement progressed during the period of high nationalism and the freedom struggle, both of which shaped its contours. Among the many achievements of the movement, the most significant were the constitutional guarantees of equal rights for women and universal adult suffrage in independent India. However, these guarantees did little to bring about social and material change in the lives of most Indian Muslim women. A new women's movement, articulated to mass and popular politics, emerged in the 1970s. Despite the longstanding and vigorous women's movement, patriarchy remains deeply entrenched in India, influencing the structure of its political and social institutions and determining the opportunities open to women and men. The negotiation and conflict between patriarchy and the women's movement are central to the constitution of the nation-state. This paper explores the issues such as employment, education and violence including sexual harassment that rocked the Indian Muslim society at greater extent. Women are thus central to the larger political and moral imagination, essential to the upholding of civic order and virtue (Eickelman and Piscatori, 2004).

Gender is the study of inequality and imbalance, along with endorsement of the social fact. Gender inequality is rooted in the social stratification which is based on the roles and responsibilities assigned to men and women and the differential valuation of their roles. Thus women positions and degree of empowerment is determined by the ways that gender identities, gender roles and gender relations are conceived at the family, household community and societal levels (Gupta and Yesudian, 2006).

Like gender, politics is everywhere. And doing politics is an immediate source to achieve the result which is due since long time. Politics is nothing except intention and action to do either in favour or against. Politics bring the world together and for developmental cause. Politics vary with space to space and giving a chance to the minority and majority to share the space equally.

Gender politics in India is a part of wider network of social relations, economic factors, identity discourse, political movement and representation. Here, I would like to investigate the contours of gender relations in India from the disciplinary of political science and spatial science where both space and politics mutually exist together but hardly supporting each other across the geographical region. Although, challenges such as education, employment and domestic violence are indeed shaking Muslim women every day with different stroke. In India, Muslim women remain in seclusion, and despite low presence in both public and private space, she seldom makes louder voice than her Hindu counterpart across the field.

Hence, the 'Islamist discourses on women that uphold the authenticity of tradition thus seek to draw boundaries not only between the Muslim and non-Muslim community but also between the "true" guardians of community and the "internal other" ' (Kandiyoti, 1991: 7–8). A key dimension of Muslim politics is the contest over the meanings attached to 'women' as symbol. The underlying belief, common to ideological formations, is that women must remain 'in their place' for political and social harmony to prevail. Unlike social conservatives, liberals and feminists, however, believe that women can remain 'in their place' and still have roles equal to men in all sphere of activity (Eickelman and Piscatori, 2004).

Gender politics is an extension of social construction in which sometimes groups are involved and sometimes individuals made a valuable participation. It is a collective effort to achieve the assignment. In South Asia, the position of Muslim women is very low irrespective to their male counterpart in the same society where both have been living since time immemorial. Every time gender politics is happening under social movement in which common participation is expected from the societies to achieve the social dream, it may be differentiated by space and time. In Indian society, the role of women has always been considered within the four walls. At the same time, whatever situation improves is because of their participation in politics and they have gradually started demanding their space in the society that is due since long years.

Indian society, which has a secular identity, provides equal rights to all religions of faith across the country, regarding caste, creed and class. Muslim population is one of the religions that is almost spread throughout the country. They are in dense population in some pockets like Jammu and Kashmir, West Bengal, Assam, Bihar, Kerala and Uttar Pradesh, where Muslim votes are the deciding factor in each and every election results. The Muslim population is very valuable in these regions. But as compared to in northern India, Muslims in the south are much better-off and are in harmony as they share power in government, which is quite absent in northern states despite having a good proportion in population. In India, Muslim women's participation in politics has been noted in large number during the Khilafat movement in the 1920s.

The various facets of the social movement in colonial India have been well documented according to the chronology. Including the Khilafat movement in which for the first time Muslim women came out from veils and openly participated to fight against colonial power for a better future. Across the freedom movement, the situation of Muslim women has received less attention among politician, scholars as well as intelligentsia. It was after a call from Gandhiji, that Muslim women made their presence felt in the national freedom movement. Many gave up *purdah* (veil) and actively participated in the Swadeshi and civil disobedience movements. Among the Indian community, particularly in Muslim community, purdah is regarded as an important part of Islamic religion and seen as historically responsible for the limited participation of women activities outside the domestic sphere. The first phase of the women's movement emerged in India in the 1920s. The immense changes has been initiated in the nineteenth century through social reform and pushed more radical changes in the range and variety of roles women could play in society. The political and economic changes of the nineteenth century had induced a societal reassessment as Indian reformers and Christian missionaries combined to press for changes in the status of women, beginning with education and raising the age of marriage. However, these goals were to be greatly expanded in the decades before Independence to include political participation, and to fight for expanded social and economic roles. At the same time, the movement's leadership remained in the hand of a few families; it nevertheless provided opportunities to a variety of emerging leaders to express their views and disseminate the message of the movement to women's group.

The leadership of the Muslim women's movement, as with the movement in other communities, tended to become identified with particular families: in Bombay, the activities of women from Tayabji, Rahimtullah and Chinoy families and in Punjab with those of Muhammad Shafi and Abdul Qadir (Lateef, 1986). The link between social reform, the status of women and the national movement proved a source of enormous strength for the national movement and of political support for the women's movement. This mutually beneficial relationship led to considerable cooperation between leaders of the national movement and the women's movement.

At the same time, 'the issue of Indian women in the political sphere first emerged during the period over extending the franchise to women' (Karlekar, 2005) and finally through 'The Government of India Act 1935' which made possible for the Indian women to become a voter, after a long struggle.

In India, there are around 60 million Muslim women who constitute world's largest electoral population. Although they (women, including Muslim women) have the right to vote and voted back in the 1920s, the situation has not improved even after we celebrated our sixtieth Independence festival with the first women president.

The government made many promises, including woman reservation provision in the parliament. Since 1970s, many talks were made about the Women Reservation Bill. And since then, many governments formed and have gone, but the Woman Reservation Bill remains waiting to pass in the houses where it is lying for more than two decades. The Woman Reservation Bill got many prime minister's sympathy but still not able to become a reality including Left coalition with the UPA government, which virtually was a government run by Mrs Sonia Gandhi. The role of a parliamentarian is susceptible and very unpredictable within the patriarchal ambient and during coalition-era government where no one party has majority in the parliament (Lok Sabha). The provision of this bill is to provide 33 per cent reservation to women in the house.

Gender politics is nothing when compared to compartmentalization of politics for either men or women, or for both.

> Since the early 1980's, India has witnessed a resurgence of politicized religion in which Hindu and Muslim communal politics alike have given a central place to gender issues. Women have figured as important signifiers of differences between groups. Sometimes they have vigorously participated in various communal projects, at other times they have spoken out against communal identity. They heightened mobilization of women has become the focus of debate in analyzing the empowerment of women. (Hasan and Menon, 2004)

Muslim women joined other women in the struggle to have access to economic resources, education and employment. The impetus of the women's movement lay somewhat diffused in the aftermath of Independence because most of the influential, educated and moneylenders of northern India immigrated to the newly created country, Pakistan. It is communal divide and most painful for Muslim women where they lost their identity and in fact even in both countries still nurse the wound of their religious identity. The position of Muslim women in the past is almost eroded with the time and the partition zeroed in on their identity. Devoid of a national or visionary leadership, the voices and experience of Muslim women came to be usurped by male Muslim claiming to represent the community. The political opportunism of the latter, combined with the failure of state programmes to alleviate women's socio-economic status, left the majority of Muslim women economically impoverished. With the dawn of the twentieth century, the impetus of social reform generated an awareness of women's issues and provided solution within legal ambit. Including much ignited debate such as Shah Bano-Muslim, personal law case created much furore across the country.

Since Independence, only some northern part experiences political ambition. In the parliament, the number of Muslim women never crosses the double digit, although once in the past during sixth parliamentary election the representation of Muslim women was around 16 per cent within women parliamentarian. After that, they never crossed a fair number of representation in the Lok Sabha election. Even sometimes, the number came down to zero, which is unprecedented for the community and also for the parliament where no Muslim woman is representing the community.

Although the number of women parliamentarian increased over time, the number of Muslim women seldom increased. Even after 60 years of Independence, the political activities among the Muslims are still the affairs of only a few families and few selected pockets, from where the women have to manage their sojourn to the parliament.

Since the first democratic election, which was held with many dreams and promises, not even a single Muslim woman could make her position as her Hindu counterpart in the existing democratic process. The situation improved little in the second parliamentary election in which Mafida Ahmed from Jorhat constituency (Assam) and Maimoona Sultan from Bhopal constituency (Madhya Pradesh) made their destiny. In the meantime, the numbers of woman increased in the third parliamentary election, but Muslim women remain in the same line. Only Zohraban Akbarbhai Charada from Banaskantha (Gujarat) and Maimoona Sultan from Bhopal constituency (Madhya Pradesh) had won the election. But subsequently in fourth and fifth Lok Sabha election, the number again heavily came down and touched zero and after that the sixth parliamentary election shows the highest number of Muslim women who manage to win the election. Among them was Rashida Haque Chaudhary from Silchar, while Akbar Jehan Abdullah made it twice, once each from Srinagar and Anantnag (J&K), and Mohsina Kidwai from Azamgarh and Merrut (UP) made their victory sign and pushed the ratio in a higher number in the parliamentary election. In the seventh parliamentary election only two managed to win the election from UP: Mohsina Kidwai (Merrut) and Begaum Abida Ahmed (Bareilly). It was only after them that Noor Bano managed the election from Rampur constituency (UP). In the fourteenth Lok Sabha election, Mehbooba Mufti from Anantnag constituency (J&K) and Syeda Rubab from Bahriach Constituency (UP) managed to win the election.

Those who managed to win the election in which all were from Congress party, except for Akbar Jehan Abdullah who belonged to National Conference party and Mehbooba Mufti (Anantnag) from JKPDP, represented only northern region in the parliament. Only nine Muslim women have served in the Lok Sabha in the past 60 years.

In the upper house, the position of Muslim women is considerably good in comparison with the Lok Sabha, except the few initial years of 1970s when there were no Muslim women in the house. And the interesting things are that out of 13, 10 were from Congress party and Najma Heptullah who later got elected from BJP after leaving Congress party. Apart from election, three Muslim women are nominated by the President of India in the house.

Across the state assemblies, the number of Muslim women who have participated in provincial government since Independence has proved to be more difficult because of vague information. Even after carefully preparing a list during the past 50 years, 26 Muslim women have been elected to the provincial legislative assemblies (Karlekar, 2005). This is indeed quite a low proportion as against their number that should be in the assemblies. Even the majority of them made their sojourn with the Congress tickets.

A more detailed examination of the selection of Muslim women politicians reveal a high degree of similarity in terms of family background, education, party affiliation and even their legacy that they carry. Most of them are from elite backgrounds and come from politically active families. Muslim women politicians, such as Mehbooa Mufti, Noor Bano and Mohsina Kidwai, are all from such politically active family where they considered their duty to fight for the cause of people and the locality and running their legacy politically.

The majority of surveyed women were unaware of the 73rd and 74th Constitutional Amendments and 'three-quarters supported reservations for women in legislatures; moreover, they expressed an interest in contesting election, especially at the local level' (Hasan and Menon, 2004). Their political awareness regarding names of party and belonging to it is good.

MUSLIM WOMEN AND EDUCATION

The dilemmas and direction of women and society are not uniform since prolonged period. They are a result of multiple factors that determine the drift of the whole cultural complex considered as a part of the social realities of the period. Among Muslim women, education from the beginning is considered as a major obstacle for social status. The level of women's social status increases positively with education. And education is considered as important indices to enhance their socio-cultural status including social mobility. It is quite well known that Muslim women are facing a number of constraints to access a better education. But at the same time, unavailability of empirical data make our claim difficult to establish this. After sixtieth year of Independence, we have no perfect mechanism to know the exact statistics regarding the number and accessibility of education to the Muslim women. While the Constitution of India promised to provide universal education to all children across caste, class and religion up to the age of 14 years, it was possible only after constitutional amendment, and it became the obligation of the State to provide and implement the programme to achieve the goal. Therefore, considerable progress has been noted in the current decade.

After several hues and cries, the UPA government set up a high-level committee to know their socio-economic status in the society as Sachar committee. The literacy rate has increased in the past five decades, and women are still lagging behind men in all the communities. The growth rate in male and female population across urban and rural areas is uneven. According to the census of India, 59 per cent of Muslims are literate as against the national average which shows it is more than 65 per cent. Muslim women fare even worse in both rural and urban areas; their lowest for work participation and education.

Countrywide survey conducted by Zoya Hasan and Ritu Menon (2004), which comprised 40 districts and spanning 12 States, gave a new data about where Muslim women stand in the Indian society.

In primary survey reports, around 58 per cent Muslim women are illiterate and merely 4 per cent are graduate and above, and 10 per cent are secondary and higher secondary passed against around 17 per cent are middle school passed compared to the primary passed, which is around 11 per cent is indeed the lowest one of them. And just around 2 per cent were getting any kind of non-formal education. The whole data unveiled the Muslim women's social status that needs remarkable efforts to change for better cause.

She divided the whole Indian Territory into four regions including both rural and urban. The rate of illiteracy is remarkably high in rural-northern part of India, which is 82 per cent and least number of illiteracy is in the rural-south where the rate of illiteracy is 30 per cent; whereas in the rural-west, it is around 61 per cent and in the rural-east, the rate of illiteracy is around is 45 per cent. However in the urban, the rate is little bit considerably to a certain mark. The rate of illiteracy is lowest in urban-south, which is around 20 per cent and the rate is worse in urban-north, where it is around 50 per cent. While in urban-east and urban-west, the rate of illiteracy is 28 per cent and 34 per cent. In the rural belt, the ratio is bit lower than the urban region, and the overall rate for southern region is respectively high compared to other regions among all classes of education.

In urban region among Muslim women, the maximum number of graduates and above higher studies are coming from the north region, which is around 19 per cent and rest from other regions are not doing well. For south, the rate is 12 per cent and also 12 per cent for the west region and around 10 per cent among the eastern region, which is lowest and needs special attention. While in urban-south, the rate of higher and senior secondary is 30 per cent, which is exclusively in better position, and rest of the other region falling inbetween the range of 10–20 per cent, which is indeed very low.

Among Muslim women who ever attended school is around 41 per cent and on regional distribution, urban areas are doing well almost in all category of education. In rural-north, it is around 14 per cent and 76 per cent for rural-south. In rural-east, the rate is 50 per cent and in rural-west it is 42 per cent. Meanwhile, the rate is little bit comfortable around urban region in which the rate is 23 per cent in urban-north and 77 per cent in urban-south, subsequently for east and west the rate is 57 per cent and 63 per cent.

Therefore on the basis of all India, the rate of Muslim women who ever attended school is indeed low, and there is the possibility to increase the rate across the Indian Territory.

Across the rural region, the Muslim women who ever attended school is poor and in which is still below 50 per cent, except the south region where rate is comfortable and reflecting a sign of improvement in comparison with other regions.

AVERAGE YEARS OF SCHOOLING

The actual status of Muslim women in the schooling is below that of Hindus in all geographical regions and quite low in the northern zone.

Table 17.1 *Schooling among Muslim and Hindu women*

Region	*Muslim women*	*Hindu women*	*Total*
North	1.6	2.7	2.2
East	2.7	3.7	3.3
South	5.0	5.5	5.4
West	3.3	3.8	3.7
All India	2.7	3.8	3.4

Source: Households from 55th round of NSS data.

In India, the average number of years for schooling that women have received is indeed very low. Among Muslims, this is 2.7 years and in Hindus 3.8 years. The differences between geographical zones are considerable and indicating a huge gap in schooling between north and south zone. While in the south, the years of schooling is good and even in the west the schooling days are good. Overall, the low average number of years of schooling of Muslim women indicates a high dropout rate for them.

EMPLOYMENT BY MUSLIM WOMEN

This is indeed true that in India majority of women work round the year for livelihood. Yet, there are few types of work that are recognized by the government for official estimation of national income. It is stipulated to be low. The data on women work participation rates show low figures among the different fields of work.

WORK PARTICIPATION RATE AMONG MUSLIM WOMEN

Among the Muslims, the work participation such as wage worker/employee is largest and followed by self-employed. The work participation rate for Muslim women is low in comparison with Hindu women. In Muslim women, the number is less for self-employed which is merely 2.70 per cent and is indeed a setback for the community. This reflects the financially weak position that pushed the community in the marginality. While the percentage for the wage worker is high, with respect to other position that is around 7.58 per cent. Being salaried worker, the number is unprecedentedly low, which is below 2 per cent. Also around 2 per cent are working as unpaid worker.

As per data available, this is carefully prepared after Hasan and Menon made a distinguished effort to unveil the Muslim workers participating across the countrywide. Among Muslim communities, embroidery/tailoring is considered as a tool to earn for family affairs because it needs little skill and even without education the work would be finished. The entire region is witness to this profession with varying degree. In the urban-east and -west, the work involved many families that include around 30 per cent and 27 per cent. In the urban zone, the profession is much popular than rural zone. Only in the southern zone the profession involved around 12.28 per cent. While in the rural belt, it is also considered as livelihood among the community, but the Muslim women are running the profession across the country in varying degrees.

Running animal husbandry business is less popular among the Muslim women. In the North zone, it is little popular among rural people, which is around 4 per cent and may be due to their religious background which is restraining them to do the work. Agricultural activities are one of them which are much popular among the Muslims and in almost all parts of the country. In the North, the rate of involvement is around 20 per cent and in the South it is 22 per cent. While in the East, the rate of doing agriculture is around 18.18 per cent and in the west the rate is quite high which is around 32 per cent.

Among Muslim women, the rate of participation in unskilled or casual work is quite high across all parts of the country. In the North, including both rural and urban, the average rate is 20 per cent. The urban-east region experiences higher rate of unskilled or casual work in the country; this is around 35 per cent while in the urban-west region the rate is 21 per cent.

Among skilled job, the rate is comparably slightly better than other categories of work. Muslim women seem to be more skilled: in the rural-north, it is around 24 per cent and 16 per cent in the urban locality. In the south, the rate is bit low and in the rural-east, the rate of skilled is 18 per cent; whereas in the urban-east, it is around 8.11 per cent. In the rural-west, the involvement rate is around 20 per cent. Even the number of white collars among Muslim women is a bit high in the north region, which is around 16 per cent and 18 per cent for rural and urban population. While in the east region, the rate is high around 18 per cent for rural and 13 per cent for urban locality. In the west zone, it is low compared to other zones in the country. Meanwhile, the working condition of Muslim women is not too good across the country, even their Hindu counterparts are doing well in all spheres, including public and private space.

SEXUAL HARRASSMENT

In India, there is hardly a day when there is no violence against women. The data given below confirm the crime rate against women round the clock and ringing a bell for further action. It is sad to say that still there is no specific data that reveal the crime against Muslim women within the four walls and across the territory. Therefore, let us consider these data to interpret the rate of crime against Muslim women in a day, and in a year.

We take the case of Imrana and Guddia as indicators to get an idea of sexual harassments against women. Imrana was raped by her father-in-law and subsequently pushed into dilemma by clergy whether she can continue relationship with her husband. She was raped, and even without her consent, the clergy announced that now she becomes the wife of her father-in-law within the ambit of Shariat rules and by force both have been separated. The case of Guddia is more strange, for her husband went missing during Kargil War when he was posted there; but subsequently, she was forced into another marriage and she started living happily when then suddenly her earlier husband appeared in her life who was missing since war days and forced her to break her second marriage. Unfortunately, she became pregnant and after her delivery, she died leaving the issue unresolved.

Therefore, both this story made much hue and cry and forced the clergy and the nobles of the Muslim society to think regarding the subject rather than announcing *Fatwa* (a binding Islamic law) immediately.

In India, every minute a women is suppressed by male in various ways. Every hour they are facing rape, molestation, kidnappings, dowry death and sexual abuses made by in-laws. The violence against women, especially domestic violence, is one of them in which women suffered most of the time within society and even by their in-laws. 'The MWS (Muslim Women's Survey) reported that approximately 20 per cent of respondents had experienced verbal and physical abuse in the marital home, over 80 per cent of it at the hands of their husbands' (Hasan and Menon, 2004).

But after several demands, Government of India brought a legislation, the Protection of Women from Domestic Violence Act, 2005, which came into force on 26 October 2006, for further check on domestic violence. Among domestic violence, sexual harassment is a kind of exploitation in which most of the time Muslim women do not raise her voice. In India, it is common knowledge that the social status of Muslim women is poor than other communities women. The data regarding domestic violence against women are same for both Hindu and Muslim women as per MWS and NFHS (National Family Health Survey, 1998–1999) report, 'although the MWS shows that Hindu women experience greater levels of violence than Muslim in all four zones' (Hasan and Menon, 2004). As per MWS, 'Muslim women, too, better off in the west and south zones, with the south zone reporting the lowest percentage 10.94' (Hasan and Menon, 2004). According to NFHS, Tamil Nadu is at the top of the list with around 40 per cent of women beaten and physically mistreated from the age of 15 years and upwards, followed by Meghalaya at 31.1 per cent; Orissa 28.9 per cent; Bihar 26.6 per cent; and Jammu and Kashmir and Uttar Pradesh at 22 per cent each. The lowest percentage is reported from Himachal Pradesh followed by Gujarat and Kerala at 10 per cent.

Even in Indian society women remain the subject of exploitations during communal conflicts. During communal conflict, women are considered as soft targets rather than providing them safe passage. During communal violence like the one in Godhra in Gujarat, Muslim women suffered much more. One form of violence, though, could be directed only against women and girls. Rape often took the form of gang rape and was followed by mutilation and finally by the destruction of evidence through the burning of the victims. In 1986, Indian Mullah made hullabaloo and pushed the government to settle the issues through legislation. In 1986, the Supreme Court of India ruled that Shah Bano, an old divorced Muslim woman, was eligible for maintenance money. However, the decision was vociferously opposed by fundamentalist Muslim leaders, who alleged that the court was interfering in their personal law. The Government gave in to the demand of these leaders, and despite nationwide protests from women, it passed an act that was ironically named Muslim Women's (Protection of Rights upon Divorce) Act.

Domestic violence is not confined to wives, but includes mothers, daughters, sisters, widows, divorced women living in the home as well as those who are in an informal relationship with the accused, including a bigamous relationship. It covers all domestic relationships in a 'shared household'. A shared household is very broadly defined to include one where the abused person lives alone or with the abuser (Kapur, 2006).

In terms of domestic violence—which is widely recognized to be increasing in India—the incidence cuts across caste, class and community. According to MWS, survey finds that over 50 per cent of the reported violence (which may, of course, be different from the actual incidence of violence) is among the Scheduled Caste and the Scheduled Tribe households, which also happen to be the poorest of the poor. Muslim women come in third (after Other Backward Castes) at 18 per cent. What is possibly more significant is that husbands were identified as the primary perpetrators in more than 80 per cent of cases.

CONCLUSION

The challenges and issues of Muslim women are wide and inevitable across the territory and require an immediate attention for improvement. The roles of Muslim women in Indian politics are very limited and marginal. The representation of Muslim women is just above 1 per cent which is considerable and alarming, whereas their Hindu counterpart is doing well, which is around 33 per cent. Unlike other politician among Muslims, the business of politics is concluded with few families and surrounded with few localities having higher proportion of population. In 60 years of Independence, there have been only eight females who could manage their path to the parliament in a different route. The representation is even below in different State legislatives which is around 26 by number after several hue and cry, and many programmes were launched across the country.

In Muslim community, education is one of the fronts where the community is lagging and more than 50 per cent peoples of the community are below literacy level. All the regions in north, east, west and south are more or less facing the same level of challenges and issues to come out from the social problem.

The employment status of Muslim women is also lower than expected. Employment is one of the important sector where Muslim women's presence is lacking. Across the rural belt, the higher rate of participation of women in agricultural activities is acknowledged, while self-employment such as tailoring, embroidery and animal husbandry is also attracting a large number of women; yet the percentage of Muslim women as wage worker, salaried and unpaid family worker is quite low.

The violence against Muslim women is quite known in the society, but due to 'introvert social status' (living within four walls and misusing the meaning of *Sharia*, an Islamic code of law), and therefore it is difficult to acknowledge the social problem. Even the domestic violence is not confined to anything particular. Rather it is found across all the relationships of female members wearing 'purdah'.

Hence, the role of Muslim women in society is quite limited and therefore may be one of the reasons for their backwardness in education, employment and frequent cause of domestic violence. Thus, there is a need for systematic involvement and enhanced participation of Muslim women in politics and other social cause to bring in equality.

REFERENCES

Eickelman, Dale F. and James, Piscatori. 2004. *Muslim Politics*. Princeton: Princeton University Press.

Gupta, Kamla and Princy, Yesudian. 2006. 'Evidence of women empowerment in India: A study of socio-spatial disparities' *Geojournal*, 65(4): 365–80.

Hasan, Zoya and Ritu Menon. 2004. *Unequal Citizen: A Study of Muslim Women in India*. New Delhi: Oxford University Press.

Kandiyoti, Denis. 1991. 'Islam and Patriarchy: A Comparative Perspective'. In *Women in Middle Eastern History*. edited by Nikki Keddie and Beth Baron, New Haven, CT and London: Yale University Press.

Kapur, Ratna. 2006. 'India: We Can End All Violence against Women', *The Times of India*, 21 November, New Delhi.

Karlekar, Karin Deutsch. 2005. 'Muslim Women in Indian Politics 1947–2002'. In *In a Minority: Essays on Muslim Women in India*, edited by Hasan and Menon, New Delhi: Oxford University Press.

Lateef, Shaeeda. 1986. *Muslim Women in India*. London: Zed Books.

http://www.comminit.com/baseline/baseline2001/baseline-301.html, accessed, 10 August 2013.

http://www.sacw.net/DC/CommunalismCollection/ArticlesArchive/MDube08032005.htmlIn, accessed 10 August 2013.

Annexure

Muslim women in Lok-Sabha and their percentage of representation

Lok Sabha Election	*Total Seat*	*Men MPs*	*Women MPs*	*Muslim Women MPs*	*Muslim Women % of Total Women*
1st (1952–1957)	499	476	23	0	0
2nd (1957–1962)	479	455	24	2	8.3
3rd (1962–1967)	543	506	37	2	5.4
4th (1967–1970)	548	516	32	0	0
5th (1971–1977)	553	527	26	0	0
6th (1977–1979)	559	541	18	3	16.7
7th (1980–1984)	565	533	32	2	6.3
8th (1984–1989)	571	526	45	3	6.7
9th (1989–1991)	531	503	28	0	0
10th (1991–1996)	534	494	40	0	0
11th (1996–1997)	545	505	40	1	2.5
12th (1998–1999)	545	501	44	0	0
13th (1999–1904)	545	498	47	1	2.1
14th (2004–Till Now)	545	500	49	2	–
Average			33.5	1.1	3.2

Source: Lok Sabha website, http//www.parliamentofindia.nic.in, accessed, 10th August, 2013

CHAPTER 18

Gender Among the Nagas of North East India

Ajailiu Niumai

This paper attempts to examine three issues related to gender in the Naga society. First, it constructs the conceptual and theoretical framework of gender and empirically analyses it by noting the cultural life of Naga women, discrimination in wages for women, traditional law of inheritance and exclusion of women in politics and religion. Second, it would examine the intervention of two prominent Naga women's organizations based in Nagaland and Manipur. Third, a question would be raised as to how the process of globalization has affected the Naga women's lives. We are living in an era of dramatic change, in a world that is being transformed by complicated financial systems and high technological revolutions into huge global market systems. Information and Communications Technology (ICT) between different tribes, castes, races, ethnic groups, states and nations has been facilitated by globalization, promising unprecedented privileges for material prosperity and larger freedom, but also threatening to compound several existing challenges of those most vulnerable. In such a complex scenario, it is essential to point out that the Naga society in the past was a simple one, confined mainly to the village in which women played their subordinate role assigned to them completely in the social, political and religious affairs. But, there have been changes in the past few years and the changing facet of women has become a vital question that needs to be further probed.

CONCEPTUAL AND THEORETICAL FRAMEWORK OF GENDER

Gender is a multifaceted reality that is culturally constructed and socially determined by the society. In other words, gender is culturally and socially constructed roles, responsibilities, privileges, relations and expectations of women and men. Because these are socially constructed, they can change over time and differ from one place to another. Gender refers to behavioral differences between males and females that are culturally based and socially learned (Appelbaum and Chambliss, 1997:218). The understanding of gender in the context of Naga culture in North East India needs to be percieved from their structure of social stratification, existing power relations between women and men, and the process of acquiring the accepted roles and behaviour. Traditionally, the birth of the girl as the first offspring in the family is considered favourable since there is a requirement of the eldest child to play a certain role, which is essential for the welfare of the family. Girls are preferred to be the eldest child as they are helpful to their parents in the discharge of domestic duties. However, the birth of a boy is generally preferred in the Naga society as the customs and traditional rules imply that the lineage of a clan and family is through a male child.

The Nagas recognized that their 'women have an important contribution to make', as quoted by a noted anthropologist and feminist Margaret Mead. However, there are traditional norms and customary laws that expect women to be subjugated to men. This paradox of recognizing women as individuals who could make important contributions and at the same time subjugated by the patriarchal system is pointed out by Lucy Zehol (1998: 2) who said, 'The fact that Naga society is patriarchal as well as patrilineal implies beyond any doubt that women are not equal to men in certain aspects of life. The patriarchal Naga society is reflected by notions such as the birth of a male child being auspicious, man as the bread winner and the protector of the society, and women being subordinate to their households'. Nonetheless, their traditional culture provides more equality between women and men as compared with the mainstream Indian society. For instance, Naga women enjoy certain privileges and status more than women in other parts of India as they do not encounter sati, do not wear purdah, pay dowry and enjoy platonic relationship with the opposite sex. Historically, social evils such as beggary, rape, female infanticide, sati, suicide and prostitution of women were not present in their culture.

Sometimes, gender is referred mistakenly only to women although it deals with the distinctive social construction of both men and women. The theoretical framework of gender in this paper is drawn from the works of Ann Oakley, Jean-Jacques Rousseau and Margaret Mead. Ann Oakley (1972: 18) states that 'gender' is a matter of culture; it refers to the societal classification into 'masculine' and 'feminine'. In other words, gender refers to a specific cultural meaning system that attaches to being a male or a female. Gender is a sexual identity of individuals in relation to the customs, traditions, ways of life and the like. The Naga society as a whole contributes to the notion of gender by influencing and moulding the community members about the ways in which men and women should behave, perform specific roles and live in a certain way. The fundamental difference between men and women is the principle of biological reproduction in which this difference overshadows the qualitative variations, skills and successes. Traditionally, the Nagas perceived that men are naturally and biologically superior to women being a patriachal society. Therefore, raising even the basic feminist questions of gender equality, women's rights and women's autonomy have often been discouraged in the society.

The Nagas' notion of gender is best illustrated by Jean-Jacques Rousseau (1762) who conducted one of the first investigations on the question of gender inequalities. He refers to biologically based inequality as 'natural or physical, because it is established by nature, and consists in a difference of age, health, bodily strength, and the qualities of the mind or the soul'. Rosseau's view on the nature of the relationship between men and women is rooted in the perception that men are stronger and thus more independent. He also believed that biological-based inequalities between men and women were relatively insignificant, whereas socially created inequalities provide the major basis for systems of social stratification. His claim on biological differences and the main task of men is to deal with the affairs of state and women to tend to domestic chores is applicable to Nagas.

On the other hand, Margaret Mead's (1935) study of the three societies in the New Guinea Islands contributed significantly to the discourse on gender. In her view, the functionalist notion of 'sex-role' was a crude precursor of the concept of gender. It suggested that men and women are socialized into sex-specific roles, namely 'instrumental' and 'expressive'. These roles were regarded as the basis of a complementary relation between men and women, which along with the sexual division of labor, contributed to a stable social order. Her analysis of gender is also apt to understand the Nagas' worldview on gender since they firmly believed that sex-roles between men and women are complementary to each other and not completely based on hegemonic relationship. Some scholars have questioned the focus of this conceptualization on 'individual' men and women who are socialized into sex-specific roles. Critics have pointed out that socialization is always a precarious achievement and that agency, interpretation and negotiation go hand-in-hand of how gender identities are actually constituted.

My acquired knowledge of the standard feminist theory from University was either Westernized (*vedishi*) or Indianized (*deshi*) which revolves around certain issues such as gender politics, sexuality, individual accomplishment, ambition, freedom and women's autonomy, liberation and the like. These feminist ideas are not strongly relevant in understanding gender among the Nagas. The feminist ideologies such as radical feminism, liberal feminism, cultural feminism, third-world feminism, ecofeminism, post colonial feminism, post structural feminism, transfeminism, marxist and socialist feminism and the like have not appealed to the Naga women owing to their cultural, historical, religious and social sphere of life. The Naga women's issues have been espoused with the larger political issue of the Nagas for self-determination, sovereignity, peace and harmony which the Naga leaders have been fighting and negotiating with the Indian state since the past several decades. Considering the above points, it is obvious that the Naga women have neglected to scrutinize their issues and position from a truly feminist perspective.

CULTURAL LIFE OF NAGA WOMEN

The social stability and harmony of the Nagas is enhanced by their hardworking women. From history, one understands that Naga women had been actively involved in life outside their homes. In the olden days, morung (dormitories) used to be the cultural and learning centres where boys and girls get trained in various skills, learnt knowledge on handicrafts, dance, songs, and the like. It also served as a voluntary organization since voluntarism was practised and carried out in the society by the members of the Morung. Morung was basically a club for youth in which they sleep in their respective dormitories. In girls' Morung, unmarried girls were made to stay together to be trained and they helped younger Naga women to shoulder social responsibilities, learn folk dance, music and participate in public life. They had their role carried out for them under the system. Social activities of the girls' Morung includes collection and giving of firewood, etc., to the destitute families. Participation in the digging of fresh water ponds for the whole village in collaboration with the corresponding boy's Morung appears prominent. There were separate morungs for both boys and girls in the Naga society. 'The dormitory system was the very basis of a village's corporate life' (Singh 1972: 75). In all the activities, the girls participate as members of girls' Morung. But as time progressed and socio-religious changes took place in the Naga society, women adapted themselves to these changes without giving up on their traditional role. The dormitory system was long gone, but the Naga women continued to participate in all the activities where her presence is required.

Till today, many women in villages involve themselves in strenuous nature of work, particularly in the shifting (*jhumming*) cultivation since agriculture is the mainstay of the economy. Women play a vital role in the process of cultivation and in maintaining the household affairs at the family level. Every Naga tribe had its own unique traditional culture, customs and ornaments with various colours, designs, sizes and members. Each of them has significance relating to an important event. Creation and designing of traditional costumes have been done since long by women. It was and is still they who weave different types of traditional colourful clothes, such as shawls and kilts, which are generally of black colours embroidered with cowries. Besides, they also make ornaments such as necklaces of beads, armlets of ivory or brass, leg rings of cane and earrings.

Again, it is women who exhibit the typical costumes of their tribe more than their male counterparts. Very often, a woman is known by the dress she wears. Yet, the weaving of her tribal costumes is not a guarantee that she will be of her original tribe because the society expects her to change her clan or tribe to the man she is married to, but the choice is hers. Empirically speaking, there is freedom with regard to the identity for a Naga woman. However, Naga women have to remain subordinate to menfolk although at the same time they act as cultural ambassador. The gender biases in cultural life are imparted through an institution such as family, marriage and community in which the role of gender is obvious. The process of acculturation has created an evolutionary crisis, and the task now is to ensure that the best of the old culture and tradition does not disappear in the zest for the new. The society has many striking features, and it should be their endeavour to preserve them. The economic prosperity would lose all meaning if the culture and tradition of Nagas are completely forgotten. Therefore, some adjustment would be necessary and they must be made, but shunned from burying the past. A balance should exist between the old and the new, between stability and change (Singh, 1972: 77).

DISCRIMINATION IN WAGES FOR WOMEN

Gender relationship continues in all aspects of economic life, making economies gendered structures. The women who lived in the villages spent most of their day economically providing for the family by tending their agricultural fields, selling goods in the market place, collecting firewood and fetching water. Women who also work in the fields are discriminated even in the payment of their wages. The Naga view of a woman is that she is considered to be weaker than man in physicality; and owing to such belief, they are given less wages. Some Naga Women's Organizations such as the Naga Women Union, Manipur (NWUM), expressed that such practice is an injustice to women and they passed a resolution by calling upon all the Naga communities to ensure that all the women are given equal wages with men for equal work (Shangkham, 1995). In some places, an equal wage is not paid to women until today. However, women have begun to question the unfair customary laws and tradition relating to unequal wages, divorce and inheritance which will ensure gender equality.

Considering the Naga women's struggle for equality, it is appropriate to connect the work of Cynthia Enloe (2004) who scrutinizes the effect of globalization on women's labour and wage ratios in her book *The Curious Feminist*. She examines the role of women in the consumerist markets, conflicts at the global level and power politics, and also reveals her specific interest in linking these themes to women's everyday lives. On the contrary, Vivian Price (2008) found that in the mainstream Indian society, women in construction work prefer their work, even if it is low paid, precarious and exhausting, to agricultural work (it pays better and is less isolating) and to domestic duties (it has less social stigma). Interestingly, Vivian Price advocated that advanced technological revolution is not going to bring about an answer to the problems of poverty encountered by poor women, if scientific changes are not grounded in a better context of sustainable development and political empowerment.

TRADITIONAL LAW OF INHERITANCE

In Naga society, women were not permitted to inherit any immovable property. A noted anthropologist cum colonial administrator J.H. Hutton (1969: 137) who extensively wrote on Naga tribes in North East India said, 'A man cannot leave real property to his daughter.' If the man does not have a male heir, the next of kin (male) could claim the property with the clan. When a daughter gets married, she may be provided and gifted with the moveable property only. At times the parents bequest their daughters agricultural fields and plot of land on the day of their marriage but not necessarily as dowry. If a Naga woman happens to be a government employee before her marriage, she maintains the house. She may construct a house or buy some land; but on her marriage, they belong to her parents or brothers. She gets nothing as per custom although she can receive gifts from her parents. Her own labour is gifted to her and not given to her as her share because she has no right of inheritance. The things brought by her to her husband's family during her marriage except for the materials adorning her body and clothings are treated as properties from then on. The Naga women are aware of discrimination against them in inheritance rights and during the assembly of the Naga Women's Union, Manipur, in Ukhrul on 3–6 October 1994, they adopted a resolution on this property inheritance issue, 'resolved to demand for equal right of inheritance of family/parental movable or immovable properties for both male and female' (Shangkham 1995: 17).

With regard to an inheritance of a married woman, the traditional custom is that as long as a couple is married and live together, the property and children belong to both the parents. However, once they separate or get divorced, the children and property belong to the husband. This reflects the intrinsic nature of Naga society as patrilineal. Divorce of any kind is a drawback to women since she does not have rights over her biological children and property. During the mid-1990s, Naga women have began to assert for their rights through the Naga Women's Union, Manipur, who took a firm resolution on divorce in 1994 during the conference at Ukhrul on 3 to 6th October. The Union states: 'It has been observed that whenever a divorce takes place, it is the woman who suffers more. A resolution was adopted that whoever (man or woman) divorces his wife or her husband should leave the house and properties for the one being divorced (Resolution No. 2). Just as a woman forfeits everything when she divorces her husband the man must also forfeit everything when he divorces his wife. This is justice to both'. The women returning to their parents' family after divorce are classified as widows. But, there is no distinction between a divorcee and a widow among the Nagas, and such women do not suffer from stigmatization and social exclusion in the society. However, it is considered a disgrace in the Naga society to have a widow in the paternal lineage. Widowhood is not regarded as inauspicious or evil, but they cannot inherit immoveable property.

An option is also open for the woman who is separated or divorced from her husband to re-marry of her choice. This is because the parents of the woman have a great concern for the unfortunate daughter, and they desire that their daughter gets re-married if this would make her life happy and comfortable. Usually, a woman who has lost her husband and has become a widow returns to the home of her parents; but if his relatives approach and request the wife of the deceased to come back to their house as widow with her children, the parents of the woman readily concede to the request without pressing for the withdrawal of the marriage bond. In a situation where a husband abuses his wife, the customary laws do not provide protection for the woman, or prosecution against the man. The question that arises here is what are the reasons for people to support the traditional customary laws? Being patrilineal in nature, Naga society wants to uphold and preserve the traditional customary laws although they are gender biased. The Naga customary laws were protected and upheld by Article 371 A of the Indian Constitution as it helped in protecting the traditional life of Nagas, but it has also led to discrimination against women.

EXCLUSION OF WOMEN IN POLITICS

Maitreyee Chaudhuri (2003) argues that the economic and political spheres are 'alien' spaces women have to enter; the 'home' is the 'natural' realm where women already exist. Her arguments holds true for Naga women since for centuries, Naga women were never encouraged to involve in political spheres although they administered their homes. The apex political body of the Naga community is the village council. Each village forming a republic empowers the citizens to participate in every decision-making directly or by their representatives who are elected in the best possible democratic manner through rising of hands or voice votes. All decisions are being taken on the basis of consensus through the participation of every male member. Hence, every male member feels personally associated with a strong and vibrant sense of belonging in the community life, and no one feels alienated (Niumai, 2003: 25). But, Naga women were debarred from political activities. In rare occasions, women would approach village council whenever they have a complaint and also to give witness for or against any case in the village court or council. Yonuo (1979: 11) affirms that Naga women were completely excluded to enter councils where men gathered to discuss political and inter-village issue. Thus, we see a constrained sphere of Naga women's participation in the political aspects.

With the change in values owing to education, modernization and globalization, the educated women themselves feel the need to take their rightful place in the society in different aspects, thereby challenging the old traditional beliefs of inequality of sexes, although majority of Naga women are not against the whole traditional system. Despite the constraints and difficulties, there is a greater participation of Naga women in the public sphere in which some of them have emerged as political leaders. For instance, Rani Gaidinliu became a legend in her lifetime due to her fearless fight against the British. From 1925 onward, she started to struggle against the British rulers in order to free the Nagas from the suppressive and exploitative foreign administration. Under the guidance of Mr. Jadonang, Rani Gaidinliu had revived and reformed the Zelianrong religion and started the 'Heraka cult' by amalgamating the tribes: Zeme, Liangmei, Rongmei and Puimei. Today, this religious sect or cult group is associated with the RSS, VHP and the BJP.

The other prominent women politicians include Mrs. Rano Mese Shaiza, a niece of the Naga leader late A.Z. Phizo who contested election with the then Chief Minister (Maitra, 1991: 60). She was elected in 1977 in the Lok Sabha from Nagaland, and she remains the only elected woman politician till today. For Manipur's Outer Constituency, Mrs. Valley Rose Hungyo contested in the Parliament election of 1989 but got defeated. Mrs. Hangmila Shaiza contested victoriously in the Manipur State Assembly election in 1990, but unfortunately she was not given any portfolio in the ministry. Therefore, years of development and progress have not resulted in a Naga woman becoming a cabinet minister in Manipur. In the history of Nagaland Legislative Assembly, there was not a single Naga woman representative. During the past general election in Nagaland, Dr. Yangerla contested from Mokokchung town but she could get 579 votes out of some 5,700 votes in her constituency. The other woman candidate, Rakhila Lakhiumong of Tuensang scored 4193 votes ranking in the fourth position. Although Yangerla and Rakhila could not win a seat in the Nagaland Legislative Assembly, they have symbolically challenged the existing patriarchal system. Rosemary Dzuvichu argued that the candidates were young educated women, which signals a need for reservation (www.morungexpress.com/frontpage/92302.html). They are positioned differently from men as women were excluded from exercising power and authority. Their customary laws prohibit women from participating in the decision-making body and considering this traditional law and customary practices, men in general and majority of women in particular are not willing to acknowledge any Naga woman politician as an 'able and efficient leader'. If women are continuously excluded in this trend, there is no hope for gender equality in their society. The psyche and attitude of the people toward women leaders need to be changed. If women have greater political power, they will emerge as more forceful and visible and make their contribution for achieving gender equality in a substantial way.

EXCLUSION OF WOMEN IN RELIGION

Traditionally, the Nagas are a religious people although they did not have a name for their religion. They live close to nature and sense its mysterious powers in the belief of the existence of a single supreme God, benevolent spirits and malevolent spirits. In the practice of the traditional religion, no woman could perform any ritual for the village as a whole even though she could perform religious rituals as an individual. The supreme God or deity was addressed reverentially as creator and sustainer of the universe. Each Naga tribe has specific names for the supreme God. For instance, the Liangmei Nagas refer to the benevolent God as 'Tingwang' or 'Arapiu' and believes that his abode is in the sky. He was worshipped affectionately and was perceived as a loving and benevolent protector who sustains life. Special sacrifice is made to the supreme God with gratitude and women hardly participated in such sacrifice at the village level. Besides the supreme God, the Nagas also believed in the existence of ancestral spirits, village deities and household deities/gods who were benevolent spirits. These deities or spirits were worshipped with reverence and offered sacrifices with food and drinks. They were believed to be the guardians or spirits of the villages and the households. 'The malevolent spirits harm human beings and bring sickness, deaths and other natural forces like storms and floods, landslides, fire, earthquakes and other unnatural phenomenon. The malevolent spirits were not worshipped but in order to propitiate or appease them lest they do harm, animal bloods and drinks were offered by spitting on them (on whom or what) to show their contempt for the spirits. All the Naga tribes believed that there is an unseen divine power behind the creation, behind the course of events and behind the destiny of mankind' (Husain,1994: 51).

In all the family rites and rituals, to propitiate the household deities, the ancestral spirits and the village deities or the supreme deity, mothers also performed some rituals. Some tribes keep a sacred place for performing ancestral worship, in which no widow is permitted to participate. Traditionally, they believed that only men should take up the religious leadership although it is the 'mothers and the grandmothers' who instill all the significant details of religious rites and rituals in their children. It is through the religious fervour of women that social fabric of the Naga society is kept knitted, and it is they who impart intrinsic religious values such as love, compassion, truthfulness and honesty that are imbued in the persona of the supreme as perceived by mothers (Pamei, 1996: 32).

Their nature of worship involved offerings or sacrifices of animals and geena (taboo), but they ceased from such practices after being converted to Christianity. The earliest Christian pioneer among the Nagas was an American Baptist missionary, the Rev. Miles Bronson. He taught the Naga people Christianity and the art of cultivating tea from about 1842 to 1852. Another Baptist missionary, the Rev. E.W. Clark was able to win few converts. In 1851, the first Ao Naga (Ao is one of the major Naga tribes), a villager from Merenkong was baptized although he was later killed during a visit to his village in a hostile attack. However, in due course the numbers of converts increased and schools were established by the missionaries. Christian endeavour or societies were organized and an attempt was made to harness the youth. The significant instrument of conversion was education. The starting of a school around 1876 at Molung in Nagaland by the Rev. E.W. Clark could be said to have been the beginning of educational work among the Nagas by the Christian missionaries (Singh, 1972, 166). The growth and impact of Christianity among the Nagas has been phenomenal, especially on their social and religious life. Life in Naga society began to revolve around the institution of the church. Gradually, women seem to be empowered through education after the missionaries' intervention, and they were even allowed and encouraged to participate in the church worship and administration. Christianity offers several role models for women than that of wife and mother. But, they are given a secondary role in the church, home and society.

Each Naga tribe and their respective villages have a church based on the background of their denominations. A huge number of Nagas were Baptist, and some of them were Presbyterian, Charismatic, Methodist, Assembly of God, Independent, Salvation Army, Good Shepherd, Roman Catholic, Seventh day Adventist and the like. Christianity upholds gender equality; but even in the contemporary Naga society, there is an instance of a man being the secretary for a women's association. This example proves that inequality even in religious matters was maintained. Gina Shangkham (1995: 18), pioneer of the NWU in Manipur, said that male dominance in religious matters is not absolutely absent (present) in the Naga society.

Women were excluded from top leadership roles within the church, and they were encouraged to take care of the Sunday school for children and involve in women's Ministry that reveals the sexual division of labour within the church. The influence of globalization and the Western countries, particularly the United States and the United Kingdom have brought about the consciousness of the need for Naga women to be ordained in Naga churches. Ordination is believed to be sacred and single women who possess divine qualities are preferred to be ordained. In fact, women are not encouraged to seek for ordination but prove themselves by their actions, behaviours and lifestyles that they are committed to serve God. The Angami tribe is the first to ordain a woman as Pastor in the Christian Revival Church in Kohima village (One of the largest village in Asia). Later, Ao Nagas have ordained two women as Pastors. Some of these ordained women are Rev. Dr. K. Kapfo, and Rev. Ajung Sojwal. However, women Pastors are not allowed to solemnize any marriage ceremony, minister in a burial service and administer the sacraments (Holy Communion), whereas male deacons can serve in the Holy Communion. Therefore, ordination did not enhance the status of women in the church and women continue to work under male authority without enjoying autonomy.

Women are kept from being fully integrated into the major roles of spiritual life of the public. This reality is affirmed by Wati Longchar, who stressed that 'though the Ao Baptist Churches have ordained a few women in the church, they are still treated like a second-class citizen. The women ordained ministers are not given full Pastoral role and injustices in the churches are still prevalent towards women. This patriarchal practice is an injustice suffered by women. As followers of Christ, both women and men must resist collectively against this biased practices in the body of Christ'. In order to make the church more inclusive, Wati Longchar suggested that participation of women should be encouraged in the church, and he proposed the 'co-pastor' model that has been adopted in other countries such as China, Indonesia, Malaysia, Singapore and the United States. (http://www.morungexpress.com/local/77399.html). An influence of migration, Westernization and globalization on Naga women may be illustrated with an example of Rev. Ajung

Sojwal from Mokokchung, Nagaland, who serves as an interim pastor in Grace Episcopal Church in Millbrook, USA. She came to the United States in 1994 for her husband Millind Sojwal's graduate studies in Princeton. Following her six months of required internship, the Bishop wanted to ordain her, but she refused since she wanted to raise her children and felt unsure whether the priesthood was her calling. After getting her Masters in Sacred Theology of the Anglican Studies from General Theological Seminary, and completed several internships Rev. Sojwal expressed her willingness to be a priest and was ordained an Episcopal priest in 2006 in the United States. Earlier, she had served as the priest at Church of our Savior in Chinatown, All Soul's Church in Harlem and as Priest Associate at All Angels Church in New York City. (http://themillbrookindependent.com/news/reverend-ajung-sojwal-arrives-interim-pastor-grace-church). Rev. Ajung is able to serve as Head of the church since she lives in United States. It is doubtful that she would be given an opportunity for such a position in the church in Nagaland. It's also interesting to note that majority of Naga women are still not favourable for change and prefer men as Head of the church. Therefore, we need to partly blame women for excluding their own womenfolk from holding high position in religious sphere.

INTERVENTION OF NAGA WOMEN'S ORGANIZATIONS

Naga women live in a conflict zone that is politically sensitive due to their people's ongoing struggle for self-determination and sovereignity. A question arises as to how women intervene or get involved in building their society that is afflicted with a complexity of social concerns, conflict and political turmoil. Most of the women's organizations are initiated by the educated women, and it is heartening to note that women's education has given the opportunity that they had not enjoyed earlier. The Census of India 2011 reveals that the female literacy rate is 70.01 per cent, whereas the male literacy rate is 82.75 per cent in Nagaland. With the growth of literacy rate, women have enabled themselves to move out of their homes, exchange their problems, ideas, evaluate their status and slowly challenge the patriachy system. Some women began to be active in various organizations, and they are keen to manifest their ability, talent, potentialities and creativities to play positive and significant roles in the society. Women's organizations such as Naga Mother's Association (NMA), NWU, Manipur (NWUM) and Naga Socialist Women's Organization, Nagalim (NSWON) held out great promises for the empowerment of women and for enhancing their status. The women social activists motivate people to take up the cause of gender justice and social evils in a stronger, bigger and better way. One finds that empowerment of women is a complicated and uphill task. The women's liberation movement, which asserts that women should be given equal job opportunities and equal pay for equal work have influenced the Naga women and their organizations and the slogan for gender equality has began to slowly penetrate in the Naga society.

Since majority of the population of Naga people are Christians, it is not surprising to see that most of the women's organizations have started as religious organizations in Nagaland; the biggest organization is the Naga Baptist Women's Association that was started in the early 1950s. There are other cultural and social organizations such as Naga Women Federation, and Naga Women Organization, but these organizations at present are not functioning actively. The third section of this paper examines the intervention of the prominent Naga women organizations, namely NMA and NWU based in Nagaland and Manipur on questions related to gender inequality and gender politics. The Naga Mother's Association and NWU were established in 1984 and 1993, respectively, and did not associate with the Indian women's liberation movement of the second wave of feminism of the 1960s and 1970s. The Naga women's organizations were formed with their own visions to empower women, focus on HIV/AIDS, drug addiction and alcoholism problems, raise voices and involve in advocacy for the cause of women living in violent and conflict zone. These women's organizations were formed mostly out of women's desire to give expression to their personality. They play a critical political role as a mediator between the Government of India and National Socialist Council of Nagaland – Issac and Muivah (NSCN-IM) and attempt for reconciliation to strengthen the ceasefire between them that exists since 1997 till today, and they also encouraged the pursuit of long-term stability in North East India.

In a sensational political situation, the NWUM had also played a magnificent role as a mediator between the NSCN-IM and the

State. In June 2012, the NWUM had intervened to prevent ethnic catastrophe in Manipur during the time when Th. Muivah, leader of the NSCN, attempted to visit his village Somdal in Manipur. During the journey, Muivah and his party members took a sojourn in Liyai Khunao, a small Poumai Naga village with 30 households situated around 25 kms south of Pfutsero town in Nagaland. Their arrival at the village has created a political chaos in Manipur due to the resistance of his entry in Manipur by the dominant Meitei community. The state-armed forces were deployed to prevent him from entry into his village and as a result, the people around the village have lived in a state of fear and insecurity since the state-armed forces had shot dead two students and injured hundreds of innocent women and children at Mao Gate on 6 May 2010. The villagers had petitioned the Deputy Commissioner, Senapati district to intervene and revoke the presence of the state-armed forces. However, their voices were not heeded. The NWUM along with Naga People's Movement for Human Rights (NPMHR) intervened and urged the Government of Manipur to remove its state-armed forces deployed at Liyai Khunao and address the concerns of the villagers. They reiterate that militarization of Naga areas in Manipur have caused violation of tribal rights and appealed to the state that military troops should be withdrawn from these areas (http://indigenouspeoplesissues.com). Another illustration worthy to be cited about the efforts of women's organization in Manipur is on Mr. Anthony Shimray's arrest in September 2010 by the Indian authorities from Kathmandu. On 8 February 2012, NWUM held a public curfew in all the four Naga dominated districts of Manipur demanding unconditional release of Anthony Shimray, the head of foreign affairs of Naga ceasefire group NSCN-IM. He was arrested on charges of helping other militant outfits of North East region in procuring arms and ammunition despite NSCN-IM being in ceasefire with the Government of India. The women's organization demanded his release from Tihar jail since his arrest was based on mere suspicion (IANS India Private Limited, 9 February 2012). Some of these pieces of evidence reveal that Naga women made sincere efforts to address the question of social justice, human rights, peace, harmony and participate as critical actor or mediator in their society.

On the other hand, they have initiated women participation in national and international forums such as the Fourth World

Women's Conference in Beijing (1995). In recent years, the contribution of NMA includes the establishment of women's cell in Dimapur, Nagaland, followed by formation of women's cell in Kohima and Mokokchung districts. The women's cell takes care of all criminal cases related to women and children, and such cells have been designated as anti-human trafficking units since human trafficking have merged in the past few years with the opening of international borders for trade through Look East Policy and globalization.

Abei-U Meru, NMA president told *The Times of India* dated 10 January 2013 in New Delhi that 'In the beginning, the biggest issue affecting homes was drug addiction. The mothers came together because it was hurting every home'. Initially, NMA aims at fighting social evils and eventually emerges as peace agents. NMA addressed the atrocities committed by the Indian army against Naga groups, women and civilians, and then years of fratricidal killings between various Naga factions. NMA made 'Shed No More Blood' its motto and every time tensions simmered, they would took off in a car on roads into the jungles of Nagaland and neighbouring states and urge leaders of various factions to have a dialogue and maintained peace. In 2010, the NMA helped calm one of the most sensational cases when two young Naga men were shot dead by the Indian army at Mao gate in Manipur. The villagers refused to claim the dead bodies for eight days and tensions escalated. NMA leaders Rosemary Dzuvichu and Meru pushed through Indian army security cordons that shrouded the bodies and took them to the victim's families. For their exemplary work and intervention in their society, the Naga Mothers Association was jointly awarded the 'Times of India Social Impact Award for life contribution for 2013' (http://articles.timesofindia.indiatimes.com).

NMA has established a Peace Team that has held advocacy meetings with Indian government officials and military officers. NMA members share the grief and agony of any mother whose son gets killed in the conflict, and they asked themselves what if the dead victim happens to be their son. Considering such ideas and philosophy of NMA, Paula Banerjee (2011) argued that one reason Naga women's peace groups remain effective is that they are able to blend the political with the social issues. The Naga women do not operate independently of their social value systems in the society. Naga women are able to achieve their goals as peacemakers because they act as agency for spaces and shun to challenge the traditional role of women. In the Naga society, women always play a substantial role in bringing about peace and harmony. They have appropriated their traditional role as a mother, wife, aunt and sister in the contemporary political arena for restoring peace. Thus, Paula emphasizes on the political contests of inclusion and exclusion that are played out in Naga women's every day lives.

These women organizations co-ordinate with the Naga People's Movement for Human Rights (NPMHR), the Naga Students' Federation (NSF), All Naga Students' Association Manipur (ANSAM) and the Naga Ho-Ho (the federation of Naga tribe council) to strengthen the peace initiative of ceasefire between the Government of India and the National Socialist Council of Nagaland (NSCN-Isaac and Muivah). Regarding women's involvement in politics, 33 per cent reservations for women in the election was proposed in Nagaland in late 1980s and early 1990s, but NSF, which is one of the powerful youth organizations based in Kohima, opposed it. In December 1998, I interviewed Mrs. Neidonuo Angami, former president of NMA and asked her whether men supported them in their fight for social justice and political representation. She expressed that some men are skeptical and did not lend support to them. She also mentioned that the NSF which was earlier dominated by men states 'Nagas are a distinct race and the role and status of women in Naga society is also peculiar. The Naga customary practices and traditions require to be protected for some more time'. They also claimed that women in Naga society do not have to clamour for such kind of women's resevation in politics or empowerment. Hence, NMA abandoned the idea of urging for reservation of women in politics during the 1990s. There were elements of tension between the women's organizations and the male-dominated organizations, but some women associations supported their men's sentiments. Thus, both the genders are involved in preventing women from questioning old practices and send across the message that 'all is well and there is no need for a change'.

However, things have changed since the 1990s, as there was a fresh proposal a few years back for implementing 33 per cent reservation for women in Nagaland, but it was rejected in the State Assembly Resolution. Women organizations including the Nagaland State Commission for Women (NSCW) were dismayed over the resolution that rejected 33 per cent reservation of seats for women in municipal and town council elections. The Joint Action Committee for Women Reservation (JACWR) was formed as a response to it, and they challenged the verdict. The Naga Mothers' Association, Watsü Mungdang, Eastern Naga Women Organization, Naga Women Hoho of Dimapur and the Tenyimi Women Organization are some of the principal Naga women's organizations comprising the Joint Action Committee. And, in November 2012, the Supreme Court of India has admitted the Special Leave Petition (SLP) of Naga women's organizations challenging the verdict of the Division Bench of the Guwahati High Court, which had earlier rejected the women groups' contest against the Nagaland government's decision to defer the municipal and town elections in the State as well as not implementing the 33 per cent reservation of seats for women in the municipal institutions. Consequently, following the petition being admitted, the Supreme Court held its first hearing on November 19, in Delhi, and had directed the Nagaland government and the State agencies in concern to respond within 6 weeks to the SPL filed by the JACWR. The assembly, too, passed a resolution exempting Part IX-A of the Constitution stating that it goes against Article 371-A of the Constitution, which states that no Act of Parliament can infringe upon the customary and traditional practices of Naga people. (The Morung Express, 20 November 2012). The women's organizations continue to demand that women's rights should be protected, as they are also citizens of the state.

The women activists argued that since 1980s, the state government has reserved one-fourth seats in Village Development Board (VDB) and one-fourth of VDB fund is allocated for women in villages. They opined that at the village level where customary and social practice are deeply entrenched by respective village councils, reservation for women in village development management committees have been implemented smoothly without any resistance or reference to violation of customary law or social practice or even Article 371-A till date by either village councils, tribal hohos or Naga Hoho. They ridiculed the state government saying Part-IX-A of the Constitution does not infringe upon Article 371-A. Some of the men dominated organizations such as Naga Hoho,

Eastern Naga People's Organization (ENPO) and Ao Senden have strongly opposed the women's protest for political representation and the way they challenge the patriarchal system (*The Times of India*, 2 October 2012). These men refused to acknowledge the fact that reservation is not about challenging the existing customary law on inheritance rights.

Some questions arise as to why the Naga men opposed 33 per cent reservation of women. What are the reasons for them to continuously prohibit women from involving in the decision-making process? Why do some of these patriarchs want their women to remain subservient to them and how long will they continue to exclude women? Are they scared to lose their power and authority and continuously uses the customary laws to exclude women even in this twenty first century? Where are the rational, intellectual and thinking Naga men who are expected to stand up for liberating and emancipating their women? These men have not realized that the 33 per cent reservation is not depriving them of power, but to give Naga women a chance to èmerge as elected leaders and exercise power as equal partners in decision-making. The former Prime Minister of India Pandit Jawaharlal Nehru said, 'To awaken the people, it is the women who must be awakened. Once she is on the move, the family moves, the village moves, the nation moves'. Nehru further said, 'You can tell the condition of a nation by looking at the status of its women'. If Naga society aspires to make progress in the true sense of the term, they need to consider the profound statements of Nehru and attempt to provide political empowerment to their womenfolk.

Being a Christian society, the present scenario needs to be scrutinized from a Biblical perspective as well since a man and woman are created to be complementary. God took the rib of Adam to make Eve as his partner, which symbolized the significance of the wife's role in husband's life. Then, God said in Genesis 1:26–27 (NIV), 'Let us make man in our own image, in our likeness, and let them rule over the fish of the sea and the birds of the air, over the livestock, over all the earth, and over all the creatures that move along the ground. So God created man in his own image, in the image of God he created him; male and female he created them'. These Scriptures reveal the essence of gender equality. However, the Naga women are sandwiched between undercurrents of traditional laws and practices. They constantly encounter the complexity of a contemporary globalised society that is undergoing the binary of change and continuity and they are also involve in mobilization, protest and challenge against the system of patriarchy in order to achieve gender equality. Nonetheless, the women's organizations have engaged themselves effectively and tactfully within their traditional space and have significantly impacted their society.

GENDER INEQUALITY AND EMPOWERMENT

Earlier, sociologists, historians and anthropologists would mention about the Naga society as a simple, egalitarian and homogenous tribal society. Their women were pereceived to enjoy certain priviledges and empowered to a large extent. However, the contemporary Naga society is not the simple society anymore. Under the influence of modernization, Westernization and globalization, their society is stratified on the basis of gender politics, backward vis-à-vis forward tribe and class hierarchy where women as the marginalized and excluded ones are still exploited. It is essential to point out that economic conditions of women do not help them drastically in climbing up the social ladder. The process of globalization has an effect on the Naga family in general and women in particular as some cases of domestic violence have began to emerge and divorce rate is also increasing at present. Domestic violence, rape, murder of women, begging, female infanticide and prostitution were not a part and parcel of Naga tradition and culture. These phenomena were never recorded in Naga history, and these are new social concerns that came as a response to globalization of mass media and acculturation of other cultures. It reminds women that the safest place for them is the home earlier, but now it is in a vacuum as they are vulnerable even inside their homes. It is a manifestation of unequal power relations, which has led to men's domination over and discrimination against women.

The basic reason for violence against women is their inferior status in a male-dominated patriachal society. Some other reasons are attributed to the prevalence of Armed Forces Special (Power) Act 1958 which gives unlimited power to state-armed forces to arrest any individual on mere suspicion, and they have often misused their power to rape and murder hundreds of women in North East India. The other causes that impinge on Naga women to their inequality are the ethnic conflict, violence perpetrated by the non-state-armed forces and their own men. In any situation of conflict and violence in Naga society, it is the women and children who suffer the most. Additionally, violence and conflict creates widows and migration that ruptures family and kinship and impoverishes them. At the same time, rape is used as a weapon of revenge in which 'women as victims' suffer from stigmatization; social exclusion, lack of access to healthcare and impoverishment as they are deprived of contributing to the family income. Hence, in such a scenario, Naga women have limited scope to be fully empowered owing to the above reasons.

None of the Naga women have been elected in the Nagaland Legislative Assembly. In Manipur, a Naga woman was elected but she could not get a cabinet portfolio. Legislations were made by the government to safeguard and promote women although the locally lived realities of Naga women tell us a different story. They do not enjoy inheritance rights nor enjoy 33 per cent of reservation in politics. Even those educated women have less opportunity to climb up the social mobility ladder to become leaders and managers in their respective institutions. In the public and private sectors, only a handful of them hold high positions and we can count them in our fingers thus, majority of them occupy the lower rung of the position. In the religious sphere, a few women have been ordained as minister in church and some were inducted as deacons and leaders for women's ministry, but they do not enjoy equal status as their male counterparts. As per Census of India 2011, sex ratio in Nagaland is 931 female for each 1,000 male, which is below national average of 940. The total population of male are 1,024,649 and female constitute 953,853, respectively. Thus, women constitute almost half of the total population, but they have a long way to achieve equality in political, socio-economic and religious spheres. They were deprived of being fully empowered and the treatment meted to women in some households, institution and public places reveals the prevailing discriminatory image and attitudes towards women.

FEMINIZATION OF POVERTY AND EMPLOYMENT

Diana M. Pearce (2011) is one of the first to theorize 'feminization of poverty' in her study of poor women in the United States. Pearce said that the feminization of poverty is not just a demographic trend or disproportionate levels of poverty among women and women-maintained families, but is about the importance of gender as a cause of poverty among women. She mentioned that since the 1980s, there has been a feminization of poverty 'trend' in the United States. Once the proportion of poor families who were women-maintained families reached about 50 per cent, it has stayed at that level, more or less, for about three decades. This is despite of some significant changes that should have decreased the feminization of poverty as American women are having fewer children, and are having them later (therefore they have more chance to finish their education and get work experience), work more years and take less time off, experience less occupational segregation, and their educational levels now are equal to and in some cases, higher than that of men. But, the feminization of poverty has not decreased because the government provides income supplements and subsidized work supports. In the context of some poor Naga women and especially elderly women, many of them do not get access to pension benefits, and they are not even aware of such welfare schemes of the Government of India. Hence, Pearce's theory on feminization of poverty may not be entirely applicable to the Naga women. However, poverty and unemployment are experiencing a feminization in Naga society since women are marginalized into disadvantaged positions, especially in the labour market. Some of the women have lower earnings as compared with their male counterparts and lack of income, illiteracy and ignorance are fundamental rationale for women's risk of poverty as it deprives them of their basic needs and capabilities.

As we begin to probe the subject of feminization of poverty and unemployment in Naga society, it is fitting to relate Amartya Sen's idea of social exclusion since Naga women suffer from deprivation of capabilities in various spheres such as employment, political and economic, their household labour not being counted as paid work, denial of inheriting immoveable property and the like. Amartya Sen's (2000) concept of poverty is link to deprivation of capabilities and shortage of income. He opines that we have good reason to value not being excluded from social relations, and in this sense, social exclusion may be directly a part of capability poverty. Sen also quoted Adam Smith who focuses on the deprivation involved in not 'being able to appear in public without shame' which is an example of a capability deprivation that takes the form of social exclusion. He argued that being excluded from social relations could lead to other deprivations as well, thereby further limiting our living opportunities. The Naga women are deprived in political spheres and have limited life chances in the globalized market economy wherein their labour force participation is rather low and thus, some of them suffer from income shortage that leads to being socially excluded to a certain extent. The labour force participation rate per 1,000 persons of age between 15 and 59 years in 2009–2010 for Naga women was 42.0 per cent and 72.9 per cent for men with the total of 57.6 per cent for the state of Nagaland (NSSO 66 Round Key Indicators of Employment and Unemployment in India, 2009–10). The Naga women are burdened in excess with domestic chores, agricultural activities and reproductive work and cultural restrictions imposed on them by the patriarchal society. In Naga Hills, forests are important mostly for hunting and shifting or jhum cultivation that have a substantial role in the livelihood of the Nagas. Naga men engage in clearing of jungles by chopping trees and burning the felled trees, bushes and weeds on fire. And the Naga women would sow the farming seeds involve in digging the fields, harvesting, threshing, winnowing and carry the farm produce in traditional baskets at their backs and store it in granaries for the whole year. Thus, women spend more time in the paddy fields, doing domestic chores such as fetching water, collecting firewood, fodder, animal husbandry and the like. The amount of time women used for walking to the fields in the hillocks is noteworthy to be reckoned with. The critical issue is that their contributions to their respective family are not acknowledged as equivalent to paid work and white-collar jobs.

Several people argue that majority of Naga women are still working in the fields and involved in low skill jobs. Besides, they have been receiving lower wages than their male counterparts as argued by the NWUM. Although women's organizations such as the NWU have taken up this issue in the past decades, the fact is that labour market continues to provide unequal income (wages) for women till today. Thus, voices of women organizations may not be fully recognized by the patriarchal society. The past years have demonstrated the feminization of poverty as cultivation of land has also become a crucial issue with an introduction of cash crops and local markets turning into subsidized economies that has further alienated the Naga women out of the decision-making process.

The sexual division of labour in Naga households, clan, kinship and traditional and cultural practices play a decisive role in altering the dynamics of who control and rule the home that ultimately determines women's entry into the labour market leaving them with limited alternatives. Things have changed nowadays for those women who are educated and work in both private and public sectors. However, majority of women remain invisible as the data state that the total percentage of working population in Nagaland stood at 49.2 per cent as per Census of India 2011. And, majority of women did not constitute the working people as per the government data. Some young Naga educated women work in the call centre (BPOs) of multi-national companies in various urban and metropolitan cities. But, most of them work in the night shifts, so their health gets affected adversely. Globalization is perceived as a means of capital accumulation wherein women are recruited in preference to men since they are cheaper. With globalization and expansion of market, job opportunity seems to have increased in the recent past yet the work participation rate of women shows that a greater proportion of literate women do not occupy high position. Literacy is perceived to have an intrinsic relationship with employment, but there has been a growing concern among sociologists, feminists and social scientists about women workers being employed in low-paying, semi-skilled and unskilled jobs further giving way to questions on why employment and literacy rate are moving in opposite directions as far as women are concerned. This social reality is relevant in understanding the dilemma of Naga women where their imbalance of work is a serious concern that needs to be addressed.

In mainstream Indian society, there has been a dialogue on the concept of unpaid labour raised by many Indian feminists and Department of Women Studies in various colleges and universities. These feminists argued that women's labour unravels the idea of time to be arduous labour for women. The Marxist feminist scholar such as Maria Meis (1982), famous for her theory of capitalist-patriarchy, studied the women lace-makers in Narsapur, Andhra Pradesh that emerged as a sensitive and pioneering study of women at the beginning of the process of globalization. Meis found out that women become part of the globalized economy by working at their homes like the lace makers in Narsapur. But, these women do not gain economically because of the middlemen who control the inputs and output prices and women have fewer chances to promote their skills, education and improve their economic status. Meis had pointed out that in patrilineal society, women's major responsibility in income earning does not necessarily lead to empowerment and gender equality that holds true for Naga women. The traditional duty of Naga women is to serve and work for sustaining their households, and it is not proper culturally for them to raise questions or object in the way feminists in other cultures do. Thus, there is a long way for Naga women to achieve gender equality and empowerment in the true sense of the term.

CHOICES, ATTIRES AND TRADE

In the traditional society, Naga women make personal choices of dress, food, selecting their spouse, enjoy social mobility and aspirations, but the choices of Naga women have changed since the past few decades. Sociologist Maitreyee Chaudhuri (2005: 27) states that a piece of 'women at home' initiates the discussion by suggesting that 'dressing for work must rank high in the list of life's arduous but inescapable chores – A dilemma', but suggests that better days are here now. Western attires are perceived to be more liberating and the consequence is a shift from khadhi handloom materials to global branded clothes. This holds true for Naga women as they shun wearing their traditional *'mekela'* or *'phanek'* (like sarong) except for traditional festivals, church services and special cultural events. The younger generation prefers to shun wearing Naga ethnic attires at homes, colleges, workplaces or markets and they feel liberated to opt for the Western clothings. The hi-tech fashion that changes dramatically and the pressure on Naga women to keep up with it has become an issue of psychological harassment for some of them. The craze for Western clothing and designer labels among the younger women is an affect of modernization and globalization.

A question was broached to some youth about their perception of an ideal woman. And the response was that an ideal Naga woman is a person who has beauty with brains and the Miss Nagaland show has become a festival that serves as a platform for these young Naga women to be in a glamour world both at the local and regional levels. The beauty pageant is making Naga women very conscious of their body, to stay slim and ensure zero size. These beauty pageants are, however, criticized by some concerned individuals who raised a question as to why exposure of beauty in a western style is considered as an important characteristic in the Naga society? They considered the pageants as a method which is not a viable mode of Naga women's empowerment. The other events such as Flower show contest portray modern Naga women as someone who is conscious of promoting natural beauty and enhance environment. One of the effects of globalization in the life styles of the contemporary Naga women is the way cable TV, social media networking and internet manipulates their time. Traditionally, Naga women are known for their hard-working nature, but some of them seem to be hooked to television. Thus, TV has become a kind of refuge for several women.

In terms of trade relations (both legal and illegal), mobility through international borders in North East India via Moreh town (one of the business centre in Manipur) and Tamu town (Myanmar) have enhanced economic activity and commercial business to a certain extent. In the past, some Nagas in general and many North Easterners in particular travel across the international borders to Myanmar and Bangladesh without passport and visa related documents. The Naga tribes live in some parts of Myanmar and it is observed that international borders have split even family and kinship. It is noteworthy to mentione that S.S. Khaplang, the leader of the National Socialist Council of Nagaland (K) is a Burmese Naga. A few Naga politicians such as the present chief minister of Nagaland, Neiphiu Rio had opened the border of Nagaland with Myanmar and facilitated social mobility through routes that are less travelled by people earlier. He states in the international conference on Myanmar at Jamia Millia Islamia in Delhi recently, 'The daily movement of Naga villagers across the border for jhumming (shifting cultivation) and other activities is a necessity'. It indicates the strategic geo-politics of the Nagas with Myanmar, and it also facilitates India's Look East Policy. The collaboration between the border international markets (particularly based in Myanmar including Thailand) and the local markets in Naga society has attracted especially the women folk to cultivate the habit of consumerist culture which is alien to their traditional culture. The markets are slowly dominating Naga women's lives in an unimaginable manner. Under the influence of globalization, some Naga women business entrepreneurs have started to travel to other South East Asian capitals such as Yangon (former capital), Tamu (commercial town in Myanmar), Bangkok and Beijing to procure commercial goods to be sold in the local market. There are several women entrepreneurs who testify that their economic status have enhanced through such small scall trade. For example, Mrs. Zoupanliu said, 'I often traveled to Bangkok and Beijing via Kolkata and Guwahati for procuring consumer goods like clothings, bags, women's accessories and upon my return, most of it would be sold out within a few months and it is lucrative'. This statement testifies the changing attitude of women in terms of engaging in small-scale business, choices and attires. And, their role has changed to a certain extent because of globalization and new opportunities are being offered to them.

The consumable goods flood the local markets in attractive packages ranging from Pepsi, Ice tea drinks to fresh juices and from canned and frozen food items to black earthen rice cookers (made by Tangkhul Naga tribe in Ukhrul district of Manipur), from genetically modified foods or high yielding varieties of crops to microwaves and fully automatic washing machines. The cross-border movement for trade (both legal and illegal) and social mobility have attributed to enhanced consumerist culture and the buying habits of some women have drastically changed over the past years and have affected their lives. The accumulation of sophisticated gadgets such as iPhones, iPods, iPads, televisions, DVDs, refrigerators, gold and diamond jewelleries, branded imported clothes, latest designer bags, cars and other goods enhance the status symbol in the contemporary society. Some women tend to pamper themselves beyond their purchasing capacity. The mass media portrays an image of a global woman as someone who can buy as much as she desires and some women become victims of such marketing strategic slogan. The introduction of various bank ATMs makes a few elite Naga women more vulnerable to purchase goods. Fortunately, the credit cards are not accepted in most shops and restaurants in Nagaland.

A wider communication and connectivity definitely enhances sharing of ideas, skills, knowledge, goods and services. However, one of the negative aspects of wider expansion is the exploitation of indigenous culture and infiltration of alien cultures, which serves as a threat to the Naga customs, values and tradition in particular. The cable TV facilitates overseas channels such as Arirang, a Korean channel, which has popularized the culture of the Korean youth among the Nagas with regard to hairstyles, dress patterns, cuisines and the like. Thus, acculturation of cultures is a rampant phenomenon, and maintaining ethnic identity has become a challenge in the globalized world and there is a need to carefully examine the impact of globalization and formulate policies to tackle the problems.

CONCLUSIONS

The purpose of this paper is to examine some generic questions of gender inequality and effects of globalization on Naga women. Three main issues were discussed from interdisciplinary perspectives, and the effect of globalization on Naga women is examined from the lens of cultural changes, empowerment, poverty, unemployment and violence against women. Considering the culture of Naga family's preference of boys over the girl child bring to our notice that though globalization has changed the garb into a more fanciful one, women are still the disadvantaged. Even if little progress has been made through globalization, it is still difficult for women to combine the obligations of work with those of family, child rearing and domestic chores. Under the rubric of globalization, Naga women encounter new forms of violence like rape, domestic violence, abused, murder, trafficking and the like. They have began their journey of challenging the patriarchal system by focusing on gender politics to a certain extent. But, the strong issues of power relations and sexuality, which the Western and Indian feminist emphasize are not largely viable in the study of Naga women owing to cultural, social and religious aspects. There are laws and policies to safeguard and empower women but they are not being implemented effectively. If the pro-women policies were implemented properly by the State and women were provided privilege to enjoy political power, then women from this part of the world could have better choices, space, freedom and opportunities in life rather than being stuck with the reality of conflict that awaits them each day.

REFERENCES

Applebaum, Richard P and Chabliss, William J. 1977. *Sociology: A Brief Introduction*. New York: Longman.

Banerjee, Paula. 2011. *Women in Indian Borderlands*. New Delhi: Sage Publications.

Bible. 1989. *The Holy, New International Version*. Grand Rapids, Michigan, USA: Zodervan.

Census of India. 2011. *Registrar General and Census Commissioner*. India.

Chaudhuri, Maitrayee. 2003. *Gender in the Making of the Nation-State, in (ed) Sociology of Gender: The Challenge of Feminist Sociological Knowledge, Sharmila Rege*. New Delhi: Sage Publications.

Chaudhuri, Maitrayee. 2005. *Feminism in India*. New Delhi: Zed.

Davids, Tine and Driel Van, Francien. 2009. The Unhappy Marriage between Gender and Globalisation, *Third World Quarterly*, 30(5): 905–920.

Enloe, Cynthia. 2004. *The Curious Feminist: Searching for Women in a New Age of Empire*. Berkeley, CA: University of California Press.

Hutton, J.H. 1969. *The Angami Nagas with Some Notes on Neighbouring Tribes*. London: OUP.

Horam, M. 1997. *Naga Polity*. New Delhi: Low Price Publications.

Hussain, Majid. 1994. Encyclopedia of India, Nagaland. Vol. XIX, New Delhi: Rima Publishing House.

Meis, Maria. 1982. *The Lace Makers of Narsapur: Indian Housewives Produce for the World Market*. London: Zed Books.

Mead, Margaret. 1935. *Sex and Temperament: In Three Primitive Societies*. Harper Perennial.

Maitra, Kiranshankar. 1991. *Nagaland-Darling of the North-East*. Delhi: Mittal Publications.

National Sample Survey Organization (NSSO). 2011. Employment and Unemployment in India Employment–Unemployment Situation in India, 66th Round, 2009–2010, Ministry of Statistics and Programme Implementation, Government of India.

Niumai, Ajailiu. 2003. 'Role of Non-Governmental Organisations (NGOs) in the Empowerment of Naga Women, UGC-DRS-SAP, Department of Sociology', Occassional Paper Series-4, University of Hyderabad, P.O. Central University.

Oakley, Ann. 1972. *Sex, Gender and Society*. London: Temple Smith.

Diana, Pearce M. 2011. The Feminization of Poverty, research paper presented in the International seminar in Valparaiso, Chile on 7 March.

Pamei, Aram. 1996. Naga Women and Culture, Raisunriang (Newslink), edited by Gina Shangkham. 2nd Issue, March, Manipur: Naga Women's Union.

Price, Vivian. 2008. "Headloads: The Technologizing of Work and the Gendering of Labor". In: edited by Ferguson, Kathy E and Monique, Mironesco. *Gender and Globalization in Asia and the Pacific: Method, Practice, Theory*. Honolulu: University of Hawaii Press.

Rousseau, Jean–Jacques. 1993. Émile (1762), Trans, Barbara Foxley. London: Dent.

Sen, Amartya. 2000. *Social Exclusion: Concept, Application and Scrutiny, Social Development Papers No. 1, Office of Environment and Social Development*. Manila, Philippines: Asian Development Bank.

Shangkham, Gina. 1995. *Naga Women Today, Raisunriang (Newslink)*. 1st Issue, October, Manipur: Naga Women's Union.

Singh, Prakash. 1972. Nagaland, New Delhi: National Book Trust.

Yonuo, A. 1979. *The Rising Nagas: A Historical and Political Study*. New Delhi: Vivek Publishing House.

Zehol, Lucy. 1998. *Women in Naga Society, West Patel Nagar*. New Delhi: Regency Publication.

NEWSPAPERS AND WEBSITES

The Times of India. Naga women's stir for 33% quota in local body elections, 2 October 2012.

Naga women's body agitates in Manipur, By Indo Asian News Service | IANS India Private Limited – Thu 9 February 2012, retrieved on 29 September 2013, Source: http://in.news.yahoo.com/naga-womens-body-agitates-manipur-163021340.html

Naga Women's Union. Manipur And Naga Peoples Movement For Human Rights: Statement On Detention Of Members, 16 June 2010, retrieved on 1 October 2013, Source: http://indigenouspeoplesissues.com

Ngullie Al. *SC directs Nagaland Government to respond on 33% women quota*, Nagaland, The Morung Express, 20 November 2012.

Times of India Impact Awards: Lifetime Contributions – Naga Mothers Association, retrieved on 30 September 2013, source: http://articles.timesofindia.indiatimes.com/2013-01-10/india/36257221_1_nma-abei-u-meru-nagaland

Reverend Ajung Sojwal arrives as interim pastor at Grace Church, retrieved on 20 September 2013, source: http://themillbrookindependent.com/news/reverend-ajung-sojwal-arrives-interim-pastor-grace-church

'Women ordained ministers are not given full pastoral role', retrieved on 10 September 2013, source: http://www.morungexpress.com/local/77399.html

CHAPTER 19

Bride Price and Patriarchal Hegemony in the Mizo Society

Hminthanzuali

Mizoram is amongst one of the Northeastern states of India bounded by Cachar district of Assam and Manipur on the north, Arakan hills of Burma on the south, Chin Hills of Burma on the east and Tripura and Chittagong hills tract of Bangladesh on the west. The inhabitants of Mizoram call themselves Mizo, which comprises various tribal groups such as *Lusei, Ralte, Fanai, Lai, Paite* and *Mara*. Ethnically, they belong to the Mongoloid stock of the Kuki–Chin group with Tibeto-Burman group of language. The Mizo society has several distinctive features in the course of its evolution and historical development from the 'Indian civilization'. Mizoram was known as Lushai Hills in colonial period (1891–1947), In the post-colonial period, it was renamed as Mizo Hills district by an act of parliament in 1954. In 1971, Mizo District was upgraded into a Union Territory and renamed as Mizoram and became the 27th state of Indian Union in 1987.

During the past decade of the nineteenth century, the region witnessed the establishment of a foreign rule that introduced two external powers in the field of politics and religion. The first agents set up their rule under the name Lushai Hills in 1891, and the latter started their mission in 1894. The repercussions of the establishment of the colonial states on the administration, law and order, and the process of social and religious transformation under Christianity were the backdrops of new social structure in the hills. Of all these, the position of women was no doubt one of the most significant changes brought about by the influence of colonialism and Christianity in the Mizo society. Consequently, due to the new gender relations introduced by the above-mentioned agencies together with the absence of Hindu caste structure, that is, dowry and sati system, many mainstream scholars argue that Mizo women enjoy better status than mainstream women (Mukhopadaya, 2002: 94).

This general observation has been recently challenged by the local feminist writers, scholars and women's associations who began to disclose the sufferings of Mizo women under the 'Mizo Patriarchy' by locating the problems within the customary law. Gradually, the need to re-think and re-construct customary law has become an insistent subject with the realization that most aspects of women's lives continue to be governed by these laws. Few studies, seminars and workshops have been carried out by scholars, writers and women's organizations on customary law and tribal women of Northeast India as well as Mizo women in particular. The issues concerning women in their studies involve inheritance rights for women, marriage customs and divorce. Nevertheless, there is no particular study on the historiography of patriarchy and the re-institution of patriarchal power within the customary law. To have a better understanding of patriarchal dominance in Mizoram, the present article historically addresses the evolution of patriarchal hegemony, the social hierarchy and the reciprocal exchange of women within the transaction of bride price in marriage custom of the Mizos.

FALLOUTS OF BRIDE PRICE

Bride price refers to payments made at the time of marriages, which is typically paid by the groom or the groom's family to the bride's family. It has been customarily prevalent among patrilineal tribal societies of Asia and Africa (Anderson, 2007: 151–74; Maitra, 2007: 2). In India, it is still practised even among the middle and lower castes of the non-tribal population (Pruthi and Sharma, 1994: 138). Various studies have put forward an explanation of the occurrence of bride price. It has been argued that bride price indicates economic conditions, societal structures, institutions and family characteristics. Generally, it has been positively characterized as a compensatory payment to the family for the loss they suffer on her departure (Rajaram, 2005: 45). Jack Goody and Tambiab defined bride price in terms of economic demands or compensatory payment as 'the transfer from the bridegroom's family and kin to the bride's family and kin-certain goods in return for which certain rights in the bride are transferred' (Goody and Tambiab, 1993: 61). Accordingly, Lipi Mukhopadaya who studied bride price amongst the tribal society of India also remarks, 'It certainly enhances the social status of a woman for whom a higher bride price is given' (Mukhopadaya, 2002: 51). Contrary to this popular observation, Shalini Randeria and Leela Visaria stated that women do not have a higher status in those society where bride price is paid for them given that with the change of residence after a marriage a woman comes under the control of her husband's family and has no rights at all (Randeria and Visaria, 2005: 71)

Gerda Lerner, a feminist historian and Gayle Rubin, a feminist anthropologist, have theoretically examined bride price from Levi Strauss's theory on 'the exchange of women' in marriages. Gerda Lerner examined how the exchange of gift or money sealed the marriages, signified the family's development of patriarchal power, economic power, and the important role it played in the consolidation of class formation in the ancient Mesopotamian and Babylonian society (Lerner, 1986: 101–22; 1998: 157). Gayle Rubin also critically observed that the formation of kinship within 'the exchange of women' specified certain rights for men, but limited women's rights to either themselves or their male kin (Rubin, 1996: 120). In the context of tribal society of Girasia in Northwestern India, Maya Unnithan Kumar stated that apart from economic rationale, bride price signified both lineage and gender hierarchies (Kumar, 1997: 190). In the history of the Mizos, marriage custom had been widely discussed particularly by the colonial ethnographers. Their observation on the traditional custom of bride price was related mostly with the economic needs and social hierarchy. For instance, the first superintendent of Colonial Lushai Hills J. Shakespear argued that marriages amongst the *Lushais* in the pre-colonial period were performed mostly because of the economic matters. In fact, after the colonial intervention it was a matter of money and amongst the ruling clans, it was meant for the establishment of the chief's power (Shakespear, 1988: 49–50). Presently, the custom of bride price has been widely practised amongst all the clans, which indeed opened an unending debate that has not yet been solved by current discourses in Mizoram. With this background in view, this paper attempts to contextualize the custom of bride price and its impact on the position of women in the Mizo society.

WOMEN'S STATUS IN MIZO SOCIETY

Mizo society is strictly based on the patriarchal system of institution where the women do not have any substantial say practically in all the main decision-making matters, whether at home or outside. Despite this, it is the women who have shouldered most of the family's burden of work. The status of women, especially in the traditional times, was very low. A woman was fully engaged with the household duties, but her status was insignificant and always subordinate to men. The history of the social background of the Mizos can be studied from the old sayings that have been handed down from generation to generation. Some of the proverbs focus on the attitudes towards women and their position during the traditional period. Famous popular adages concerning the women are *'Hmeichhe thu thu ni suh; Chakai sa sa ni suh'*, which means flesh of the crab is no meat; words of a woman are no words, *'Hmeichhe finin tuikhur ral a kai lo'*, which means the wisdom of women does not reach beyond the village stream, *'Hmeichhia leh Vau sam loh chu an pawng tual tual'*, which means uncontrolled wives and untrimmed grass in the fields both become unbearable, *'Hmeichia leh Palchhia chu thlak theih a ni'*, which means worn-out fencing and a woman can be replaced, *'Hmeichhia leh Chakaiin Sakhua an nei lo'*, which means women and crabs do not have religious rites. *'Hmeichhe tawng menah thlak suh; hmeichhia leh uipui chu lo rum lungawi mai mai rawh se,'* which means do not pay heed to what a woman says; let a woman and a dog bark as they please.

According to oral tradition, these attitudes towards women are found in the history of the different clans of the Mizo. As it portrayed women as holding an inferior place in the society – faithful housewives to their husbands who could be divorced by her husband at any time, passive, un-knower and sometimes as bearing extreme or brutal character – the proverbs prohibited her right of self-expression or to explore her knowledge in public. Thus, for men, proverbs emerged as one of their hegemonic tools to validate their control over women. Even today, it is being constantly used as a reminder for women to maintain her role and cultural stability.

TRADITIONAL MARRIAGE SYSTEMS AND PATRIARCHAL DOMINANCE

The question on the nature and origin of women's subordination in the formation of culture has been a long rumination amongst the feminists in their study of women in history in which different alternative explanations are given. While patriarchal dominance has been recognized as the genesis of women's subordination, for Levi Strauss, 'the exchange of women' marks the beginning and the cause of women's subordination, which in turn reinforces a sexual division of labour by instituting male dominance (Levi-Strauss, 1969: 489; Lerner, 1986: 24). If it was male's hegemony in the family and male's constructed culture that dominated Mizo women, the circulation of women in the form of marriage may also give us some explanation to understand patriarchal hegemony and women's oppression in the formation of Mizo culture.

Marriages, according to Levi Strauss, are the most basic form of 'gift' exchange, which constitutes male bonds in which women are the most precious of gifts, and culture depends upon that tie (Rubin, 1996: 116). From his androcentric analysis, feminists have pointed out the centrality of the woman as the desired object to secure male bonds instead of forging male–female relation. Others have not looked so much at the woman in this system of exchange, but at the male bonds it establishes (Newman, 1987: 21). Given the diverse forms of marriage amongst the different clans and families, a closer look at the marriage systems is needed—transaction of bride wealth, that is, bride price and the marriage alliances amongst the ruling clans. In this context, it is important to look at the structure of exchanges which characterize patriarchal ties, supremacy and oppression of women in the formation of Mizo culture.

Amongst all the Mizo clans, marriages were mediated through the transaction of *'man'* or bride price. During the traditional period, the price differed according to the clans. *Sial* (*Mithun*) or bison was the most valuable item of bride price, and there was no fixed amount with regard to the number of *Sial*. Sometimes, it was also paid in terms of articles such as gongs, guns, beads and *Puan* or loincloth. It was from the nineteenth century, when the *Sailos* consolidated their power in Dungtlang village, that bride price was properly given in terms of *sial* as most of the historical evidences of bride price in the early eighteenth century were mainly in the form of these articles (Sangkhuma, 2000: 31–6).

The traditional Mizo custom of *Man* or bride price has been one of the most contentious issues amongst the writers and scholars. Chatterji says, 'The institution of marriage in the Mizo Society, with all its inner details of agreement, etc., also goes to establish a significant place for the woman in the Mizo society ... In fact, the marriage price may well be looked upon as the prestige value rather than the sole price of commodity' (Chatterji, 1975: 8). Like Chatterji, in their attempt to study women's status in marriage system, many scholars have simply drawn vague conclusions by glorifying bride price as the symbol of women's high status, but failed to observe the enhancement of patriarchal hegemony and control over women within this custom. First, patriarchal legitimacy emerged in the arrangement of marriage and distribution of *Man*. Before the settlement of *Man*, both the families had to meet up with each other and make negotiation. The initiative was first taken from the boy's side by sending *Palai* or negotiators particularly men, to the girl's family (Kipgen, 1996: 79). *Man* was divided into *Manpui* or main price and *Mantang* or subsidiary price. The main price or *Manpui* went to the bride's father. Only in the absence of either the father or the nearest male relatives or if the girl was born outside wedlock was a mother authorized to claim *Manpui*. The subsidiary price known as *Mantang* was distributed between the bride's paternal uncle (*Palal*) and maternal uncle (*Pusum*) and then to the girl's paternal aunt (*Ni Ar*) and her elder sister (*Naupuakpuan*). The recipient of *Palal* was an adopted trustee, who was expected to protect her in her future. Besides, the recipient of *Pusum* had great responsibilities in the house of the newly married couple and they could not perform ceremonies such as *Khuangchawi* and *Chawn* without him (Zawla, 1976: 95). For this reason, Kipgen, a Mizo theologian, also agreed with Chatterji to assume the bride price as a prestige value for women. Similarly, Dokhuma a Mizo well-known writer also argued that the distribution of subsidiary prices or *Mantang* shows that a woman was not de-humanized and sold as a commodity as the price stand only for a marriage price, not for a woman's price (Dokhuma, 1992: 144).

Although it was her parents who received the negotiators as well as the price, all the final decisions and settlement were made by the father and other male members in the family. They (men) fixed the price and received the large share of the bride's price. The first gender-defined role for women was to be those who were exchanged in marriage transactions. The observed gender role for men was to be those who did the exchanging or who defined the term of the exchanges (Lerner, 1986: 214). Henceforth, the custom of bride price defined gender role and insured male hegemony in the family to confirm that women belonged to men, needed to be protected and controlled by men.

The famous Mizos' welcoming word of a newborn female child says, 'Oh! She will become a beautiful maid and would bring a handsome price' (Hminga, 1987: 26–7). This old saying reveals the obscured economic reason and gender division of labour in the 'circulation of women' in bride price. Accordingly, a number of scholars and writers have elaborated this position to signify women's lower position in the Mizo society and for this reason Vanlaltlani observed that a girl was by and large taken as an economic asset or a moveable commodity and sold like the most valuable domesticated animals at the cost of her parents (Vanlaltlani, 2005: 20). Here, a society's demand on women's productive labour emerged. Perhaps due to the communities' dependency on jhumming cultivation along with gender division of labour, first importance was given to productive labour in the selection of the wife. Generally a woman was assessed through her contribution to jhumming, her ability in weaving and other domestic works (Lianthanga, 1999: 137). This observed fact has led to the assumption that a woman's productive labour was one of the objects in the custom of bride price. Economically, marriage then appears as a benefit for the bridegroom's family, but a great loss for the bride's family. Hence, economic needs of the family fostered and made a woman equivalent with *Sial*, so she was 'given' and 'received' reciprocally by the two families in her marriage. In this context, bride price appears as a compensation given to the bride's family from the bridegroom's family. Perhaps, being equivalent to domesticated animal, as H.S. Luaia, one of the first Baptist Pastors in the Southern part of the hills, commented, a woman was called '*Ran ngo*' or fairer domesticated animal (Luaia, Interview, 19 January 2007). Consequently, she was exchanged or bought to be controlled by her new owner without having any rights over her own economic production for the completion of patriarchal power.

The position in a clan hierarchy and position in a marriage system were also intimately linked, which resulted to the diverse form of *Man*. Amongst all the clans, the chief's daughter fetched the highest price. It is generally believed that the bride price has its good side, as the higher price would make the position of the wife more secure and marriage more permanent. Apparently, the position of *Lai* and *Mara* women in the family was much more secure than the *Lusei* women who fetched lower prices. On the contrary, to constitute bride price as the sign of a woman's status would be a fallacy as it only signified her higher status compared to women of other clans and families, but not to men. Despite the higher price they had to pay, every man intended to marry a woman from the higher clan/sub-clan. This custom was a common practice among the *Lai* (Pawi Chanchin, 1988: 142). This custom had a deep connection with their sacrificial ceremonies. For instance, in the sacrificial ceremonies of *Sechhun*, performed by the *Lais*, a sacrificial animal '*Sial*' was tied with a rope known as *sehrui*, and it was only a man of '*hnamtha nei*', (who married a girl from the respectable clan) who could hold *sehrui*. Meanwhile a man of '*hnamchhe nei*' (those who married a girl from the lower or inferior clan) was not allowed to touch *sehrui* (ibid.: 106). This social practice then reveals that women were exchanged with her equivalent prices in marriage not only to signify men's status in the society but to reinforce hierarchical formation as well.

The impact of social hierarchy, on the contrary is that bride price along with dowry also differed according to clans and families. There, prices are higher among the *Lai*, *Mara* and the *Paite* as compared with the *Luseis*. Amongst all the clans, the chief's daughter fetched the highest price. Generally, price differed according to the number of *Sial* they had to pay. Being the owner of family's property/production, payment of *Sial* and other articles for a bride price depended upon the economic status of men. It is also stated that the daughter of the chief also brought a number of female slaves with her on the day of her wedding. We have a good example with regards to this. According to the historical record, the *Lusei* chief *Suakpuilala* raided Adampore in the Cachar area and procured 32 Bengalee women to accompany his sister *Vanhnuaithangi* to her husband's house in 1865 (Chatterjee, 2000: 82). In this form of marriage, exchange of women emerged as an initial step or a strategy to expose men's economic power to the other groups of men.

A 'gift' or exchange of women in marriage for the Mizos also somehow emerged with political alliances to establish the purity of lineage and power relations as well. A feminist anthropologist Gayle Rubin argued that the result of a gift of women is more profound than the result of other gift transactions, because the relationship thus established is not just one of reciprocity, but one of kinship (Rubin, 1996: 117). An important custom that was commonly connected with marriage and lineage system was the examination of the family history. This was because they believed that physical appearance and all the characters could be inherited by their descendants. The chief's family was more careful in this regard. For instance, in the case of the *Sailo* ruling clan, if a chief's son searched for a wife in another village, the prospective wife was placed on a bed enclosed by a curtain by the mother and the girl would stand only with her skirt to be examined by the chief's son (Zawla, 1976: 93). J. Shakespear, the first superintendent of Lushai Hills, stated that among the chiefs, the desire to marry another chief's daughter limited the young man's choice and marriage among first cousins was more frequent than among the commoners (Shakespear, 1988: 49). Therefore, the marriage between the common man and the chief's daughter was very rare. It is also said that if a common man fell in love with the chief's daughter, it could endanger his life. For instance, during the early nineteenth century, a chief's daughter *Laltheri* fell in love with *Chalthanga*, a common man. But she could not marry him and later on, her brothers' men killed *Chalthanga* (Zawla, 1976: 265).

As a result of constant wars amongst the different clans, many chiefs also carried out matrimonial alliances as a means to strengthen their political linkages – to consolidate their relationship with other ruling clans and to make peace with their neighbouring enemies. There are a number of evidences in Mizo history to prove the existence of such a practice. The best documented case was: In the mid-nineteenth century, the greatest *Sailo* chief *Lallula's* son Mangpera married *Pi Buki* a daughter of a

Palian chief, *Lalrihua*. In the beginning, there was a constant hostility between the *Palian* and *Sailo* chiefs. But this matrimonial alliance brought peace between these two clans (Lalthanliana, 2000: 440). In another sense, the custom of concubinage and the exchange of women as 'gift' had some relations. When a chief or a wealthy man chose to take a concubine, he was required to pay a price to her family equal to the bride price. But as in the case of a real wife, the whole amount was rarely given especially when it was the chief that desired a concubine. Often, the chief could get away with paying some favours and small gifts to the girl's father. Fathers gave their daughters willingly at this concession because being associated had its advantages for him (Parry, 1988: 38).

Accordingly, marriages for the Mizos in pre-colonial period formed different strategies for the formation of social hierarchy, patriarchal alliance and power. It was not only between the two families an alliance was made, 'but between the two groups of men in which a woman was only figured as one of the objects in the exchange' (Lerner, 1986: 47) to consolidate men's social, economic and political power between the two groups. In short, to some extent, it may also be surmised that a bride price indeed superficially valued the status of women; but in practice, it was only their reproductive labour that was valued to strengthen patriarchal hegemony in the society.

COLONIALISM AND THE CONSTRUCTION OF TRADITIONAL PATRIARCHY

After the British occupation, superintendent of the Lushai Hills was the head of the district in whose hands was placed the extra-judicial powers to settle disputes. However, he did not interfere with the administration of the district on his own except in exceptional cases. The superintendent selected certain 'chiefs', and vested them with certain powers, thus, keeping with the old social and political traditions. For the efficient administration in the hills, a pamphlet titled '*A Monograph on Lushai Customs and Ceremonies*', the first printed document on the customary laws of the Mizos, was compiled in the year 1928. It consists of important *Lushai* customs such as the chief and village administration, marriage customs, divorce, inheritance, sexual offences, and so on, ceremonies such as funeral ceremonies, sacrifices and feasts.

N.E. Parry who compiled, 'A monograph on Lushai Customs and Ceremonies' stated that Mizo chiefs of different clans such as *Sailo* and those of *Zahau, Hualngo, Fanai* and *Hnamchawm* chiefs, who commonly followed *Sailos'* customs, were consulted before the compilation of the pamphlet. Out of the 56 chiefs he consulted, there were no female chiefs and more than half of the chiefs belonged to *Sailo* clan (Parry, 1988: ii). Thus, the traditional customs, laws and ceremonies mentioned in the monograph were mostly based on *Sailos'* tradition compiled from the definition and interpretation of men that did not reflect women's voices. Along with the exclusion of women's voices, traditional patriarchal law was re-instituted or confirmed in a written form. Accordingly, administration of the hills was dominated by colonial and *Lusei* or *Sailo* patriarchal thought where women were always subjected to the authority of a patriarch.

Given that the customs were recorded for the efficient government of the colonial officers, modifications were also being made. But in the case of bride price and its distribution, rather than ruling out or limiting men's power, old customs was reinforced except that the price had to be paid in cash or in terms of *Sial* that was equivalent to ₹ 40 (Biaksiami, 1982: 3–4). The immediate impact of the Colonial's fixation of bride price was the reinforcement of social or clan's hierarchy. Take, for example, the *Sailo* who held the highest price as the price of a bride worth *Sesawm* or ten bison, for other *Lusei* ruling clans such as *Zadeng, Thangluah, Palian* and *Rivung* the price was fixed at *Seriat* or eight bison and the price was fixed between *Sesarih* or seven bison and *seruk* or six bison amongst the commoners (Sangkima, 2002: 28). To persuade and win the confidence of the chiefs, the colonizers reinforced bride price as one of the hegemonic instruments of their government. With the support of colonial power, the *Sailos* and other ruling clans therefore continued to preserve their traditional authorities through the traditional norms of 'the exchange of women' in marriages.

DISCOURSES ON BRIDE PRICE DURING THE POST-COLONIAL PERIOD

The early post-colonial period witnessed rapid transformation of social and political condition of in the hills. One of its impacts was the growth of consciousness amongst the educated women that led to the formation of the first women's organization, *Mizo Hmeichhe*

Tangrual Pawl in 1946. The first women's conference was organized on 26–28 January 1948 in Aizawl. In the conference, it was proposed that women's agenda should be included in the political process of Mizo hills. Realizing the problems of women within the customary law, they drafted few points that degraded their position from the issues concerning bride price, divorce, inheritance, adultery, etc. Regarding the custom of bride price, the assembly passed the resolution for the submission of its eradication to the district council as the price often created problems for the women in the family (Zoram Hriattirna, 15 June 1955: 1–3). During the process of the formation of Mizo District Council, the organization repeatedly requested the authorities to include women representative in the council.

As early as the inauguration of the District Council in 1952, the assembly reviewed and revised the existing laws on Mizo customs that was modified under colonial government and eventually the Mizo Hnam Dan or Mizo Customary Law of 1956 was amended in 1960. In the District Council Assembly, the Mizo *Hnam Dan* or Mizo Customary Law was a contentious issue particularly on the custom of marriage in 1955–1960. After a debate on whether to follow Christian Marriage Act, Indian Marriage Act or the existing Mizo Hnam Dan or Mizo Customs, it was decided that the practice of the traditional norms of marriage would continue. To begin with, the tradition of sending *Palai* or negotiator had to be continued as it was before.

Despite their inclination to 'colonial traditionalism', there was a long debate on the eradication of bride price. One of the members of the council Ch Saprawnga, who put forward the question on the context of bride price and its eradication, argued that on the ground of humanity *Man* or bride price symbolized the selling of a woman and suggested for the redefinition of its meaning to a '*lawmman*' or 'reward'(Zoram Hriattirna, 15 June 1955: 1–3). Another member, Lalbuaia also recommended to give due importance to the decision of the two families and was against to reinforce the practice as an obligatory custom. In contrast Tuikhurliana, who supported its eradication, urged his anxiety of loosing men's power as he argued, 'whenever there is a *man* we the men are the owners, but if *man* is eradicated, we will lose our authority, though women's rights will be limited' (Zoram Hriattirna, 15 June 1955: 1–3). The discussions and debates of the assembly however reflected the traditional patriarchal thought and the council members were very sceptical about gender equality. For majority of the members, 'it is the father who has the absolute power in all the family matters.' As such, many of them could not stand their ground. To support the continuity of 'colonial traditionalism', Ch Saprawnga also changed his position and in the end he was opposed to its eradication. Finally, the suggestion of bride price eradication was declined and the assembly supported its continuity in such a way that the custom had a good side for the expansion of family and clan relationship. When it was amended in 1960, the customary law states, 'In all the marriages the practice of bride price has to be decided between the two families. If the marriage is mediated through bride price, the father will be the main recipient. If the bride has no father, the price will go to her brother and her nearest male relative respectively. But in the case of *Falak* (a bastard) the mother will be the main recipient'. And all the marriages has to be registered in the Village Council (Zoram Hriattirna, 15 November 1955: 2).

There was also a long debate on the increase of the price and finally an increase was made mostly in favour of the bride's male relatives. *Manpui* was fixed at ₹ 100, but if a bride had a dowry, it would be increased to ₹ 120 and the *Mantang* was distributed amongst the relatives and it was continued to extend and strengthen their respective clan or family ties in the future. Perhaps the district council's support to the abolition of chieftainship led to the eradication of bride price fixation in terms of clans that led to the elimination of traditional social hierarchy that symbolized bride price as a symbol of clan and family status.

When Mizoram was still a Union Territory of India, a committee on Mizo Customary Law was formed in 1980 to reform the existing law modified under the Mizo District council. After the hills attained the status of statehood, they compiled a new customary law and named it '*Mizo Hnam Dan*'. The committee reinforced the compulsory practice of bride price and defined its meaning by stating, 'Man does not denote buying or selling, it only symbolizes the new relationship between the families of the bride and the groom' (Mizo Hnam Dan, 1956: 13). The price has been fixed at ₹ 420 that has to be distributed according to the norms of the traditions. This price is followed to the present day. The traditional perspective on economic demands of the women has gradually faded out; however, the distribution of mantang reflected the traditional custom of 'exchange' for the patriarchal bonds in the family or clan. In short, the new state government did not bring traditional patriarchal hierarchy to an end in the Mizo society.

CONCLUSION

To conclude, the present paper shows that bride price for the Mizo is a symbol of women's status that signifies patriarchal power in the family. In the pre-colonial period, it symbolized gender and social hierarchy, economic or reproductive demands and lineage or family ties that led to the 'exchange' of women between the two groups of men to strengthen patriarchal power. During the colonial period, along with the process of the discontinuity of the old customs, the colonizers' politics on the inclination of traditional norms led to the official fixation of the price in terms of money. The colonial's definition of bride price then was eventually redefined during the post-colonial period that gave the symbolic meaning of bride price for the strengthening of family and clan relationship. Presently, bride price has become a complicated practice as a result of new social relation. Marriage custom has changed, but the symbolic meaning of bride price in relation to women has not changed. In this context the disadvantage of bride price for women is that in spite of the present definition of its meaning the word 'buying' is still in vogue. Given to the new social relation most of the families also misused the existing customary law on the distribution of *Mantang*. The immediate impact is the expansion of new patriarchal relationship or power to symbolize new social hierarchy. As a result of the present situation, bride price has become a contentious issue amongst the Women's Organizations. Their main fallouts on bride price are, either the abolition or increase of the price. Meanwhile, the 'new patriarchy' is anxious of loosening its control over women and is therefore in favour of bride price to symbolize cultural identity. Thus from the point of view of the new patriarchal society, the practice of bride price proves advantageous since for the 'new patriarchy' it is a means to preserve their cultural or traditional identity and power. The women who are the first victims of patriarchy do not have any say in this matter. A serious consideration needs to be taken not only in the issue of bride price but also the related issues of gender that arises because of the existing male constructed customary law.

REFERENCES

Anderson, Siwan. 2007. 'The Economics of Dowry and Bride Price', *Journal of Economic Perspectives*, 21(4): 151–74.

Biaksiami. 1982. *Mizorama Hmeichhe Tangrual Pawl Ding Hmasa Ber MIZO HMEICHHE TANGRUAL PAWL*. Aizawl, Mizoram.

Chatterjee, Suhash. 2000. *Mizo Chiefs and Chiefdom*. New Delhi: M.D Publication.

Chatterji, N. 1975. *Status of Women in the Earlier Mizo Society*. Aizawl, Mizoram: Tribal Research Institute.

Dokhuma, James. 1992. *Hmanlai Mizo Kalphung*. Mizoram: J.D. Press Publication.

Ferdandes, Walter. 2002. *The Indigenous Issue and Women's Status in Northeast India*. Paper Submitted at Indigenous Rights in Common Wealth Project, South and Southeast Asia Regional Expert Meeting. New Delhi: Indian Conference on Indigenous Tribal Peoples (ICITP) India International Centre.

Goody, Jack and S.J. Tambiab. 1993. *Bridewealth and Dowry*. London: Cambridge University Press.

Hminga, C.L. 1987. *The Life and Witness of the Churches in Mizoram*. Lunglei: Literature Committee, Baptist Church of Mizoram.

Kipgen, Mangkhosat. 1996. *Christianity and Mizo Culture*. Jorhat, Assam, India: Mizoram Theological Conference, Eastern Theological College.

Kumar, Maya Unnithan. 1997. *Indentity, Gender and Poverty: New Perspective on Caste and Tribe in Rajasthan*. New York: Baghahn Book.

Lalthanliana. 2000. *Mizo Chanchin (1900 Hma Lam)*. Aizawl, Mizoram: Vanbuangi Gas Agency.

Lerner, Gerda. 1986. *The Creation of Patriarchy*. Oxford: Oxford University Press.

Lerner, Gerda. 1998. *Why History Matters, Life and Thought*. Oxford: Oxford University Press.

Levi-Strauss, Claude. 1969. *The Elementary Structures of Kinship*. Boston: Beacon Press.

Lianthanga, C. 1999. *Hmanlai Mizo Nun*. Aizawl, Mizoram: Mizoram Publication Board.

Luaia. Personal Interview, 19 January 2007.

Maitra, Sudeshna. 2007. *Dowry and Bride Price*. Prepared for the International Encyclopedia of the Social Sciences, 2nd ed., February 2007.

Mizo Hnam Dan (Mizo Customary Law) Mizo Hnam Dan (Customary Law). 1956. Enforced with effect from 1956 vide Mizo Hnam Dan (Operation Order), 1957 as amended in 1960, 1996. Compiled by The Committee on Mizo Customary Law, Law and Judicial Department, Government of Mizoram, Aizawl, Mizoram.

Mukhopadaya, Lipi. 2002. *Tribal Women in Development*. Publication Division, Ministry of Information and Broadcasting, Govenrment of India, 2002.

Newman, Karen. 1987. 'Portia's Ring: Unruly Women and Structures of Exchange in the Merchant of Venice', *Shakespeare Quarterly*, 38(1): 19–33.

Parry, N.E. 1988. *Lushai Custom: A Monograph on Lushai Customs and Ceremonies*. Aizawl, Mizoram: RI Offset Printers on behalf of Tribal Research Institute.

Pawi, Chanchin. 1988. *Tribal Research Institute*. Aizawl, Mizoram.

Pruthi, Raj and Bela Rani, Sharma. 1994. *Encyclopedia of Women, Society and Culture*. New Delhi: Anmol Publication.

Rajaram, Indira. 2005. 'Economies of Bride Price and Dowry'. In: *Dowry and Inheritance*, edited by Srimati Basu, Kali for Women.

Randeria, Shalini and Leela, Visaria. 2005. 'Sociology of Bride Price and Dowry'. In: *Dowry and Inheritance*, edited by Srimati Basu, New Delhi, Kali for Women.

Rubin, Gayle. 1996. 'The Traffic in Women'. In: *Feminism and History*, edited by Scott J.W., Oxford: Oxford University Press.

Sangkhuma, Z.T. 2000. 'Mizo Hmeichhia Leh Inneihna'. In: *Hmeichhiate leh Mizo Hnam Dan (Seminar Papers on Women and Mizo Customary Law)*, edited by Zohmangaiha, Aizwl, Mizoram: Valcolm Publication.

Sangkima. 2002. 'Women and Politics in Mizoram through the Ages', *Historical Journal of Mizoram*, 3(1): 28–38.

Shakespear, J. 1988. *The Lusei-Kuki Clan*. Aizawl, Mizorm: Tribal Research Institute.

Vanlaltlani, T. 2005. *Mizo Hmeichhiate Kawngzawh*. Aizawl, Mizoram: Mizoram Publication Board.

Zawla, K. 1976. *Mizo Pi Pute leh An Thlahte Chanchin*. Aizawl, Mizoram.

Zoram, Hriattirna. *(District Information)*, Aijal, 15 June 1955, p. 13.

Zoram, Hriattirna. Aijal, 15 November 1955, pp. 1–8.

CHAPTER 20

How Socio-cultural Factors Influence the Health-Seeking Behaviour of Women During Pregnancy in Rural Bangladesh

Faisal Ahmmed and Tofayel Ahmed

The use of health services is related to availability, quality and cost of services as well as the social structures, religious faith, health beliefs and personal characteristics of the users. According to the World Health Organization, over half a million women succumbed to death each year from complications of pregnancy or childbirth. The situation of pregnancy- and childbirth-related morbidity and mortality is worse in Bangladesh because of low utilization of maternal health services (Nuruzzaman, 2009). The reduction in levels of maternal mortality and improvement of maternal health has been central policy goals since the inception of Fourth Population and Health Program in Bangladesh in 1992. Efforts to address these issues have recently gained considerable momentum with the formulation of the National Strategy for Maternal Health. This strategy is predicated on the 'Three Delays Causal Framework' that affects safe motherhood service utilization and outcomes: delays in making the decision to seek care, delays in reaching a medical facility and delays in receiving adequate treatment or management at the facility and emphasizes the provision of emergency obstetric care to resolve this endemic problem.

Although the maternal mortality ratio in Bangladesh has declined from more than 600 in 1980 to 322 in 2004, it is still one of the highest in the world. Pregnancy- and delivery-related deaths account for 20 per cent of the death in women of reproductive age. The unavailability of trained service providers, low utilization of services by pregnant women, along with the infrastructure difficulties, together contribute to the high rate of maternal deaths in Bangladesh. As well, the utilization of maternity care provided by trained professionals during and after delivery is alarmingly low in Bangladesh. While there have been some improvements in the recent years, about half of the pregnant women still do not seek any antenatal care (ANC). Similarly, women's awareness of potentially life-threatening conditions during pregnancy, delivery and after delivery is comparatively lower in Bangladesh than many countries. Everyday on an average, 32 mothers die during delivery. About 70 per cent of pregnant women do not have access in emergency pregnancy support and 78 per cent of the mothers' mortality is due to this reason (Ministry of Health and Family Welfare, 2009).

There exists urban–rural discrepancy in maternal mortality and the statistics is skewed in relatively 'socially conservative' districts. For instance, maternal mortality is higher in Sylhet than any areas in Bangladesh (Prothom Alo, 19 December 2009). Bangladesh Demographic and Health Survey 2007 reveals that at national level, 85 per cent delivery takes place at home and only 18 per cent women receive support from health services. This survey mentioned that this number is 5 per cent low in Sylhet division. Only 10 per cent of pregnant women in Sylhet division give birth in different government and private health centres. Similarly, the government statistics indicate that at national level 46 per cent of rural women seek health support during pregnancy, whereas it is much lower in rural parts of Sylhet division. It is customary in Sylhet that people avoid rural health and family-planning workers, union heath and family welfare centres, satellite clinics or any other health facility for seeking support during pregnancy and safe delivery.

There are several social, religious and economic barriers that prevent pregnant women from seeking services from health facilities. The conventional economic views promotes that the government health facilities located in rural areas provide free ANC, delivery and post-natal care services, yet the cost related to medicines, transportation and surgical operations in the case of complications discourages poor women to seek services from these facilities. Due to unconsciousness and less or no contact with mainstream services, the situation of indigenous women is more vulnerable. This economic view may explain part of the puzzle yet social stigma generated through patriarchal structure deserves some credit. For instance, a prevalent perception among male is that pregnancy is a natural process for women, and it will pass normally and thus no extra care and support is needed in this phase of life. Men (and sometimes along with women) promote superstitions such as not taking much food during pregnancy, arguing that extra feeding will increase the growth of the foetus and will affect normal delivery.

The disarray in health-seeking behaviour is strongly associated with inferior status of girls and women in Bangladesh. This is mainly due to entrenched dysfunctional gender relations brought about by dated social and cultural practices and is reinforced by literalist interpretations of religious texts, especially the Quran and other similar texts. Under the umbrella of *purdah* and the sometimes self-serving interpretation of the Quran by men, certain values and practices of Bangladesh society have made applicable to the daily living experiences of the rural poor women (Reza and Ahmmed, 2009). These women have to exist in an environment that is marked by a 'forced poverty of social relationships' (ibid.) that requires them to be confined to their living quarters free from exposure to outsiders, mainly males. This is done, so she is taught, in order to preserve their modesty vis-à-vis the outside world. Overriding all of these, the poor rural woman is treated as if her body and her future are not hers to own and manage. Naturally, this has a trickle-down effect on any health-seeking behaviour of women. As data on this issue are scarcely limited, the researchers found conducting research on the topic important and they conducted a study on the pregnant women of *Dawdik* village of Sylhet district. This article is the outcome of the research that systematically explained the health support-seeking behaviour of pregnant women, influence of their male counterparts in shaping health-seeking behaviour, their health problems during pregnancy as well as their coping mechanisms. It also analysed the male's perceptions on health issues of pregnant women.

METHODOLOGY

With the objectives of an in-depth exploration on health-seeking behaviour of pregnant women in rural area, the research project used a qualitative design. The goal of the qualitative design is to represent the participants' reality as faithfully as possible from their points of view (Morgan and Kunkel, 2001). In order to ensure an in-depth exploration on psychological, social, religious, gender and cultural perceptions on maternal health during pregnancy, and to explore women and community peoples' knowledge and the deeper causes of neglecting women's health care, the qualitative design could help the researchers to gather information through the use of multiple methods of data collection that includes interview, conversation and observation. Since the findings of qualitative research is heavily dependent on reliable data (Patton, 1990), the researchers paid special attention in the field work phase and worked as major tools of data collection from the participants.

Although Sylhet district is comparatively an economically solvent area than other districts of Bangladesh, many people of the district live in remote villages in acute poverty. Illiteracy and unconsciousness rules many parts of their lives. The study was conducted within four remote villages of Sylhet district. A list of villages was made based on recent census report. The list was further narrowed down to four villages using random sampling technique. The researchers visited these areas and engaged in formal enquiry, informal discussions with pregnant women with the aim of identifying awareness and access of the utilization of maternal health facilities as sources of cooperation with the research project. The team also investigated male's perception and community's outlook on these issues. All pregnant women and their respective male family members living in the selected villages regarded as the population of the study and all of them were interviewed as the respondents of the research. Due to the socio-cultural and religious barriers, collecting data from the pregnant women was difficult to male researchers. In order to compensate that limitation, the research team included female research associates. Moreover, support was sought from NGO health workers, local traditional birth attendants (TBAs) and older women of the respective families. Recruitment of the participants was made based on their personal interest. Before formal interview, the research team identified the participants and visited them frequently, made rapport with them and motivated them to speak with the research team. Before appearing before the research team, pregnant women obtained assent from their husbands and/or their mothers-in-law.

OBJECTIVES

The study was conducted in order to explore the health status of rural pregnant women and their medical support–seeking behaviour in general. However, the specific objectives are as follows:

- To know the present health status of rural women during pregnancy.
- To know the availability of health-related services that are provided in the rural area.
- To know the health-seeking behaviour of the pregnant women.
- To identify the socio-cultural, religious and male influences towards shaping existing health-seeking behaviour.
- Aiming to provide information to the development program planner for designing and implementing need-based development interventions for the pregnant women.

MAJOR FINDINGS

General Characteristic of the Participants

The research team found 632 married women in the studied villages. Among them, 84 were pregnant. Early marriage was strongly prevalent among the participants. Out of 84 participants, 72 got married in the age of 15–20 years. All four villages were Muslim dominated, and naturally majority of the participants were from Muslim faith. Literacy rate was found to be very poor among the pregnant women. More than half of them were illiterate. Almost all of the participants were found to be engaged in household activities except one who was a primary school teacher. Two-third of the participants reported that the current one was their third and fourth experience of pregnancy. About half of the participants were living in joint family where most parts of their lives were guided by their mothers-in-law. Almost all of the husbands of the participants were farmers.

Present Health Status

Healthy pregnancy was barely seen among the participants. Pregnancy-related complications were found alarming among two categories of participants—women aged under 18 years and women experiencing third and fourth pregnancy. Birth spacing is a significant indicator for good health of pregnant women, but majority of the participants who delivered for the second time or more had maximum 18 months gap between the pregnancies. Pregnancy under the age of 18 years was not uncommon. We found nine individuals who got married at the age of 14 years and became pregnant at the age of 17 years. Due to not having control over their body, pregnancy was imposed upon them by their husband's family members. Despite not having physical ability, few of their husbands imposed pregnancy upon them without their assent. We asked participants whether their husbands took their opinion on child birth. We found none who had a role in decision-making on having child. One participant mentioned,

> It is in fact not necessary to ask any wife before having a baby in our society. Husbands will take decision or it shall be imposed by mother in-law or other influential family member of husband's family. As the girl come to her husband's house at her immature age, she can not raise her voice over husband about her personal wellbeing, she has to accept everything. It is said that, pregnancy is normal and common matter among married women. In many cases pregnancy is unplanned and is the result of lack of use of contraception. Sometimes want for boy baby force an women to accept repeated pregnancy in our area.

Among these participants, four were experiencing severe complications. About two-third of the pregnant women from both of those groups were experiencing problems such as oedema, abdominal pain, body ache, headache and back pain. Only one-third of the participants reported that they were not experiencing any major complications.

Birth Plan

Since birth is considered as a natural process, majority of the community people view that they should not make any specific plan for birth. Almost all of the villagers mentioned that they do not take any preparation for safe delivery. They even do not know the possible date of delivery correctly. Importance of safe delivery is not known to them. All practices and behaviours related to delivery are based on their traditional belief and experience. Few of the traditional preparations even cause serious harm to both infant and mother. At home, the room where baby is given birth is known as *Atur Ghar*. According to the villagers, this place should be closed and secured free or fresh air should not pass into the room as evil spirit may enter into the room with air that can harm the infant. The mother and the infant have to spend few days in captivity. Thus, a separate place is prepared as part of birth plan. Instead of medical arrangement, many villagers go to traditional healers and collect *Tabiz* for the safety of infant and mother. One of the participants who was the mother-in-law of a pregnant woman viewed,

> We arrange everything at our home. Once pain is started, we call upon a female neighbor who has experience in delivery or we deal the case on our own. I have taken some preparation, I have cleaned the place where baby will be born and will stay for few days along with her mother and I made some blanket for her. We have collected Tabiz from the clergyman of nearest mosque. This shall help us as it is formed with God's words. We also have planned to consult a traditional healer who can prescribe some herbal medicine for pain free and risk free delivery.

Due to not having personal autonomy to take decision, most of the women cannot make birth plan personally; they have to rely upon their husbands or other family members. One of our participants who was pregnant told,

> I am sick, but my husband or my mother in-law does not consider it seriously. They view it as usual. As this is my first experience, I have consulted with my mother and my mother requested my husband to take me at my mother's house so that she can support me. My husband agreed and I shall go to mother's house. My baby shall be born there.

We asked her about possible arrangement to be taken by her mother. She told that there is a TBA in their village who supports all villagers and she would arrange the attendant's support. We found only about 15 per cent of the participants who were conscious about the importance of birth plan, and they consulted medical professional regularly. All of these women told that they will go to the hospitals, health centres or clinic for safe delivery. This group had good understanding about the importance of safe delivery.

Perception on Health Support During Pregnancy

Due to massive awareness, camping regarding safe motherhood by few NGOs, most of the pregnant women are found to be conscious about health during pregnancy. But the general perception of the studied villagers was ambiguous. It might be because of partial awareness camping targeting women and adolescent girls only. The study team conducted three focus group discussions with male residents of every village and almost all of male residents did not know about the importance of regular health care during pregnancy. Even in most cases, the husbands of pregnant women had poor understanding about this topic. Despite having deep interest to get proper medical service, pregnant women could not afford or arrange it due to the mis-cooperation of their husbands. One of the husbands viewed that,

> We do not know about its importance. My mother, wife of my sisters never went hospital during pregnancy for any support. We think it is a natural process and baby shall be born automatically. God has given the baby and he will see her wellbeing.

Superstition is also another significant factor explored by the research team. One of the mothers-in-law of a pregnant woman told,

> No one should go outside in the whole period of pregnancy. Going outside is dangerous. Any evil spirit can attack the pregnant woman. So we do not allow them to go outside.It is the common perceived idea of community people that pregnancy is a natural process and extra support and treatment is not mandatory at this stage. Most of the villagers believe that it is not essential to go to hospital during delivery, rather, the support of TBA is enough for this. Few of the participants viewed,God has a decision what will happen. We are nobody to change the fate. Therefore we should trust upon god.

Religious misinterpretations sometimes restrict women from receiving medical supports for physicians who are male. One of our participants failed to arrange regular check-up as her husband forbid her to go to the male medical doctor. He described how she was restricted,

> My husband told me that our religion never permits to go to another male who may see or touch any parts of your body. As the physician is a male, I should not go there. He collected some water and oil purified by a local clergy man with holy words (commonly known as Pani Pora) and suggested to drink and use regularly. My husband believe that these two items shall ensure my safety and good health, evil spirit shall not touch me and my baby shall be a pious one.

ACCESS IN EXISTING HEALTH SERVICES

Our research sites were located about 11 km distance from divisional headquarters of Sylhet city where both government and private health services are found to be available. However, one union health centre and an *upazila* health complex were located at closer distance to their villages. All of those hospitals, health centre and clinics have maternal health support service and many of them provide services free of cost. But mainly due to lack of consciousness villagers visit those hospitals occasionally. 'Pregnancy is a natural process and this time shall pass naturally, why should we go to the hospitals or health support centres? Our mothers and sisters advised us to remember almighty God, he will see our wellbeing'—this was the common perceptions among a large number of participants. However, a small number of participants were conscious about the importance of receiving treatment and advice from the medical practitioners and they regularly visited their care givers. They could arrange it as their husbands cooperated with them.

According to the participants, religion was another significant factor that restricted them from going outside for treatment during pregnancy. It was observed that the women of the study area led their lives in a conservative manner. Their male counterparts and family usually do not allow them to go outside for any purposes. Few of our participants noticed that they were allowed to consult physician if the physician was a female. Almost all of the participants informed that they were not allowed to go outside the home alone; the husband or any male member of the family helped them in outside affairs occasionally if the male member had available time to do that. Traditionally in rural areas, the general well-being of women is widely neglected. It might be because of the inferior status of women (Ahmmed and Reza, 2006). A group of women who had basic education viewed that their status was low inside the family, their life was controlled by male members, they had no freedom and they could not do anything as per their own desire. They reported that they are totally dependent on their husbands and that is why their well-being dependent on the desire of their husbands. The study observed that health issues of women are not properly addressed by their counterparts or by other family members. Even in many cases, mothers-in-law and sisters-in-law, who have experienced complications related to pregnancy, avoid the importance of health support of women during pregnancy and always discourage them to go to hospital and clinics. Those realities sometimes restrict women in receiving medical supports closer to their community. However, few women were found who had regular contact with health workers of local NGOs. These health workers frequently visited pregnant women's houses as part of their duties. This group of participants also visited satellite clinics and tried to follow the advices of medical professionals. Trained TBAs are another source of support for few pregnant women. TBAs are trained by NGOs and villagers usually rely upon them. Two reasons were identified for such attitude—(a) TBAs are known to the villagers and the pregnant women have easy access to them as they live inside the village; (b) family members usually support to receive suggestions from TBAs, and there is no or minimum cost of services provided by TBAs.

CONCLUSION

In Bangladesh, only 13 per cent of the pregnant women get support from skilled and professional birth attendants. The maternity mortality rate is 320 within 10 million in Bangladesh. Safe maternity can reduce the death of mother and infants and can help to develop a healthy nation. In addition, it can help in reducing infant mortality rates and developing mother's health status that are prime targets of the Millennium Development Goal (MGD) in connection to health. Without changing the behaviour of rural people of Bangladesh it is difficult to achieve MGD in connection to health. Data show that despite having different health services, majority of the rural people avoid receiving those services. Even government's cost-free services fail to attract large number of people mainly because of their perception regarding health services. Pregnancy is considered as a normal process and most of the rural people still rely on traditional healing process for overcoming critical health situation during pregnancy. Mass media, especially electronic medias can play a vital role in changing people's attitude. In addition with perception and lack of knowledge about the health issue during pregnancy, the research explored few areas that need to be addressed properly. Government health workers usually avoid visiting houses/villages regularly at research areas. Although NGO's health staffs arrange regular visit, they spend inadequate amount of time in counselling, which is essential to change people's perception and understanding about health during pregnancy. The research team found no arrangement to organize group/community meeting on health issue with villagers which could help to motivate villagers to receive existing medical services closer to their community. Due to poverty, many people cannot reach medical support centres. Weekly clinic can be arranged at the middle of two villages so that they can receive treatment inside their village.

The research explored that due to some complex formalities and due to the non-professional behaviour of medical staffs, few people avoid receiving treatment from government health centres. Thus, government health centres should introduce one-stop and easily accessible health services for rural poor. Medical should be trained in a way so that they can deal their client professionally. Simultaneously, Union Health Centres should be upgraded so that all supports regarding pregnancy and delivery are available there, and responsibility of medical staffs should be ensured through intensive supervision. As people have good trust upon TBAs and as they have easy and quick access to TBAs, government should take massive program to train all TBAs in a way so that they can provide appropriate suggestions and emergency assistance to rural pregnant women. Government can use rural spiritual leaders and community leaders in creating awareness about pregnancy-related health services under the guidance of local self-government. A special chapter on pregnancy health can be added in the text book of lower secondary grade. This can create an understanding about the importance of pregnancy health among children and ultimately can help them in their personal and community life. To reduce the maternity mortality rate, the Government of Bangladesh has taken some operational steps, such as: to deliver birth with the help of skilled birth attendants, to provide financial support for bearing the cost of birth delivery and to provide nutritious food package to the malnutritious pregnant women. These steps should be implemented in such a way that all people who are in need can benefit from the support of the government.

It is noteworthy to mention that it is difficult for the government to take the whole responsibility regarding the quality health support for pregnant women in rural areas. Therefore, government–NGO cooperation can strengthen the impact of existing services as well as this cooperation can create new areas and understanding for better health services of rural pregnant women.

REFERENCES

Ahmmed, M.F. and Reza, M.H. 2006. 'Violence Against Women at Family Level: Some Observations', published in (in Bengali), *Annual Bengali Journal of Bangladesh Public Administration Training Centre*. 9th Year Issue, Kartik, 1411: 83–104.

Hasan, Reza M. and Faisal, Ahmmed. 2009. 'Structural Social Work and the Compatibility of NGO Approaches: A Case Analysis of Bangladesh Rural Advancement Committee', *International Journal of Social Welfare*, 18: 173–82.

Hossain, Imtiaz. 2009. 'Maternal Health Situation in Sylhet Division (written in Bangla)', Prothom Alo, 19 December 2009.

Ministry of Health and Family Welfare. 2009. *Annual Report* on Reproductive Health. Ministry of Health and Family Welfare, Bangladesh Secretariat.

Morgan, L. and Kunkel, S. 2001. *Aging: The Social Context* (2nd edition). California USA: Pine Forge Press.

Nuruzzaman, M.H. 2009. 'Affecting Maternal Health Services Utilization Married Adolescents and their Use of Maternal Health Services in Bangladesh', *Internet Journal of Health*, http://www.britannica.com/bps/additionalcontent/18/36122546, accessed 27 December 2009.

Patton, M.Q. 1990. *Qualitative Evaluation and Research Methods*. California 91320, USA: Sage Publications.

Contributors

Rekha Pande is Professor and Head of the History Department and a joint faculty in the Centre for Women's Studies at University of Hyderabad, Hyderabad. Her work is in the interdisciplinary area of history and women's studies. She has published in the area of women's history, cultural history, women and the Bhakti movement, socialization and family, girl child, child labour, women's work, health, violence against women, women's movement and impact of globalization on women. Besides her contributions in number of journals, both in India and abroad, she has to her credit eight books: *Journey's into Women's Studies: Crossing Interdisciplinary Boundaries*, edited (2014); *Globalization, Technology Diffusion and Gender Disparity: Social Impacts of ICTs*, coedited (2012); *Divine Sounds from the Heart* (2010); *Women in Nation Building: A Multi-dimensional Perspective*, coedited (2007); *Religious Reform Movement in Medieval India* (2005); *Gender Issues in the Police* (2000); *Child Labour in the Beedi Industry* (1998); and *Succession Struggle in the Delhi Sultanate* (1990). She has been the editor of *International Feminist Journal of Politics (IFJP)* and *Foreign Policy Analysis*. She received the International Visiting Fellowship in the School of Policy Studies, University of Bristol, UK; Academic Fellow, University of Buffalo, USA; and International Visiting Scholar, at Maison De Research, Paris. She is the member of board of studies of many universities in India. She can be contacted at panderekha@gmail.com

U. Joan Fairhurst, Professor Emeritus, University of Pretoria, South Africa, is a geographer whose academic interests lie in the field of social geography with an emphasis on the cultural, socio-political and economic facets. She pioneered Geography of Gender in South Africa. She was involved in the work of the Institute for Women's and Gender Studies at the University of Pretoria since its inception and served as interim director for a period. Apart from serving on the Council of the Society for South African Geographers (as President in 1997–1998), Joan Fairhurst has been involved with the work of the International Geographical Union, as a full member on the South African National Committee, a corresponding member with its Gender and Education Commissions, and as organising secretary for the International Geographical Union 2002 Regional Conference held in Durban (South Africa) in 2002. She can be contacted at joanfair@global.co.za

N.A. Flipsen has gained international working experience for the past years on several large collaboration projects, most of which are located in Africa. Her research interest are empowerment and gender issues in the context of ICT. Her main focus in the international setting is guidance of students, course development, managerial aspects, setting up international partnerships and project development. As an employee within the Information and Computer Science Department, she became interested in how gender issues develop in the ICT sector. She can be contacted at nicole.flipsen@cs.ru.nl

Th. P. van der Weide is currently a full-time professor in Information Retrieval and Information Systems (IRIS) in the Digital Security section of the Institute for Computing and Information Sciences (ICIS) at the Radboud University in Nijmegen. His main research interests include information systems, information retrieval, hypertext and knowledge-based systems. He is involved in the Information Foraging Lab, an interdepartmental research group focusing on the development of models and techniques supporting modern knowledge workers. He is also involved in an extensive research programme with public universities in Uganda, supported by Nuffic. He can be contacted at tvdw@cs.ru.nl.

Shauna Wilton is an Associate Professor of Political Studies at the Augustana Campus of the University of Alberta in Canada. In general, her research focuses on the politics surrounding diversity, culture, gender, ethnicity and nationalism. She is also engaged in research exploring the use of women's bodies as markers of group differences within popular and political publications and as part of this project, has received a Shastri Indo-Canadian Institute Fellowship. In the past few years, she has published articles in the *International Journal of Canadian Studies, Social and Legal Studies*, the *Canadian Journal of Information and Library Sciences*, as well as numerous book chapters. She can be contacted at swilton@ualberta.ca

Indira Mahendravada is Professor, Department of Economics, University of Mysore, Mysore. She obtained her Ph.D from Institute for Social and Economic Change, Bangalore. She teaches research methodology, natural resource economics and environmental economics, gender and development. Her areas of research interest are development issues, policy analysis, participatory research and gender studies. She has published nearly forty research papers and attended several national and international conferences. She can be contacted at mahindira@yahoo.com

Smarak Swain is a Bachelor of Technology from Indian Institute of Technology, Kharagpur and is presently pursuing his Masters in Taxation and Business Laws from NALSAR Law University, Hyderabad. He has authored a book on *Applied Psychology: India Specific and Cross-Cultural Perspectives* and has edited a collection of essays on *Social Issues of India*. He is working in the Indian Revenue Service (IRS) and is presently posted as Assistant Commissioner of Income Tax in Bhubaneswar. He has an immense interest in behavioural sciences and doubles up as an independent scholar in the field. He can be contacted at smarak@gmail.com.

Leila Bijos is a Professor in Law at Universidade Catolica de Brasilia, and is a special advisor for International Programs. She has been invited to visit and lecture in many foreign universities in Japan, the Republic of China, Ecuador, Switzerland, Spain, South Africa and Iran. She is a former Visiting Scholar at the Center for Iberian and Latin American Studies (CILAS) and at the Center for US-Mexican Studies, UCSD. She has been a consultant for the Japan International Cooperation Agency (JICA), the Special Secretariat of Women, Presidency of the Republic, Ministry of Health and Ministry of Education. Bijos has published several articles on various subjects in international and Brazilian reviews and newspapers, related to international politics, gender, human rights, migration and sustainable development. She can be contacted at lbijos@ucb.br

Sita Vanka is currently Professor and Dean at the School of Management Studies, University of Hyderabad, Hyderabad. She has over two decades of teaching experience in the areas of public policy management, women studies, educational management, human resource management and entrepreneurship. As a trainer, she has successfully conducted training programmes for the top management, middle management and operational level. As a researcher, she has conducted research in the areas of entrepreneurship, human resource management, women in management. As a consultant, she was involved in assignments of both public and private sectors. She is a reviewer and advisory committee member of several journals. She can be contacted at sita_vanka@yahoo.co.in

Lalit Joshi is Professor in the Department of History at the University of Allahabad, Allahabad. He was also involved with a research and teaching programme at Syracuse University from 1987–1990. His area of research include cultural globalization and the history of Indian and world cinema, and has published extensively in Hindi and English in international and national journals and anthologies. His publications include *House Full* (2002), *Bollywood Texts* (2011) and two forthcoming titles *The Cultural Globalization of India* and *Revisiting Allahabad*. Professor Joshi has also been providing occasional archival and other assistance to the Hindi film industry. He can be contacted at lalitvjoshi@gmail.com

M.N. Rajesh is a Lecturer in the Department of History at the University of Hyderabad, Hyderabad. His main areas of interest are technology and gender and the history and politics of the Tibetan region. He has a Master's degree in history from Jawaharlal Nehru University (JNU) and also completed his M.Phil. and Ph.D. from JNU. He has also worked as a reader in the Centre for Women's Studies in the University of Hyderabad. He has published on the aspects of Indian and Tibetan history and technology. Subsequently he expanded his interests to the role of internet activism with reference to the Tibetan movement. He can be contacted at sherabling@yahoo.com

Neaz Ahmed is Professor of Social Work at Shahjalal University of Science and Technology, Syhet, Bangladesh. He obtained his BSS (Honours) and MSS in Social Welfare from the Institute of Social Welfare and Research, University of Dhaka, Bangladesh. His research focuses on marriage and divorce, marital satisfaction, social work intervention for physically and mentally handicapped, correctional services for juvenile delinquency, child labour, human rights and ethnic minority issues. He has published a good number of articles in national and international journals. He has published *Divorced Women in Bangladesh* (2007) and *Research Methods in Social Sciences* (2007). He has participated and presented his scholarly works in different national and international seminars and workshops. He is serving as an active member of the editorial board of the *Annual Review of Ethnic Affairs*. He can be contacted at nahmed1973@gmail.com

Olugu Ukpai is a Doctoral Law candidate at the Reading University's School of Law. He is the Director of Women's Legal Empowerment and Social Accountability (WOLESA). Broadly, his work is in the interdisciplinary area of law, gender, culture, religion, African history, environmental practice and development. He is an international consultant on gender and development, law, policy, and feminist jurisprudence with African concentration. Ukpai is a recipient of West African Research Association (WARA) Fellowship (2011) and Canadian Commonwealth Scholarship (2005–2007). He holds the University of Reading's Doctoral Scholarship (2009–2013), Federal Government Scholarship (2003–2004) and a University Scholarship (1996–2000). In 2010, he received the Xn Foundation Prize for 'Outstanding Achievements and Excellence' at Kent University in the United Kingdom and 'Global Citizen Award' from Canada. He can be contacted at oluukpaiolu@yahoo.com

Lipi Ghosh is Professor and Director of the Centre for South & South East Asian Studies, University of Calcutta. She was formerly a Visiting Associate to the Indian Institute of Advanced Study, Shimla (1997), Visiting Scholar and Visiting Professor to *Maison des Sciences de l'Homme*, Paris (1986, 1997, 1998), Visiting Faculty to the School of Oriental and African Studies, London, under British Academy Award (1999), and Ford Asia Fellow and Visiting Scholar in the Institute of Thai Studies, Chulalongkorn University,

Bangkok, Thailand (2000). She has also been awarded the Visiting Scholarship to SEAP, Cornell University, USA. She was also a Charles Wallace Visiting Scholar to SOAS in 2004, Visiting Scholar to the Centre for Women Studies & Gender Relations, University of British Columbia, Canada, 2005; and Visiting Faculty to the Nalanda Srivijya Centre, Institute of South East Asian Studies, Singapore, 2010. Her research interest are ethnicity, minority and cultural studies in context of South and Southeast Asia with special reference to gender studies. She has also published many academic articles in several reputed national and international journals. She can be contacted at lipighosh@gmail.com

B. Ratna Kumari is currently the Director, Dr. Durgabai Deshmukh Centre for Women's Studies, Andhra University (AU), Visakhapatnam. She won the Best Thesis Award for her doctoral in 1992. She also received Best Researcher Award (2007) and Best Academician Award (2009) by AU. She has received the LWF Fellowship (Geneva), DAAD Fellowship (Germany) for her scholarship in economics, women's studies/gender studies. She is the author of five books, including *Gender and Globalization: A Comparative Perspective of Europe and India* (2010). She can be contacted at ratna_cws@hotmail.com

R. Jayasree is Professor, Department of Women's Studies and Dean of the School of Social Sciences, Humanities and Management in S.P. Mahila University, Tirupati. She has published in the area of reproductive health behaviour of women; sex workers sexual behaviour and reproductive health; oral health problems of tobacco chewers; new reproductive technology; utilization of maternal and child health services by the rural adolescents and adult women; and reproductive health of adolescents and unmarried youth. She has been the Convener of the Sexual Harassment Cell, SPMVV and Member, Board of Studies for Women's Studies in a large number of universities. She can be contacted at jayaretna@rediffmail.com

Rebecca John is currently working on her doctoral thesis, entitled *Scandal, Governmentality and Legal Discourses on the Modest Woman: Case Studies of Sexual Harassment in Public Spaces of Kerala* at the Centre for the Study of Law and Governance, Jawaharlal Nehru University, New Delhi. She can be contacted at johnrebecca@gmail.com

K.M. Ziyauddin is an Assistant Professor-cum-Assistant Director at the Centre for the Study of Social Exclusion and Inclusive Policy, Maulana Azad National Urdu University, Hyderabad. He did his M.Phil. in Social Medicine and Community Health at Jawaharlal Nehru University, New Delhi and Ph.D. in Sociology, School of Economics, University of Delhi, Delhi. He can be contacted at ziyakm@rediffmail.com

Ajailiu Niumai is Associate Professor, Centre for the Study of Social Exclusion and Inclusive Policy (CSSEIP), University of Hyderabad (UoH), Hyderabad. She is also the joint faculty at the Centre for Women's Studies, UoH. In 2006–2007, she was nominated as the First Fellow of CARTHA, a non-profit organization based in Iowa City, USA. Her area of research interest includes gender, NGOs and development, children at high risk, Indian diaspora philanthropy and tribal studies. She has presented over thirty papers in seminars and conferences in India and also made presentation in the University of Iowa, USA, University of Wisconsin, Madison, USA and University of Surrey, UK. She can be contacted at aniumai@yahoo.co.uk

Hminthanzuali is an Assistant Professor, Department of History and Ethnography, Mizoram University, Aizawl, Mizoram. She obtained M.A., M.Phil. and Ph.D. from the University of Hyderabad. She works in the interdisciplinary area of history and gender studies. Her research interests include gender and oral tradition, gender and colonial reforms, gender and armed conflict and women's indigenous knowledge systems, particularly in the region of North East India. She has contributed number of research papers and articles on gender/women's issues in various reputed journals, books and conferences in India and abroad. She can be contacted at hmingthanzuali@gmail.com

Faisal Ahmmed is Associate Professor of Social Work, Shahjalal University of Science and Technology, Sylhet, Bangladesh. His main areas of research interest are ethnic minority, aging, indigenous peoples, minority and marginalized people, child labour, public health and violence against women. He has published a number of articles in national and international journals. Two of his scholarly works are published as books from Germany. He is working on indigenous, minority and gender issues for social justice through research and publications. Dr. Ahmmed is working as the Editorial Chair of the *Annual Review of Ethnic Affairs*, the only specialized journal in Bangladesh which publishes research articles on indigenous issues. He can be contacted at fahmmedsust@yahoo.com

Tofayel Ahmed is serving as Associate Professor of Business Administration at Leading University, Sylhet, Bangladesh. His major scholarship covers the area of productivity and profitability. Dr. Ahmed has deep interest on different social issues including gender development and indigenous and marginalized people. A good number of his scholarly works are published in reputed journals. He has participated and presented his works in national and international seminars. Dr. Ahmed is affiliated with different voluntary organizations to serve the disadvantaged people of Sylhet region in Bangladesh. He can be contacted at fahmmedsust@ yahoo.com

Index